COMMERCIAL DIVER
BASIC MANUAL
2th Edition

Alex Fatum

ISBN-13: 9798880484300

Cover design by: CUSADU
Library of Congress Control Number: 2018675309
Printed in the United States of America

DESCRIPTION

This book comprehensively covers the mandatory training program for diving specialists, offering valuable insights for both professional divers and apprentices. It delves into the fundamentals of the physical properties of the environment, exploring their impact on human physiology during immersion. The content includes breathing gas mixtures, detailed descriptions of diving gear and equipment, maintenance rules, and storage conditions. Practical exercises for diving descents, crucial for divers, are presented, enhancing trainees' technical skills.

The textbook addresses the organization and procedures of diving descents in various conditions, such as rapid currents, night dives, ice dives, and overhead environments like sunken ship compartments or caves. Decompression and non-decompression dive tables are explained. Special diving tools, from manual to hydraulic, are discussed, along with recommendations for underwater welding, cutting, and working with concrete. The book covers the technology of hydraulic structure construction, principles of hydrology, and various diving works for different specialties.

Ship-related diving operations, search and recovery of sunken objects, engineering diving in civil construction and oil fields, diving operations in the fishing industry, and rescue diving are all explored. Authored by specialists, the book makes complex subjects understandable for divers and students alike. It serves as a teaching aid for professional-technical schools, technical colleges, and diving training centers, aligning with the training program for third-class divers.

CONTENTS

I CHAPTER

FUNDAMENTALS FOR CALCULATING ABSORBED BREATHABLE GAS IN DIVER'S BREATH

In the first chapter, the textbook provides a detailed description from which one will learn about the physical characteristics of the environment, such as atmospheric air and the measurement of atmospheric pressure for calculating the respiratory gas absorbed by the human body underwater. It also covers fundamental topics such as the properties of the aquatic environment, buoyancy of a diver, pressure on the human body underwater, underwater visibility, propagation of sound and light, and the spread of shockwaves in water.

§ 1. Physical properties of the environment

Our planet is surrounded by a gas envelope called the atmosphere. The thickness of this envelope from the Earth's surface to interplanetary space reaches 1000 kilometers. Under the influence of gravitational forces, known as gravity, the main mass of atmospheric air, more than 80% of the total mass, and about 90% of all water vapor in the atmosphere, are located in the lower layer of the atmosphere in polar regions from 8 to 10 kilometers, in temperate latitudes from 10 to 12 kilometers, at the equator 16-18 kilometers. With increasing altitude, the mass, pressure, and temperature of the air decrease. Therefore, the higher above the Earth's surface, we measure the air density, the less it is. One liter of air weighs 1.293 grams at normal atmospheric pressure of 760 millimeters of mercury column and a temperature of 59 °F (15°C).

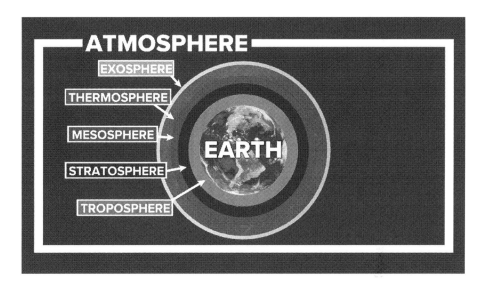

Fig. 1. Earth's atmosphere: troposphere, stratosphere, mesosphere, thermosphere, exosphere

Properties of atmospheric air

Earth's atmospheric air is a mechanical mixture of several gases, the main ones being nitrogen, oxygen, argon, and carbon dioxide. In addition, the air contains inert gases such as neon, helium, methane, krypton, hydrogen, xenon, nitrogen oxides, propane, ozone, chlorine, ammonia, as well as many other gases in small quantities. Besides gases, the air has various impurities, including dust, water vapor, combustion products, and sea salts. Knowledge of the composition and pressure of gases helps calculate optimal gas mixtures for breathing used by divers underwater.

Nitrogen – a gas that does not burn or support combustion, has no odor or taste, and is colorless. The main component of the air is 78.13%. Under normal conditions, it is neutral to the body. One liter of nitrogen weighs 1.25 grams. At normal atmospheric pressure, about one liter of nitrogen is dissolved in the human body. Nitrogen is one of the essential elements for plant nutrition, as it is part of proteins and nucleic acids, enzymes, and chlorophyll molecules.

Oxygen – a gas that does not burn but supports combustion, has no odor or taste, and is colorless. The main component of the air is 20.9%. In its pure form, it is not dangerous. One liter weighs 1.428 grams. Oxygen's main property is its ability to readily combine with other substances, forming so-called oxides. Life on Earth is impossible without oxygen. To sustain life, oxygen maintains a continuous process of oxidizing nutrients, releasing energy. Even brief interruptions in its supply lead to the cessation of vital functions in the organism. Normal human activity occurs when consuming about 21% oxygen in the breathing mixture. Minor fluctuations of 1-2% oxygen are not felt by humans, but a decrease in oxygen content to 18.5% in inhaled air leads to oxygen deprivation.

Argon is a gas that does not burn or support combustion, has no odor or taste, is colorless, and is poorly soluble in water. The density under normal conditions is 1.7839 kg/m3, with a weight of 1.78 grams. It constitutes 0.93% of the volume and 1.3% of the mass, making it the most common inert gas in the Earth's atmosphere, with 9.34 liters present in 1 m^3 off air.

Carbon Dioxide – a gas that does not burn or support combustion, is almost odorless (in high concentrations, it has a slightly alkaline "soda" smell), and is colorless. It is 1.5 times heavier than air, with one liter weighing 1.98 grams. It is a compound of carbon with oxygen, formed during the burning and decay of organic substances. The human body continuously produces carbon dioxide through the oxidation of food. An excess of carbon dioxide, at a partial pressure of 0.03 atmospheres, corresponding to 3% in the air, acts as a poisonous gas.

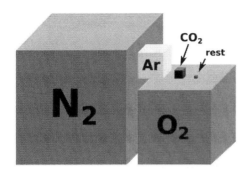

Fig. 2. Percentage ratio of gases in the air

Other gases in the air, present in small quantities, do not have a significant impact on the human body. The amount of water vapor in the air, ranging from 0.2% to 4% by volume, has a substantial influence on the human body. At high temperatures, the air can contain more water vapor, while lower temperatures result in less vapor, leading to the formation and evaporation of mist. At the same temperature, humid air is lighter than dry air because water vapor is significantly lighter than the gases in the air. This phenomenon is observed in cloudy weather. The normal content of water vapor in inhaled air is considered to be 1–1.5%. A high content of water vapor in the air disrupts the regulation of heat release and absorption, while a lower content causes excessive moisture loss by the body.

Measurement of atmospheric pressure

Since air consists of gases with weight, it exerts pressure on the Earth's surface and all objects on it. The magnitude of atmospheric pressure was first measured in 1643 by Italian scientists Torricelli (Evangelista Torricelli) and Viviani (Vincenzo Viviani), who conducted experiments with mercury, allowing them to detect the presence of air pressure. The experiment involved sealing a glass tube with one end and immersing it in a vessel of mercury. The scientists released all the air from the tube, causing it to fill with mercury, and then raised it with the closed end submerged in the metal. The weight of the mercury pulled the liquid metal downward, creating a partial vacuum at the sealed end of the tube, leaving an empty space above the mercury. As atmospheric pressure increased, the mercury in the open vessel rose, and when it

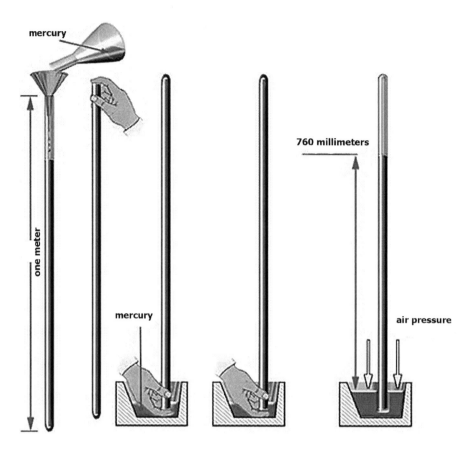

Fig. 3. Experiment with mercury to demonstrate atmospheric pressure

decreased, it fell. The constructed device became the first mercury barometer. Upon measurement, it was found that the height of the mercury column in the tube was 760 mm, and the weight of the mercury was 1.033 kg. Thus, at sea level, the atmospheric pressure is 760 mm of mercury, equivalent to a force of 1.033 kg per 1 cm². This pressure is called atmospheric barometric pressure.

If a tube of the same diameter is filled with water instead of mercury, the column of water corresponding to normal atmospheric pressure will be 10.33 meters because water is 13.6 times lighter than mercury. Thus, 760 mm of a mercury column equals 1.033 kg/cm², which is equivalent to a 10.33-meter water column. In technology and diving, the unit of pressure is taken to be 1 kg/cm^2, which equals 10 meters of water column and corresponds to 735.6 mm of a mercury column or 0.968 atmospheres. Therefore, 1 technical atmosphere (bar) is equal to 1.01325 barometric atmosphere (bar). For the convenience of calculations, the technical atmosphere is accepted as the unit of pressure, equal to 1 kg per 1 cm^2 of area.

Interestingly, Earth's gravity imparts weight to the air, approximately 1 kilogram per square centimeter. The density of air is about 1.29 kg/cm^3, meaning a cube with a side length of 1 meter filled with air weighs 1.29 kilograms. Imagine that the air above your head exerts a weight of about 250 kilograms on a person standing upright! The human body doesn't get flattened because there is air inside the body, balancing the external air pressure. The same principle applies to diving. The pressure of the surrounding environment is counteracted by the internal pressure in the human body due to the increased pressure of the breathing gas mixture used by the diver.

Pressure on the human body underwater

When diving underwater, a person experiences pressure not only from atmospheric air but also from the water. With every 10 meters of depth, the pressure increases by 1 atmosphere. This pressure is called excess pressure. The sum of excess and atmospheric pressures (measured from zero - vacuum) is called absolute pressure or cumulative pressure. At a depth of 10 meters, a diver is under 2 atmospheres of pressure. Absolute pressure is measured by the formula:

$$P = p + 1$$

where:

P - is the absolute pressure in atmospheres;

p - is the excess pressure in atmospheres.

Task 1. Using the formula, determine the pressure on the diver at depths:

3 meters _____ 9 meters _____ 15 meters _____

Compressibility of gases

All gases consist of very small particles in constant motion, taking up a large volume. The force of attraction between gas molecules is much less than in liquids or solids. Unlike solids, gases take the shape and volume of the vessel they are in. With increased pressure, gases compress, reducing their volume, and they become more elastic. Correspondingly, when pressure decreases, gases can expand. Gases also have the ability to change their volume with temperature variations.

At increased pressure, air compresses easily, significantly reducing its volume.

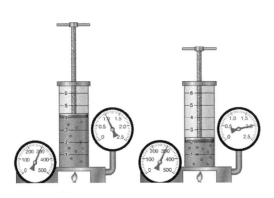

Fig. 4. Compressibility of gases

The pressure of compressed air is measured by an instrument called a manometer.

In 1662, Irish scientist Robert Boyle experimentally established that, at a constant temperature, the volume occupied by a gas changes inversely with pressure. Fourteen years later, in 1676, French scientist Edme Mariotte independently discovered this law.

Fig. 5. Manometer

Today, one of the fundamental gas laws bears the name Boyle-Mariotte. The essence of this law is that the pressure of a gas and its volume are inversely proportional: as pressure increases, the volume of the gas decreases, and vice versa.

In mathematical terms, this statement is expressed as the formula:

$$P = C/V$$

where:

Fig. 6. Robert Boyle

P - is the gas pressure, V - is the gas volume, and C - is a constant under specified conditions.

In general, the value is determined by the chemical nature, mass, and temperature of the gas. For example, take air with a volume of 30 liters (C) at atmospheric pressure and begin compressing it. Changes in volume will occur as follows:

Pressure in atmospheres (P)	1	2	3	4	5	6	7	8	9	10	11	15
Volume in liters (V)	30	15		7,5	6		4,28	3,75		3	2,72	

Task 2. Fill in the empty cells in the table above using the Boyle-Mariotte formula. The relationship between the pressure of air and its volume is established by the formula:

$$P1 \times V1 = P2 \times V2$$

where: P - is the absolute pressure of the gas in atmospheres;

V - is the volume of the gas in liters.

Fig. 7. Edme Mariotte

For calculations in diving, this law has practical applications.

Example 1: Determine how much uncompressed air is in a 12-liter tank if the air pressure in it, according to the pressure gauge, is 200 bar.

Solution: Transforming the Boyle-Mariotte formula, we get:

P_1=201 bar, V_1=12 liters, P_2=1 bar;
$V_2 = (P_1 \times V_1) / P_2 = (201 \times 12) / 1 = 2412$ liters.

Example 2: Determine how much compressed air a diver, under a pressure of 3 bar according to the pressure gauge, will receive if 120 liters of air per minute without pressure are supplied for breathing.

Solution: First - recall the formula for absolute and excess pressure P_2=p+1=3+1=4 bar.

Second - transform the Boyle-Mariotte formula:

P1= 1 bar, V1= 120 litres, P2 = 4 bar;

$V2 = (P1 \times V1) / P2 = (1 \times 120) / 4 = 30$ liters/minute.

The calculations above are valid only for constant temperature. In practice, more accurate calculations are used in diving with the application of formulas that determine the dependence of gas volume and pressure on temperature.

This law was derived by the French scientist Joseph Louis Gay-Lussac in 1802. The law is expressed by two formulas:

$$V1 / T1 = V2 / T2 \quad \text{or} \quad V1 \times T2 = V2 \times T1$$

at constant pressure (P);

$$P1 / T1 = P2 / T2 \quad \text{or} \quad P1 \times T2 = P2 \times T1$$

at constant volume (V);

where: V1 and V2 are the initial and final volume of the gas at constant pressure;

P1 and P2 are the initial and final absolute pressure of the gas at constant volume;

T1 and T2 are the initial and final absolute temperature of the gas.

Absolute temperature of the gas is measured from absolute zero (-273°C). This is the minimum temperature that a physical body can have in the universe, with zero on the scale corresponding to the temperature at which air "loses all its elasticity." To determine the absolute temperature of the gas, add the temperature in degrees Celsius to the value of 273°.

For example, at an air temperature of 25°C, the absolute temperature of the air will be 273 + 25 = 298°C.

Using Gay-Lussac's law, we can perform more accurate calculations related to diving descents. For example, suppose we need to determine the pressure in a diver's tank during an underwater descent, where the air pressure on the surface according to the pressure gauge is 232 bar, the air temperature is 28°C, and the water temperature is 4°C. Transforming the Gay-Lussac formula, we get:

$P_2 = P_1 \times (T_2 / T_1) = P_1 \times (273 + T_2) / (273 + T_1)$;

Substituting the values: $P_1 = 232$ bar, $T_1 = 28$°C, $T_2 = 4$°C;

we get: $P_2 = 232 \times (273 + 4) / (273 + 28) = 213,5$ bar

Task 3. Using the Gay-Lussac formula, determine the pressure in the diver's tank during an underwater descent, where the air pressure on the surface according to the pressure gauge is 180 bar, the air temperature is 15°C, and the water temperature is 7°C.

Joseph Louis Gay-Lussac

Fig. 8. Joseph Louis Gay-Lussac

Partial gas pressures

It is known that atmospheric air exerts a force of 760 millimeters of mercury – this is the total pressure of gases making up the air. Additionally, different gases present in the composition of air or breathing gas mixtures have distinct properties and affect the human body differently. To understand the impact of a specific gas on a diver under increased pressure, it is essential to know the partial pressure of that gas. The pressure of one gas in a gas mixture is called partial pressure and depends on the percentage content of the gas in the gas mixture and the total pressure. The total pressure of gases is equal to the sum of the partial pressures of gases.

As the total pressure increases, the partial pressures of individual gases increase, and under these conditions, gases affect the body differently than under normal atmospheric pressure. It has been established that under certain pressure, the action of nitrogen on the human body is narcotic. Therefore, dives to depths exceeding 40 meters are recommended to be conducted using gas mixtures containing helium, which has a weaker narcotic property compared to nitrogen. Oxygen-helium mixtures are not optimal for breathing. Starting at a pressure of 10 atmospheres, signs of helium narcosis manifest in the human body, including rhythmic tremors of the upper limbs and torso, along with changes in the functions of the central nervous system. Helium exposure causes rapid body cooling and alters the voice (resulting in a nasal tone). For example, the narcotic effect of inhaling argon only occurs at barometric pressures above 2 atmospheres. In 2014, the World Anti-Doping Agency recognized argon as a doping substance.

To avoid narcotic anesthesia, it is recommended to use gas mixtures with several components, ensuring that the partial pressure of oxygen in the final gas mixture is not less than 120 millimeters of mercury. The calculation of partial pressure uses the percentage content of gases in the mixture by weight. In diving practice, the composition of the breathing gas mixture for a diver is usually calculated by volume. Discrepancies in calculation methods are minor and have no practical significance. The partial pressure of a gas is expressed in absolute atmospheres, millimeters of mercury, or as a percentage of gas content, normalized to standard pressure. The partial pressure of gas in a mixture in absolute atmospheres is determined by the formula:

$$\textbf{P gas} = \textbf{P} \times \textbf{N} / \textbf{100}$$

P gas - partial pressure of the gas in atmospheres or bar;

N - percentage content of the gas in the mixture;

P - total pressure of the gas mixture, bar.

This formula has practical application for calculating the partial pressure of the composition of the breathing gas mixture for a diver.

Example 1. It is necessary to determine the partial pressure of nitrogen and oxygen when supplying air to a diver under a pressure of 3 bar.

As it is known, the percentage content of nitrogen in the air is 78%, and oxygen is 21%. Substituting these values into the formula given above, we get:

partial pressure of nitrogen: $PN_2 = 3 \times 78 / 100 = 2,34$ bar;

partial pressure of oxygen: $PO_2 = 3 \times 21 / 100 = 0,63$ bar.

Calculation of partial pressure in millimeters of mercury is carried out using the same formula. For example, let's consider the partial pressure of gases in atmospheric air in millimeters of mercury (mmHg).

$O_2 = 20,9\%$, $N_2 = 78,13\%$, $Ar = 0,93\%$, $CO_2 = 0,03\%$.

$P O_2 = 760 \times 20,9 / 100 = 158,84$ mmHg;

$P N_2 = 760 \times 78,13 / 100 = 593,788$ mmHg;

P Ar = 760 × 0,93 / 100 = 70,68 mmHg;

P CO_2 = 760 × 0,03 / 100 = 2,28 mmHg.

It is known that during submersion, air compresses, and despite the fact that the percentage content of any of the gases remains unchanged in compressed air, its partial pressure will increase proportionally to the depth of submersion. The partial pressure of a gas in percentage content, normalized to atmospheric pressure, is calculated by multiplying the percentage content of the gas by the absolute pressure of the gas mixture.

Example 2. It is required to determine the partial pressure of carbon dioxide in percentage content, normalized to standard pressure. For instance, a diver is supplied with a breathing gas mixture at a pressure off 4.5 bar, and the carbon dioxide content in the mixture is 0.03%.

By multiplying the percentage content of carbon dioxide in the mixture (0.03%) by the total pressure of 4.5 bar, we obtain the partial pressure of carbon dioxide equal to 0.135%.

Example 3. At a depth of 40 meters, the partial pressure of oxygen will be not 158.84 millimeters of mercury, as at the surface, but five times greater. At the same time, the percentage content of oxygen in the air mixture remains unchanged.

PO_2 = 760 × 20,9 × 5 / 100 = 794,2 mmHg.

Solubility of gases

Understanding the relationship between the gaseous environment and the human body under increased pressure involves exploring the solubility of gases in liquids. Any gas, when in contact with a liquid, dissolves in it, and the dissolution process is always exothermic. Since gas molecules are not bound to anything, there are no energy costs associated with breaking any chemical bonds. Consequently, the solubility of gases decreases with increasing temperature. For example, if you leave a glass of cold water in a warm room, bubbles of gas, which is air dissolved in the water, will appear on the inner surface of the glass over time, due to heating.

Unlike liquids, any gas differs in that it does not have a constant concentration in its own phase. The content of gas in a unit volume changes with pressure. This affects the equilibrium between the liquid and the gas, and consequently, the solubility of the gas depends on pressure. For instance, when opening a bottle of carbonated water, vigorous release of gas bubbles is observed, emphasizing the connection between pressure and gas solubility. The dependence of gas solubility on pressure follows a law described in 1803 by the English chemist William Henry. The solubility of a gas in a liquid is proportional to the pressure of the gas above the liquid's surface.

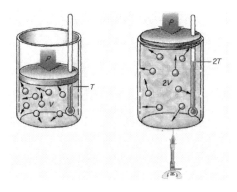

Fig. 9. Dependence of gas solubility on pressure and temperature

Imagine a closed container in which equilibrium has been established between a certain gas and the same gas dissolved in a liquid: Gas X <=> Gas X in a dissolved state in the liquid. With an increase in gas pressure by adding it to our closed container, the equilibrium will shift in a way that the pressure will decrease slightly—some of the gas will transition into the liquid, and the concentration of the gas in the liquid will increase. Consequently, solubility will increase. The dissolution of a gas in a liquid occurs until the gas pressure above the liquid equals the pressure of the gas already dissolved in it.

If multiple gases dissolve simultaneously, the dissolution of each occurs independently of the others. Passing a gas stream (bubbling) through a liquid causes the gas to dissolve according to the created pressure. The volumetric solubility of gases in a liquid depends on their partial pressure, temperature, and the chemical nature of the gas.

§ 2. Basic properties of the aquatic environment

Composition and properties of water

Water is a colorless liquid, representing a chemical compound of hydrogen and oxygen. Freshwater, in comparison to air, is denser and heavier. Calculating the weight of these two mediums per unit volume is straightforward. As we know, one liter of air weighs 1.293 grams, while one liter of water weighs 1000 grams; therefore, water is 773 times heavier than air. In determining the specific gravity of liquids and solid bodies, water serves as a conventional unit. Distilled water, at a temperature of 4°C, plays this role, where one milliliter of water equals one gram in weight.

Seawater is denser than freshwater, with an average specific gravity of 1.025 g. Due to its ability to dissolve various substances, natural water contains a certain amount of different chemical elements. The density and specific gravity of water depend on the substances dissolved in it. On average, chloride sodium (table salt), potassium, magnesium, calcium, and other chemical elements in seawater constitute 2-4% of its volume, making it denser and heavier than freshwater. It's worth noting that the salt content in seas is not uniform; for example, one liter of water from the Atlantic Ocean contains 35 grams of salt, while one liter of water from the Black Sea has about 20 grams.

In addition too salts, various gases are dissolved in water. For instance, the amount of oxygen in water is twice that in atmospheric air, but it is in a chemical compound with hydrogen, and the dissolved oxygen per liter of water is approximately 6 milliliters. Under the influence of temperature, water density changes. Freshwater has the highest density at a temperature of 4°C, and with an increase or decrease in temperature, water density decreases slightly. For example, with an increase in temperature to 20°C, the density of freshwater decreases by only 0.2%. The density of water changes more significantly under the influence of salinity. The density of seawater is 2-3% higher than that of freshwater. However, these density fluctuations in water are of little importance for diving; therefore, in all calculations related to diving, the density of water is considered equal to one.

Like any liquid, water is almost incompressible under pressure. Therefore, with increasing diving depth, the density of water remains practically unchanged. For example, at a depth of 100 meters, the density of water increases by approximately 0.05%. Significant for diving are the heat capacity and thermal conductivity of water. The heat capacity is 3.5 times greater than that of air, and thermal conductivity is 25 times greater than that of air. This means that the human body in cold water loses heat much faster and in larger quantities than in the air.

The human body on the Earth's surface experiences constant air pressure equal to 16-18 tons per square meter of its body surface. However, this pressure is not felt because external pressure is balanced by internal pressure in the lungs and air cavities of the body. During dives, in addition to atmospheric pressure, the pressure of the water also acts on the human body. When submerged underwater, to avoid feeling the pressure of the surrounding environment, it is necessary to maintain the condition of equal external and internal pressure. To achieve this, air or a breathing mixture is supplied to the diver under pressure equal to the pressure exerted by the surrounding water. Water pressure increases proportionally with depth. It increases by 1 bar for every 10 meters. It follows that a diver at a depth of 10 meters experiences a pressure of 2 bar, and to stabilize pressure, the supply of a breathing mixture under a pressure of 2 atmospheres is required.

Task 1: What pressure should the supply of a breathing mixture be for a diver at a depth of 38 meters?

Buoyancy of a diver

One of the fundamental concepts in diving is the idea of positive and negative buoyancy. According to the physical law attributed to Archimedes in the 3rd century BCE, any object submerged in water loses weight equal to the weight of the water it displaces. When a body is immersed in water, two opposing forces act on it: gravity and buoyancy. The force of gravity (or the weight of the body), directed vertically downward, seeks to submerge the body, while the water impedes the immersion, attempting to push the submerged body to the surface. This force is called buoyancy force, lifting force, or hydrostatic buoyancy force, and it is also known as Archimedean force.

Fig. 10. Greek scientist Archimedes

When the force of gravity is greater than the buoyancy force, the body sinks freely, having negative buoyancy. If the weight of the body is less than the buoyancy force, the body floats on the surface. When these forces are equal, the body is in a state of equilibrium, meaning that the sum of forces is zero, and the body has neutral buoyancy.

Example 1. A piece of iron with a volume of 1 dm³ (1 liter) weighs 7800 grams. Submerged in water, it will sink because its buoyancy force, equal to 1000 grams, is less than its weight.

Example 2. A wooden block with a volume of 1 dm³ (1 liter) weighs 600 grams. When submerged in water, it remains on the surface, displacing 0.6 dm³ (600 milliliters) of water. It will float on the surface, having a reserve of positive buoyancy of 400 grams.

The average specific gravity of a person's body during exhalation fluctuates between 1.021 and 1.098. Since the average specific gravity of water is 1, we see that the human body has a slight negative buoyancy. This explains why a person who cannot swim will sink. However, if they take a deep breath and lie on the water's surface, their body acquires positive buoyancy.

The buoyancy of a diver depends directly on the type of diving equipment. The volume of a diver in ventilated diving equipment increases, thus increasing their positive buoyancy by 5-10 kg. A diver using scuba gear has positive buoyancy up to 5 kg. Thus, in any diving gear, a diver acquires some positive buoyancy that needs to be offset for submersion. To give the diver negative buoyancy, weights are included in the equipment, worn on the belt. These weights can also be metallic plates attached to the back with special straps. Lead is commonly used as the weighting metal. Soft weights are made of lead in the form of small balls the size of a pea, and they are placed in small pouches, usually inserted into special pockets in the diver's vest.

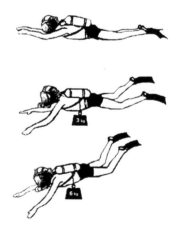

Fig. 11. Diver's buoyancy

Also, to achieve negative buoyancy, divers use special diving boots with metal soles, toes, and heels, usually made of brass. When a diver descends underwater in gear, their buoyancy is adjusted so that it equals zero or has a slight negative buoyancy of 0.5 to 1 kg. It should be noted that if a diver has to work on the seabed, a negative buoyancy of 2 to 8 kilograms is required. It is also essential to consider that when diving with scuba gear, as the air in the tank is consumed, the diver loses weight underwater overall.

Buoyancy of the diver is influenced by the density or specific weight of water. In seawater, a diver has greater buoyancy than in freshwater because salty water is denser and has more buoyant force. This also applies to water temperature approaching 4°C; the colder the water, the higher its density, requiring more weights for comfortable diving.

In dry-type diving suits, diving suits, or diving helmets, the volume of air around the diver during descents must be adjusted towards negative buoyancy. During manual lifting of heavy objects during ascents, the diver increases buoyancy towards the positive side. If it is necessary to rest on the seabed, the diver vents from their suit an amount of air that allows them to comfortably maintain negative buoyancy, avoiding being squeezed by the surrounding medium.

Water, being denser compared to air, poses a significant obstacle to the diver's rapid movement. The resistance to movement for a diver swimming horizontally is much less than for a diver walking on the seabed. To reduce water resistance, a diver walking on the seabed has to move forward sideways or with a certain tilt of the torso forward.

When in a current, the diver may need to move by crawling and use various devices to facilitate movement. Frequently used tools include walking lines, supports, picks, and knives. The dense medium complicates the diver's work with hand tools; hammer or hammer blows are much weaker than in the air. For underwater work, it is recommended to use a heavier tool in weight and less bulky.

In places with a lot of silt during dives, the diver faces additional significant resistance to their movements. When performing certain types of work in heavy diving gear, it is necessary to maintain the diver's vertical position. The ability to easily return to a vertical position during tilts directly depends on the correct mutual arrangement of the center of gravity and the center of buoyancy of the diver.

The most balanced state is considered when the centers of gravity and buoyancy lie in one vertical line, with the center of gravity located approximately 20 cm below the center of buoyancy. In cases where the center of gravity is higher than the center of buoyancy, the diver may overturn headfirst and be thrown to the surface. The same fate awaits the diver if a lot of air accumulates in the lower part of the drysuit during descent. To avoid flipping upside down, the diver must thoroughly vent the air through the venting valves before submersion.

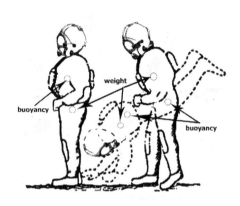

Fig. 12. Location of the center of gravity and buoyancy center of the diver

Underwater visibility

Water, due to its greater density, has the property of significant light dispersion and absorption. Sunlight or light from other sources above the water's surface is extensively reflected, especially in rough waters. The penetration of light into the water and the illumination of objects in it depend on the surface brightness, depth, and water transparency. With increasing depth, illumination rapidly decreases. For example, in seawater with good visibility, at a depth of three meters, we only get 50% of the illumination at the surface.

Fig. 13. Underwater visibility

As the diving depth increases, the penetration of sunlight decreases. As the angle of incidence of rays decreases, the number of rays reflected from the water's surface increases, reducing the number of rays penetrating underwater. Visibility also significantly decreases in murky water, where suspended solid particles strongly scatter light rays. The human eye, in direct contact with the aquatic environment, perceives visible objects as blurry and distorted.

To improve underwater vision, a layer of air, separated from the aquatic environment by transparent glass or polymer, is needed for the human eyes. These can be masks, suits, helmets, or goggles for underwater swimming. The air between the eye and the glass enhances the refractive ability of the eye lens, as light rays enter the eye not from the water but from the air layer. Reflected light rays from objects pass to the diver's eyes through water, glass, and air, refracting each time they transition from one medium to another, magnifying objects in the diver's eyes by about one-third of their natural size.

Divers use artificial lighting to improve visibility, which is not effective in murky water.

Due to the optical properties of water and the influence of light filtration, there is a sharp change in color perception underwater. Light penetrates the water and interacts with its molecules, causing scattering and absorption of different wavelengths. With increasing diving depth, there is a change in the color spectrum due to light absorption by water. Changes in the color spectrum can vary depending on the lighting at the dive site, visibility conditions, water transparency, and the content of suspended particles in the water. Here are the main changes that occur with increasing depth:

Red Color: Red is the first color absorbed by water. Already at a depth of about 5-10 meters, red shades begin to disappear, and objects that appear red on the surface may appear more gray or brown underwater.

Orange Color: At a shallow depth of up to 5-10 meters, reflected light retains most of the spectrum, and color shades remain bright and saturated. However, with increasing diving depth, light absorption occurs, and at a depth of 10-15 meters, it becomes less noticeable. Objects with orange shades may look paler or more yellowish.

Yellow Color: At a depth of about 20-30 meters, the yellow color begins to lose its intensity. Objects with yellow shades may appear more green or gray.

Green and Blue Colors: Green and blue colors are maintained at depths exceeding 30 meters. Objects in the water at this depth may appear more saturated with blue or green tones.

Purple Color: Purple color can also be seen at depths greater than 30 meters, as it has a shorter wavelength and is less susceptible to water absorption.

White Color: White color is best perceived by human vision, so tools and equipment are often painted white, additionally applying strips of reflective paint that make the diver's gear more visible when illuminated by artificial light.

Sound propagation. hearing underwater

The most important organs for hearing are the ears. To understand the basic principles of the human auditory system, it is necessary to know the structure and processes of this mechanism. The ear is divided into the outer ear, middle ear (tympanic cavity), and the inner ear, known as the cochlea. The outer ear consists of the auricle and the auditory canal extending into the thickness of the temporal bone. This auditory passage begins at the auricle and ends at the tympanic membrane, which separates it from the middle ear. The tympanic membrane is very thin and sensitive to pressure.

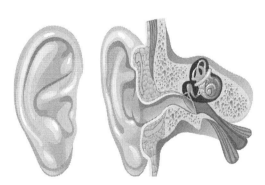

Fig. 14. Outer middle and inner ear

The middle ear is an air-filled cavity behind the tympanic membrane. It represents a small chamber located within the thickness of the temporal bone, connected to the nasopharynx by the Eustachian tube, which equalizes pressure on both sides of the tympanic membrane. The tympanic cavity is connected to the nasal cavity by the Eustachian tube, so it always contains air. The smallest bones of the human skeleton—the malleus, incus, and stapes —are also located in the middle ear; they are responsible for transmitting sound vibrations from the outer ear to the inner ear. Atmospheric air outside presses on the tympanic membrane through the auditory canal, while the air in the tympanic cavity from the inside, entering through the Eustachian tube, equalizes the pressure. The same process occurs during a diver's descent underwater. Through the Eustachian tube, a breathing gas mixture enters the tympanic cavity, exerting pressure on the tympanic membrane from the inside with a force corresponding to the depth of the dive. As a result, the pressure on both sides of the tympanic membrane remains the same, preventing damage to the tympanic membrane, and the diver does not experience painful sensations.

The process of equalizing pressure is called "clearing." In one out of a thousand cases, persistent Eustachian tube blockage is observed, usually due to improper development or obstruction after inflammation of the middle ear. Sometimes, temporary blockage of the Eustachian tube occurs with a cold, angina, or upper respiratory tract infection. In these cases, the mucous membrane of the tube swells, the lumen narrows, and it becomes clogged with mucus.

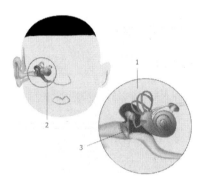

Fig. 15. Middle and inner ear: (1) - middle ear; (2) - eustachian tube; (3) - tympanic membrane

During underwater descents, when the Eustachian tube is poorly passable, and the pressure in the tympanic cavity does not equalize with the surrounding pressure in time, divers experience a specific condition called ear barotrauma (injury caused by a change in air pressure, affecting typically the ear or the lung). This condition leads to the rupture of the tympanic membrane, accompanied by sharp pain.

The inner ear is located deep within the bone tissue, consisting of the vestibule and semicircular canals responsible for the sense of balance and body positioning in space, and the cochlea filled with a special fluid. Here, sound vibrations reach in the form of vibrations. Inside the cochlea is the organ of Corti (a structure in the cochlea of the inner ear which produces nerve impulses in response to sound vibrations), which is directly responsible for hearing. It contains about 30,000 hair cells that capture sound vibrations. Sound waves vibrate

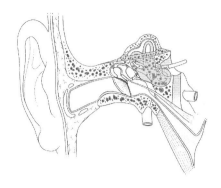

Fig. 16. Inner ear

the tympanic membrane, auditory ossicles, and the membrane of the organ of Corti. Nerve impulses from the hair cells of the organ of Corti are transmitted through the auditory nerves to the auditory center, located in the temporal lobe of the brain. Interestingly, each hair cell responds to a specific sound frequency, and the death of these cells results in hearing impairment. When they die, a person can no longer hear sounds of that frequency.

Sound propagates in water at a speed close to 1500 meters per second, which is nearly five times faster than in the air. However, underwater, humans hear less well due to the characteristics of the human auditory system, which is located in the inner ear. Sound waves reach it in two ways: through air and bone conduction. With air conduction, sound waves travel at a speed of approximately 330 meters per second, passing through the external auditory passage, causing vibrations of the tympanic membrane, and entering the inner ear through the auditory ossicles of the middle ear, irritating the endings of its auditory nerve. With bone conduction, sound vibrations are transmitted unhindered to the auditory apparatus through the bones of the skull, and the range of audibility depends mainly on the tone of the sound. The higher the pitch, the farther the sound is heard. It is proven that bone conduction is 40% lower than air conduction. Bone conduction of sound simultaneously provides sound perception to both ears, making it impossible for a diver to determine the direction of the sound and orient himself underwater. Hearing underwater depends on the type of equipment used. During descents without a helmet, divers hear quite well, while in a neoprene-fitting helmet, sound perception decreases. The worst hearing occurs in a voluminous helmet with an air layer. Sound vibrations are dispersed and absorbed, reaching the eardrums last, passing through the helmet and the layer of air between the helmet and the ear. It should be noted that sounds produced on the surface are practically inaudible underwater, just as underwater sounds cannot be heard on the surface. Therefore, to hear underwater sounds, it is necessary to enter the water at least knee-deep. In this case, sound vibrations through the bones will be transmitted to the skull bones and, through them, to the inner ear. When diving headfirst into the water, the sound volume increases several times. Various underwater communication systems are used for communication between divers, depending on water conditions such as diving depth, water turbidity, and the presence of interference. These include underwater radios and radiophones, as well as devices with text messaging communication functions. All these systems have limitations on the range of signal transmission and the depth at which they can operate. In the absence of underwater communication systems, divers use primitive sound sources to convey conditional signals and exchange messages among themselves. The most common signals include messages like "Everything is okay," "Everyone stop and stay in place," "Attention, danger approaching," "Urgent assistance needed," and "Everyone surface immediately." Sounds produced by rattles, hammers, or striking a metallic object on a cylinder serve as sources of such signals. For example, the audibility range of knife hits on a cylinder is about 150 meters. Orientation underwater by sound, for divers with little experience, is practically impossible. In the air, sound reaches one ear a fraction of a second (approximately 0.0001 seconds) earlier than the other. Therefore, a person can determine the direction of the sound source with an accuracy of 1-3°. Underwater, the speed of sound is five times faster, and sound is perceived almost simultaneously by both ears, so they cannot perceive the difference in the time of sound arrival and determine the direction of the sound source.

Propagation of shock waves in water

Underwater explosions are characterized by an instantaneous increase in pressure. The speed of the shock wave is equal to the speed of sound propagation. In water, explosive energy spreads in the form of a shock wave and hydrodynamic forces. The shock wave creates compression and rarefaction in water, causing oscillations and the spread of energy in all directions. Hydrodynamic forces can induce flows and water displacement, causing damage to objects in their path. In an air explosion, due to its compressibility, the impact of the shock wave diminishes quite quickly as it moves away from the explosion site. A shock wave in water propagates five times faster, and due to the low compressibility of water, it significantly attenuates more slowly, acting over a much greater distance from the explosion site. With an increase in the depth of the explosion, the shock wave spreads much farther due to the better conductivity and density of the medium, but the intensity of the wave decreases with the distance from the explosion source.

Fig. 17. Explosion underwater

Underwater explosions can have serious consequences for the environment and living organisms at much greater distances than in the air. Fish and other aquatic organisms can be damaged or killed as a result of the explosion. Plants and corals may also be damaged due to the strong shock wave and changes in water pressure. For example, if an explosive charge equivalent to 3 kilograms of TNT is safe for a person at a distance of 50-70 meters in the air, it will be safe in the water at a distance of about 2000 meters. Therefore, when conducting explosive work, it is crucial to strictly adhere to all recommendations and instructions established by competent organizations or government authorities to ensure the safety of divers and objects underwater.

Checkpoint questions for chapter one:

1. What are the main gases in the composition of atmospheric air, and what is their percentage ratio?

2. Name the property of oxygen and its significance in human life.

3. Name the property of carbon dioxide and its impact on the human body.

4. What is atmospheric pressure?

5. What are technical atmosphere, absolute atmosphere, and excess atmosphere?

6. How does the volume of gas change with changes in pressure?

7. How does the volume and pressure of gas change with changes in temperature?

8. What is partial pressure of a gas?

9. How is the partial pressure of a gas calculated in a gas mixture?

10. What is the weight of one cubic meter of air?

11. Until what depth does gas dissolve in liquid?

12. What is the significance of the specific heat and thermal conductivity of water for diving descents?

13. How does water pressure change with increasing depth?

14. What does Archimedes' principle express?

15. Under what conditions of gas mixture delivery will a diver at a depth of 10 meters not experience discomfort?

16. How does buoyancy force differ from the weight force of a diver?

17. How is light distributed in water? Which spectrum of rays is best visible to the human eye?

18. How does sound propagate in water? How does the tonality affect sound propagation?

19. What are the differences in the propagation of shock waves in air and in water?

20. Calculate the buoyancy force of a wooden block weighing 1200 grams and with a volume of 1.2 dm³. Will this block remain afloat or sink?

21. Will a wooden block weighing 1200 grams and with a volume of 1.2 dm³ sink if it is immersed in saltwater at a temperature of 4°C?

II CHAPTER
PHYSIOLOGY AND PATHOLOGY OF UNDERWATER IMMERSIONS

Chapter two of the textbook is dedicated to the physiological aspects of diving, providing a foundation for understanding the changes and processes that impact the human circulatory and respiratory systems in underwater conditions.

The chapter includes a comparison of breathing gas mixtures based on oxygen, such as air, Nitrox, Heliox, and others. Information is presented on factors influencing the amount of dissolved gas in the human body and the effects of gases on the human body under pressure. The toxicity of gas components in breathing mixtures, as well as the toxic or narcotic effects of individual gases in breathing gas mixtures, is discussed. The calculation of the partial pressure of various gases at different depths is also presented.

Additionally, the chapter contains information on the mechanisms of body temperature regulation and heat dissipation, covering thermogenesis, heat loss through the lungs, and heat loss through the skin.

§ 3. Influence of environmental pressure on gas exchange and human circulation

With an increase in ambient pressure exerted during a diver's descent, the most significant changes occur in the functioning of the respiratory and circulatory systems. To understand the specific alterations in these systems, it is essential to comprehend the processes of blood circulation and gas exchange under normal conditions for the human body. The circulatory system consists of the muscular organ—the heart—and blood vessels: arteries, veins, and capillaries. Arteries carry blood from the heart to the periphery, while veins return it from the periphery to the heart. Gas exchange between blood and tissues occurs in the smallest vessels connecting arteries and veins, known as capillaries. The heart has two halves separated by a vertical septum. Each half is divided horizontally into two chambers: the upper is called the atrium, and the lower is the ventricle. The left side of the heart contains oxygen-rich arterial blood, while the right side contains oxygen-poor but carbon dioxide-rich venous blood.

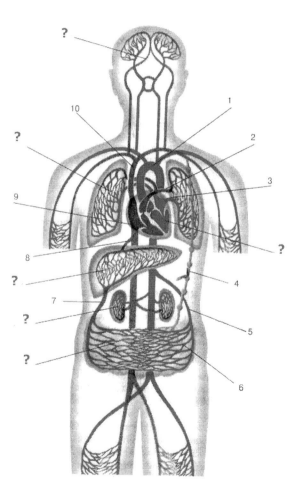

Valves in the septa between the atria and ventricles open in the direction of the ventricles, allowing blood to flow only in one direction. Not all heart chambers contract simultaneously. Initially, both atria contract, and blood passes through the valves into the ventricles. Then, both ventricles contract, and blood moves from them into the blood vessels. After ventricular contraction, the cardiac muscle remains relaxed for some time, and then the entire cycle repeats.

Fig. 18. Human organs

Pulmonary circulation

The pulmonary circulation begins with the contraction of the right ventricle, directing venous blood into two pulmonary arteries. The right artery leads to the right lung, while the left one leads to the left lung. In the lungs, arteries branch into capillaries, forming a multitude of lung capillaries with very thin walls. Thin arteries branch into capillaries and approach the lung's air sacs, called alveoli. Here, they facilitate gas exchange: carbon dioxide from the veins diffuses into the alveolar air, while oxygen from the alveolar air enters the blood, binding with hemoglobin. The blood becomes arterial, and hemoglobin transforms back into oxyhemoglobin, causing the blood to change color from dark to bright red. Capillaries carrying oxygenated blood merge first into small and then into larger vessels—pulmonary veins—that return arterial blood to the heart. Two pulmonary veins, carrying arterial blood, lead from each lung to the left atrium, concluding the pulmonary circulation. Blood flows into the left ventricle, initiating the systemic circulation.

Systemic circulation

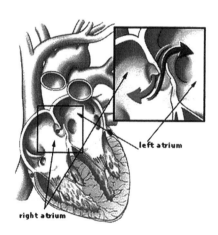

Fig. 19. Circulation in the Heart

When the left ventricle contracts, blood is ejected into the aorta – the largest artery. Branches from the aortic arch supply blood to the head, arms, and torso. In the thoracic cavity, arteries branch from the descending aorta to organs within the chest, while in the abdominal cavity, arteries supply organs of the digestive system, kidneys, muscles of the lower body, and other organs. Arteries deliver blood to all organs and tissues, extensively branching, narrowing, and gradually transitioning into blood capillaries. In the capillaries of the systemic circulation, oxyhemoglobin in red blood cells breaks down into hemoglobin and oxygen. Tissues absorb oxygen for biological oxidation, and the resulting carbon dioxide is carried away by blood plasma and hemoglobin in red blood cells. Nutrients in the blood are delivered to cells. Afterward, blood gathers in the veins of the systemic circulation. Veins from the upper half of the body drain into the superior vena cava, while those from the lower half drain into the inferior vena cava. Both veins carry blood to the right atrium of the heart, concluding the systemic circulation. Venous blood passes into the right ventricle, restarting the pulmonary circulation. Thus, every drop of blood sequentially goes through both circulatory systems—one after the other.

The circulation in the heart pertains to the systemic circulation. From the aorta, an artery branches off to the heart muscles. It encircles the heart like a crown and is consequently called the coronary artery. Smaller vessels diverge from it, breaking down into a capillary network. Here, arterial blood releases its oxygen and absorbs carbon dioxide. Venous blood collects in veins, which merge and, through several channels, flow into the right atrium. In the human body, blood moves through two circulatory systems: the pulmonary—between the heart and lungs—and the systemic—between the heart and all other organs. Blood, a liquid tissue of the body, fills the blood vessels. As it flows through various body regions, blood delivers oxygen and nutrients, becomes enriched with carbon dioxide and other metabolic by-products, which are eliminated from the body through excretory organs.

In the liquid part of the blood, called plasma, suspended are the so-called formed elements: erythrocytes (red blood cells), leukocytes (white blood cells), and thrombocytes – blood platelets. Erythrocytes, numbering 4-5 million in one cubic millimeter, predominate in the blood. An erythrocyte is a cell without a nucleus, characterized by a disc-like shape, almost entirely filled with a substance called hemoglobin. Hemoglobin forms an unstable chemical compound – oxyhemoglobin – with oxygen. This compound has the property of breaking down into hemoglobin and oxygen in an environment where oxygen is insufficient. Tissues of the body, sensing the need for oxygen, constitute such an environment.

Red blood cells have a relatively short lifespan and are constantly replaced by new ones. It has been scientifically proven that 800 billion erythrocytes die daily, approximately 1/30th of the entire blood volume. These losses are replenished by the influx of fresh erythrocytes produced in the red bone marrow and also formed in the liver in the fetus. Red bone marrow is the primary source of erythrocyte formation in adults. It is a soft tissue located inside bones such as the pelvic bones, sternum, ribs, and the upper part of the thigh. Special cells called stem cells have the ability to differentiate into various types of blood cells, including erythrocytes.

Stages of erythrocyte maturation take place in the red bone marrow, where they undergo the process of erythropoiesis (erythropoiesis is a subtype of hematopoiesis, during which red blood cells are formed). In the fetus, during development, erythrocytes are also formed in the liver. From the early stages of embryonic development, the liver serves as a temporary site for the formation of blood cells, including erythrocytes. This continues until the bone marrow becomes the primary source of erythrocyte formation. When erythrocytes reach maturity, they leave the red bone marrow or liver and enter the bloodstream, where they perform their functions. There are significantly fewer leukocytes in the blood, ranging from 4000 to 11000 in one cubic millimeter. Leukocytes, or white blood cells, play a crucial role in the human immune system and perform various functions aimed at protecting the body from infections, diseases, and other harmful influences. They can move independently and play a key role in the human immune system. They activate and move to the site of inflammation, where they help fight infection and contribute to tissue regeneration. Platelets, or blood platelets, play an important role in the human body, especially in the blood clotting process and the prevention of bleeding. There are about 300,000 of them in one cubic millimeter of blood. When a blood vessel is damaged, platelets activate and aggregate, forming a platelet plug or clot. This process is known as platelet aggregation. The platelet plug, or clot, forms a primary plug that prevents further bleeding and creates a temporary seal in the damaged vessel. Activated platelets release blood clotting factors such as thromboxane and serotonin, which help strengthen and sustain blood clotting.

These factors contribute to the narrowing of the damaged blood vessel and the reinforcement of the platelet plug. Platelets also regulate the influx of new platelets to the site of injury. They release substances such as thrombopoietin, which stimulate the bone marrow to produce new platelets. In addition to blood clotting, platelets, during the repair of damaged tissues, release growth factors that stimulate tissue regeneration and healing. Interacting with immune cells, platelets participate in the body's immune response, including inflammation and fighting infection. It is important to note that a normal platelet count in the blood is crucial for maintaining normal blood clotting function; if blood did not clot, even a minor scratch could cause life-threatening bleeding. In addition to the closed circulatory system, there is an open lymphatic system that allows clearing intercellular spaces from unnecessary substances. The drainage of lymph carries away from the tissue fluid everything formed in the process of cell life, including microorganisms that have entered the internal environment, dead cell parts, and other unnecessary residues. Additionally, some nutrients from the intestines enter the lymphatic system. All these substances enter the lymphatic capillaries and flow into the lymphatic vessels.

Passing through lymph nodes, lymph is purified and, freed from foreign impurities, enters the jugular veins. The primary purpose of the heart is to ensure the continuous movement of blood through the vessels. If the heart stops, a person dies within 5-6 minutes. The human body contains about 5 liters of blood, approximately 5-8% of body weight. One complete circulation of blood takes about 30 seconds. In the resting state of the human body, the heart of a healthy person contracts 70-75 times per minute, ejecting 60-80 milliliters of blood with each contraction into the aorta. In a day, the heart pumps more than 8000 liters of blood. The velocity of blood flow depends on the condition of the person: at rest or during physical exertion. The higher the physical load, the faster the blood circulation, and during physical exertion, the heart contracts up to 150 times per minute, and the amount of blood ejected with each contraction can increase to 180 milliliters. As blood travels through the blood vessels, it experiences a certain resistance from the vessel walls. The smaller the diameter of the vessels as they move away from the heart, the greater the resistance to blood flow. To overcome this resistance, blood enters the vessels from the heart under a certain pressure. The highest pressure in the vessels is noted at the moment of contraction of the heart ventricles. This pressure is called maximum arterial pressure. In a healthy person, it is approximately 110-130 mm Hg. Art. At the moment of relaxation of the ventricles, the pressure in the vessels will be minimal, approximately 60-80 mm Hg. Art. The smallest pressure is observed in venous blood in the hollow veins at the point of their entry into the right ventricle of the heart. The heart, as it were, draws venous blood from the hollow veins. When on the surface of the earth, the human body feels almost the same atmospheric pressure on all areas of the body. When submerged underwater, the human body will experience different pressures on the upper and lower parts of the body. With an average height of a diver of 170 cm, the pressure difference will be 130 mm Hg. Art. As a result, different conditions for blood flow are created in the upper and lower parts of the body. The pressure in the veins located above the level of the heart will be lower than at the point of entry of the hollow veins, so the outflow of venous blood from the head and upper extremities is difficult, and the veins of the head, neck, and arms become filled with blood. In the lower parts of the body, the natural outflow of blood is facilitated by the increasing pressure of the water, which tries to "squeeze" blood from bottom to top. At the same time, opposite conditions are created for the flow of blood through the arteries. In the direction of lower pressure, blood will flow easily, and as it passes to the lower parts of the body, blood will encounter increasing resistance. As a result of uneven water pressure relative to the depth of immersion of the human body, blood redistribution occurs in the human body, and the load on the heart increases. In addition to this, the lower extremities of the diver, insufficiently supplied with blood and tightly compressed by a wetsuit, cool faster than other parts of the body.

§ 4. Influence of pressure on human respiration

Processes and organs of respiration

To sustain life in the human body, continuous absorption of oxygen by cells and the removal of carbon dioxide, which is formed during oxidative processes, are necessary. These two processes constitute the essence of respiration. Air, or any respiratory gas mixture containing oxygen, is inhaled through the nose or mouth and passes through the respiratory pathways. Inhalation involves the contraction of the diaphragm and intercostal muscles, leading to the expansion of the chest and the creation of negative pressure in the lungs. The respiratory gas mixture passes through the respiratory pathways, including the nasal cavity, pharynx, trachea, and bronchi. The bronchi divide into numerous tiny tubes called bronchioles, which lead to miniature air sacs that make up the human lungs and are called alveoli. There are about 700 million alveoli in the lungs. The diameter of each air sac is approximately 0.2 mm, and their total surface area is about 90 square meters. Passing through the air-conducting respiratory pathways, air or another respiratory gas mixture enters the pulmonary sacs. Alveoli are the site of the main gas exchange in the lungs. In the walls of the alveoli are numerous microscopic capillaries that surround the alveoli. The wall of the pulmonary sac and capillary together has a thickness of only 0.004 mm. Capillaries contain oxygen-rich blood, and the air in the alveoli contains oxygen and carbon dioxide. Here, diffusion occurs, where oxygen passes from the alveoli to the blood in the capillaries, and carbon dioxide passes from the blood to the alveoli. This process is determined by the difference in gas concentrations between the alveoli and the capillaries.

As we already know from the previous material, oxygen bound to hemoglobin in red blood cells is transported to the tissues of the body through the circulatory system. Carbon dioxide, formed as a result of gas exchange in the tissues, returns to the lungs through the circulatory system and is released into the alveoli for subsequent exhalation.

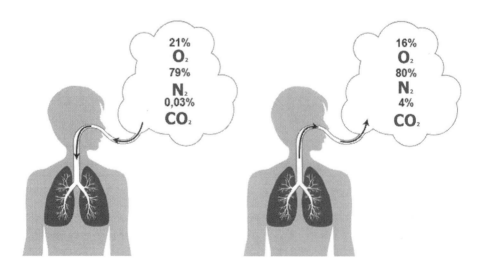

Fig. 20. Diffusion process

Outside, the lungs are covered with a smooth, slightly moist membrane - the pleura. The same membrane covers the walls of the chest cavity formed by the ribs and intercostal muscles on the sides, and by the diaphragm or chest muscle below. The lungs are not fused with the walls of the chest cavity; they are just tightly pressed against them. This is because there is no air in the pleural cavities, which are narrow slits. Inside the lungs, in the alveoli, there is always air communicating with the atmosphere, so there is atmospheric pressure in the lungs. It presses the lungs against the chest walls with such force that the lungs cannot detach from them and passively follow them when the chest expands or compresses.

Breathing occurs as follows. During inhalation, by the effort of respiratory muscles, the chest expands. The lungs, passively following the chest, draw in air through the respiratory pathways. Then, due to its elasticity, the chest decreases in volume, the lungs compress, and excess air is expelled into the atmosphere - exhalation occurs.

With each inhalation, a person takes in 500 milliliters of air into the lungs, and exhales the same amount. This air is called tidal air. If, after a normal inhalation, an additional deep inhalation is made, an additional 1500–3000 milliliters of air will enter the lungs. This is called inspiratory reserve. With a deep exhalation after a normal exhalation, it is possible to remove 1000–2500 milliliters of the so-called expiratory reserve air, after which about 1000–1500 milliliters of residual air still remain in the lungs. The sum of tidal, inspiratory, and expiratory reserve air is called the vital capacity of the lungs. It is measured using a special device called a spirometer. In different people, it ranges from 3000 to 7000 milliliters. The larger the lung volume, the longer a diver can stay underwater. Human breathing is regulated by special nerve cells, the so-called respiratory center, which is located near the cardiorespiratory center in the medulla oblongata. The respiratory center is very sensitive to an excess of carbon dioxide

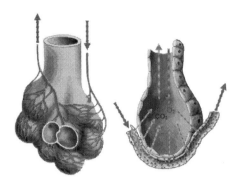

Fig. 21. Gas exchange process

in the blood. An increase in the carbon dioxide content in the blood irritates the respiratory center and accelerates breathing. A sudden decrease in the carbon dioxide content in the blood or alveolar air causes apnea - a brief cessation of breathing for up to a minute and a half. Holding one's breath by an act of will for one minute is considered a normal indicator for the human body. While at rest on the earth's surface, a person takes 16 to 20 breaths. As we already know, with each inhalation, 0.5 liters of air enter the lungs; making 20 breaths, we get 10 liters of air per minute. This value is called the minute ventilation, or pulmonary ventilation. Not all the air entering the body during inhalation reaches the alveoli. The respiratory pathways of a person, such as the trachea, large and small bronchi, occupy a volume of about 175 cubic centimeters. The air occupying this volume does not participate in the breathing process and is removed during exhalation without reaching the alveoli. During inhalation, the alveoli are filled primarily with the air that filled the respiratory pathways at the end of exhalation, in other words, air containing a lot of carbon dioxide and water vapor. The volume of the respiratory pathways, in which air not involved in breathing is located, is called the dead space. After a diver turns on the breathing apparatus, the magnitude of the dead space increases due to the addition of the volume of the valve box with pipes, and the conditions of pulmonary ventilation worsen slightly. During physical work, the minute ventilation increases to 20–30 liters per minute, and during heavy work, it can reach 100 liters per minute or more. Being underwater, even without performing any work, is a significant load on the body, so the volume of air consumption underwater significantly increases. The resistance to breathing is of great importance when working underwater. As the diving depth increases, the compressed air that a diver breathes becomes denser. The size of the respiratory passages, the cross-sectional area of the throat and bronchi, remains unchanged, and when breathing compressed air, a person has to exert more effort to pass the same volume of gas into the lungs, but denser. Therefore, prolonged exposure of a person to increased pressure leads to rapid fatigue of the chest muscles. Similarly, the horizontal position of a person floating on the surface, who experiences uneven pressure on different parts of the body, also leads to fatigue. The head of a floating person is at the level of the water surface or above it, therefore, when breathing in the lungs, atmospheric pressure is maintained.

The swimmer's chest is submerged at a depth of 30-40 cm, and it is already pressed upon by a column of water equal to 0.03–0.04 kilograms per square centimeter. The surface area of the chest is approximately 600–650 cm2; therefore, the total water pressure on the entire chest of the swimmer is 8–12 kilograms. This pressure provides additional resistance, which the swimmer overcomes during inhalation due to the strength of the chest muscles. The force of the respiratory

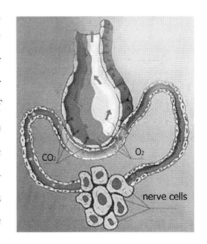

Fig. 22. Special nerve cells

muscles of the chest is capable of overcoming up to 110 mm Hg, which corresponds to a diver being at a depth of 150 cm. Inhalation will be more difficult when the body is in a vertical position underwater because the pressure on the lower part of the chest will be greater than on the upper part. The optimal condition is swimming underwater in a horizontal body position; in this case, the pressure on the chest is uniform. Scientifically proven, when underwater, one can breathe through a tube at a depth of no more than 1 meter. At greater depths, respiratory muscles cannot overcome the additional column of water pressing on the chest. When breathing through a tube, the inhaled air is depleted of oxygen and has a slight excess of carbon dioxide. Coupled with increased respiratory resistance, this leads to stimulation of the respiratory center, increased breathing, and shortness of breath. The primary condition for human breathing underwater is the equality of air pressure in the lungs with the external water pressure. To balance the external water pressure on the chest, air or a gas mixture is supplied to the lungs under pressure corresponding to the depth. Currently, this is done in three ways: through a short tube (up to 40 cm) for a surface swimmer, using autonomous breathing apparatus, and by supplying air from the surface to isolating devices.

Influence of increased air pressure on the diver's body

The human body consists of 65-70% liquid. As is known, water and other liquids practically do not compress under pressure, so a gradual and slow increase in the pressure of fluids and the breathing mixture is not felt by the tissues of the human body. However, the human body has a number of hollow organs filled with gases: the lungs, intestines, tympanic, frontal, and maxillary sinuses are connected to the nasopharynx and the middle ear by relatively narrow channels. If these channels are blocked or not fully open, the permeability of compressed gas will not be able to equalize with the changing external pressure, leading to painful sensations and specific diseases in divers. Conditionally, a diver's stay underwater (or in a recompression chamber) can be divided into three stages: the first is the descent period, during which pressure on the body increases, called compression; the second is the period when the diver is at the maximum depth under the greatest pressure, and the period of pressure reduction, called decompression.

To avoid specific diving-related illnesses, it is necessary to understand the characteristics of each of these periods. During the compression period, the diver's body is subjected to rapidly increasing ambient pressure. This rapid pressure change can lead to the onset of negative pathological processes in the tympanic cavity and accessory sinuses of the nose, located in the upper jaw, frontal, and ethmoid bones. Due to pressure imbalance in the tympanic cavity with external pressure, a rupture of the eardrum, called ear barotrauma, may occur. In some cases, after pressure in the ears, toothache may arise because the branches of the trigeminal nerve simultaneously serve the eardrum and the teeth of the upper and lower jaws. Increased pressure may cause pain in an individual tooth affected by caries. During rapid descent, a "squeeze" can occur in the diver due to insufficient air supply in the diving suit or untimely pressure equalization under the mask.

During the period when the diver is at maximum depth, due to violations of safety rules in diving, functional shifts in the human body may occur, depending on the increased partial pressure of gases in the breathing mixture or the low ambient temperature. A significant aspect is the period of stay at

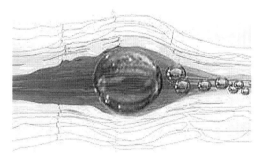

Fig. 23. Bubbles that can block blood vessels

maximum depth, during which excess saturation of the body tissues with nitrogen or other inert gases occurs. The consequences of this phenomenon manifest during the ascent of the diver to the surface.

During the decompression period, tissues of the human body gradually release excess nitrogen. If the ascent of the diver occurs too quickly, due to a decrease in absolute and partial pressures, part of the dissolved nitrogen in the body will transition to a free state and be released in the form of bubbles, which can block blood vessels and cause decompression sickness. If the diver voluntarily delays exhalation and does not timely remove the excess expanding air from the lungs, barotrauma of the lungs may occur during the ascent. Also, during the ascent of the diver, there is an increase in the volume of gases in the intestines, which can cause abdominal pain.

To avoid negative effects on the human body during the ascent period, it is advisable to use decompression tables.

The influence of changes in the partial pressure of individual gases on the human body Nitrogen, oxygen, and carbon dioxide, in the proportions that make up the air, are harmless to the human body under normal atmospheric pressure. With a change in the partial pressure of all or individual gases, the human body experiences their negative effects. When a diver descends to a depth of more than 40 meters and breathes compressed air, the diver enters a state reminiscent of mild alcohol intoxication. At a partial pressure of 5-6 atmospheres, inexplicable euphoria appears, and with further descent, the effect of nitrogen on the human body intensifies, coordination is disrupted, orientation is lost, and visual and auditory hallucinations begin. At a pressure of 12-13 atmospheres, sleep occurs. After pressure is reduced, all these phenomena disappear without a trace. With a significant increase in the partial pressure of oxygen in the inhaled air, oxygen poisoning occurs. The initial signs of oxygen poisoning include a tingling sensation in the fingers of the hands and feet, twitching of facial muscles, especially the lips and eyelids, and spasmodic twitching of the fingers. A feeling of restlessness arises. General convulsions and loss of consciousness then quickly follow. Carbon dioxide, present in the air up to 1%, does not have a harmful effect on humans, but when diving to 40 meters, its percentage content increases fivefold, reaching 5% in terms of atmospheric pressure. At such a concentration, carbon dioxide poisoning occurs in humans. Increased carbon dioxide content can result from a violation of the rules for using breathing apparatus or malfunctions in diving equipment. All gases in the gas mixture, when breathed in, dissolve in the blood and tissues of the body. According to the laws of physics, the amount of gas dissolved in a liquid will be proportional to the pressure of the gas above the liquid and the temperature at which the dissolution occurs. The amount of gas dissolved in the tissues of the human body depends on the time spent under pressure and the physical load.

Breathing gas mixtures for divers

A breathing gas is a mixture of gaseous chemical elements and compounds used for respiration.

Air is the most common and only natural breathing gas. However, other gas mixtures or pure oxygen are also used in breathing apparatus and closed living environments, such as scuba tanks, rebreathers, diving suits, submarines, hyperbaric chambers, and medical life support and first aid equipment. Methods used to fill diver's cylinders with gases other than air are called gas blending. Breathing gases for use at pressures below normal atmospheric pressure typically consist of pure oxygen or oxygen-enriched air to provide an adequate amount of oxygen for maintaining life and consciousness or to support higher levels of exertion than would be possible using air. Usually, additional oxygen is supplied as pure gas added to the breathing air during inhalation or through a life support system. Oxygen is a crucial component of any breathing gas at partial pressures ranging from 0.16 to 1.60 bar at atmospheric pressure. Oxygen is typically the only metabolically active component unless the gas is an anesthetic mixture. Some amount of oxygen in the breathing gas is consumed by metabolic processes, while inert components remain unchanged and primarily serve to dilute oxygen to the appropriate concentration; therefore, they are also known as diluent gases. Thus, most breathing gases are a mixture of oxygen with one or more inert gases. Breathing gases for hyperbaric use have been developed to enhance the characteristics of normal air by reducing the risk of decompression sickness, shortening decompression time, reducing nitrogen narcosis, or providing safer deep-sea dives. A safe breathing gas for use under elevated pressure possesses four main characteristics: - The gas must contain sufficient oxygen to sustain life, consciousness, and the breathing rate of the user. - The gas must not contain harmful impurities. Carbon monoxide and carbon dioxide are common poisons that can contaminate breathing gases. - The gas must not become toxic when inhaled under high pressure, such as underwater. Oxygen and nitrogen are examples of gases that become toxic under pressure. - The gas must not be too dense for breathing. The work of breathing increases with increasing density and viscosity. Maximum ventilation decreases by about 50% when density is equivalent to air at 3 bar, and carbon dioxide levels become unacceptably high at moderate gas density exceeding 6 g/liter. A gas density of 10 g/liter or more may cause uncontrollable hypercapnia even at very low work levels, which can lead to potentially fatal consequences.

Gas analysis

Gas mixtures generally need to be analyzed either in the process or after mixing for quality control. This is especially important for breathing gas mixtures, where errors can impact the health and safety of the end-user. Most gases that may be present in diving cylinders are difficult to detect because they are colorless, odorless, and tasteless. For some gases, electronic sensors such as oxygen analyzers, helium analyzers, carbon monoxide detectors, and carbon dioxide detectors exist. Oxygen analyzers are typically located underwater in rebreathers. Oxygen and helium analyzers are often used on the surface during gas blending to determine the percentage of oxygen or helium in the breathing gas mixture. Chemical and other gas detection methods are used for periodic testing of the quality of compressed breathing air from air compressors designed to fill scuba cylinders.

Common breathing gas mixtures for diving

Air - a mixture of 21% oxygen, 78% nitrogen, and approximately 1% other gas impurities, mainly argon (for calculation simplicity, the last 1% is usually considered as nitrogen). Being inexpensive and easy to use, it is the most common gas for diving. Due to nitrogen causing nitrogen narcosis, a safe depth for most divers is considered to be around 40 meters (130 feet), although the maximum working depth of air at an allowable partial pressure of oxygen of 1.6 bar is 66.2 meters (218 feet).

Oxygen - pure oxygen is primarily used for accelerating shallow decompression stops at the end of deep dives. The risk of acute oxygen toxicity rapidly increases at pressures exceeding 0.6 bar. Oxygen is widely used in rebreather-type breathing apparatus.

Nitrox - a mixture of oxygen and air, typically referring to mixtures containing more than 32% oxygen and 68% nitrogen. This breathing gas mixture can be used as a tool for accelerating in-water decompression stops or reducing the risk of decompression sickness, thus extending dive time.

Trimix - a mixture of 18% oxygen, 35% nitrogen, and 45% helium, often used by divers for deep dives instead of air to reduce nitrogen narcosis and avoid the risk of oxygen toxicity. The purpose of trimix is to reduce the narcotic effects of nitrogen and oxygen, thereby extending the depth limit for diving. The mixture composition is denoted as A/B, where A is the oxygen content percentage, and B is the helium content percentage (e.g., Trimix 10/50 contains 10% oxygen and 50% helium).

Heliox - a mixture of oxygen ranging from 11% to 20% and helium ranging from 89% to 80%, known among divers as the "bottom mix." It is used during deep dives to eliminate nitrogen narcosis. To avoid oxygen toxicity, the oxygen content in the mixture is calculated based on partial pressure, either at the maximum depth or the depth of primary work.

Heliair - a form of trimix easily blended from helium and air without using pure oxygen. It always has an oxygen-to-nitrogen ratio of 21:79, with the remaining gas being helium.

Oxygen-hydrogen-helium mixture of gases (Hydrox) - a mixture of oxygen, helium, and hydrogen used for dives below 130 meters, up to 500 meters. However, hydrogen narcosis begins to take effect at greater depths. The mixture is explosive due to the combination of these volatile gases, so hydrogen is only added to gas mixes with low oxygen content.

Hydrogen - a gas mixture of hydrogen and oxygen used as a breathing gas for very deep dives. It is explosive and falls into the category of explosive gases. Applicable at depths from 70 to 700 meters.

Neox - a mixture of oxygen and neon, sometimes used in deep-sea diving. It is rarely used due to its cost. Additionally, symptoms of decompression sickness caused by neon ("neox bends") have a poor reputation, as they are widely reported to be more severe than symptoms caused by a similar oxygen-helium mixture.

Classification of breathing gas mixtures based on oxygen content

Breathing gases for underwater dives are classified according to their oxygen content. The boundaries set by authorities may vary slightly, as the consequences gradually change depending on the concentration and individual organisms, making them not precisely predictable.

Normoxic - it contains approximately 21% oxygen, not significantly different from its content in the air. This mixture ensures continuous safe use at atmospheric pressure and dives up to 66 meters (at an oxygen partial pressure of 1.6 atmospheres).

Hyperoxic (Oxygen-Enriched) - in this gas mixture, the oxygen content exceeds 21%. It is primarily used as an intermediate or travel gas during prolonged use, resulting in measurable physiological effects. Special handling procedures are sometimes required due to increased fire hazard. Associated risks include oxygen toxicity at depth and the potential for combustion if breathing apparatuses are stored and used carelessly.

Hypoxic - it has an oxygen content less than 21% and is used for deep-sea dives. There is a significant risk of a physiological effect resulting in a short-term loss of efficiency due to hypoxia on the surface or near it.

Individual components of gas mixtures

Breathing gases for underwater dives are composed of a small number of gas components that give the mixture unique characteristics not found in atmospheric air.

Oxygen (O_2) must be present in every breathing mixture because it is essential for the metabolic processes of the human body that sustain life. The human body cannot store oxygen for future use, as it does with food. Deprivation of oxygen for more than a few minutes leads to loss of consciousness and death. Tissues and organs in the body, especially the heart and brain, suffer damage if deprived of oxygen for more than four minutes.

Filling a diving cylinder with pure oxygen costs about five times more than filling it with compressed air. Since oxygen supports combustion and causes corrosion in diving cylinders, it should be handled with caution, especially when mixing gases. Historically, oxygen was obtained through fractional distillation of liquid air, but increasingly, it is produced using non-cryogenic technologies such as pressure swing adsorption and vacuum swing adsorption.

The oxygen content of a breathing gas mixture is sometimes used in its naming. The oxygen fraction determines the maximum depth at which the mixture can be safely used to avoid oxygen toxicity. This depth is called the maximum operating depth. The concentration of oxygen in the gas mixture depends on the fraction and pressure of the mixture and is expressed as the partial pressure of oxygen.

Hypoxic mixtures contain less than 21% oxygen, although the 16% threshold is often used, and they are intended for breathing at depth as a "bottom gas," where higher pressure increases the partial pressure of oxygen to a safe level. Trimix, Heliox, and Heliair are gas mixtures commonly used for hypoxic mixes and are used in professional and technical diving as deep-breathing gases.

Normoxic mixtures contain the same oxygen fraction as air, 21%. The maximum operating depth of a normoxic mixture can reach only 47 meters (155 feet). Trimix with oxygen content from 17% to 21% is often described as normoxic because it contains a high enough oxygen fraction to be safely breathed at the surface.

Hyperoxic mixtures contain more than 21% oxygen. Enriched Air Nitrox (EANx) is a typical hyperoxic breathing mixture. Compared to air, hyperoxic mixtures cause oxygen toxicity at shallow depths but can be used to reduce decompression stops by more quickly eliminating dissolved inert gases from the body.

The partial pressure of any gas component in a mixture is calculated as follows: partial pressure = total absolute pressure × volumetric fraction of the gas component. For the oxygen component:

$$PO_2 = P \times FO_2$$

where:

PO_2 - partial pressure of oxygen;

P - total pressure;

FO_2 - volumetric fraction of oxygen.

The minimum safe partial pressure of oxygen in a breathing mixture is usually 16 kPa (0.16 bar). Below this partial pressure, a diver may be at risk of losing consciousness and death due to hypoxia, depending on factors including individual physiology and the level of exertion. When a hypoxic mixture is breathed in shallow water, it may have an insufficiently high PO_2 level for the diver to remain conscious. For this reason, normoxic or hyperoxic "transport mixtures" are used at moderate depths between the "bottom" and "decompression" phases of a dive.

The maximum safe PO_2 content in a breathing mixture depends on the duration of exposure, the level of physical exertion, and the safety of the breathing equipment used. It typically ranges from 100 kPa (1 bar) to 160 kPa (1.6 bar). For dives lasting less than three hours, 140 kPa (1.4 bar) is commonly considered, although the U.S. Navy allows dives with PO_2 up to 180 kPa (1.8 bar). At high PO_2 levels or longer exposures, the diver risks oxygen toxicity, leading to seizures.

Each breathing mixture has a maximum operating depth determined by its oxygen content. For therapeutic recompression and hyperbaric oxygen therapy, a partial pressure of 2.8 bar is commonly used because, when conducting therapy in a hyperbaric chamber, there is no risk of drowning if a person suddenly loses consciousness. For longer periods, such as saturation diving, a pressure of 0.4 bar can be sustained for several weeks.

Oxygen analyzers are used to measure the partial pressure of oxygen in a gas mixture.

Divox is designed for breathing oxygen suitable for divers. In the Netherlands, pure breathing oxygen is considered medicinal, unlike industrial oxygen used for welding, which requires a doctor's prescription. The diving industry registered Divox as a trademark for breathing oxygen to bypass strict rules regarding medical oxygen, making it easier for divers to obtain oxygen for mixing breathing gas.

In most countries, there is no difference in the purity of medical and industrial oxygen, as they are produced by the same methods and manufacturers but have different labeling and documentation. The main difference lies in the extensive traceability requirements for medical oxygen, making it easier to identify the exact trace of a batch of oxygen in case of purity issues.

Aviation-grade oxygen is similar to medical oxygen but may have lower moisture content. **Nitrogen (N_2)** is a diatomic gas and the main component of air, the cheapest and most common breathing gas mixture used for diving. It causes nitrogen narcosis in divers, limiting its use for shallower dives. Nitrogen can also cause decompression sickness.

Equivalent air depth is used to assess the decompression requirements of **Nitrox** mixtures (oxygen/nitrogen). Equivalent narcotic depth is used to assess the narcotic activity of trimix (oxygen/helium/nitrogen). Many divers consider the narcosis level induced by a dive to 30 meters (100 feet) while breathing air to be a comfortable maximum. Nitrogen in a gas mixture is almost always obtained by adding air to the mixture.

Helium (He) is an inert gas that is less narcotic than nitrogen at equivalent pressures (there is actually no evidence of any narcosis from helium) and has much lower density, making it more suitable for deeper dives than nitrogen. Helium is equally capable of causing decompression sickness. Filling with a helium mixture is significantly more expensive than filling with air due to the cost of helium and the cost of mixing and compressing the mixture. Since helium has six times greater thermal conductivity, it is not suitable for inflating drysuits due to its poor thermal insulation properties compared to air, which is considered a good insulator. The low molecular mass of helium (molecular mass of monatomic helium = 4 compared to the molecular mass of diatomic nitrogen = 28) increases the pitch of the breather's voice, which can hinder communication. This is because the speed of sound is higher in a gas with a lower molecular weight, which increases the resonant frequency of the vocal cords. Helium leaks from damaged or faulty valves faster than other gases because helium atoms are smaller, allowing them to pass through smaller gaps in seals. Significant amounts of helium are found only in natural gas, from which it is extracted at low temperatures through fractional distillation.

Neon (Ne) is an inert gas, occasionally used in deep-sea commercial dives, but it is very expensive. Like helium, it is less narcotic than nitrogen, but unlike helium, it does not distort the diver's voice. Compared to helium, neon possesses superior thermal insulation properties. **Hydrogen (H_2)** has been used in gas mixtures for deep-sea dives, but it is highly explosive when mixed with more than 4-5% oxygen (e.g., oxygen present in the breathing gas mixture). This limits the use of hydrogen for deep dives and imposes complex protocols to ensure that excess oxygen is removed from the breathing equipment before inhaling hydrogen. Similar to helium, it raises the pitch of the diver's voice. A mixture of hydrogen and oxygen used as a breathing gas for divers is sometimes called Hydrox. Mixtures containing both hydrogen and helium as diluents are called Hydreliox.

Many gases are unsuitable for use in breathing gas mixtures for diving. Here is a non-exhaustive list of gases that are undesirable components for breathing gas mixtures:

Argon (Ar) is an inert gas that is more narcotic than nitrogen, making it generally unsuitable as a breathing gas mixture for diving. Argon is used in decompression research. It is sometimes used to inflate drysuits for divers who use helium as the main breathing gas mixture due to argon's excellent thermal insulation properties. Argon is more expensive than air or oxygen but significantly cheaper than helium. Argon is a component of natural air, making up 0.934% of Earth's atmospheric volume.

Carbon Dioxide (CO_2) is formed as a result of metabolic processes in the human body and can cause carbon dioxide poisoning. When a breathing gas mixture recirculates in a rebreather or life support system, carbon dioxide is removed by scrubbers before the gas is reused.

Carbon Monoxide (CO) is a highly toxic gas that competes with carbon dioxide for binding to hemoglobin, hindering the transport of oxygen in the blood. It is a poisonous substance in cases of carbon monoxide poisoning. It is usually formed due to incomplete combustion and is present in the exhaust gases of internal combustion engines. CO in the air drawn into the air compressor during tank filling cannot be stopped by any filter. The exhaust gases of all internal combustion engines running on oil-based fuels contain some amount of CO, making them a particular problem on boats, where the compressor intake cannot be arbitrarily moved to a desired distance from the engine exhaust. The heating of lubricating materials inside the compressor leads to their vaporization sufficiently for them to be available to the compressor's intake system. In some cases, hydrocarbon lubricating oil can be drawn directly into the compressor cylinder through damaged or worn seals, and the oil may (and usually will) then ignite due to the tremendous degree of compression and subsequent temperature rise. Since heavy oils burn poorly, especially with improper atomization, incomplete combustion leads to the formation of carbon monoxide. A similar process can potentially occur with any solid material containing "organic" (carbon-containing) substances, especially in tanks used for hyperoxic gas mixtures. If the air filter of the compressor fails, ordinary dust containing organic substances (as it usually contains humus) can enter the cylinder. A more serious danger is that air particles in boats and in industrial areas where cylinders are filled often contain combustion products in the form of carbon particles (these are what make a dirty rag black), and they pose a more serious hazard when entering the cylinder. Carbon monoxide is usually avoided as much as practically possible by placing the air intake in uncontaminated air, filtering solid particles from the intake air, using appropriate compressor design and lubricating materials, and ensuring that operating temperatures are not excessive. If the residual risk is excessive, a hopcalite catalyst can be used in the high-pressure filter to convert carbon monoxide into carbon dioxide, which is much less toxic.

Hydrocarbons (CxHy) are present in compressor lubricants and fuel. They can enter diving cylinders due to contamination, leaks, or incomplete combustion near the air intake. They can act as fuel during combustion, increasing the risk of explosion, especially in gas mixtures with high oxygen content. Inhaling oil mist can damage the lungs and ultimately lead to lung degeneration with severe lipid pneumonia or emphysema.

Moisture content. During the gas compression process in a diving cylinder, moisture is removed from the gas. This is beneficial for preventing corrosion inside the cylinder but means that the diver will be inhaling very dry gas. Dry gas extracts moisture from the diver's lungs underwater, contributing to dehydration, which is also considered a predisposing factor for decompression sickness. This leads to discomfort due to dryness in the mouth and throat, causing thirst in the diver. This problem is mitigated in rebreathers because the reaction with soda lime, which removes carbon dioxide, returns moisture to the breathing gas mixture. In this case, the temperature of the exhaled gas and relative humidity remain relatively high, and a cumulative effect occurs due to repeated inhalation. In hot climates, open-circuit diving can accelerate heat exhaustion due to dehydration. Another issue related to moisture content is the tendency of moisture to condense when the gas pressure drops through the regulator; this, combined with a sharp temperature decrease, including due to decompression, can lead to the freezing of moisture into ice. Regulator icing can cause the moving parts to jam and the regulator to malfunction. This is one of the reasons that scuba regulators are usually made of brass and chrome-plated (for protection). Brass, with good thermal conductivity, quickly transfers heat from the surrounding water to the cold, just-compressed air, helping to prevent icing.

§ 5. Heat exchange in the human body in water

The human body is warm-blooded, meaning its body temperature is sufficiently high and independent of the surrounding environment. The surface temperature of the human body is 36.6°C, and the temperature of internal organs is 38°C. Normal fluctuations in body temperature depending on the time of day and age are very insignificant and do not exceed a few tenths of a degree. In case of body cooling, body temperature can drop to 34°C, and in many diseases, it can rise to 41°C. The temperature of the human body is regulated by two processes: heat generation and heat dissipation. Nutrients entering the body with food are the source of heat generation. When these substances oxidize, a certain amount of heat is released. For example, the breakdown of 1 gram of fat releases 38.9 kJ (9.3 kcal) of energy, which is twice as much as the breakdown of 1 gram of proteins or carbohydrates, each providing 4.1 kilocalories of heat. The generated heat goes to maintain a constant body temperature. If the processes of heat generation and dissipation are in equilibrium, the temperature is maintained at the required level, and a person does not experience either heat or cold. The human body can adapt to the temperature of the surrounding environment up to a certain limit. For example, at high air temperatures, a person sweats heavily, increasing heat dissipation by evaporating water from the skin surface. To maintain a constant body temperature, the human body uses thermoregulatory mechanisms triggered by thermoreceptors. Such sensors are located on the body's surface, and at temperatures above 45°C and below 10°C, they provide a rapid physiological response that a person perceives as pain.

Other sensors are located in the hypothalamus and spinal cord. They come into operation when a drop in temperature becomes life-threatening. When internal temperature begins to rise (hyperthermia), blood vessels dilate to increase the surface area of contact with the external environment, acting like a car radiator. Sweat is produced, which evaporates from the skin's surface, cooling it. Breathing becomes more intense to get rid of excess heat through the lungs. With a decrease in the ambient temperature, oxidation processes of food intensify, and the body tries to reduce heat loss. When the temperature decreases (hypothermia), blood vessels narrow to reduce heat loss through the skin. As a result, all liquid moves to internal organs. This leads to a negative side effect: increased diuresis and, consequently, dehydration. The body focuses on heating internal organs and minimizes heat exchange with the external environment. Metabolism and breathing intensify to produce more heat to compensate for heat loss. Thermogenesis peaks in 15-20 minutes. After that, activity decreases as energy reserves are depleted, and two hours later, its production drops by half.

In water, the human body is more susceptible to rapid cooling due to larger heat losses than in the air. This is because the aquatic environment is significantly denser and has a higher heat capacity compared to air. Therefore, during underwater dives, divers wear wetsuits to reduce heat loss. If a diver wears a dry-type wetsuit, which prevents body contact with water, the warm clothing under the wetsuit creates a barrier of air between the diver's body and the aquatic environment. This barrier, heated by the diver's body, allows the human body to reduce heat dissipation to the external environment. It is also worth noting that if a diver uses a wet-type wetsuit, due to the specific properties of the material from which the wetsuit is made, neoprene creates a barrier of small air bubbles between the diver's body and the aquatic environment. This helps retain heat around the body, preventing its loss. Neoprene has hydrophobic properties, meaning it repels water and prevents it from penetrating the material. This allows the wetsuit to remain dry inside and prevents it from becoming waterlogged. In cases where underwater dives without wetsuits are necessary, measures are taken to prevent body cooling. The main measure is to limit the time spent underwater. The maximum allowable time in the water at a water temperature above 16°C is 30 minutes, at a temperature of 14°C, it is 20 minutes. Diving without wetsuits at a temperature below 14°C is not allowed!

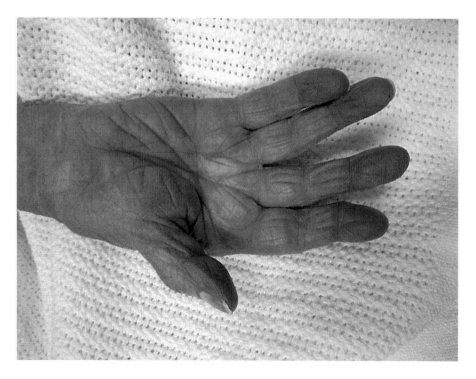

Fig. 24. Hypothermia

The effect of cold on the body

Sudden and unexpected exposure to cold activates the skin's thermoreceptors, triggering thermoregulatory defense mechanisms: hyperventilation, strong shivering, and vasoconstriction. At very low temperatures, fainting and respiratory failure may occur. This neurological response is triggered even if the internal body temperature has not dropped below the normal mark. Divers experience slow, prolonged body cooling during extended deep dives. Nervous reactions are reduced and, in some cases, unnoticed. Peripheral vessels constrict from the beginning to reduce heat exchange through the skin and maintain the temperature of internal organs. When thermogenesis fails to cope with heat loss, the diver's body temperature starts to drop. The diver does not feel this and is unaware of the slow onset of dangerous hyperthermia. When the temperature of internal organs reaches 36°C, the person's reactions and thinking become slow and erroneous, making it dangerous to continue diving in such a state. Additionally, radical physiological changes hinder the normal elimination of inert gases from the body tissues, increasing the risk of decompression sickness. Hypothermia leads to vascular constriction, reducing the amount of blood circulating through peripheral tissues and, consequently, impeding the removal of inert gases from them. Since heat loss and hypothermia risk significantly increase with depth, a diver must monitor their condition during the dive.

Thermogenesis - the production of metabolic energy

The typical value for metabolic heat energy produced by the human body at rest is about 60 watts. It is distributed approximately as follows: various organs: 30 watts; the nervous system: 12 watts; respiratory muscles: 6 watts; other muscles: 12 watts. Total: 60 watts.

The thermal energy generated during moderate exertion can reach 300 watts, for example, during prolonged swimming with fins or running at a speed of 8 km/h. This energy is produced due to increased muscle activity. Note the increased value for respiratory muscles: various organs: 30 watts; the nervous system: 10 watts; respiratory muscles: 60 watts; other muscles: 200 watts. Total: 300 watts.

Such a level of heat energy production cannot be sustained for long. After two hours of continuous exertion, energy production drops to 125 watts. Gas consumption provides more useful information for calculating the level of thermogenesis: 8 l/min (at rest) 100 watts; 20 l/min (at the bottom) 250 watts; 10 l/min (decompression stops) 125 watts.

Heat loss

As is known, heat is simultaneously formed and released into the surrounding environment. Heat dissipation from the body occurs through the skin and lungs. Heat loss through the skin occurs:

1. During the evaporation (sweating) of water from the skin's surface, causing the body to lose about 25% of all heat.

2. Through radiation (radiation) of heat rays if the body temperature is higher than the surrounding environment.

3. Through conduction (conduction) aimed at heating the layer of air in contact with the body surface, consuming about one-third of the heat.

4. Through convection (heat transfer by fluid/gas movement).

Heat loss during breathing (through the lungs) occurs due to the heating of the inhaled gas and its humidification (latent heat).

When passing through the regulator, the gas pressure drops sharply. At a depth of 40 meters at the beginning of bottom time, the pressure of the bottom gas decreases from 300 bar to 13 bar in the first stage and from 13 to 5 bar in the second with each inhalation. With rapid cooling, the gas temperature drops to very low values, sometimes below 0°C. The final temperature of the inhaled gas depends on the water temperature, gas volume, and mass. The deeper you go, the colder the water becomes, the greater the gas volume you consume, and the colder the inhaled gas becomes. We cannot feel such a low temperature of inhaled gas because we do not have thermoreceptors in the respiratory pathways (trachea and lungs). Therefore, the body's reaction, characteristic of hypothermia and aimed at reducing heat loss, will not be activated in time.

The lungs at the alveoli level are ideal heat exchangers due to their very large surface area. They instantly heat and humidify the inhaled gas to the core temperature of 38°C. Bronchi and trachea are poor heat exchangers; the gas that remains in them is heated only partially.

At rest, a person inhales about 0.5 liters of gas on average with one breath; with moderate loads, gas consumption increases, tripling, and the residual volume is about 0.15 liters. Thus, only 85% of the inhaled gas is heated to the internal body temperature. At a depth of 40 meters, a diver's gas consumption increases by 5 times compared to the surface. This means that at depth, a diver's body loses heat through the lungs 5 times faster than on a cold day on the surface. Aware of the danger of such heat loss, divers who dive in cold water use external sources to heat the breathing gas mixture.

For example, when breathing through a two-meter regulator hose, heat losses are reduced. Depending on the water temperature, the actual temperature of the breathing gas mixture delivered to the diver's respiratory organs will be several degrees higher than when breathing from a standard-length hose. The time the air spends in the long hose before inhalation is sufficient for it to absorb some heat from the surrounding water. Therefore, divers diving in cold water are recommended to use two-meter hoses on each of the regulators. Currently, there are closed-circuit breathing apparatuses that deliver warm and humidified gas on inhalation, thereby reducing heat losses through the respiratory organs. However, when it comes to regular scuba diving apparatuses, humidified gas cannot be used in the scuba for several reasons, so the human body has to humidify it in the lungs. This humidification is achieved by water evaporating from the internal walls of the alveoli. Evaporation involves the transfer of heat (since energy is required to convert liquid water into water vapor) and a subsequent temperature drop. This energy is called "latent heat." Humidifying the inhaled gas not only depletes the energy from the human body's lungs but is also one of the main causes of dehydration, and dehydration, in turn, can trigger decompression sickness. The deeper the diver descends, the more breathing gas their body consumes, and consequently, the greater the mass of gas that their body humidifies and heats. The energy expenditure is independent of the diving depth but depends on the quantity of breathing gas consumed by the diver. This ratio is approximately 10 watts with a breathing rate of 20 liters per minute. The energy used to heat the inhaled gas is proportional to the mass of the gas and depends on the gas properties.

The formula is as follows:

$$\text{Heat losses} = Cp \times 0.8 \, (38 - IT) \times Q \times P / 60 + LV$$

where:

IT - temperature of the inhaled gas;

Q - volume of inhaled gas (liters per minute);

P - absolute pressure;

Cp - heat capacity of the gas;

LV - latent heat.

A gas with high heat capacity (hereinafter Cp) requires more energy to heat up to a given temperature and, accordingly, releases more energy when cooling down, and all of this takes more time. Therefore, it will be a better insulator. On the other hand, a gas with low heat capacity heats up quickly and cools down quickly. It releases energy easily and is a poor insulator. For nitrogen and oxygen, Cp is approximately the same, about 1.31 W/1°C.

For helium, Cp = 0.93 W/1°C. The heat capacity of the mixture is calculated taking into account the proportion of gases in the mixture. Three examples of using gas mixtures for breathing are provided below: the first with air as the bottom mix, the second with helium and oxygen (heliox), and the third with trimix.

Example 1. A diver has a gas consumption of 20 liters per minute while breathing. He breathes air at a temperature of 2°C at a depth of 50 meters. What will be his heat losses through the lungs?

Heat losses = $1.31 \times 0.8 (38 - 2) \times 20 \times (6/60) + 10 = 85.5$ W.

Example 2. A diver descends to 80 meters with heliox 10/90, water temperature is 2°C. Heat capacity of the mixture:

$$(0.10 \times 1.31) + (0.90 \times 0.93) = 0.97 \text{ W/1°C.}$$

What will be the heat losses?

Heat losses = $0.97 \times 0.8 (38 - 2) \times 20 \times (9/60) + 10 = 93.6$ W

If air is used in this example, it will result in 123.2 W.

Example 3. A diver descends to 80 meters with trimix 16/40 at a temperature of 2°C.

Heat capacity of the mixture = $(0.16 \times 1.31) + (0.40 \times 0.93) + (0.44 \times 1.31) = 1.16$ W/1°C.

What will be the heat losses?

Heat losses = $1.16 \times 0.8 (38 - 2) \times 20 \times (9/60) + 10 = 110$W

Heat losses through the skin

The heat of the human body warms the gas inside the drysuit through radiation and conduction. Convection moves heat to where it will escape from the suit faster. This poses a very difficult task for calculation; there are no two absolutely identical people with the same weight and identical subcutaneous fat. However, we can attempt a rough calculation to have a basis for choosing thermal protection.

Conductivity plays a more significant role in heat transfer through the suit. Fourier's law states that the amount of thermal energy transferred from a hot body to a cold one, divided by an insulating layer, is proportional to the temperature difference between the two bodies. The proportionality coefficient depends on the surface, nature, and geometry of the layer and is called thermal conductivity (W/°C). The lower the thermal conductivity value, the better the insulating properties of the separating layer. If we apply values for calculations, where T1 is the hot body of the diver, and the cold body T2 is the water, we get a formula to calculate heat losses through the skin:

$$(Q) = (T1 - T2) / (1/H1+1/H2+1/H3+...)$$

where:

Q : amount of heat;

T1: temperature of the hot body;

T2: temperature of the cold body;

H1: conductivity of the 1st layer;

H2: conductivity of the 2nd layer;

H3: conductivity of the 3rd layer.

Examples of conductivity values for various insulating layers:

Air layer = 8;
Peripheral fat layer (large build) = 15;
Peripheral fat layer (normal build) = 30;
Peripheral fat layer (slim build) = 50;
Adjacent water layer (almost stagnant) = 70;
Adjacent water layer (moderate flow) = 300;

Mountain polypropylene 1st layer = 400;

Fleece 10 mm = 7;

Fleece 7.5 mm = 10;

Fleece 5 mm = 14;

Fleece 10 mm + argon = 4;

Fleece 10 mm + helium = 30;

Neoprene 7 mm = 20;

Neoprene 5 mm = 30;

Compressed neoprene 4 mm = 40;

Crushed neoprene 2 mm = 80;

Trilaminate = 300.

Example 1. Calculate the diver's heat loss through the skin. Let's assume the diver is 1.75 m tall and weighs 72 kg. He uses a trilaminate drysuit and a 7.5 mm fleece undergarment. The suit is inflated with air. The water temperature is 2°C, and the flow is moderate, at 1.5 knots. What are the expected skin heat losses?

$$Q = (38-2)/((1/50) + (1/300) + (1/10) + (1/300)) = 285 \text{ W};$$

Skin heat losses = 285 W.

Convection - the transfer of heat by the movement of liquid or gas. We can use the water around the diver in our model as a boundary layer of very high conductivity. This is more important in a loose membrane suit than in a tightly fitting neoprene drysuit. A wet drysuit can be considered an additional fat layer since, if it fits snugly, it has a similar conductivity value. Some undergarments do not prevent strong convection and therefore have high conductivity. The more gas circulation is restricted, the better the thermal insulation properties. Sweating away from the body prevents it from evaporating in contact with the skin, reducing further cooling. Some materials are designed for this purpose. However, note that other underlayers must also conduct this moisture to settle as condensation on the inner surface of the suit. Some insulators have impermeable outer shells that prevent this, and internal fibers become saturated with condensed moisture, losing their insulating properties.

To calculate the overall heat losses, it is necessary to sum up the skin heat losses and the heat losses during breathing. And to obtain the heat balance, it is necessary to subtract the total heat losses from thermogenesis. To more accurately determine the thermal balance of a diver's body, it is necessary to calculate it for different phases of the dive, taking into account a specific profile and decompression schedule. Studies have shown that the reduction in internal body temperature can be calculated using the formula:

cooling (ºC/hour) = (thermogenesis – heat losses) / body weight

So, the internal body temperature of a diver with a height of 176 cm and weight of 72 kg will decrease by 1ºC in just 53 minutes. Regular diving with trimix takes much longer. A decrease in the internal temperature of the human body by even 1ºC can lead to slowed thinking, loss of orientation, uncoordinated movements, apathy, tremors, and increased breathing. The body will respond to the temperature drop (to maintain internal temperature at 38ºC) by increasing metabolism. However, as studies show, the body cannot continuously generate energy, and energy production decreases after two hours of continuous stress on the human body.

It is important to understand that the presented calculations are approximate. Heat losses are difficult to quantitatively assess and usually exceed the values obtained. Whether you dive in cold waters in a drysuit or in tropical seas in a wetsuit, heat loss is a risk that always exists in deep or prolonged dives. Every diver should remember that in an emergency situation, such as a disruption in the supply of breathing gas due to a hose rupture or a similar incident, an unexpected inhalation from emergency equipment with a denser or very cold composition of breathing gas can lead to a fatal psychoneurological reaction. This reaction results in choking due to throat constriction. It is also worth considering that hypothermia tends to accumulate. Repeat daily heat losses lead to the body's inability to resist the cold.

Checkpoint questions for chapter two:

1. Explain the circulatory system in humans.
2. What changes occur in the circulatory system of a person submerged underwater?
3. What are the peculiarities of breathing for a person underwater?
4. What processes must occur in the human body to achieve pressure equilibrium for a diver compared to the surrounding environment during descent?
5. What is minute ventilation, and what factors influence it?
6. What determines the amount of dissolved gas in the human body?
7. How does nitrogen affect the human body under pressure?
8. At what depths does the narcotic effect of nitrogen manifest?
9. How do Nitrox and Heliox respiratory gas mixtures differ?
10. Which gas components in a breathing mixture are toxic?
11. How is the partial pressure of one of the components in a gas mixture calculated?
12. Name the most common respiratory gas mixtures and their characteristics.
13. List three main classifications of respiratory gas mixtures based on oxygen content.
14. How is the temperature of the human body regulated?
15. How does the human body release heat?
16. What is thermogenesis?
17. How does heat loss occur through the lungs?
18. How does heat loss occur through the skin?
19. How long can a person stay in the water without a wetsuit at 16°C, 14°C, and 13°C?

III CHAPTER
DIVING GEAR

Chapter three of this textbook provides a detailed overview of the purpose, construction, and functionality of various diving equipment essential for underwater descents. The chapter covers the fundamental devices and principles of operation of scuba sets, the construction of high-pressure cylinders, different diving regulators, and buoyancy compensators. Comprehensive descriptions are given for the structure and operating principles of rebreathers and hose equipment.

Various types of wetsuits, mask constructions, diving helmets, snorkels, fins for diving, and underwater lights are discussed. Detailed explanations are presented for the structure and basic principles of operation of diving instruments such as a pressure gauge, compass, depth gauge, diving computers, underwater metal detectors, underwater video recording devices, and underwater drone robots. Practical care advice for diving equipment is also provided.

§ 6. Classification of diving equipment

Fig. 25. Diving work equipment

Diving equipment refers to a set of items that sustain the life of a diver underwater for a specific period. The complex of devices is worn and secured on a person before diving.

The main objectives of diving equipment are:
1. Providing the diver with air (or gas mixture) for breathing under pressure equal to the ambient pressure.
2. Creating the necessary buoyancy (or stability) for the diver to move underwater and perform various tasks.
3. Ensuring thermal and insulating protection for the diver from cold or contaminated water.
4. Ensuring the safety of the diver during underwater descents and ascents.
5. Establishing communication between the diver and the surface or other divers underwater.

Conventionally, diving equipment is classified as heavy or light, and based on how it perceives external environmental pressure, equipment is divided into soft and hard.

In heavy equipment, the diver's head is in a metallic or carbon helmet into which air (or a special gas mixture for breathing) is supplied, and the body is isolated from water by a soft watertight suit - a drysuit. To offset buoyancy, a set of weighted items is included in the heavy equipment, which divers do not use in light diving equipment. (Helmets and boots for divers made of metal (brass or copper)).

Regular drysuits belong to soft diving equipment; they do not perceive external pressure, unlike hard diving equipment, which includes hard suits, rescue capsules, and submersibles.

Diving suits are further divided into wet and dry types. Wet suits are diving clothes made from a special material - neoprene (foamed rubber). Microbubbles inside the neoprene material serve as a kind of air buffer between the environment and the diver's body. They help retain heat in the human body during underwater dives and create positive buoyancy for the diver. However, this buoyancy changes during descent due to the compression of neoprene with increasing depth. Microbubbles, due to the increasing pressure of the surrounding environment, decrease in volume, leading to thinning of the material and partial reduction of the drysuit's positive buoyancy.

Dry suits of the dry type include drysuits with a ventilation system in the undersuit space, through a valve system for supplying and venting air or a special gas (e.g., argon). Suits of this type do not allow water to enter and achieve this by using sealing cuffs (obturators) on the hands and neck and waterproof zippers with a special design. Dry suits can be made of neoprene or other materials with water-repellent properties. Trilaminate (pressed nylon/butyl/polyester) is commonly used, and for special dives in aggressive environments, rubberized materials resistant to the negative effects of oil products are used.

Depending on the tasks and the depth of the dive, mandatory diving equipment is additionally equipped with items necessary for each specific underwater dive. This equipment includes instruments: watches, depth gauges, compasses, pressure gauges, and underwater computers, as well as special underwater equipment designed for specific underwater tasks, such as photo-video equipment, underwater metal detectors, diver sonars, means of underwater communication, underwater welding apparatus, and various other underwater tools.

Usually, the mandatory equipment for underwater dives includes: a drysuit, a diving mask and snorkel or helmet, fins or diving boots with metal soles and protective inserts, a weight belt, a diver's knife, an underwater flashlight, a whistle and a diver's buoy, and equipment providing the diver with a breathing gas mixture.

By the method of providing the diver with breathing underwater, the equipment is divided into four types:

1. Open-circuit equipment.
2. Ventilated equipment.
3. Combined diving equipment.
4. Regenerative equipment and injector-regenerative equipment.

Hose equipment includes devices where the diver, from the surface or from an underwater apparatus, receives compressed air or another breathing gas mixture through a hose, either from a compressor or from transport cylinders.

In figure 28, you can see the components of the ventilated diving equipment:

1 - Air control system for simultaneous maintenance of one to three divers; the mixed gas panel with communications is designed for surface supply air diving down to a maximum depth of 40-100 meters sea water (msw).

2 - Hose for supplying a breathing mixture of gases and wires for a telephone, flashlight, and video camera.

3 - The Divex lightweight, airless helmet is designed to be used with its own waterproof neoprene collar or directly over a drysuit.

4 - Neck dam.

5 - Dry suit and air supply and release valve integrated into the dry suit.

Fig. 26. Composition of ventilated equipment

6 - The Arvest harness was designed to allow the diver to don a single harness instead of the four separate items previously required: recovery harness, bail-out bottle harness, tool harness, and weight belt. This "waistcoat-style" harness distributes the load evenly around the body, providing secure and comfortable support for a fully kitted diver.

7 - Rubberized dry-type diving gloves with a quick-release mechanism for attaching to the sleeves of a dry suit.

8 - Diving knife.

9 - Diving boots.

Ventilated equipment (Venturi Vent) operates on the principle of continuous delivery of compressed air to the diver from the surface through a hose, providing air circulation inside the drysuit and helmet. This type of air supply allows the diver to obtain the required gas volume for breathing, maintain a comfortable temperature through ventilation, and discharge excess carbon dioxide into the water through relief valves.

Open circuit breathing system equipment

This is based on the principle of pulsating air delivery to the diver through an open breathing circuit, with the diver exhaling directly into the water. This equipment is subdivided into air-balloon, hose, and combined types. Combined diving equipment includes both a hose-supplied delivery of breathing mixture to the diver through surface-supplied hoses and, simultaneously, the presence of autonomous gear for the diver's use in case of necessity. Air-balloon equipment includes all types and varieties of scuba diving equipment, where the diver becomes completely autonomous and carries compressed air cylinders or another breathing gas mixture.

Combined equipment is universal, as it integrates both the air-balloon system and the hose system, using the gas mixture from the cylinders as a reserve or emergency, while the main source of the gas mixture consumed by the diver is the hose supply.

In figure 27, you can see the components of the composition combined diving equipment:

1 - Air control system for simultaneous maintenance of one to three divers; the mixed gas panel with communications is designed for

Fig. 27. Composition combined diving equipment

surface supply air diving down to a maximum depth of 40-100 meters sea water (msw).

2 - Transport cylinders containing a compressed mixture of breathing gases.

3 - Hose for supplying a breathing mixture of gases and wires for a telephone, flashlight, and video camera.

4 - The Divex lightweight, airless helmet is designed to be used with its own waterproof neoprene collar or directly over a drysuit.

5 - Breathing gas mixture flow regulator.

6 - Neck dam.

7 - Dry suit.

8 - Air supply and release valve integrated into the dry suit.

9 - The Arvest harness was designed to allow the diver to don a single harness instead of the four separate items previously required: recovery harness, bail-out bottle harness, tool harness, and weight belt. This "waistcoat-style" harness distributes the load evenly around the body, providing secure and comfortable support for a fully kitted diver.

10 - Rubberized dry-type diving gloves with a quick-release mechanism for attaching to the sleeves of a dry suit.

11 - Diving knife.

12 - Diving boots.

As you may have already noticed in the picture, we can see the high-pressure cylinder on the back of the diver. This cylinder contains a mixture of breathing gases, allowing the diver to breathe. If necessary, the diver can disconnect from the external hoses and become fully independent for movement. To take advantage of the autonomous supply of breathing gas, the diver needs to have a helmet of a different design than the one shown in picture 26. In the design of a diving helmet for autonomous breathing, a diving regulator must be built in. The most common helmets of this type are those produced by Kirby Morgan. In picture 28, you can see the structure of such a helmet.

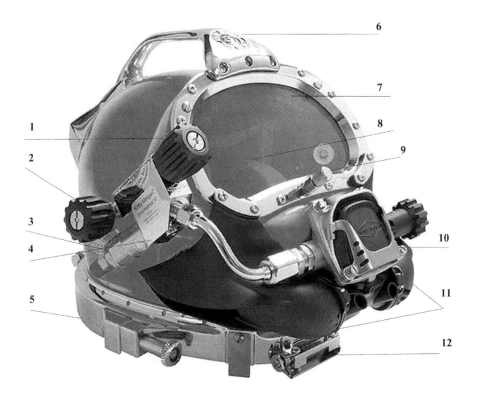

Fig. 28. Composition the Kirby Morgan 37 helmet

Diving Helmet Structure:

1. - Glass defogging and water purging valve.

2. - Reserve air supply valve.

3. - Non-return valve. Prevents a drop in air pressure in the helmet in case of damage or "pinching" of the primary air supply hose.

4. - Threaded fitting for connecting the drysuit inflation hose, etc.

5. - Neck ring. Secures the helmet to the diver's head, preventing accidental removal.

6. - Helmet carrying handle

7. - High-strength polycarbonate view window.

8. - Rotating mask inside the helmet for the nose part of the head. Maintains a low CO_2 concentration in the helmet.

9. - Nose block/clamp. Balances pressure in the middle ear.

10. - Breathing regulator (optional).

11. - Gas exhaust deflector directs exhaled gas away from the view window.

12. - Lock for securing the neck clamp.

It is worth noting separately the ventilated gear with copper and brass diving helmets, which can be classified as historical diving equipment. Such helmets, suits, and accessories are primarily supplied worldwide to historical diving clubs. The helmets are manufactured at a diving equipment factory in the Chinese city of Wuhu using traditional methods. This diving equipment is not a replica but is indeed intended for diving descents and is widely used in China and some other countries.

By the method of connecting the helmet to the drysuit, historical ventilated equipment is divided into three-bolt and twelve-bolt types. The three-bolt equipment is used for underwater emergency rescue, lifting operations, and other work at depths up to 60 meters.

Twelve-bolt equipment is used for underwater work in river and lake conditions, as well as in seaports and harbors when performing various types of underwater technical work at depths up to 30 meters.

In three-bolt equipment, the flange of the diving helmet is clamped between the helmet flanges and the neck dam using three bolts with nuts. In twelve-bolt equipment, the drysuit is attached to the neck dam using overlays and twelve bolts, while the helmet is connected to the neck dam with a special lock.

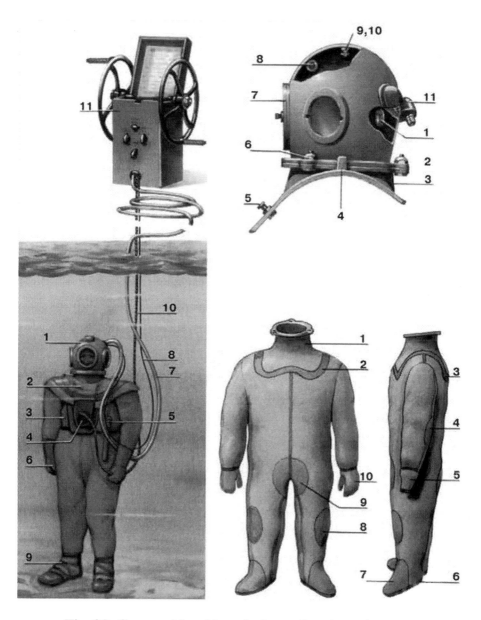

Fig. 29. Composition historical ventilated equipment

In Figure 29 you see Fig. 29. Composition historical ventilated equipment:

The composition of ventilated equipment includes: (1) – diving helmet; (2) – neck dam; (3) – drysuit (rubberized or diving shirt); (4) – front diving weight; (5) – knife with a Marcellus belt; (6) – diving gloves; (7) – air hose; (8) – signal line (cable or strong rope); (9) – diving boots; (10) – telephone wire; (11) – hand air compressor (diving pump).

Diving helmet structure: (1) – main valve (removable air valve); (2) – flange of the bowl; (3) – neck dam; (4) – hook; (5) – eyelet; (6) – nut on the bolt; (7) – front window socket; (8) – phone installation point; (9) – phone clamp; (10) – telephone wire input; (11) – air supply hose attachment point.

Main parts of the diving suit: (1) – flange; (2) – front yoke; (3) – back yoke; (4) – elbow pads; (5) – cuff; (6) – sole; (7) – toe; (8) – knee pads; (9) – apron; (10) – gloves.

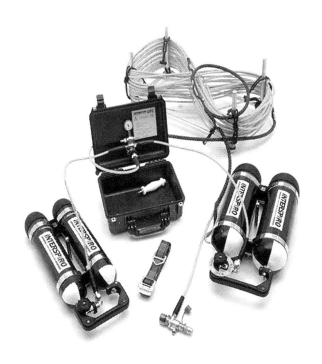

Fig. 30. Air hose equipment

Unlike ventilated equipment, regenerative equipment does not have a gas volume. The diver's breathing is carried out directly into the respiratory apparatus in a closed breathing circuit. Carbon dioxide produced during breathing is absorbed by a chemical composition, then the mixture is enriched with oxygen and delivered on inhalation. This type of breathing apparatus is called a rebreather. A rebreather (from the English prefix "re-" indicating the repetition of an action and English "breath") is a breathing apparatus. The operating principle is as follows: the gas mixture intended for breathing enters the diver's lungs from the breathing bag through a non-return valve. In the lungs, the gas concentration of this mixture changes; oxygen decreases, and carbon dioxide increases. Upon exhalation, this mixture, through another non-return valve, enters the canister of the chemical absorbent, which absorbs carbon dioxide, and the remaining gas mixture is returned to the breathing bag. Oxygen is separately supplied to the breathing bag, renewing its portion in the breathing mixture necessary for the diver.

Fig. 31. Rebreather

Injector-regenerative equipment combines the operation of two previous systems, providing the diver with air and artificial gas mixtures using ventilation and injection methods. The characteristic features of this equipment include the complete or partial restoration of the gas mixture in the regenerative system. The supply of breathing gas from the surface is mainly done by the injector to fill the diving suit during underwater immersion. The duration of the diver's stay underwater depends on the duration of the regenerative system's operation. When using this equipment for dives up to 40 meters deep, an air-oxygen mixture is applied, and above 40 meters, an oxygen-helium mixture is used. If the injector-regenerative device is not needed, it can be removed, and the equipment is then used as a conventional ventilated one.

Fig. 32. Injector regenerative diving equipment

§ 7. SCUBA diving equipment
(self contained underwater breathing apparatus)

Fig. 33. Scuba diver

Autonomous equipment for diving with scuba devices is designed for short underwater descents. The most common device for underwater dives is SCUBA, which allows the diver to maintain a constant source of air during the descent. Most SCUBA devices consist of three mandatory components, including: a high-pressure tank, an air supply regulator, and special devices holding the tank(s) with the breathing gas on the diver's body.

The main components of SCUBA include:

Diving cylinders. The cylinder contains compressed air or gas mixtures such as air, nitrox, or heliox, serving as a source of breathing gas for the diver. Cylinders can have different capacities, and the choice depends on the duration and depth of the dive.

Fig. 34. SCUBA view from the back

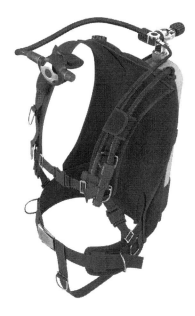

Fig. 35. SCUBA front view

Pressure regulator. Pressure regulators are connected to the cylinder and regulate the airflow from the cylinder to the diver. They reduce the gas pressure from a higher level in the cylinder to atmospheric pressure, providing the diver with the ability to comfortably breathe underwater.

Attachments of cylinders to the diver. Straps, backplates, and buoyancy control devices (BCD) are used to attach cylinders to the diver. In traditional diving, the scuba tank is worn on the back like a backpack. In sidemount diving, cylinders are attached to the sides on both sides of the diver. The simplest way to attach the "backpack" is when the cylinder (or several cylinders fastened together with metal clamps) is attached to a special backplate using straps or bolts. This backplate is equipped with special straps that secure the diver. The most common way to attach the cylinder to the diver is to use a buoyancy compensator. In addition to securing the cylinder and other diving equipment, buoyancy compensators are used to control buoyancy, allowing the diver to change their position in the water, ascend, descend, or remain at a specific depth without the need for constant use of muscles to maintain the desired position. A common feature of the buoyancy compensator is the presence of an inflatable gas chamber, which serves as a kind of waterproof bag that, when needed, is filled with air or gas using a special control called an inflator. When filling the air chamber with gas, the diver gains positive buoyancy, becoming more buoyant according to Archimedes' principle. In other words, by inflating the buoyancy compensator's chamber with gas, the diver increases the volume of the submerged body while maintaining the same mass in the water. To achieve negative buoyancy and descend to depth, the diver uses exhaust valves through which air or another gas mixture is vented from the buoyancy compensator's air chamber into the surrounding environment.

Cylinders for scuba diving

Cylinders for scuba diving have their peculiarities; they differ in volume, the material from which they are made, and various types of valves. They have a cylindrical shape, rounded, flat, or concave bottom on one side, and an elongated neck with internal threads on the other side. A valve is screwed into this thread, serving to fill the cylinder

Fig. 36. Rubber boot, handle, mesh

with air or another breathing gas mixture and to release the gas flow during the dive.

Cylinders used for diving come in various volumes and materials. The modern industry primarily manufactures cylinders from three main materials: steel, aluminum, and carbon. Steel cylinders are made from high-alloy steel with additions of chromium and molybdenum, and depending on the manufacturer, they are coated with a protective layer of zinc or a protective polymer both inside and outside.

The main disadvantage of steel cylinders is their relatively high susceptibility to corrosion compared to cylinders made of other materials. However, they have several advantages. With relatively low cost

Fig. 37. Steel cylinder

compared to aluminum and carbon cylinders, they are more compact, heavy, and durable. With the same external dimensions, steel cylinders have a larger volume and generally withstand higher working pressures, providing the diver with a longer dive time. Another advantage of steel cylinders is that they have a low buoyancy level (usually negative buoyancy), both when empty and when full.

The main advantage of aluminum cylinders is their relatively low susceptibility to corrosion. This is explained by the ability of aluminum alloys to create a protective oxide film. In case of corrosion on the metal surface, this film prevents the lower layers of aluminum from further oxidation. A small drawback of aluminum cylinders, compared to steel ones, is their dimensions.

Since the strength of aluminum is inferior to steel, aluminum cylinders need to have thicker walls to hold gas at the same pressure compared to steel cylinders. Despite the fact that the weight of aluminum is three times less than the weight of steel for the same volume of gas, aluminum cylinders will have a larger size but will retain the advantage of lower weight. Aluminum cylinders usually have a high buoyancy level when empty and negative buoyancy when full.

Fig. 38. Aluminum cylinder

A significant advantage of carbon cylinders compared to aluminum and steel is their relatively light weight. They are made from a metal composite material, epoxy resins, and carbon fiber, making them lightweight and durable. Carbon cylinders have positive buoyancy, both when empty and when full.

As for the disadvantages of carbon cylinders, their manufacturer indicates a relatively short service life (up to 15 years), which is specified on the cylinder itself. This is due to the fact that the epoxy resins used in the production of composite cylinders begin to decompose. All cylinders have specific markings around the neck of the cylinder, containing safety and identification information. This information is applied by the manufacturer and is controlled by authorities responsible for approving cylinders for use (usually such checks are carried out once every two years).

Fig. 39. Carbon cylinder

Fig. 40. Marking

The marking, stamped on the neck as the manufacturer's emblem, contains the following mandatory information:

1. The name or logo of the company that manufactured the cylinder, allowing identification of the manufacturer and assessment of quality and compliance with standards.

2. Factory serial number of the cylinder.

3. The year and month of manufacture of the cylinder.

4. The weight of the cylinder without the valve.

5. The volume of the cylinder, indicating the amount of air that can be contained inside, is specified in liters for countries using the metric system or in cubic feet for countries using the imperial measurement system (such as the USA and the UK).

6. The material of the cylinder, from which the cylinder is made, such as "AL" for aluminum cylinders, "STEEL" for steel cylinders, or "CARBON" for carbon cylinders.

7. The working pressure, usually denoted by the Latin letters "WP" and indicated in BAR or PSI (pounds per square inch). Diving cylinders are designed for high pressure. The maximum allowable operating pressure for the cylinder is called the working pressure. This is important information for safe use and control of filling and pressure in the cylinder.

The test pressure, usually designated by the Latin letters "PT," is indicated in BAR or PSI (pounds per square inch). The maximum allowable pressure used for testing the cylinder to approve it for operation is called the test pressure, and it is typically 150% of the working pressure. Each cylinder must have a stamp or a label from the inspection body that conducted the high-pressure cylinder test and approved it for further use. The approval should include the name or trademark of the organization that performed the inspection, the month, and year of the inspection.

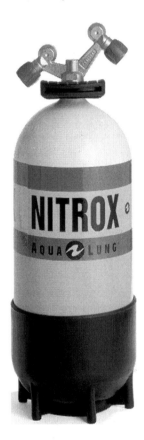

Fig. 41. Cylinder nitrox

Depending on the manufacturer and region, markings on cylinders may include additional information about certification and compliance with specific safety standards. For example: AIR COMPRIME (compressed air) or NITROX. It is important to note that cylinder markings may vary slightly depending on the region or country of manufacture. Before using any type of cylinder, always follow the recommendations and requirements of the manufacturer.

The choice of cylinders for underwater dives depends on the diving tasks, planned duration, and depth. Often, divers prefer the most common cylinders in the diving region. For example, in Ukraine, divers most commonly use SCUBA equipped with a single-cylinder single-valve DIN 200 system, which includes 15-liter steel cylinders with a working pressure of 230 bar. This means that a diver, using diving equipment with such a fully filled cylinder, takes 3450 liters of breathing gas underwater (15 liters multiplied by the working pressure of 230 bar, resulting in 3450 liters).

Divers in Germany, Poland, and Sweden prefer to use 10-liter steel cylinders, while in the UK, they prefer 12-liter steel cylinders. In the USA, most divers prefer to use SCUBA with a single-cylinder single-valve INT (YOKE) system, and in this region, aluminum cylinders with a volume of 11.1 liters (80 lbs) and a working pressure of 207 bar (3000 psi) are most common. The weight of such a cylinder in water, when filled with breathing gas at the working pressure of 207 bar, is -0.7 kilograms, and the weight of the same cylinder in water at a residual pressure of 35 bar is +1.5 kilograms. These values significantly affect the positive and negative buoyancy of the diver.

In most diving descents, divers use air as a breathing gas mixture for immersion. To calculate the weight of air in a filled cylinder, it is necessary to recall the previously studied material on the physical properties of air. As we already know, one cubic meter of air (1000 liters) weighs 1.29 kilograms. To calculate the weight of gas in the cylinder, you need to multiply the gas pressure in the cylinder according to the pressure gauge by the volume of the cylinder capacity. As a result, we obtain the amount of gas contained in the cylinder in liters. Knowing the initial weight of gas for a specific volume, we convert the obtained volume in liters into weight units.

It should be noted that in the American and English traditional systems of measurement, the imperial measurement system is used. For example, the unit of pressure, mechanical stress, and Young's modulus (modulus of elasticity) is measured in pounds per square inch (pound-force/square inch, psi). 1 PSI (psi) = 0.0689475729317831 bar. To calculate the equivalence of volumes between different cylinder designations in the USA and Europe, it is necessary to use a table that indicates the corresponding approximate values of volumes. Cylinders marked: S100 lbs have a volume of about 12.9 liters; S80 lbs has a volume of about 11.1 liters; S63 lbs has a volume of about 8.7 liters; S50 lbs has a volume of about 7.1 liters; S40 lbs has a volume of about

5.5 liters; S30 lbs has a volume of about 4.2 liters; S19 lbs has a volume of about 2.6 liters; S13 lbs has a volume of about 1.8 liters; S06 lbs has a volume of about 0.8 liters.

Check your knowledge by completing the following tasks:

1. Calculate the weight of air in a filled cylinder with a volume of 12.9 liters and a working pressure of 300 bar?

Answer: _____

2. What will be the weight of air in a cylinder with a volume of 15 liters at a residual pressure of 35 bar?

Answer: _____

3. What will be the weight of air in a cylinder with a volume of 1 liter at a residual pressure of 150 bar?

Answer: _____

4. What will be the weight of air in a filled cylinder with a volume of 11.1 liters and a working pressure of 207 bar?

Answer: _____

5. What will be the weight of air in a filled cylinder with a volume of S19 lbs at a working pressure of 5000 psi?

Answer: _____

Valve

The main element of every cylinder is the valve mechanism. The purpose of this mechanism is the same for all types of high-pressure cylinders. The valve serves to retain gas under pressure in the cylinder. The operating principle is very simple. The outlet pipe has an external thread that screws into the cylinder neck. From the pipe screwed inside the cylinder, a small 5-10 cm gas intake tube is extended. Some manufacturers install a porous filter at the end of this tube to prevent any particles from the cylinder from entering the valve. Valves with a conical thread are usually sealed with a thread sealant like Teflon tape. In the past, lead cord was used to seal such valves. Valves with a cylindrical thread are sealed with a ring-shaped rubber gasket. Conical threads have two thread standards and are usually used for oxygen-containing cylinders. As for the cylindrical thread inside the cylinder, according to the European standard EN 144, the necks of steel

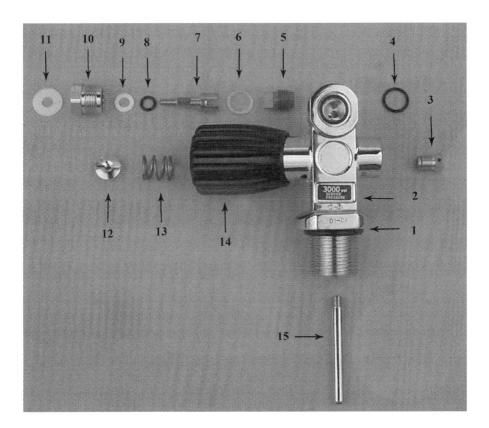

Fig. 41. Valve internal parts: (1) cylinder sealing ring; (2) valve housings; (3) pressure relief valve; (4) regulator o-ring; (5) locking mechanism; (6) spacer metal ring; (7) valve mechanism control lever; (8) O-ring; (9) Teflon gasket; 10 pressure screw; (11) teflon gasket; (12) fixing nut; (13) pressure screw spring; (14) valve adjustment knob; (15) suction tube or filter.

cylinders use M25x2 thread, necks of aluminum cylinders produced in the USA use 3/4-14 NPS thread (National Pipe Straight thread), and necks of carbon cylinders produced in Europe use M18x1.5 thread. Inside each valve, there is a shut-off valve that has a right thread, i.e., it opens counterclockwise. Some companies make shut-off valves with a ball device; for example, the shut-off cylinder valve from the Italian company Scubapro opens by turning the lever 90 degrees. According to the mounting systems of reducer mechanisms to the cylinder valve, valves are divided into three main groups.

Yoke mounts (INT)

Fig. 42. Yoke system valve

The working part of the valve, through which the breathing gas mixture exits, does not have a thread, making it different from the valves of other systems. Due to the special shape of the valve head, a yoke-like fastening located on the reducer, visually resembling a clamp, is used to connect the reducer to the cylinder valve. When tightening the fastening bolt of the reducer, the bolt's edge rests in a special recess located on the back of the valve head. The sealing of the connection between the reducer regulator and the cylinder valve occurs due to a rubber ring and a special silicone grease.

DIN system mounting

The working part of the valve, through which the breathing gas mixture exits, has an internal thread with a diameter of 5/8 inch. Depending on the number of thread turns, 5 or 7, DIN system mounts are divided into two groups: DIN200 and DIN300, respectively. As the

Fig. 43. DIN system valve plus adapter (washer) for INT

name suggests, the DIN200 mounting system has a shorter thread and is used with cylinders and reducers with a working pressure of up to 232 bar. The DIN300 mounting system has a longer thread and is used with cylinders and reducers with a working pressure of up to 300 bar. Regulators equipped with reducers with DIN300 mounting systems can be used with cylinders equipped with valves with DIN200 mounting systems. Cylinders equipped with valves with DIN300 mounting systems can only be used with regulators equipped with the same DIN300 mounting system.

Nitrox/Oxygen system mounting

Special attention should be given to three types of mounts of reducers to cylinder valves that contain oxygen (Oxygen) or nitrox-based gas mixtures. The green wheel catches the eye immediately, and in the Yoke mounting system, a green rubber sealing ring is visible in the valve head. The first type of Nitrox/Oxygen system valve mounts externally resembles the DIN system valve. However, common standards for the use of oxygen-enriched gas mixtures differ from the DIN system

Fig. 44. Nitrox/Oxygen system valve

in that the internal thread of the M26x2 valve has a larger diameter than the DIN system with sizes of 5/8. These valves are mainly used for cylinders installed in rebreathers, such as the Poseidon Se7en.

Fig. 45. Oxygen cylinder valve

The second type of valves for cylinders containing Nitrox/Oxygen gases is valves with external thread Sp 21.8 (W21.8), which are usually used for cylinders with a volume of up to 5 liters, and external thread Sp 27.8 (G3/4) for cylinders larger than 5 liters. Usually, the valve bears the manufacturer's mark containing the following information: the mounting system of the reducer to the valve, DIN, or INT(Yoke); the thread standard for attaching the valve to the cylinder. In Europe, the EN 144 standard is most often used, which involves the use of M25x2 thread, while in the USA, the 14 NPS standard is used, which uses 3/4 thread; the size of the valve outlet thread G5/8; the working pressure of the valve (usually 230 bar and 300 bar for European standards or 3000 psi, 5000 psi for American standards. To solve certain tasks, divers and technical specialists servicing diving equipment use adapters that allow attaching reducers of one mounting system to cylinder valves of another system. It is important to know that cylinders designed for Nitrox/Oxygen gases can be used for air, but after such use, before filling them with Nitrox/Oxygen gases, cylinders and valves must undergo oxygen cleaning by a qualified specialist. It is strictly prohibited to fill Nitrox/Oxygen gas mixtures into cylinders that have not undergone oxygen cleaning!

Single-tank scuba diving has gained the most popularity worldwide. Depending on the diver's tasks, qualifications, and diving training schools, cylinders used for dives can be single-valve or double-valve. Single-valve cylinders are used by divers diving in pairs or small groups. Regulators connected to such cylinders have two lung regulators. One lung regulator is used by the diver carrying the scuba tank throughout the underwater dive, and the second lung regulator (usually yellow) is intended for the diving partner in case of regulator failure. Double-valve systems are used by divers diving in challenging conditions with strong currents, in icy or highly polluted water.

Fig. 46. Cylinder valve

To increase the volume of the breathing gas mixture, some divers use two cylinders on their back, called "sparks." The use of sparks provides the diver with better underwater stability due to weight distribution and reduced water resistance. Typically, the valve system of paired cylinders has two valves and a central valve (called a manifold with an isolating valve), allowing the diver, if necessary, to combine the breathing gas mixtures in different cylinders into one common volume or fill each cylinder with a different breathing gas mixture.

Fig. 47. Spark manifold

An important advantage of using a dual-valve system for single-tank equipment or twin-tank setups is the ability to use two independent regulators that, by duplicating each other, enhance the diver's safety level during dives. In the event of a failure of one regulator, the diver shuts off the valve of the non-functioning regulator and breathes through the second functional regulator. The presence of two or more independent regulators in diving equipment is a mandatory factor for solo dives. It should be noted that according to Gay-Lussac's law, at the point of gas expansion due to pressure reduction, there is a sharp drop in the gas temperature. By opening the cylinder valve without a regulator attached to it, you can observe how the upper part of the cylinder quickly becomes covered with frost. Any gas or gas mixture in the cylinder under high pressure, when exiting through the small opening in the cylinder valve, rapidly cools, cooling the cylinder neck to sub-zero temperatures. Moisture in the air condenses and freezes on the cylinder valve. According to the same law, the reverse effect is observed during gas compression, which occurs during the filling of cylinders, leading to an

Fig. 48. Photo of scuba gear with two cylinders

increase in its temperature. Therefore, when filling a cylinder with compressed air or any other breathing mixture from a compressor or a larger capacity transport cylinder, the filled cylinder heats up.

Regulator

As you already know from the previous material, the human body can inhale if the gas supplied to its lungs equals the ambient pressure (Ambient Pressure). This task is accomplished by the main component of scuba diving equipment, called the regulator. The construction of the regulator is based on mechanisms and valves that respond to changes in ambient pressure. Comfortable breathing and staying underwater are achieved through a two-stage system that reduces the high pressure of the breathing gas mixture in the cylinder to the ambient pressure of the diver.

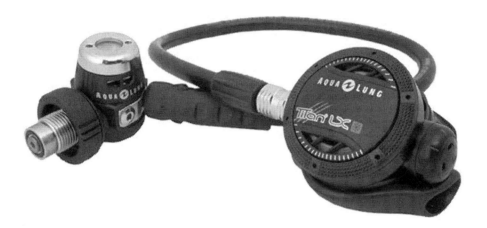

Fig. 49. Regulator

Diving regulators with a two-stage reduction mechanism typically consist of a regulator (first stage) and a demand valve (second stage). The regulator reduces the pressure of the air coming from the cylinders and maintains it constant during the operation of the demand valve. The operation of the regulator is determined by a valve, the movement of which upward, under the influence of compressed air from the cylinders and the spring, holds the flexible diaphragm and the spring.

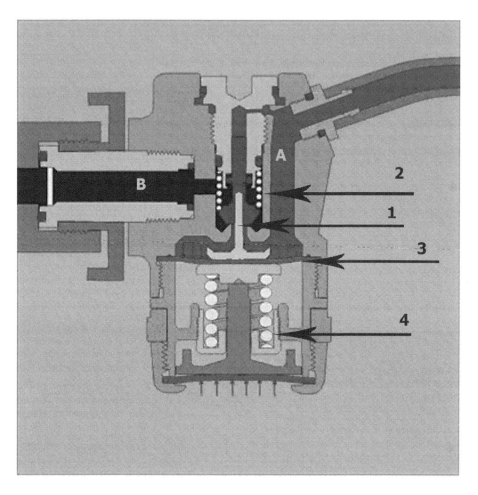

Fig. 50. Scheme (First stage)

With the regulator attached to the cylinder, when the cylinder valve is opened, air from the cylinder enters the regulator chamber "B". The pressure in this chamber rises, leading to the initiation of the diaphragm "3" flexing upward, compressing the spring "4". When the air pressure in chamber "B" reaches a certain level, determined by the spring force, the elasticity of the membrane, and the pressure in chamber "A", the valve "1" under the influence of the spring "2" and compressed air will close the opening in the seat. This stops the flow of air from chamber "B" to chamber "A," and the pressure in chamber

"A" equals a predetermined pressure of the regulator, which is 8-10 bar higher than the ambient pressure. Air from chamber "A" enters the demand valve (second stage) of the regulator, which, through its mechanism, reduces the air pressure to the ambient pressure at which the diver can inhale.

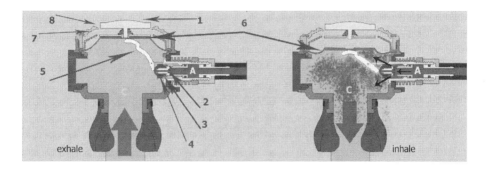

Fig. 51. Operation principle of the demand valve

During inhalation, the pressure in chamber "A" drops, disrupting the balance between the pressure in this chamber and the ambient pressure. The diaphragm bends inside the chamber and presses on the lever. The lever, moving and compressing the spring, opens the valve, allowing air from chamber "B" to be supplied to chamber "A" and then to the second stage during inhalation. After completing the inhalation, the system returns to a balanced state. The cycle repeats with the next inhalation.

In a demand valve operating on the principle of single-stage pressure reduction, high-pressure air from chamber "A" of the regulator is reduced to the required breathing pressure. In such a demand valve, the supply of high-pressure air to the inhalation chamber (C) is controlled by a valve (2), which is held closed by a spring (3) and the pressure of the air. The needle of the valve (4) is supported by a lever (5), which is pivotally mounted on the air supply mechanism of the demand valve. The upper end of the lever (5) is in contact with a rigid plate attached to the central flexible rubber diaphragm (6), which presses against the button (1) in the cover of the valve body (7). The membrane (6) is hermetically attached to the cover, forming a movable wall for the inhalation chamber. The cover has holes (8), allowing the external pressure to act on the entire area of the membrane, causing it to bend into the inhalation chamber when this pressure increases. The demand valve is configured so that when the pressures in the inhalation chamber (1) and the external environment are equal, the valve closes.

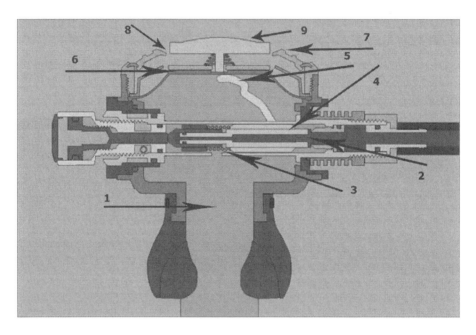

**Fig. 52. Principle of operation of the demand valve
with an ejector**

During inhalation, the pressure in the inhalation chamber (1) decreases, and the flexible rubber membrane (6) bends downward under the pressure of the external environment, pressing on the lever. This lever transmits pressure to the needle valve, lowering the valve and compressing the spring. As a result, air from chamber "A" of the regulator, compressed air, enters chamber (1), from where it goes during inhalation. When inhalation is completed, the pressure in chamber (1) equalizes with the pressure of the external environment. The spring returns the valve and lever to their original position, closing the valve and stopping the flow of air from chamber "A" of the regulator. The breathing resistance is a fundamental characteristic of any scuba regulator and is determined by its design. This resistance can be characterized by two main values. The first value is the breathing resistance, which depends on mechanical reasons caused by the design of the components and assemblies of the apparatus and their manufacturing, i.e., the force of springs, the transmission ratio of handles, friction in axial connections, and the pressure of air on the valve. All these factors determine the resistance of the scuba regulator when breathing in the atmosphere at normal (atmospheric) pressure. The absolute value of the breathing resistance in the air for most regulator designs is usually about 40-60 mm of water column. The second value is the resistance of the regulator for breathing underwater. This value is more important because it determines the characteristic of the regulator in the environment for which it is intended to operate. The breathing resistance underwater varies for different regulators and generally depends on the design of the scuba or rebreather and the diver's position underwater at any given moment. The location of the demand valve near the mouth provides minimal resistance when breathing in a horizontal position underwater since the distance from the center of the lungs to the scuba regulator will be minimal in this case. With the demand valve located near the mouth, the supply of air under pressure equal to the water pressure at the center of the diver's chest occurs when the diver is in a horizontal position. The breathing resistance will be small and will approach the resistance of breathing in the air. This event explains the presence of a significant number of demand valve designs. However, in a vertical position, the demand valve has high resistance during inhalation, and when tilted, air overflows, resulting in high resistance during exhalation.

Demand valves (second stages) with an ejector in the schematic are similar to regular demand valves and differ only in the presence of a tube diverting air from the valve opening into the inhalation tube. In such a device, the tube, together with the inhalation tube, forms an ejector or, as it is called, a jet pump. Compared to demand valves without an ejector, where lung effort is required to maintain a vacuum in the device throughout the entire inhalation period, devices with an ejector reduce lung working time by approximately 75%. This significantly facilitates breathing, and demand valves with jet devices have good operational characteristics.

In regulators with an amplification system, there are three parallel membranes: the controlling membrane detecting fluctuations in lung pressure, the transmitting membrane (of smaller diameter, rigidly connected to the first one), and the valve membrane, rigidly connected to the pin of the demand valve. The space between the transmitting and valve membranes is filled with silicone fluid. The presence of a hydraulic amplifier provides multiple amplification of the initial impulse, allowing the regulator size to be reduced. The total force supplied by the hydraulic amplifier is proportional to the ratio of the areas of the valve and transmitting membranes. All modern regulators are two-stage. Two stages of the regulator allow maintaining a constant supply of the breathing gas mixture to the diver's respiratory organs, regardless of the diving depth and ambient pressure.

In addition to the basic components for comfortable breathing and staying underwater, a diving regulator may include additional features, such as breathing (inhalation) control systems and airflow management. Depending on how the first-stage valve operates based on the pressure of the breathing gas mixture in the cylinder, regulators are classified as balanced and unbalanced. Regarding ambient pressure, regulators are categorized as balanced and overbalanced.

Unbalanced regulators

When talking about balanced or unbalanced regulators, it implies the balance of the first-stage valve concerning the residual pressure of the breathing gas mixture in the cylinder. The operation of the unbalanced regulator's valve directly depends on the residual pressure in the cylinder. Compressed air coming from the cylinder, in a way, assists the spring in opening the valve. Therefore, the higher the pressure in the cylinder, the faster the valve opens, allowing the first-stage chambers to be filled with the compressed breathing gas mixture. The lower the pressure in the cylinder, the slower the valve opens, and accordingly, the slower the first-stage chambers are filled. The diver needs some effort to inhale from the regulator. This demonstrates the unbalance of the regulator.

Balanced regulators

In this type of regulators, the air pressure in the lung system remains constant regardless of changes in ambient pressure. An additional pressure balancing mechanism is used to compensate for depth changes. Practically all regulators are balanced concerning the pressure of the water column. This is the so-called hydrostatic balance of the regulator. It implies that the setting pressure in the regulator chamber does not depend on the pressure of the water column. As known, every 10 meters of the water column add 1 bar to the ambient pressure. Regulators are designed so that the pressure in the regulator chamber also increases by 1 bar for every 10 meters of water thickness. Thus, the difference between the pressure in the regulator chamber and the water pressure remains constant, ensuring equal loading on the second stage of the regulator at different working depths. For example, at the surface, the setting pressure of the Poseidon Jetstream regulator in the first-stage chamber is 10 bars. At a depth of 20 meters, where the excess pressure of the water column is 2 bars, the pressure in the regulator chamber is 12 bars. The setting pressure remains equal to 10 bars (12 bars in the regulator chamber minus 2 bars of water column pressure equals 12 bars).

Over-balanced regulators

Even if a regulator is hydrostatically balanced and has a balanced first-stage valve that operates independently of the air pressure in the cylinder, divers feel increased effort during inhalation at greater depths. This is because at depth, due to the increasing ambient pressure, air has greater density and viscosity. As air passes through channels and sections, frictional force increases, resulting in less air reaching the diver's lungs per unit of time. To ensure a consistent air supply regardless of depth, engineers invented the over-balanced regulator. Over-balance means that the setting pressure of the regulator increases with depth. This is done to compensate for the increasing density and viscosity of air at greater depths, ensuring a consistent air delivery per unit of time both at the surface and at depth.

Fig. 53. Aqualung Legend first stage

The principle of operation of over-balanced regulators is that the setting pressure increases with depth. For example, at the surface, the setting pressure of the Aqualung Glacia regulator is 9.5 bar, and at a depth of 20 meters, the pressure in the second-stage chamber is 12.3 bars. Thus, with an excess pressure of the water column of 2 bars, the setting pressure of the over-balanced regulator is 10.3 bars (12.3 - 2 = 10.3 bars), not 9.5 bars as would be expected with a balanced regulator.

There is also a classification of regulators based on their resistance to the water temperature in which the dive takes place. Since the breathing gas mixture cools the most when exiting the cylinder in the first stage of the regulator, each inhalation creates a "freezing effect" around the valve seat. This area starts absorbing heat from the regulator body and the surrounding water. After some time, the temperature of the valve seat stabilizes but remains below freezing. Any moisture in the gas turns into ice, and the regulator goes into free flow. In this case, the intermediate pressure will increase, and the second stage will continuously deliver gas. In the event of such a failure, it is necessary to switch to an alternative air source and shut off the cylinder by closing the valve in front of the jammed regulator.

To prevent this situation, the breathing gas mixture in the cylinder must be dry enough. This is why compressors are equipped with systems for both filtration and drying of water vapors in the air. The colder the environment, the colder the breathing gas mixture becomes, and the more likely the regulator is to freeze. According to the European standard EN 250, which defines the requirements, testing, and labeling of open-circuit self-contained diving apparatuses for compressed air, all regulators are divided into two groups: warm water regulators, which can be used in water temperatures above 10°C, and cold water regulators, intended for use in water temperatures below 10°C.

The EN250 standard establishes a lower limit: the work should not exceed 3 J/l, and the best modern regulators provide work up to 0.6 J/l. To obtain certification for use in water temperatures below 10°C, the regulator must undergo a test conducted under standard conditions: depth of 50 meters, breathing intensity of 62.5 l/min, compressed air pressure of 50 bars, water temperature of +4°C (plus-minus 0.2°C), exhaled mixture temperature of +28°C, humidity of the exhaled mixture more than 90% (the last two parameters are relevant during regulator testing on the stand). In these conditions, the regulator must last for 5 minutes. Regulators that pass this test are suitable for cold water dives with temperatures up to +4°C. The standard does not regulate further temperature decreases in the water.

The first stage, also known as the regulator, is the most important component of the regulator system. The first stage connects to the cylinder with compressed air (or any other breathing gas mixture). When the cylinder valve is opened, the gas mixture under excess pressure in the cylinder enters the regulator, which reduces it to intermediate pressure and directs the gas flow through the hose to the second stage. Intermediate pressure in the regulator is defined as the pressure that exceeds the ambient pressure by 8-10 bars (approximately 120-145 psi) depending on the regulator model and manufacturer. The difference between intermediate pressure and the pressure of the air exiting the second stage regulator (ambient pressure) is the setting pressure of the regulator. At the surface, the intermediate pressure equals the setting pressure.

Regulators have valves in their design that prevent the backflow of gases and maintain constant intermediate pressure in their system. Depending on the model and manufacturer, first stages are divided into two main types of diving regulators based on the control element: diaphragm and piston regulators. They have different designs and operating principles. One of the key performance indicators of the

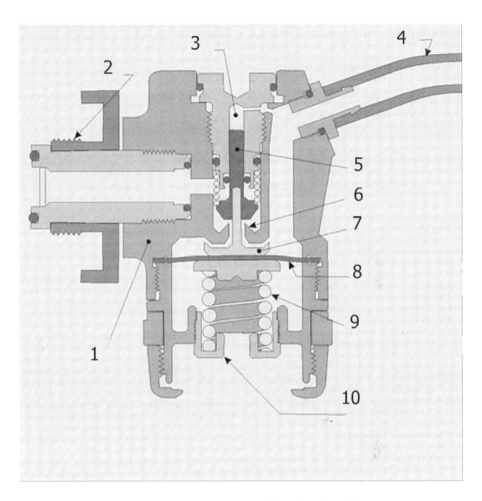

Fig. 54. Main parts (First stage): (1) - body; (2) - DIN system attachment to the cylinder; (3) - balancing chamber; (4) - medium-pressure hose; (5) - diaphragm valve; (6) - valve seat; (7) - valve pusher; (8) - main diaphragm; (9) - main spring; (10) - adjustment nut.

first-stage regulator is the magnitude of pressure drop in the regulator chamber during inhalation. This value indicates how much the pressure in the regulator chamber must decrease for the valve to open and air supply to the second stage to begin in the initial phase of inhalation.

To check this, screw in a 3/8" low-pressure gauge into the regulator port. Design features of piston regulators fundamentally prevent this value from being less than 1 bar. While the most common diaphragm regulator has a pressure drop in the regulator chamber of 0.5 bar.

Piston type regulators

Next, we will take a closer look at the principles of operation and the structure of different types of regulators. The first stage contains a piston that moves back and forth in response to changes in ambient pressure. During inhalation, the diver's piston opens, allowing air to pass into the second stage. Piston regulators usually have a simple design, are easy to maintain, perform well at great depths, and are predominantly used in warm water. Below are some models of piston diving regulators from a variety of well-known manufacturers available on the market: Scubapro MK2, Scubapro MK21, Scubapro MK25, Aqua Lung Calypso, and others. In turn, piston first stages are divided into unbalanced and balanced.

Unbalanced piston first stage

The control of this stage is the piston (1), the lower part of which acts as a valve. At the end of the piston, a removable valve cushion (2) is attached. The valve seat (3) is firmly fixed in the body. If the regulator is not loaded, the valve is open because the piston is pushed back by the spring (4). When the cylinder valve is opened, compressed air flows through the filter (5) into the high-pressure chamber (6). Then, through the open valve into the "A" cavity of the regulator chamber (7). Further through the piston passage channel "B," air in the piston (1) passes into the "C" cavity of the medium-pressure regulator chamber (7). At the surface, when the pressure in the regulator chamber (7) reaches 9.2 bar, the force from the air pressure on the upper part of the piston overcomes the spring force (4), and the pressure on the cushion of the cylinder valve's outgoing compressed air closes the valve. During inhalation, a vacuum is created in the "A" cavity of the regulator chamber, reducing the pressure in the "C" cavity accordingly. Under the action of the spring (4), the piston moves up -

the valve opens, allowing air to flow in during inhalation. After the inhalation is stopped, the regulator chamber (7) fills with air to the set pressure, and the valve closes. In this design of the regulator, the pressure of the cylinder's compressed air directly affects the valve. Compressed air entering from the cylinder helps the spring (4) open the valve. Therefore, if the pressure of the compressed air in the cylinder is low, the valve opens more slowly, leading to slow filling of the regulator. This is manifested in the unbalance of a simple piston regulator.

Hydrostatic balance of the Aqualung Calypso regulator

When diving, water enters through the holes (8) into the hydrostatic chamber (9). Under the pressure of the water column, the piston (1) moves toward the "C" cavity of the regulator chamber, opening the valve. As a result, an additional amount of air enters the regulator chamber to close the valve and compensate for the

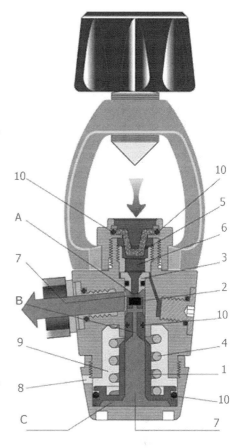

Fig. 56. Structure of the unbalanced piston regulator Aqualung Calypso: (1) - piston; (2) - valve cushion; (3) - valve seat; (4) - spring; (5) - filter; (6) - high-pressure chamber; (7) - regulator chamber; (8) - hydrostatic plug; (9) - hydrostatic chamber; (10) - O-rings; **A** - regulator chamber cavity; **B** - piston passage channel; **C** - regulator chamber cavity.

water pressure, thereby increasing the pressure in the regulator chamber by the amount of the water column pressure. Aqualung Calypso regulators have a removable valve seat (3) made of high-strength stainless steel. The likelihood of damaging such a seat is very low, but even if the seat is damaged, it is easily replaceable. Some piston-type regulators have a seat that is part of the brass body. The likelihood of damage to the brass seat is higher, and in case of damage, the entire body needs to be replaced.

Balanced Piston first stage

Let's consider the principle of operation and the device of a balanced piston regulator - the Aqualung Pioneer. The controlling element of the balanced piston regulator is the piston (1). The valve cushion (2) is firmly attached to the regulator body. The end of the piston serves as the valve seat. If the regulator is not loaded, the valve is open because the piston is pushed back by the spring (3). When the cylinder valve is opened, compressed air flows through the filter (4) into the high-pressure chamber (5). Then, through the open valve and the passage channel in the piston (6), air enters the regulator chamber (7). At the surface, when the pressure in the regulator chamber (7) reaches 9.2 bar, the forces from the air pressure on the upper part of the piston overcome the spring force (3), and the piston closes the valve. During inhalation, a vacuum is created in the regulator chamber (7), reducing the pressure, and under the force of the spring (3), the piston opens the valve, allowing air to pass during inhalation. When inhalation stops, the regulator chamber (7) fills with air to the set pressure, and the valve closes. In this design, the pressure of the cylinder's compressed air does not affect the valve's operation, so the inhalation efforts are independent of the amount of air in the cylinder, making the regulator balanced.

Fig. 55. Filter

Hydrostatic balance of the Aqualung Pioneer regulator

When diving, water presses on the diaphragm (8) of the hydrostatic chamber (9), which is filled with silicone oil. Through the diaphragm (8) and silicone oil, the water column pressure is transmitted to the piston (1), which moves towards the regulator chamber (7), opening the valve. As a result, an additional amount of air enters the regulator chamber to close the valve and compensate for the water pressure, thereby increasing the pressure in the regulator chamber by the amount of the water column pressure. The silicone-filled chamber ensures the regulator's resistance to freezing. The hydrostatic chamber of most balanced piston regulators from other manufacturers is open to water access. Instead of the diaphragm (8), these regulators have openings. In this case, the regulator can be used in water not colder than 10°C (according to the EN250 standard). The "weak point" of a balanced piston regulator is the sealing ring (10), which bears the maximum loads, as it isolates the high-pressure chamber. It is precisely because of its wear that

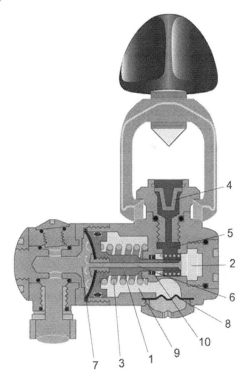

Fig. 57. Diagram of the Balanced Piston Regulator Aqualung Pioneer: (1) - piston; (2) - valve cushion; (3) - spring; (4) - filter; (5) - high-pressure chamber; (6) - piston passage channel; (7) - regulator chamber; (8) - diaphragm; (9) - hydrostatic chamber; (10) - piston sealing ring (O-ring).

air "trickling" from the first stage regulator underwater often occurs. Also, over time, the valve cushion becomes unable to hold the set pressure, leading to the regulator being set to free-flow. The valve cushion, all sealing rings, and the filter must be replaced during periodic technical maintenance of the regulator. The set pressure of this regulator is not adjustable, as its value is determined by the design developed by the manufacturing plant.

Diaphragm regulator

The first stage contains a diaphragm that separates high-pressure air from intermediate pressure. During the diver's inhalation, the diaphragm opens, allowing air to pass into the second stage. Diaphragm regulators usually have high sensitivity to pressure changes and good performance at low temperatures.

Membrane balanced first stage

Let's examine the design and principles of operation of the membrane-balanced regulator using the example of the first stage Aqualung Titan. The controlling element of the membrane-balanced regulator is the membrane (1). It is connected to the valve (3) through the push rod (2), which is pressed against the valve seat (4) by the force of two springs (9) and (10). The valve seat (4) is firmly fixed in the regulator body. If the regulator is not loaded, the valve is open under the action of the spring (5). When the cylinder valve is opened, compressed air flows through the filter (6) into the high-pressure chamber (7). Then, through the open valve and the passage channel in the regulator's intermediate pressure chamber (8). At the surface, when the pressure in the regulator's intermediate pressure chamber (8) reaches 9.2 bar, the force from the air pressure on the membrane (1) overcomes the spring force (5), the membrane (1) evens out, and under the action of springs (9) and (10), the valve closes.

During inhalation, a vacuum is created in the regulator's intermediate pressure chamber (8), reducing the pressure, and the membrane (1), under the force of the spring (5), bends towards the regulator's intermediate pressure chamber (8) and, through the push rod (2), overcoming the force of springs (9) and (10), opens the valve, allowing air to pass during inhalation. When inhalation stops, the regulator's intermediate pressure chamber (8) fills with air to the set pressure, and the valve closes. One of the main elements of the balanced membrane regulator is the balance chamber (11), inside which air is under pressure equal to the pressure in the regulator's intermediate pressure chamber (8). As a result, the valve's operation does not depend on the pressure of the compressed air coming from the cylinder. In the regulator's valve mechanism, unlike many similar designs, the valve guide (12), located inside the balance chamber (11), is suspended between two springs (9) and (10). As the pressure in the cylinder decreases, the spring (10) pushes the valve guide upward, compressing the spring (9). This increases the stroke of the valve and the effective cross-section of the valve. This design provides a difference in the action of the valve mechanism when the pressure in the cylinder changes, stabilizing the volume of the delivered air. The set pressure of the first stage is adjusted using the nut (13), which regulates the degree of compression of the spring (5) and, consequently, the pressure of the spring (5) on the membrane (1). Bending into the regulator's intermediate pressure chamber (8), the membrane changes the pressure in this chamber. The Aqualung Titan first stage model includes the Air Turbo system. Under the membrane in the regulator body, there is an additional hole (17) leading to the regulator chamber. When the air in the regulator chamber is depressurized, occurring as a result of inhalation from the second stage, additional injection occurs through the Air Turbo channel. As a result, the membrane responds more quickly to inhalation, providing a more stable air delivery throughout the inhalation phase.

Hydrostatic balance of the Aqualung Titan first stage

When submerged, water penetrates through the hole in the adjustment nut (13) into the hydrostatic chamber (14). Under the pressure of the water column, the membrane bends towards the regulator's intermediate pressure chamber (8), opening the valve. As a result, the pressure in the regulator's intermediate pressure chamber increases by the amount of the water column pressure, and thus, the valve closes, compensating for excess water pressure. The hydrostatic chamber of the Aqualung Titan first stage in the SUPREME version is sealed by a membrane, isolating the spring (5) from the external environment. The water column pressure is transmitted to the main membrane (1) through the silicone membrane (15) via the push rod (16). This is the so-called "dry chamber." It ensures the regulator's resistance to

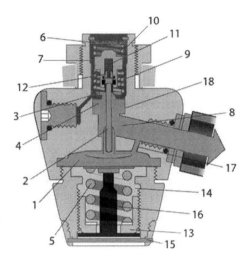

Fig. 58. Diagram of the membrane-balanced regulator Aqualung Titan: (1) - membrane; (2) - push rod; (3) - valve; (4) - valve seat; (5) - spring; (6) - filter; (7) - high-pressure chamber; (8) - intermediate pressure chamber; (9) - spring; (10) - spring; (11) - balance chamber; (12) - valve guide; (13) - adjustment nut; (14) - hydrostatic chamber; (15) - silicone membrane; (16) - push rod; (17) - Air Turbo channel; (18) - sealing rings (O-rings).

freezing and protects the hydrostatic chamber from contamination. Other manufacturers' membrane regulators, to ensure resistance to freezing, assume filling the hydrostatic chamber with silicone oil or a similar substance. A cap or an additional membrane is installed over such a chamber. Through this membrane and silicone oil, the pressure of the surrounding environment is transmitted to the main membrane.

During the technical maintenance of membrane regulators, it is necessary to replace the membrane, the valve seat cushion, all sealing rings, and the filter.

Superbalanced membrane first stage

The main difference in the operation of this regulator is the design of the hydrostatic chamber (1). Its mandatory element is the dry chamber. The hydrostatic chamber is closed by a silicone membrane (2) and transmits the pressure of the surrounding environment to the main regulator membrane (4) through the push rod (3). In the Titan regulator, the diameter of the silicone membrane of the dry chamber is calculated so that with each increase in the pressure of the surrounding environment by 1 bar, the pressure in the regulator chamber also increases by 1 bar. Thus, the set pressure of the regulator remains constant

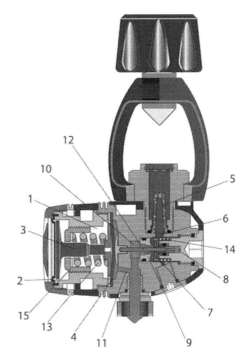

Fig. 59. Diagram of the superbalanced membrane regulator Aqualung Legend: (1) - hydrostatic chamber; (2) - silicone membrane; (3) - push rod; (4) - main membrane; (5) - filter; (6) - high-pressure chamber; (7) - valve; (8) - balancing chamber; (9) - valve seat; (10) - regulator chamber; (11) - Air Turbo channel; (12) - push rod; (13) - spring; (14) - spring; (15) - adjustment nut.

regardless of the depth. In the Legend regulator, the diameter of the silicone membrane of the dry chamber is slightly larger than that of the Titan regulator with the same diameter of the main membrane. Therefore, with an increase in external pressure, due to the difference in the areas of the two membranes, the pressure in the regulator chamber increases by a larger amount with increasing depth. That is, the set pressure of the Legend regulator increases with depth. As a result of the increased set pressure at depth, air passes through the channels more quickly, compensating for its increased density. Thus, the dry chamber of the superbalanced Legend regulator provides not only protection of the first stage of the regulator from cold water and contamination but also serves as the main mechanism ensuring superbalance. Since the set pressure of the superbalanced first stage increases with depth, ordinary (unbalanced) second stages of regulators are not suitable for it, as they will respond to an increase in set pressure as a safety valve. Balanced second stage regulators are designed to work with superbalanced regulators.

Second stage

The second stage, usually called a demand valve or octopus, equalizes the intermediate pressure of the breathing gas coming from the regulator (first stage) to the ambient pressure of the diver's environment. The demand valve has a valve system that opens during the diver's inhalation and closes during exhalation, providing only one-way airflow. Usually, the diver breathes through the mouth, holding the second stage with an ergonomic silicone mouthpiece. Depending on the design, some diving regulators have the technical capability to deliver air to special full-face masks, allowing the diver to breathe through the nose.

Second stages are divided into downstream and upstream systems for delivering breathing gas to the diver during descent. The two main types differ in how they control the flow of intermediate pressure air directed to the diver's respiratory organs during inhalation and exhalation. Let's examine each type in more detail:

Fig. 60. Aqualung Legend second stage

Downstream (Demand) air delivery systems are the most common type of demand valves. As the name suggests, the valve mechanism delivering breathing gas to the diver opens with the flow of air moving from the first stage. Second stages of this type operate on the principle of creating low pressure during inhalation. When the diver inhales, the human body draws air into the lungs, creating a small low-pressure in the demand valve's chamber. At this moment, the valve releasing air into the water during exhalation closes due to ambient pressure, and the membrane, enclosed in the second stage housing, begins to move towards the diver's respiratory pathways. This membrane, with its rigid center, slightly presses on a lever connected to the intake valve and located under the purge button. Exiting the seat of the intake valve in the second stage allows the breathing gas mixture in the hose under intermediate pressure to flow freely, filling the demand valve's chamber and the diver's lungs with the required amount of gas for inhalation. At this moment, the first stage fills the chambers of the second stage with intermediate pressure. During exhalation, the pressure in the diver's lungs, as well as in the diver's respiratory system and the chambers of the second stage, becomes higher. This leads primarily to the reverse movement of the membrane, which stops pressing on the purge lever. Consequently, this results in the closure of the intake valve in the second stage, which, under the action of a spring, sits back in the seat, blocking the airflow from the first stage, and opens the exhaust valve for exhaled air to be released into the environment. In the event of a malfunction in the first stage, increasing intermediate air pressure will open the valve, and the demand valve in the malfunctioned regulator will go into free flow, continuing to supply air to the diver (excessive supply, leading to a rapid release of the breathing gas mixture from the tank). Many downstream second stages from various manufacturers are equipped with a Venturi flow adjustment system for the injection of the breathing gas mixture into the diver's respiratory organs, called the Venturi.

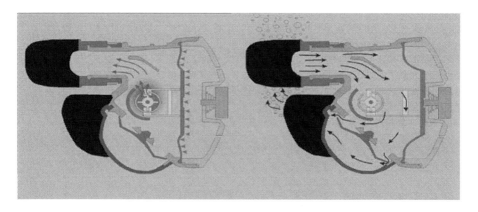

Fig. 61. Venturi effect

The Venturi effect is a consequence of Bernoulli's law, according to which the pressure of a gas or liquid is inversely proportional to the speed of its movement. Many of us have seen this law demonstrated in physics classes. Take a sheet of A4 paper, fold it, and tear it in half.

Then, holding two resulting paper strips parallel to each other at a distance of 5-10 cm, blow through the channel that forms. Instead of the expected divergence, the strips will come together. This happens because the pressure of the air moving between the strips decreases compared to the pressure of the air on the external side of the strips.

Fig. 62. Diver with a scuba

The membrane of the demand valve behaves in the same way during the inhalation phase when the second stage valve is already open. The airflow moving in the demand valve's air chamber has lower pressure compared to the pressure on the external side of the membrane, causing the membrane to bend further into the air chamber—resulting in the spontaneous injection of air. This continues until the airflow stops, and we begin to exhale. This effect helps the diver during the inhalation phase.

Deflector - is regulator for the second stage.

Downstream second stages are divided into two categories: unbalanced and balanced.

Unbalanced second stage

Unbalanced second stages reduce the force of the airflow coming from the first stage by means of the spring force of the valve, which is manually adjusted from the intermediate pressure hose side. By removing the air supply hose, a hex key (or other necessary tool) is inserted into the air supply hole and turned in 5-15 minute intervals. This can reduce the load on the spring holding the intake valve, lowering the resistance on inhalation to an extremely low level in manual adjustment mode. Thus, the operation of the intake valve of the regulator is adjusted to the set pressure values of the first stage, regardless of the manufacturer. In terms of their operating principle, all second stages are very similar. Let's consider the device and operation using the example of the Aqualung Calypso demand valve.

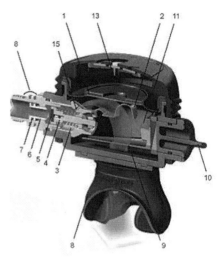

Fig. 63. Aqualung Calypso Second Stage: (1) - membrane; (2) - lever; (3) - spring; (4) - valve stem; (5) - valve seat cushion; (6) - valve seat; (7) - O-ring; (8) - heat exchanger; (9) - Venturi valve; (10) - Venturi adjustment lever; (11) - air chamber; (13) - water chamber; (14) - diaphragm; (15) - hole to the valve body.

The controlling element of all known second stages is the diaphragm (1). It separates the housing of the demand valve into two chambers - the air chamber (11) and the water chamber (13). The air chamber always maintains pressure equal to the ambient pressure, i.e., the pressure in the water chamber. It is at this pressure that we can take a breath. Inhalation is done from the air chamber (11), and exhalation also occurs into this chamber. Therefore, during exhalation, automatic pressure equalization occurs on both sides of the diaphragm - the air chamber is filled with exhaled air to the pressure of the surrounding environment, and excess air is vented through a one-way flutter valve for exhalation.

Consider a hypothetical situation in which a diver with a regulator in their mouth holds their breath on the surface and begins to descend. As the depth increases, the ambient pressure acts on the diaphragm of the demand valve, causing it to bend towards the air chamber. In doing so, it presses on the lever (2). The lever opens the valve, and air from the first stage under pressure enters the air chamber of the demand valve. The influx of air continues until the pressure in the air chamber (11) increases and becomes equal to the water pressure. At this point, the diaphragm (1) returns to its original position, and the valve closes. Thus, the air chamber of the demand valve still maintains pressure equal to the ambient pressure, and the demand valve is ready for the diver to inhale. This principle is fundamental to the operation of the second stage of any regulator. When inhaling in the air chamber (11) of the second stage, there is a rarefaction, causing the diaphragm (1) to bend downward and press on the lever (2). The lever, connected to the valve stem (4) and overcoming the force of the spring (3), moves the valve. A replaceable valve seat cushion (5) is attached to the end of the valve, away from the valve seat (6). Through the open valve and the opening (15), air rushes into the air chamber of the demand valve (11) and through it, facilitating inhalation. When inhalation stops and exhalation begins, air fills the chamber (11) to the ambient pressure, and the diaphragm (1) returns to its original position, closing the valve under the influence of the spring (3). Excess exhaled air exits through a one-way flutter valve located at the bottom of the air chamber of the demand valve. A deflector covers it, protecting the valve from external influences and diverting bubbles of exhaled air.

The second stage of this regulator is equipped with a Venturi adjustment system with a switch (10) located on the outside of the housing, in the form of a 90-degree rotatable lever (the Venturi switch is called the "pre-dive"/"dive" mode

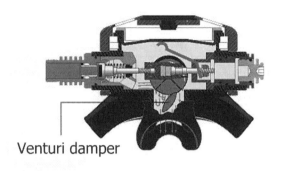

Venturi damper

Fig. 64. Venturi valve

switch). The Venturi system inside the housing consists of a valve (9) that redirects the airflow inside the air chamber of the demand valve. In the "maximum" position, the channel is fully open for airflow, and the injection is maximally engaged. Before diving, the lever is switched to the "minimum" ("Pre-Dive") position. Once underwater, to make breathing easier, the switch is moved to the "maximum" ("Dive") position.

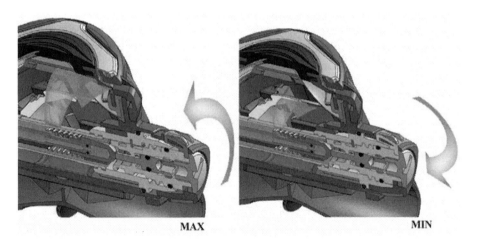

MAX   MIN

Fig. 65. Manual adjustment

Adiabatic gas expansion

As is known, according to Gay-Lussac's law, at the point of adiabatic gas expansion (expansion of gas due to a drop in pressure from higher to lower), there is a sharp drop in the temperature of the gas. You can observe this phenomenon by opening the valve of a tank without a connected regulator - the upper part of the tank quickly becomes covered with frost. The reverse is also true - during adiabatic gas compression, its temperature increases. Therefore, when filling a tank with air from a compressor, the tank heats up. In the demand valve at the point of air outlet from the valve (let's call it the "cold point"), the temperature of the air drops to about -30°C. Since the diver's body exhales moist air, moisture condenses at the point where the lever attaches to the valve stem, where the temperature is low. This condensed moisture can turn into ice and cause the lever (bypass) to jam, which, in turn, can disrupt the operation of the second stage, leading it to free flow. To ensure resistance to freezing, second stages are equipped with a heat exchanger (8), which transfers heat from the water to the "cold point" and to the metal parts of the valve mechanism, preventing the formation of ice crystals on metal surfaces. At the same time, the lever (2) has a Teflon coating, also preventing the formation of ice crystals on it. Let's also consider the operating principles and the diagram of a more frost-resistant unbalanced demand valve, the Aqualung Titan.

In the illustration, it can be seen that the attachment point of the lever is shifted towards the opposite side of the "cold point," i.e., the air outlet from the valve. Moreover, the

Fig. 66. Aqualung Titan second stage

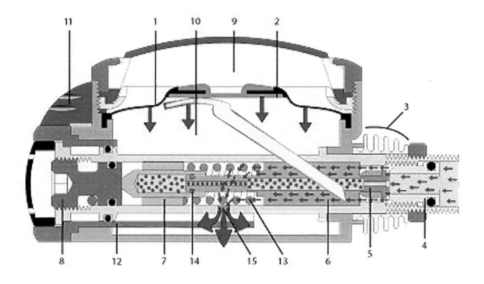

Fig. 67. Unbalanced demand valve Aqualung Titan: (1) – diaphragm; (2) – lever; (3) – heat exchangers; (4) – valve seat; (5) – O-ring; (6) – valve seat cushion; (7) – spring; (8) – valve stem; (9) – Venturi valve; (10) – deflector; (11) – thermal insulator; (12) – stem; (14) – exhaust valve; (15) – air chamber.

valve stem consists of three parts (8, 12, 13). The middle part is a plastic bushing (12), serving as a thermal insulator. Thus, the low temperature of the air from the "cold point" is not transmitted to the lever (2). The lever itself has a Teflon coating, which also prevents the formation of ice crystals on the lever. The second stage has powerful heat exchangers (3), which transfer heat from the water to the metal parts of the valve mechanism, also preventing the formation of ice crystals on metal surfaces. This second stage operates as follows: When inhaling in the air chamber (15), there is a rarefaction, causing the diaphragm (1) to bend downward and press on the lever (2). The lever, connected to the valve stem (8) through the stem (13) and thermal insulator (12), overcomes the force of the spring (7) and moves the valve. A replaceable valve seat cushion (6) is attached to the end of the valve, away from the valve seat (4). Through the open valve, air rushes into the air chamber of the demand valve (15) and through it, facilitating inhalation. When inhalation stops and exhalation begins, air fills the chamber (15) to the ambient pressure, and the diaphragm (1) returns to its original position, closing the valve under the influence of the spring (7). Excess exhaled air exits through a one-way flutter valve (14) located at the bottom of the air chamber of the demand valve. A deflector (11) covers it, protecting the valve from external influences and diverting bubbles of exhaled air. The demand valve is equipped with a Venturi adjustment, which is a valve (9) redirecting the airflow in the air chamber (15).

Balanced second stages

A balanced second stage has a compensating chamber in its mechanism, slightly reducing the force of the airflow from the first stage. This helps decrease the load on the springs and reduces inhalation resistance to an extremely low level. The large cross-sectional area of the nozzle ensures the intake of a significant amount of air, crucial for any physical activity underwater. The operation of the demand valve is independent of the first stage's preset pressure, allowing second stages of this design to be used with first stages from any manufacturer without additional adjustments.

Using the Aqualung Glacia LX second stage as an example, let's examine the operation of the breathing apparatus during the inhalation and exhalation phases.

During inhalation in the second stage air chamber (10), there is a rarefaction, causing the diaphragm (1) to bend downward, pressing on the lever (2). The lever, connected to the valve stem (6) through the stem (13), overcomes the force of the spring (13), moving the valve. A replaceable valve seat cushion (5) is attached to the end of the valve, away from the valve seat (4). Through the open valve and then through the hole (15) in the valve mechanism cylinder, air rushes into the breathing apparatus's air chamber (10), facilitating inhalation. When

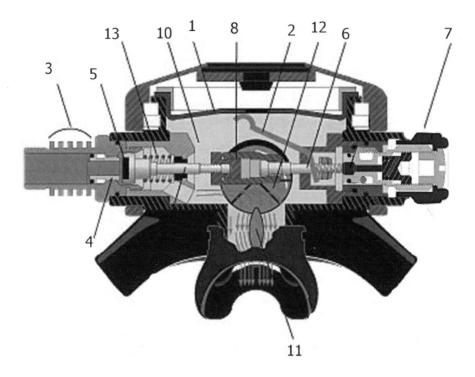

Fig. 68. Aqualung Glacia LX second stage: (1) – diaphragm; (2) – lever; (3) – heat exchangers; (4) – valve seat; (5) – valve; (6) – adjustment stem (7) – breathing gas delivery adjustment knob; (8) – Venturi valve; (9) – Venturi valve; (10) – second stage chamber; (11) – Venturi valve switch; (13) – supply valve spring.

inhalation stops, and exhalation begins, air fills the chamber (10) to ambient pressure, and the diaphragm (1) returns to its original position, closing the valve under the influence of the spring (13). Excess exhaled air exits through a one-way flutter valve (4), located at the bottom of the second stage's air chamber. A deflector (5) covers it, protecting the valve from external influences and diverting bubbles of exhaled air. To prevent freezing, the second stage is equipped with a heat exchanger (3), and for easy inhalation, it features a Venturi adjustment system (11). The Venturi system consists of a valve (12), which closes and redirects the airflow coming into the air chamber from the opening (15).

In addition to the Venturi adjustment, the second stage has a breathing resistance adjustment screw (1), which, through the pusher (2), changes the compression degree of the spring (3), thereby affecting the effort required to open the second stage valve. This manual adjustment allows controlling air consumption. With the screw fully tightened, inhalation resistance is maximum, allowing very economical air consumption. With the screw fully loosened, inhalation resistance is practically absent, and the demand valve operates in a very light mode, forcefully delivering air.

Let's consider the fundamental structural difference between balanced and unbalanced demand valves. The fundamental schematic of a balanced second stage's device resembles the structure of a diaphragm-balanced first stage regulator. The valve stem has a through hole through which air from the first stage, at intermediate pressure, enters the balancing chamber. An O-ring prevents air from the balancing chamber from entering the breathing chamber. Thus, in addition to the spring force, the valve is supported from the inside, in the balancing chamber, by the air pressure equal to the intermediate pressure. In other words, unlike an unbalanced demand valve where the spring has to overcome the pressure of compressed air coming from the first stage, in a balanced demand valve, the compressed air at intermediate pressure partially compensates for the spring force to close the valve. This design allows significantly reducing the spring force, thereby reducing the effort required to open the valve. This is why breathing from a demand valve does not depend on the magnitude of the intermediate (preset) pressure. However, being a downstream second stage, as the pressure between the first and second stages increases, the demand valve may go into free flow. However, the critical intermediate pressure, at which the demand valve acts as a relief valve, is much higher than that of unbalanced demand valves and is about 18-20 bar.

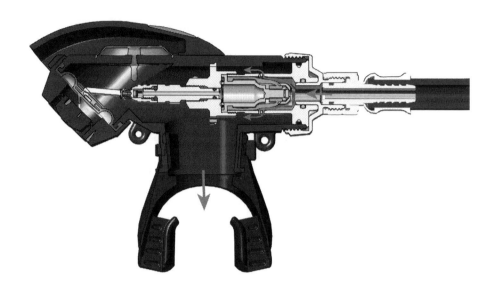

Fig. 69. Operating principle of the counterflow gas delivery system Poseidon XSTREAM

Counterflow gas delivery systems (Xstream). The design of the counterflow second stage is such that the valve closes with the airflow coming from the first stage. By opening the cylinder valve, the breathing gas pressure, decreasing through the first stage to intermediate pressure, flows through the hoses to the second stage. The mechanism of the second stage has two valves, large and small. As the pressure increases, the large valve expands, closing the openings for further airflow. In this position, the regulator remains pressurized, and the second stage does not allow air for inhalation. When the diver inhales, creating a pressure drop in the second stage chamber, the diaphragm bends, slightly pressing on the bypass lever. The lever is connected to the small valve, which opens slightly, leading to the abrupt opening of the large valve and the openings for the passage of the breathing gas from the hose. Air rushes through the openings into the hollow chamber of the second stage and then into the diver's respiratory tract. During exhalation, the exhaled gas fills the same chamber of the second stage to ambient pressure, causing the diaphragm to return to its original position.

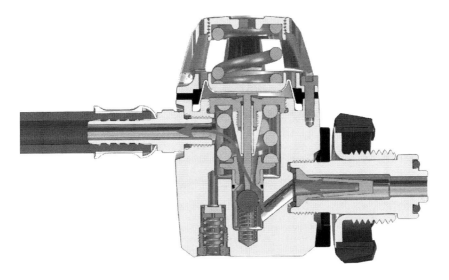

**Fig. 70. Operating principle of the Poseidon XSTREAM
first stage**

The small valve, not feeling the pressure of the lever, closes, and inside the demand valve, there is a repeated increase in pressure, leading to the return of the main large valve to its original position, closing the supply of breathing gas. In case of a malfunction in the first stage and an increase in intermediate pressure, the hose supplying air to the second stage may rupture under increasing pressure. To prevent such situations, a relief valve is integrated into the gas mixture supply hose from the regulator, which releases excess pressure. As can be seen from the description, the designs of counterflow second stages look more technologically complex, but they compensate for their exceptional performance in extreme conditions, providing the diver with easy inhalation regardless of the depth. These regulators include: Poseidon XSTREAM, Poseidon Jetstream, Hollis 500SE, Sherwood Genesis.

Fig. 71. Freezing of regulator parts

Special mention should be made of regulators used for diving in extreme conditions, in freshwater with temperatures close to 0°C, and in saltwater with temperatures down to -3°C. Diving in cold water environments imposes special requirements on the regulator because the freezing of any stage of the regulator can disrupt the pneumatic system, leading to either spontaneous free flow from the second stage or a cessation of air supply.

Laboratory tests and practical use of regulators of any design in water with temperatures above +7°C have shown that the likelihood of freezing regulator parts in the first and second stages is negligible. However, when operating the regulator at ambient temperatures below +7°C, this risk sharply increases, especially with increased diver breathing intensity or when diving to depths close to 40 meters. This is because, with large airflows, according to Gay-Lussac's law, the regulator's components are more intensively cooled due to the increased flow of expanding air. The degree of regulator cooling depends on many factors, primarily pressure differences and the amount of gas exiting per unit of time. At the point where air exits the valve, the temperature drops to approximately -30°C; however, the regulator does not freeze because the relatively warm water surrounding it heats the regulator's reducing devices, preventing moisture from freezing, even if it condenses. A decrease in the ambient temperature creates a higher probability of freezing for surfaces in contact with the cold water that experience friction.

Manufacturers of freeze-resistant regulators employ various technological solutions that boil down to several methods. In the first stages, the hydrostatic chamber is isolated from the surrounding water by filling it with silicone liquid and sealing it with a special gasket. An isolated dry chamber is used to protect the valve mechanism from the intrusion of cold water. Air has thermal conductivity orders of magnitude lower than silicone, and this solution has practically eliminated the possibility of freezing in the first stage. Configurations and diameters of technological channels are altered using Teflon coatings in places where the airflow velocity changes sharply. To protect against freezing in the second stages of regulators, all metallic parts of demand valves are coated with a layer of Teflon (polytetrafluoroethylene) or another special coating. This special coating prevents moisture from freezing at critical points and inhibits regulator freezing. Heat exchangers are installed on demand valves, eliminating the freezing of the valve mechanism. (The second stage bodies, made of metal, act as heat exchangers themselves.) The ultimate freeze resistance of the regulator is determined by the manufacturers' experience and the continuous improvement of the models they create. In most cases, regulator freezing during dives is caused by a violation of operation, storage, or maintenance rules. For example, the presence of moisture inside the regulator leads to a malfunction. Moisture inside can condense and freeze. Divers should be prepared for an emergency situation where any regulator can freeze. If a diver encounters a regulator free-flowing, resulting in spontaneous air delivery, it is necessary to close the cylinder valve supplying air to the malfunctioning regulator and switch to an alternative air source. More information about emergency situations during dives can be found in the chapter "Diving."

Dual-hose design regulators

In your practice, you may come across diving equipment that has been mass-produced since 1955. The company Aqua-Lung released the Aqualung Mistral regulator, which has a dual-hose design and combines the first and second stages in one housing. Mistral had a monstrous overall breathing

Fig. 72. Dual-hose design regulators aqualung mistral

performance by modern standards – 4.5 J/l; nevertheless, this circumstance did not prevent divers, both amateurs and professionals, from successfully using this regulator for many years. Interestingly, regulators AVM-1M, AVM-3, "Podvodnik 1," and "Ukraine," produced at that time in the country then called the USSR, had almost identical designs to the Aqualung Mistral. Let's take a closer look at the structure and basic principles of operation of the Aqualung Mistral 1955 regulator.

In 2006, the company Aqualung introduced a modern regulator designed in the style of the 1950s. One of the tasks set by the Aqualung engineers was to ensure that the new generation regulator met the stringent requirements of European standards, EN 250 and

Fig. 73. Mistral 2006 - back to the future

Fig. 74. Jacques-Yves Cousteau — the inventor of the SCUBA

EN 144-3, and EN 13949 (which determine the possibility of using regulators with Nitrox mixtures and pure oxygen). The Mistral regulator, within the EN 250 standard (with a maximum allowable total breathing performance of 3 J/l), delivers 1.9 J/l at a depth of 50 meters, with a breathing intensity of 62.5 l/min, and at a pressure of the supplied compressed air of 50 bar.

The Mistral regulator is essentially a two-stage regulator; it has the first stage of the Titan regulator and operates on the same principle as ordinary modern regulators with two stages of compressed air reduction. The only difference in the dual-hose design is that the second stage of the regulator has an inhalation hose and an exhalation hose, connected to each other on one side by a valve box with a diffuser.

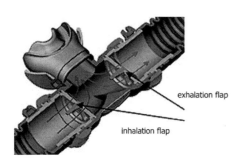

exhalation flap

inhalation flap

Fig. 75. Valve box equipment with a diffuser Mistral

To maintain the regulator and gain direct access to the duckbill non-return valves for inhalation and exhalation, it is necessary to unscrew the corrugated hoses from the valve box with a diffuser using fastening nuts. The design of the valve box with a diffuser is similar to that of rebreathers. On the other side, both corrugated hoses connect to the second stage of the regulator, which is attached directly to the first stage. The conglomerate of the first and second stages is connected to the cylinder valve, so both stages are located behind the diver's back. Air from the first stage is delivered to the second stage through a short medium-pressure hose. The obvious advantage of this design is that bubbles of exhaled air are released behind the diver's back, away from the ears, and do not irritate the diver's hearing with excessive noise. Both stages of the regulator are fully protected from the environment by dry chambers, making it ideal for dives in cold or contaminated water with a high concentration of suspended matter.

Technical specifications of the Aqualung Mistral regulator: First stage: Balanced diaphragm linear mechanism Maximum working pressure: 300 bar for DIN, 232 bar for YOKE 4 ports 3/8" UNF, 1 port 7/16" UNF Setting pressure: 9.5 bar ± 0.5 bar Flow rate: 1400 l/min at YOKE = 200 bar Body made of brass with matte chrome finish Removable YOKE seat,

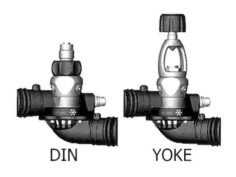

DIN   YOKE

Fig. 76. First stage of the Titan regulator

spring: stainless steel Filter: bronze with nickel plating O-rings: EPDM Second stage: Dual-hose, downstream valve Valve box with a diffuser and non-return valves Valve opening force: between 2.5 and 4 mbar Body and valve box made of impact-resistant plastic Diffuser, corrugated hoses, valves, membrane, duckbill made of silicone Adjustable valve seat: nickel-copper Length of hoses: 630 ± 5 mm and 245 ± 5 mm Weight: Mistral Yoke – 1960 g, Mistral Din – 1820 g Compatibility with NITROX: 40% O2 for DIN or YOKE version; 100% O2 for EN 144-3 standard version. Certification: EN250: 2000 cold water regulator. The breathing performance curve of the Mistral regulator at a minimum input pressure of 50 bar and a diving depth of 50 meters is total breathing performance: 1.9 J/l, and air consumption at a breathing intensity of 62.5 l/min. At the same time, the maximum permissible limit is 3.0 J/l.

Diving devices

Devices used by divers to gather information during underwater dives are called diving instruments. These include: underwater watches, compass, pressure gauge, depth gauge, thermometer, various underwater computers with sensors.

Underwater Watch. Any mechanical or electronic watch that is waterproof and can function at depths corresponding to the requirements of the planned dive is considered a diving instrument. Many modern diving watches are designed for determining the current time underwater by a diver. The watches have an electronic mechanism with backlighting or an

Fig. 77. Underwater watch

arrow mechanical mechanism of pocket watches, mounted in a waterproof stainless steel case. The dial is phosphorescently painted with 12 divisions and numbers. The clock hands are also coated with phosphorescent paint. The working depth of the watches for immersion is up to 100 m.

Underwater Compass. It is an essential tool for divers, especially when performing tasks related to navigation and exploring the underwater environment and detecting objects. The underwater compass, like many other instruments, is not equipped with a specially reinforced casing to compensate for the pressure of the surrounding

Fig. 78. Underwater compass

environment; instead, it contains a liquid that ensures the proper functioning of the instrument under increased pressure conditions. The magnetic underwater compass operates on the principle of a magnetic disc made of fluorescent material, which freely rotates horizontally. The disc has markings for cardinal directions, degrees in a circle, and a pointer arrow that, in the absence of external magnetic fields, points to the North Pole. On the outer part of the compass, there is a rotating dial with degrees, which serves as a specific reference and is set by the diver in the direction needed for specific tasks at the beginning of the dive.

Depth Gauge. Underwater depth gauges track the current and maximum depth of a dive. They can be mechanical or electronic. Inside each diving depth gauge is a liquid that ensures the proper functioning of the instrument under increased pressure conditions. The depth gauge consists of a scale in the form of a dial with a flexible diaphragm-sensitive element inside the device. Measurement limits of depth range from 0 to

Fig. 79. Underwater depth gauge

70 meters. In mechanical depth gauges, two needles are used. One of them, the finer one, is manually set by the diver to zero before the dive, and during the dive, the thicker needle pushes it towards increasing depth. When reducing depth or ascending, this needle remains at the mark of the diver's maximum depth throughout the dive. The second needle is directly dependent on the pressure of the surrounding environment on the rubber valve located in the depth gauge housing. Due to this pressure, the diver sees information on the current dive depth on the scale arranged in a circle. The main

allowable error of readings at an ambient temperature of 20±5°C does not exceed ±2.5% of the upper limit of measurement.

In electronic depth gauges, depth readings are displayed on the screen and indicated numerically (in meters or feet).

Fig. 80. Underwater pressure gauge

Pressure Gauge. The most important diving instrument that is part of the regulator set is the pressure gauge. This device is designed to measure the residual pressure of the breathing gas mixture in the cylinder. The pressure gauge can be electronic or mechanical. It is connected to the high-pressure port of the first stage regulator through a high-pressure hose. The device is usually placed in a metal or plastic housing, in a protective rubber cover. Through impact-resistant thermoglass, a readable scale in bar or psi is visible. The protective cover of the pressure gauge, in which several diving instruments are located, is called the instrument console. Instruments placed in the console can be electronic or analog. Often, in addition to the pressure gauge, console instruments include a compass, depth gauge, and thermometer. Some pressure gauges connect directly to the regulator via a threaded connection.

Fig. 81. Miniature pressure gauge

The universal dive computer, installed on the console with a high-pressure hose, connects to the first stage of the scuba regulator. Such computers are multifunctional, providing all necessary information about depth, time, cylinder pressure, decompression status, and direction on one easily readable screen. One of the

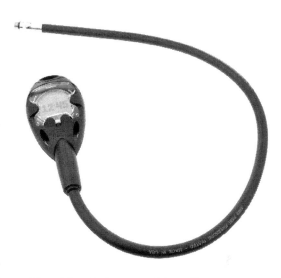

Fig. 82. Universal Dive Computer

advantages of these devices is a three-dimensional compass; some models of such computers do not have a digital compass and instead use a traditional magnetic compass, typically mounted on the console above the computer screen.

Almost every one of such computers provides visual and auditory depth and pressure signaling, alerting the diver when their air supply is running low. Typically, all computers of this kind have simple controls: an easily readable dot matrix display and electroluminescent backlight.

Many modern computers can operate in multiple gas management modes, such as Nitrox, Air, and Gauge, to maximize bottom time and extract the most from each dive. When using enriched air, such a computer can be programmed for Nitrox mixes with oxygen content ranging from 21% to 100%, and adjust the partial pressure of oxygen in the range of 0.5 to 1.6 bar. In Gauge mode, it can also function as a depth gauge and timer with profile memory. Flexible decompression occurs using contemporary mathematical algorithms employed in diving tables, providing continuous decompression for the diver's optimal ascent time and additional protection with a series of deep stops between the maximum depth and the ceiling. In Nitrox mode, the diver can expedite decompression by switching to a gas mix with a higher oxygen percentage.

Underwater Computer. Various electronic devices used by divers to monitor and track specific parameters during underwater dives are called diving computers. These devices range from sophisticated dive computers to electronic dive watches, differing in the set of useful functions. Providing useful information for the diver is their main task. Some of them have hose connections to the regulator through a high-pressure port, others are digital wristwatches with access to cylinder data through a transmitter, and some electronic diving devices are not connected to the scuba tank at all. Most of these devices have the following functions. **Depth Gauge.** Diving computers track the current dive depth. They can display depth information in meters or feet and warn the diver with sound and light signals if certain depth limits are exceeded. Clock Function. Typically, all dive computers track dive time, allowing the diver to monitor the duration of the dive, including bottom time and decompression stops.

Compass function. Designed for underwater navigation, the dive computer provides information about the direction of the dive, helping the diver orient in the underwater environment. A circular indicator with cardinal points is displayed on the computer screen, along with a graphical

Fig. 83. Underwater Computer

representation of an arrow pointing in the direction. Numeric values also indicate the current direction in degrees. Bottom Timer Function. Its main function is to count down the time from a set value to zero. The user can set the desired time for the timer, usually by entering a numerical value using buttons or the device's touch screen. After setting the time, the timer starts counting down in reverse. The remaining time until zero is displayed on the screen, usually in minutes and seconds. The timer may also have sound or vibration alerts to notify the user when the countdown is complete. Some bottom timers are activated only after being immersed in water. Underwater computers provide information about required decompression stops during ascent. They can display recommended stop times and warn of the need to follow decompression procedures to prevent decompression sickness. Diving computers alert the diver if safe limits for dive time, depth, or ascent rate are exceeded. They can also track air supply and warn of the need to return to the surface. Some diving computers have the ability to record dive data, such as depth, time, temperature, and other parameters. This data can be used for dive logging or analysis to improve safety and efficiency. Specialized diving computers allow divers to program various gas mixes, such as nitrox, and provide information on depth and dive time limits for each gas mix.

Transmitter. Sometimes, instead of or in parallel with a pressure gauge, a special electronic sensor called a transmitter is installed in the high-pressure port, which performs the functions of a pressure gauge by transmitting residual gas pressure readings in the tank to a special diving

Fig. 84. Underwater computer and transmitter

computer via radio waves. Information about the amount of gas mixture in the tank allows the diver to control the consumption of breathing gas during the dive. Depending on the manufacturer, diving computers support simultaneous communication with multiple transmitters installed on different cylinders. Depending on the tasks of the underwater dive, especially during group dives or with a large number of stage cylinders, information about residual pressure in each cylinder allows the dive instructor to check, monitor, and if necessary, adjust the current plan of the diving descent.

Attaching tanks to a diver

In traditional methods of underwater descent, the scuba tank is worn on the diver's back like a backpack. There are several types of tank attachments.

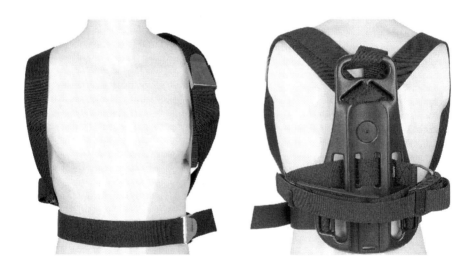

Fig. 85. Plastic backplate with straps

The simplest method of attachment is when a single tank is secured to a metal or plastic backplate using one or two special straps (usually nylon straps, 5 cm wide, with special metal or plastic buckles). To prevent the straps from sliding on the tank, rubber inserts are placed on them. This backplate is equipped with shoulder, waist, chest, and crotch straps that secure the tank to the diver.

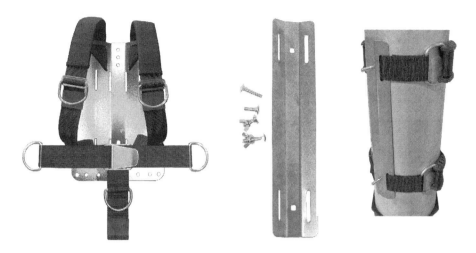

Fig. 86. Metal backplate with straps

The same method applies to the attachment of a tank block consisting of two or more tanks fastened together with metal clamps. These clamps are secured to a special ergonomic diver's backplate using a pair of bolts. The backplate is also equipped with shoulder, waist, chest, and crotch straps that secure the tanks to the diver.

The most common type of tank attachment to a diver is a buoyancy compensator, commonly known as a **BCD**

Fig. 87. Buoyancy compensator

(Buoyancy Control Device). Let's delve into it in more detail. Traditionally, a buoyancy compensator is a vest with an inflatable bladder that allows the diver to control buoyancy during the dive. To increase buoyancy, ascend to the water's surface, and comfortably stay afloat, the diver, by pressing the control button on the inflation valve, fills the buoyancy compensator's chamber with air. If depth needs to be maintained or buoyancy decreased for depth control, the diver releases air from the buoyancy compensator's chamber into the surrounding environment through special exhaust valves.

The primary purpose of buoyancy compensators is buoyancy control. The larger the capacity of the compensator's air chamber, the greater its lifting force and, consequently, the wider the range of buoyancy adjustment. The design and volume of the air chamber vary for each buoyancy compensator. An optimal air chamber for a vest corresponds to the weight of the equipment in the water, considering that the air tank becomes lighter by a few kilograms by the end of the dive. Factors such as the total weight of the equipment, the type and thickness of the wetsuit, the number of weights, water temperature and density, and the weight of special equipment carried by the diver during the dive should also be taken into account. For warm water dives in a three-millimeter neoprene wetsuit, a compensator with a 12-liter capacity is sufficient. For dives in a 7-9 millimeter wetsuit or a dry suit, the buoyancy compensator should have a chamber volume of more than 18 liters. The first buoyancy compensators resembled lifebuoys, with an air chamber shaped like a bubble, worn from the front, requiring divers to insert their heads into the central hole. Later, the air chamber was placed around the diver's body, and the "lifebuoy" took on the form of a vest. Adjusting the buoyancy of such a diver's vest or "bubble" was done through a corrugated hose with a valve, as it had to be inflated by mouth. To release air, the diver had to raise the hose towards the surface and press the button, which turned the inflation valve into an exhaust valve.

The control device for managing buoyancy is called an inflator. Later, a separate inflation hose for the buoyancy compensator was invented, supplying gas to the chamber from the first stage of the regulator. Some inflators, in addition to the standard buoyancy control functions, have an integrated second-stage regulator (breathing system).

Fig. 88. Buoyancy compensator inflator

Modern inflators allow for quick and precise buoyancy adjustment by inflating and deflating the chamber as needed. However, the function of inflating the buoyancy compensator by mouth has persisted to this day. Most models of modern buoyancy compensators attach the inflator to the compensator using a special corrugated hose and a quick-release mechanism for the inflation hose. On many models equipped with a corrugated hose, there is a traditional air release valve on the right shoulder,

Fig. 89. Buoyancy compensator inflator with integrated breathing regulator

which is controlled by a cable inside the corrugated hose. To release air from the buoyancy compensator, it is not necessary to raise the arm with the control device towards the surface; it is enough to pull the inflator, stretching the corrugated hose.

In i3 systems for managing the buoyancy of the compensator, an integrated type inflator (control device) is used. It is attached directly to the buoyancy compensator's air chamber on the left side, in the

diver's abdominal area. It is connected to an inflation hose with a quick-release mechanism from the first stage of the regulator, and a cable from the air release valve, which is located on the shoulder of the buoyancy compensator. During descent, the diver presses the lever down to inflate the compensator, and during ascent, pulls the lever up to release air. Just like in a traditional buoyancy compensator, the buoyancy chamber can be

Fig. 90. Buoyancy compensator with integrated inflator

inflated by mouth by blowing into a special hose with a mouthpiece and a valve, which is folded in the front part of the compensator on the left side. Each buoyancy compensator has several air release valves located at its top and bottom, which the diver uses as needed.

When the diver tilts the head down, air is released from the internal buoyancy compensator chamber by pulling the cable of the valve located at the bottom of the compensator. In a vertical body position, the valves in the shoulder area of the compensator are used, including the exhaust valves in the inflator control device. When opening the exhaust valve, air from the buoyancy compensator exits into the water and rises vertically to the surface. If you open the air release valve, which is below the level of the air bubble inside the buoyancy compensator, the air chamber of the buoyancy compensator will fill with water. The classic buoyancy compensator, as we see it today, appeared only in 1985. It took the form of a vest with adjustable buckle mechanisms and detachable shoulder straps (ADV) that allow the diver to adjust the BCD to their individual parameters. The shape of the air chamber follows the contours of the vest (except for the shoulder straps), ensuring even distribution of air around the diver's waist, back, and shoulders. Even distribution of air positively affects the diver's center of gravity, allowing them to be in a comfortable vertical position on the water's surface when needed. A well-fitted buoyancy compensator on the diver's body provides not only comfort but also efficiency in buoyancy control. To increase comfort, many manufacturers, taking into account the structural features of the male and female body, produce buoyancy compensators designed for men or women, respectively.

The main inconvenience of classic vest-type buoyancy compensators is the squeezing of the diver from the sides when the air chamber is filled. This problem was solved in the late 90s with the introduction of wing-type compensators with a rear buoyancy chamber. During underwater descents using a steel, aluminum, or carbon backplate equipped with straps between the backplate and the cylinder (twinset), the BCD (Buoyancy Control Device) system began to be placed. This introduced an

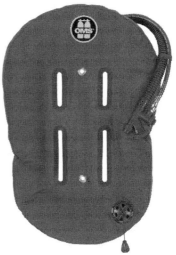

Fig. 91. Wing type
buoyancy compensator

inflatable chamber that does not squeeze the diver during inflation and can be of arbitrary shape and volume. Depending on the appearance, wings are divided into two types – they can be horseshoe-shaped or have a bubble shape. Wings used for solo diving have a redundant compensation system, and such wings are called dual-inflator wings. Inside the protective cover, limiting the wing's volume, there are two separate inflatable chambers. Each chamber has two inflators, separately connected to the regulator, and each of these chambers has its own air release valves. Although wing-type buoyancy compensators perform the same functions as vest-type compensators, wings, along with their advantages, have their disadvantages. Due to the position of the inflatable chamber, the balancing capabilities of wing-type compensators are extremely limited. Imbalance leads to the appearance of a turning moment, causing a shift in the center of gravity towards the front of the abdomen and chest. This makes the wing tend to tip the diver face down from a vertical position.

Fig. 92. Wing type buoyancy compensator

An alternative to traditional scuba diving is **the sidemount** style, with a side-mounted configuration of cylinders. Sidemount diving involves placing air cylinders to the sides of the diver. Instead of a single large cylinder or twin cylinders used in traditional back-mounted diving, sidemount divers use two or more cylinders positioned on the sides of their bodies. Therefore, buoyancy compensation systems differ in attachments, placement, and appearance from traditional buoyancy compensators. The Buoyancy Control Device (BCD) used in sidemount diving also has a watertight chamber, exhaust valves, and an inflator

Fig. 93. Sidemount buoyancy compensator

connected to one of the regulators on the breathing gas cylinder or a separate regulator on a small-volume cylinder used exclusively for the BCD system.

Sidemount is widely used in various fields, including cave diving, underwater exploration, and technical dives, where increased maneuverability and better stability during descents are required. Additionally, the placement of cylinders in sidemount configuration allows divers to easily detach from one cylinder and continue the dive or ascent using another cylinder if needed.

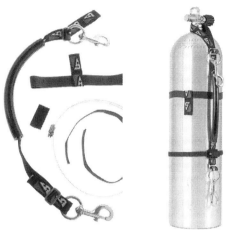

Fig. 94. Attaching additional cylinders to the diving equipment

Fig. 95. Back view sidemount buoyancy compensator

It's helpful to know the terms and abbreviations used by different manufacturers to distinguish the designs in their buoyancy compensators:

BCD (Buoyancy Control Device): Traditional vest-type buoyancy compensator.

ADV: Traditional vest-type buoyancy compensator with adjustable and separable shoulder straps. The buoyancy chamber is distributed around the waist, back, and shoulders.

D-rings: All modern buoyancy compensator models are equipped with D-shaped rings located at various points on the compensator for secure and convenient attachment of numerous accessories and diving equipment. They are typically made of metal or high-strength plastic.

SL (Self-Adjusting): Indicates the presence of an integrated weight pocket system.

SLS (Self-Adjusting Lumbar Support): A self-adjusting system for redistributing the load to the lumbar region, designed to transfer the load from the back to the hips. The load redistribution is achieved through the use of a special roll at the bottom of the compensator, filling voids in the lumbar area.

i3 (Airtrim): Integrated inflator system in the compensator that controls inflation and deflation without a corrugated hose.

Wing: The buoyancy chamber of the buoyancy compensator is located entirely on the back and covers the cylinder (or twinset) from both sides when inflated. This provides a more streamlined shape to the front of the torso and allows for the attachment of various additional accessories to the front of the compensator's harness system.

FUSION: Combination of ADV and wing. The Fusion design provides a unique advantage in terms of comfort and buoyancy distribution due to the careful design of the air chamber shape.

TDS (Tri-load Distribution System): A three-direction load distribution system that distributes the weight of the loaded compensator to three points through a tri-glide and rotating buckles. The system is designed to facilitate a diver's movement on land in full gear.

TAS (Torso Adjusting System): Length adjustment system for the backplate, providing vertical adjustment of the compensator's back according to the diver's torso length.

ISS (Internal Support Structure): Internal support structure design to provide additional rigidity to the buoyancy compensator, especially when a cylinder twinset is attached to the vest.

EVA: Buoyancy compensator designs specifically for women. The air chamber and harness system for women are specially designed to conform closely to the contours of the chest, waist, and torso, even when the compensator is fully inflated.

§ 8. Rebreather
(CCR - Closed Circuit Rebreather)

Oxygen-regenerative autonomous breathing apparatus (Rebreathers) involve the use of pure oxygen for breathing. The term "Rebreather" is derived from two English words: re-breathe - repeated inhalation. A rebreather is a recirculating breathing apparatus in which, unlike a

scuba (Self-Contained Underwater Breathing Apparatus), exhaled breathing mixture is not entirely discharged into the water or is not discharged completely (Closed Circuit Rebreather (CCR)). The exhaled mixture is processed to enable repeated breathing. To achieve this, carbon dioxide is removed from the mixture, and oxygen is added to it; then the enriched mixture is delivered for inhalation.

Fig. 96. Rebreather

History of rebreathers

The first commercially practical rebreather for underwater diving was designed and built by the engineer-diver Henry Fleuss in 1878 while working for Siebe Gorman in London. His autonomous breathing apparatus consisted of a rubber mask connected to a breathing bag, with about 50–60% oxygen supplied from a copper reservoir. Carbon dioxide was absorbed by a "filter," passing the diver's exhalation through a bundle of string soaked in a solution of potassium carbonate (K_2CO_3). This system allowed for dives lasting up to three hours. Fleuss tested his device in 1879, spending an hour in a water tank, and a week later, he dived to a depth of 5.5 meters (18 feet) in open water, experiencing decompression sickness when hastily pulled out of the water by assistants. This apparatus was first used in a working environment in 1880 by Alexander Lambert, the lead diver on the Severn Tunnel construction project, who successfully navigated 1000 feet (300 meters) in the dark to close several underwater doors in the tunnel. Fleuss continuously improved his apparatus by adding a demand regulator and cylinders capable of holding more oxygen at higher pressures. Sir Robert Davis, head of Siebe Gorman, perfected the oxygen rebreather in 1910, inventing the Davis Submerged Escape Apparatus. It was the first rebreather mass-produced and primarily intended for emergency escape for submarine crews, but it soon found widespread use in recreational diving. The equipment included a rubber breathing bag containing a canister of barium hydroxide to absorb exhaled carbon dioxide. At the bottom end of the bag, a high-pressure steel cylinder filled with oxygen was placed, equipped with a regulating valve connected to the breathing bag. Opening the cylinder valve allowed oxygen to enter the bag, creating pressure equal to the surrounding environment. The equipment also included an emergency buoyancy bag at the front to assist the owner in staying afloat. In 1911, Draeger from Lübeck tested a semi-closed rebreather system for standard diving gear, using an injector system for gas circulation through a scrubber and a breathing circuit that included the entire internal part of the helmet. Soon after, it was put into operation and was available in two versions: the DM20 oxygen rebreather for depths less than 20 meters and the DM40 nitrox rebreather for depths up to 40 meters. Minimizing breathing effort and using a mouthpiece-free helmet was possible thanks to pneumatic gas circulation. The US Navy developed a Mark V variant for dives with heliox. They were successfully used during the rescue of the crew and salvage of USS Squalus in 1939. The Mark V mixed-gas helmet with heliox was based on a standard helmet with a scrubber canister installed at the back of the helmet and a gas injection system that recirculated breathing gas through the scrubber to remove carbon dioxide, allowing helium savings. Gas delivery to the diver was controlled by two valves. The "Hoke valve" controlled the flow through the injector into the "aspirator," which passed gas from the helmet through the scrubber, and the main regulating valve was used for emergency shutdown, to open the circuit for helmet flushing, and to provide additional gas during heavy work or descent. The flow rate of the injector nozzle was nominally 14 liters per minute at a pressure of 7 bar above atmospheric pressure, which was 11 times the volume of injected gas through the scrubber. Throughout the 1930s and during World War II, the British, Italians, and Germans developed and widely used oxygen rebreathers to equip early divers. The British adapted Davis's underwater rescue apparatus, and the Germans adapted Dräger submarine escape rebreathers for their divers during the war. Italians developed similar rebreathers for the combat swimmers of the Decima Flottiglia MAS, especially the Pirelli ARO. In 1939, US Major Christian J. Lambertsen invented an underwater oxygen rebreather for free diving, which was adopted by the Office of Strategic Services. In 1952, he patented a modification of his apparatus, this time called SCUBA (an acronym for "Self-Contained Underwater Breathing Apparatus"), which later became a common English word for autonomous breathing equipment for diving and then for activities using this equipment. After World War II, military divers continued to use rebreathers as they do not produce bubbles that would reveal the presence of divers. The high percentage of oxygen used by these early rebreather systems limited the depth at which they could be used due to the risk of convulsions caused by oxygen poisoning.

In 1995, Dräger introduced a semi-closed circuit rebreather called Atlantis. In Japan, Grand Bleu produced a rebreather called Fieno. In 1996, Cis-Lunar Development Labs in the USA mass-produced the MK-IV rebreather. In 1997, Ambient Pressure Diving in the UK manufactured the closed-circuit Inspiration rebreather with electronic control, followed by the KISS from Jetsam Technologies. By 1998, French cave diver Olivier Isler used the fully redundant semi-closed RI 2000 rebreather during the revival of the Dou de la Colle in France.

Rebreathers provide specific advantages for underwater biological research, particularly for dives that depend on unobtrusive observation or require a covert approach to wildlife for capture or tagging. They are also beneficial for prolonged underwater stays or operations at relatively deep depths beyond 50 meters. One of the pioneers in using rebreathers for scientific purposes was Walter Stark, who invented the first electronically controlled closed-circuit rebreather for use in underwater biological research. Soon after, it was utilized in the Tektite II project for biological research during the exploration of the underwater world. By the mid-1980s, the interest in using rebreathers for scientific cave diving coincided with amateur exploration activities known as technical diving. Underwater filmmakers Howard Hall and Bob Cranston began using rebreathers to observe marine life underwater with less risk of influencing their behavior. The primary advantage of closed-circuit rebreathers for biological research dives is the absence of noise and disturbances caused by bubbles of exhaled gas, which are known to have a disruptive impact on animal behavior. This proved particularly effective when divers needed to approach or capture animals such as sea otters and significantly facilitated the recording of animal sounds. The use of rebreathers reduces issues associated with multiple dives and decompressions, allowing divers to undertake a single extended dive without the need to return to the surface or shore between multiple dives, especially where continuous observation is desirable. The ability to maintain a constant partial

Fig. 97. MK series rebreather

pressure of oxygen significantly increases dive time at moderate depths without the need for decompression. Such dives can allow for a single multi-level dive where previously multiple open-circuit dives were required. Equipment and training costs can sometimes be quickly offset by increased efficiency in accomplishing tasks in a single dive in a single day. Significant cost savings on helium diluent are possible for deeper dives, especially in remote locations where helium costs can be ten times higher than in industrial areas. Training for using rebreathers consists of two aspects: First, general training for the rebreather class, including the theory of the operation principles of major rebreather types and general knowledge of the physiological impact on the human body during underwater descents. Second, specific training for working with a particular rebreather model, covering details of preparing the rebreather for operation, user testing, maintenance, and user troubleshooting. Specialized training also includes courses on normal operational and emergency procedures specific to each rebreather model. Transition training from one model to another, if the equipment is similar in design and operation, requires only the second aspect of training. The fundamental procedures necessary for using each rebreather model are usually detailed in the operating manual and the training program for that rebreather. However, there are several common procedures that are applicable to all or most types. Assembly and functionality check before the dive. Before use, the scrubber canister must be filled with the appropriate amount of absorbent material, and the device must be checked for leaks. Usually, two leak tests are conducted, known as positive and negative pressure tests, checking the airtightness of the breathing circuit at lower and higher internal pressures than external. The positive pressure test ensures that the device will not lose gas during use, and the negative pressure test ensures that water will not enter the breathing circuit, where it could damage the scrubber medium or oxygen sensors.

Testing and calibration of oxygen sensors are part of the pre-dive checks for rebreathers in which they are used.

Rebreathers with electronic control may have an automatic sensor check procedure that compares the readings of all cells using diluent and pure oxygen as calibration gases. Therefore, calibration is usually limited to an oxygen partial pressure of 1 bar, which is not optimal, as specified values typically exceed 1 bar. Specialized calibration chambers are required for calibration at more than one bar, where cells can preferably be tested and calibrated at pressures ranging from 1.6 to 2 bars in pure oxygen.

Pre-breathing the apparatus (usually about 3 minutes) shortly before entering the water is a standard procedure. This ensures that the scrubber material heats up to the operating temperature and operates correctly, and the partial pressure of oxygen in the closed-circuit rebreather is properly controlled. To prevent flooding of the internal circuit, the dive/surface valve (or activate the emergency valve) must be closed before removing the mouthpiece from the mouth to prevent water from entering the loop. This action should be taken when replacing the mouthpiece. In many rebreathers, there are no automatic shutdown valves (DSV), so only the diver can prevent flooding. Operating the DSV or BOV (a DSV valve equipped with an additional second stage) is usually performed with one hand while holding the mouthpiece with the teeth, but in some cases, both hands are required if the mouthpiece is not in the mouth. Rebreather divers need to conduct oxygen monitoring. The partial pressure of oxygen is crucial for the rebreather and is monitored at frequent intervals, especially at the beginning of the dive, during descent when temporary increases can occur due to compression, and during ascent when the risk of hypoxia is highest. In electronically controlled rebreathers, the control system performs this task, and the diver is alerted to deviations from the set value by an alarm signal. On some rebreathers, the diver can manually assist the injection system in adjusting the mixture, regulating the required partial pressure of oxygen, and adjusting buoyancy changes associated with depth changes. Oxygen content recovery in the cycle occurs during "scrubber washout," which is considered the safest method to restore the mixture in the loop to an optimal oxygen level. It works only when the partial pressure of oxygen in the scrubber itself does not cause hypoxia or hyperoxia, for example, when using normoxic diluent (normoxic mixes contain the same oxygen fraction as air — 21%, and the maximum working depth of normoxic mix can reach 47 meters), and observing the maximum working depth of the diluent.

The technique involves simultaneous loop ventilation and diluent introduction. This flushes out the old mixture and replaces it with fresh gas with a known oxygen fraction.

Fig. 98. Pre-breathing with the apparatus

161

Loop drainage. Regardless of whether the considered rebreather has the ability to capture any water ingress, training for rebreather operation will include procedures for removing excess water. The method will depend on the specific unit's design since there are numerous places in the loop where water can accumulate, depending on the details of the loop architecture and where water penetrates. These procedures mainly address water entering through the mouthpiece, as this is a common problem.

With certain rebreather models, the diver has the opportunity to monitor carbon dioxide levels. The accumulation of carbon dioxide poses a serious risk, and most rebreathers lack electronic carbon dioxide monitoring. The diver must be constantly attentive to signs of this problem.

The dive surface valve (DSV) is a compact and reliable diverter that does not require additional bail-out valve (BOV) functionalities. The mouthpiece has a front switch for opening and closing the breathing circuit. All DSV valves are equipped with mushroom-shaped silicone valves.

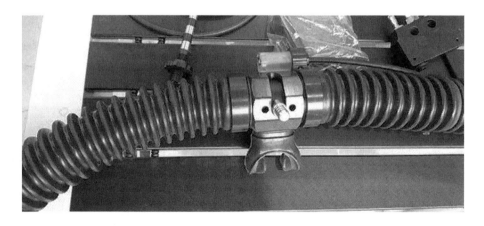

Fig. 99. Dive surface valve (DSV)

Emergency bail-out valve (BOV)

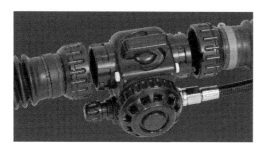

Fig. 100. BOV

The Emergency bail-out valve combines open and closed circuit mouthpieces in one housing. The diver can quickly switch to emergency gas supply through the second stage without removing the mouthpiece from the mouth.

Two manual addition valves, located on the mouthpiece, one for oxygen and one for diluent, replace standard addition valves that pass through the shoulder to the gas block.

Fig. 101. Manual addition valves (MAV)

Fig. 102. Automatic diluent valve (ADV)

The automatic diluent valve (ADV) operates on the same principle as a standard regulator. The membrane inside compresses when negative pressure is applied, opening the valve that adds diluent to the loop.

Emergency procedures

To act confidently under stressful conditions, let's consider each possible rebreather failure separately, which is more likely to occur, as well as effective emergency procedures that the diver must perform to avoid serious consequences.

Chain breakage rescue by switching the rescue valve to break the chain. This is easy to do and works well, even when the diver is in a hypercapnic state, as there is no need to hold one's breath at all. This is a simple procedure, and in most cases, all that needs to be done is to turn the valve handle on the mouthpiece unit by 90°.

The Emergency bail-out valve (BOV) is a control valve for the open circuit installed on the rebreather mouthpiece with a manual mechanism for switching from the closed circuit to the open circuit. The position selecting the open circuit control valve can replace the closed state of the dive surface valve (DSV) since the breathing circuit is effectively sealed during emergency rescue. The Emergency bail-out valve allows the diver to switch from the closed loop to the open loop without the need to change mouthpieces. This can save time in an emergency, as the automatic emergency valve is ready for immediate use. This can be crucial in a situation of severe acute hypercapnia when the diver physically cannot hold their breath long enough to change the mouthpiece. Gas delivery to the BOV is often done from the onboard diluent cylinder, but measures can be taken to supply external gas using quick-connect fittings.

Chain breakage rescue by opening the emergency valve already connected to the full-face Mask, or in some cases, by breathing through the nose. This also does not require removing the mouthpiece. A suitable full-face mask model with an additional port for a lung demand valve is required for this. The procedure requires the supply valve on the open circuit regulator to be open, and usually, the rebreather's dive/surface valve is closed.

Chain breakage rescue by closing the DSV valve and replacing the rebreather mouthpiece with a separate lung demand valve. This is simple but requires the diver to hold their breath while switching mouthpieces, which may be impossible in cases of hypercapnia. An alternative to emergency circuit opening is rescuing the rebreather by closing the DSV mouthpiece of the main rebreather and switching to the mouthpiece of the independent emergency rebreather. This does not disable the circuit for opening but has logistical advantages in dives where the volume of sufficient open circuit gas to reach the surface may be excessive, and the second rebreather is less bulky. There may be an intermediate step where the diver jumps to break the loop on the diluent gas when preparing the rescue rebreather.

Independent open circuit system

Additional cylinders are heavy and bulky, but larger cylinders allow the diver to carry more gas, providing protection during ascents on deeper and longer dives. The breathing gas mixture must be carefully selected to be safe at all ascent depths; otherwise, more than one set may be required. For extended penetrations or mandatory decompression obligations, several open-circuit emergency cylinders may be needed to provide an adequate amount of gas. In such cases, selected mixtures can be optimized to match the worst-case scenario of the planned profile. Emergency gas supply can be provided from the rebreather diluent cylinder, from independent cylinders, or, for depths less than approximately 6 meters, from the rebreather oxygen cylinder. In all cases, during rescue, the rebreather loop must be isolated from water to avoid flooding and gas loss, which could adversely affect buoyancy. It may be necessary to close the gas supply valves on the cylinders to prevent a malfunctioning control system or a free-flowing ADV from continuing to add gas to the circuit, which would also adversely affect buoyancy, possibly depriving the diver of the opportunity to stay at the depth necessary for decompression. Chain Breakage Rescue is usually considered a good option when there is uncertainty about the problem and whether it can be resolved. The rescue procedure depends on the details of the rebreather's design and the rescue equipment chosen by the diver. The dive buddy should remain with the rebreather diver who needs emergency measures until the diver safely surfaces, as the buddy will likely be needed at that time.

Rebreather device

Each rebreather utilizes two hoses - one for delivering the breathing gas mixture to the mouthpiece and the other for returning the exhaled mixture to the breathing circuit. In the design of each rebreather, there is an integrated capacity (absorber canister) in the breathing circuit, filled with a chemical substance actively absorbing carbon dioxide. In all rebreathers, the method of removing carbon dioxide is the same.

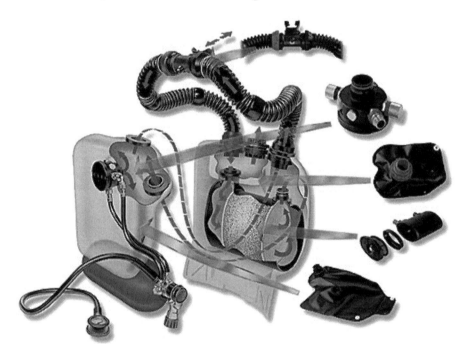

Fig. 103. Rebreather device

The addition of oxygen to the mixture occurs differently in various types of rebreathers. Since the breathing mixture is not exhaled into the water but returned, rebreathers have a capacity to which it can be returned (breathing bag). The breathing mixture in this capacity has the same pressure as the surrounding underwater environment.

Rebreathers can operate in both closed and semi-closed breathing loop modes. Semi-closed circuit rebreathers are divided into those with an active or passive system for delivering the breathing gas mixture. Among the existing types of devices, devices with a circular closed breathing scheme are the most widespread. Inhalation in this device is carried out from an elastic breathing bag with a capacity of 6–8 liters, providing the deepest inhalation and exhalation. In this bag, a portion of oxygen is supplied from the cylinder through a dosing device. During inhalation through the inhalation tube, oxygen enters the diver's lungs.

The exhaled gas mixture, thanks to the presence of corresponding valves in the exhalation tube, enters the absorber box and then again into the breathing bag. The absorber box contains 1–2 kilograms of a chemical substance that absorbs carbon dioxide, thus purifying the exhaled air. As an absorbent, granulated lime chemical absorbent (HPI GOST 6755-53) is used, consisting of grains sized 2.5–5.5 mm of calcium oxide hydrate (96%) and sodium hydroxide (4%). One kilogram of such lime absorbent can bind up to 100 liters of carbon dioxide. There are also rebreathers in which, in addition to the usual carbon dioxide absorbent, regenerative substances based on sodium peroxide are used. Such a regenerative substance can not only absorb carbon dioxide but also release oxygen.

The principle of operation of the regenerative rebreather is that the diver's consumption of fresh breathing mixture is compensated not only by supplying oxygen from the cylinder but also by the release of oxygen by the regenerative substance. The breathing apparatus has an oxygen supply mechanism, usually consisting of a reducer, a dosing device (bypass), and a minimum pressure indicator. This mechanism reduces the high pressure of oxygen from the cylinder to the working pressure and provides a continuous and uniform (metered) supply of oxygen from the apparatus cylinder to the breathing bag.

Primarily due to the danger of oxygen poisoning, dives in simple devices not equipped with special computers that control the valve system are limited to a depth of 20 meters. With the use of a second diluent (diluting agent – nitrogen-oxygen gas mixture, trimix, heliox) cylinder, dives with depth restrictions are conducted:

40 meters - the maximum depth for air as a diluent – the depth for which all operating parameters are guaranteed (CO_2 absorption, O_2 control);

110 meters - trimix testing depth as a diluent – testing depth;

150 meters - heliox testing depth as a diluent;

WARNING - dives deeper than 100 meters are associated with the following additional risks – the mechanical strength of the device nodes is not guaranteed. The presence of an air cavity in the sound alarm (buzzer) will eventually lead to its failure; some other elements may also fail.

Majority of rebreather types provide a significant extension of no-decompression limits. This is achieved by increasing the oxygen fraction and decreasing the inert gas fraction in the breathing gas mixture. This advantage is particularly pronounced at depths up to 30 meters. Deeper descents will yield approximately double the time gain. For this reason, there is a substantial reduction in decompression time for decompression dives. If you conduct sufficiently long dives, decompression with a rebreather will take much less time. For instance, spending an hour at a depth of 30 meters with a closed-circuit rebreather (CCR) requires only an 11-minute decompression compared to 74 minutes if you were breathing air in an open-circuit system.

All rebreathers can be divided into two major groups based on their action principles: fully closed-circuit rebreathers and semi-closed-circuit rebreathers. In closed-circuit rebreathers (CCR), the exhaled mixture is completely processed, and after removing carbon dioxide, pure oxygen is added. It can't be said that the mixture from these types of rebreathers does not vent into the water; rather, it doesn't vent during constant-depth swimming. During ascent, i.e., when external pressure decreases, the breathing mixture expands, and the excess is vented into the water through an overpressure relief valve.

Semi-closed-circuit rebreathers (SCR) differ from closed-circuit ones in that the mixture from the breathing circuit is vented even during constant-depth swimming, but the amount of vented mixture is much less than with a regular scuba. Removing part of the mixture is necessary because to maintain the required oxygen level in the breathing mixture, artificial breathing mixtures such as Nitrox, Trimix, and Heliox are used here. Therefore, it is necessary to remove excess inert gases: nitrogen and helium.

In turn, both closed-circuit and semi-closed-circuit rebreathers can be of several types based on the principle used to maintain the optimal composition of the breathing mixture.

CCOR - Closed circuit oxygen rebreather

Oxygen rebreathers of the closed-circuit type are the ancestors of rebreathers in general. The first such device was created and used by the British inventor Henry Fleuss in the mid-19th century while working in a flooded mine. Closed-circuit oxygen rebreathers have all the main components typical of any type of rebreather: a breathing bag; a canister with a chemical absorbent; breathing hoses with a valve box; a bypass valve (manual or automatic); an overpressure relief valve; and a high-pressure cylinder equipped with a regulator.

Oxygen rebreathers operate on pure oxygen, meaning the diver breathes a gas mixture with a partial addition of pure oxygen. This principle simplifies the design and reduces the size. The operating principle is as follows: the breathing gas mixture from the breathing bag, after passing through a non-return valve into the diver's lungs, then through another non-return valve, carrying exhaled carbon dioxide along with remnants of the breathing gas mixture, enters the canister with a chemical absorbent. There, carbon dioxide is absorbed by caustic soda (sodium hydroxide, lye, caustic soda – NaOH), and the remaining oxygen is returned to the breathing bag. Caustic soda acts as a catalyst, and the main absorption of carbon dioxide occurs with calcium hydroxide. The oxygen consumed by the diver is replenished from an oxygen cylinder, which is supplied to the breathing bag through a calibrated nozzle at a rate of approximately 1-1.5 liters per minute or added by the diver using a manual valve. During descent, the compression of the breathing bag is compensated either by the automatic bypass valve or by the diver using a manual valve.

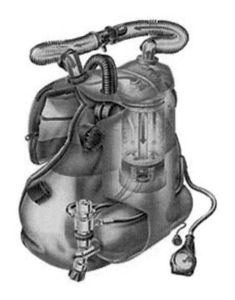

Fig. 104. Schematic diagram of a rebreather

When opening the cylinder valve, oxygen passes through the first stage regulator to the automatic bypass (second stage regulator) and the manual bypass. During inhalation, oxygen from the automatic bypass enters the inhalation bag and the inhalation hose through a non-return valve into the mouthpiece box and through the demand valve into the diver's lungs. During exhalation, the mixture (remaining oxygen with carbon dioxide) passes through a non-return valve and the exhalation tube into the absorbent canister, where it is purified from carbon dioxide and then returns to the breathing bag. The mouthpiece box has a special valve that allows blocking the entry of the mixture into the demand valve (and water into the breathing circuit). A pressure gauge is connected to the regulator to monitor the oxygen pressure in the cylinder. When oxygen is consumed from the breathing bag, the deficiency is replenished during the next inhalation using the automatic or manual bypass. During ascent, excess mixture from the breathing bag is vented into the water through an overpressure relief valve. To eliminate bubbles, mesh caps or sponges are placed on the overpressure relief valves. This simple device is very effective and reduces the diameter of bubbles to 0.5 mm. Such bubbles completely dissolve in the water within half a meter and do not reveal the diver at the surface.

Limitations inherent in closed-circuit oxygen rebreathers are primarily due to the use of pure oxygen, the partial pressure of which is a limiting factor based on the depth of the dive. Toxicity is manifested in two forms: pulmonary (measured in OTU - Oxygen Tolerance Units) and convulsive

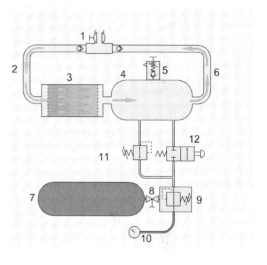

Fig. 105. Rebreather diagram: (1) valve box with one-way valves and a manual valve to close the circuit; (2) exhalation hose; (3) chemical absorbent canisters (also called absorbent cartridges or scrubbers); (4) counterlung (gas mixing bag); (5) buoyancy control valve; (6) inhalation hose; (7) oxygen cylinder; (8) valve; (9) reducer (first-stage regulator); (10) pressure gauge; (11) automatic gas supply valve; (12) manual gas supply valve.

(measured by its impact on the central nervous system CNS - Central Nervous System). The maximum safe partial pressure of oxygen for divers is considered to be 1.6 bar (usually 1.4 for prolonged exposures), and only in emergency cases is a temporary increase to 2.0 bar and 3.0 bar allowed by the French Navy. The dive depth is limited to 6 meters in warm water with minimal physical exertion. In the German Navy, this limit is 8 meters. Considering that some inert gas remains in the breathing circuit of the apparatus, the maximum diving depth with such devices is limited to 7 meters.

In closed-circuit rebreathers (CCR) the exhaled mixture is entirely processed, and after removing carbon dioxide, pure oxygen is added. It cannot be said that the mixture from these types of rebreathers does not escape into the water; rather, it does not escape during constant-depth swimming. During descent, i.e., with a decrease in external pressure, the breathing mixture expands, and the excess is released into the water through the ventilation valve.

Depth and dive time calculations

Since breathing occurs almost with pure oxygen, the calculations are very primitive. The limiting factor is the partial pressure of oxygen. Therefore, the maximum dive depth (MOD — Maximum operating depth) is calculated as:

$$\textbf{MOD [m]} = (\textbf{ppO}_2 - \textbf{1}) \times \textbf{10}$$

where: ppO_2 — allowable partial pressure of oxygen in bars (usually 1.6). In reality, as mentioned earlier, the maximum depth does not exceed 7 meters.

The maximum dive time due to the toxic effects of oxygen (CNS and OTU) is calculated using standard procedures, which you will become familiar with in the chapter on diving using Nitrox-based gas mixtures. The scrubber time limit (STL — Scrubber time limit) is calculated as follows:

$$\textbf{STL [min]} = \textbf{SCSCV/ViO}_2$$

where: SC — (Scrubber coefficient) absorbent capacity of 1 kg of absorbent (for Draeger Sorb and SodaLime from 120 to 150 l/kg).

SCV — (Scrubber Canister Volume) is the amount of absorbent in the canister in kilograms; ViO_2 — (Volume Inhaled O_2) is the diver's minute volume of oxygen consumption in liters per minute (oxygen consumption volume is approximately equal to the volume of exhaled carbon dioxide).

The most well-known representatives of this type are the Draeger LAR-V (Germany) and Oxy Max (England). A simple homemade closed-circuit oxygen rebreather was created by a cheerful American homemade rebreather consisted of a "Nescafe" can (absorbent canister), a 0.5-liter oxygen cylinder connected to a high-pressure regulator with a buoyancy compensator inflator (breathing hose and manual bypass valve), and a plastic bag with an image of Mickey Mouse (breathing bag). The apparatus functioned reliably because, apart from the materials used and the image of Mickey Mouse, it did not differ from the rebreathers used by Italian and English combat swimmers during World War II. Another homemade (also Made in the USA) closed-circuit oxygen rebreather used a regular hot water bottle as the breathing bag.

CCCR - Closed Circuit Chemical Rebreather

Closed-circuit oxygen rebreathers with chemical regeneration of the breathing mixture and a pre-prepared mixture Similar in design to rebreathers of the previous type, but differ in the principle of replenishing the oxygen content in the mixture. The point is that, unlike absorbent substances that simply absorb carbon dioxide, the canisters of such apparatus are charged with a regenerating substance that, when absorbing 1 liter of carbon dioxide, releases approximately 1 liter of oxygen. Despite their small size, these devices have fantastic autonomy. For example, using a typical representative of this group -

the Soviet IDA-71 apparatus, it was possible to swim underwater for 6 hours.

Regenerative substances are very capricious in use. When water enters the absorbent canister, a foamy alkali is released, creating the infamous "caustic cocktail" that scares divers talking about rebreathers. This "cocktail" can cause significant damage to the oral cavity, throat,

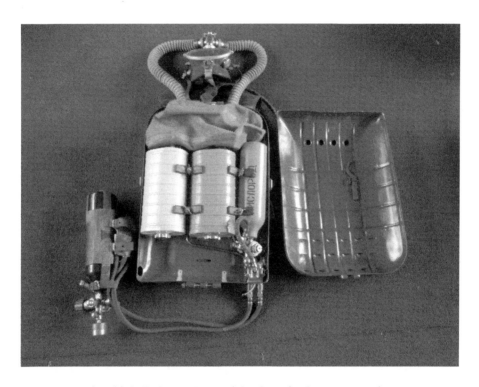

**Fig. 106. Rebreather with chemical regeneration
of the breathing mixture**

trachea, and even the lungs of the diver. Conventional absorbent substances behave much more calmly. It is known that alkali is released when wet, but without a violent reaction, and the entry of water can be determined not by tasting the mixture but by the difficulty of breathing. Most modern rebreathers have traps for water or hydrophobic membranes in their design. The purpose of such devices is to intercept water that has entered through the demand valve and prevent it from reaching the absorbent. Usually, the second breathing bag (exhalation bag) is used as traps, which also helps reduce the exhalation resistance of the rebreather. We will consider the basic principles of the operation of this type of rebreather using the example of the IDA-71, which was manufactured in the last century. This rebreather has two differences from rebreathers without chemical regeneration. The first is the presence of a backflush valve - a mechanical device that, at a depth of 10-12 or 18-20 meters (its adjustment is impossible), stops the supply of pure oxygen to the breathing bag and begins supplying a mixture consisting of 40% oxygen and 60% nitrogen. The second feature is the presence of two absorbent canisters in the IDA-71. The first one is charged with a regular absorbent based on caustic soda (calcium hydroxide), and the second one is charged with substance O3 (o-three), created based on sodium peroxide. (Sodium peroxide, Na_2O_2 - yellowish-white crystals, or substance "OK-Ch", containing asbestos). Substances O3 and OK-Ch can not only absorb carbon dioxide but also release oxygen. Every diving specialist knows about the chemical properties of O3 and similar substances: "...these substances are extremely flammable. Ignition and explosion occur upon contact with any organic, combustible lubricant materials, or inorganic flammable substances." The main instruction for use states: "If work with the O3 apparatus is completed, the cartridge must be left open until the reactions in it are completely stopped; otherwise, the consequences can be catastrophic.

CATEGORICALLY PROHIBITED — to seal used regenerative cartridges. Below is a verbatim account from a diving specialist about the results of an experiment using substance O3: "I swam until O3 was completely depleted. When pouring out the substance, I unscrewed the bottom plug and tried to remove the substance, but it clumped together. Right away, I broke off a dry twig and tried to crush the clumped pieces in the cartridge. Literally two seconds later, flames erupted inside the cartridge. However, not the entire volume was burning, but one of the pieces that I managed to shake out immediately. Following the piece, the substance began to sprinkle, and upon contact with the fire, it started burning with a red-blue color." The principle of operation of a chemical rebreather is that the diver's oxygen consumption is compensated for by the release of oxygen by substance O3. Thus, there is no excess of the breathing mixture (at least theoretically), and the apparatus does not release gas bubbles, earning the right to be called "closed." Since the rate of oxygen release by substance O3 is not constant and depends on many unpredictable factors, such as water temperature, it is impossible to accurately determine the oxygen content in the rebreather's breathing bag.

Oxygen-regenerative breathing apparatus with a pendulum breathing scheme usually operate on a regenerative substance that absorbs carbon dioxide and releases oxygen. The apparatus scheme involves passing the breathing mixture through the regenerative box twice: during inhalation and exhalation. The oxygen supply mechanism allows adding oxygen to the breathing bag from the cylinder as the volume of the breathing mixture in the bag decreases during a dive. Oxygen-regenerative breathing apparatuses are lightweight and compact. The apparatus body is made of aluminum sheet in the form of a box inside which brackets are attached to give rigidity to the body and to attach the oxygen cartridge's regenerative cartridges. On the inside of the body, there are two loops for attaching the chest, waist, and shoulder straps, three screws, a bracket, and a buckle for attaching the apparatus suspension system straps, and an identification mark; on the waist belt, there is a buckle for attaching the nitrogen-oxygen cylinder.

The valve box is designed to connect and disconnect the diver to the rebreather and to distribute the inhaled and exhaled gas flow. The distribution of inhaled gases and the gas mixture exhaled through the corresponding valves proceed as follows: during inhalation, a vacuum is created inside the valve box, as a result of which the exhalation valve is pressed even more forcefully against the seat, and the inhalation valve opens, allowing the gas mixture from the breathing bag to pass during inhalation. When the diver inhales, the pressure in the valve box increases, the inhalation valve closes, and the exhalation valve opens, allowing the gas mixture with a low oxygen level and enriched with carbon dioxide to pass into the regenerative cartridge. The breathing bag is an eight-liter capacity made of elastic rubberized fabric, designed to store a reserve of the gas mixture. Regenerative cartridges are used to store substance O3 and to maintain the chemical absorbent. Each cartridge consists of an outer case, an inner case, and two covers. On each cartridge cover, there are inlet and outlet nozzles through which the cartridge is connected to the breathing bag nozzles. The second cover has a built-in charging nozzle, closed with a cap nut - a plug with a gasket. The regenerative cartridge consists of: a cartridge case; an inner box; an inhalation nozzle; an exhalation nozzle; a grid; a bumper ring; a gasket; and a cap nut.

In the upper part of the inner cartridge, there is a grid and a mesh used for the uniform distribution of the moist mixture exhaled over the entire surface of the substance. Inside the inner casing are rings that prevent the passage of the gas mixture, inhaled between the cartridge walls and the chemical substance, facilitating the regeneration of the gas mixture in the cartridge. Next, the mixture, through the annular gap between the outer and inner casings and through the inhalation nozzle, enters the breathing bag. This gap is also used as a heat-insulating layer, preventing the cooling of the substance. The cap nut has a protrusion, the height of which indicates the amount by which the cartridge should not be underfilled with substance O3 during charging, as it heats up to 180°C and expands during operation. The lung automatic device is used for the automatic supply of gaseous oxygen or nitrogen-oxygen mixture in case of its shortage during inhalation, as well as for equalizing the pressure of the gas mixture in the "apparatus-lungs" system with the ambient pressure. The direct-action lung automatic device of the IDA-71 apparatus is installed on the low-pressure line and operates with oxygen supplied to a pressure of 6-8 kgf/cm². The supply of gaseous oxygen to the valve seat is made through a nozzle with a filter. The seat is closed by a valve under the action of a spring. The sealing of the seat connection with the valve is due to the pressure of gaseous oxygen on the valve and the efforts of the spring. The height of the lever arms is adjusted by the internal adjusting screw, and the resistance to opening the valve is adjusted by the external adjusting screw. When the submembrane cavity is discharged and when there is excess pressure in the submembrane cavity (during rapid descent, depth drops, falling into a pit, etc.), it bends down, acting on the upper lever, which presses on the lower one. The lower lever overcomes the force regulated by its spring, which abuts against the stem of the outgoing valve from its seat, and gaseous oxygen passes into the submembrane cavity, connected to the breathing bag. As a result, oxygen enters the breathing bag and the diver's lungs until the pressure in the "apparatus-lungs" system equalizes with the ambient pressure. Let's assume that the pressure in the submembrane cavity is lower than in the supermembrane one. The membrane will bend sequentially, and the valve will open, meaning that gaseous oxygen will enter the "apparatus-lungs" system. Thus, only when the pressure is equalized, the membrane returns to its original position, the levers are regulated by the releasing valve under the action of the spring, which, under the pressure of oxygen, tightly presses against its seat and blocks the access of oxygen to the bag. The oxygen cylinder with a reducer has a working volume of one liter, a working pressure of 200 bar, and is painted in light blue or white. The reducer is screwed into the cylinder neck with glycerin cement. A pressure gauge connected to the high-pressure triple indicates the oxygen pressure in the cylinder after the valve is opened. Oxygen is charged into the cylinder through a high-pressure nozzle, closed with a cap nut with a chain. A low-pressure hose connecting the reducer to the apparatus is connected to the low-pressure nozzle. The nitrogen-oxygen cylinder is made in one housing with a shut-off valve. It is used for descents to depths exceeding 20 meters and is designed to maintain the gas mixture: oxygen - 40%; nitrogen - 60%.

Nitrogen-oxygen cylinder is attached to the diver's belt and connected to the rinsing device socket. The rinsing device is activated at a depth of 12-17 meters and is designed to flush the "lungs-apparatus" system with oxygen when the diver ascends from a depth of more than 20 meters and with a nitrogen-oxygen mixture when the diver descends to a depth of more than 20 meters. It also automatically switches the gas supply between oxygen and nitrogen-oxygen mixture when ascending from a depth greater than 20 meters and descending, respectively. The reducing regulator is used to reduce the pressure coming from the oxygen cylinder. In order to reduce the size and disconnectable connections of the regulator, it is structurally made in one housing with a shut-off valve having a gland seal. When the valve spindle is rotated counterclockwise, the valve moves away from the seat, allowing oxygen from the cylinder to flow through. When rotated clockwise, the valve closes the seat, and the flow of oxygen from the cylinder stops. The relief valve is used for the automatic equalization of the gas mixture from the "lungs-apparatus" system to prevent barotrauma to the diver's lungs and rupture of the breathing bag when the diver surfaces, as well as in case of excessive supply of the gas mixture to the "lungs-apparatus" system. This pressure relief valve, housed in a casing, has a membrane that simultaneously serves as a spring-type valve. The threaded valve prevents water from entering the breathing bag. The membrane opening is adjusted by rotating the adjusting screw. In order to more fully utilize the capacity of the breathing bag in all positions of the apparatus, the relief valve has a compensator—a corrugated tube through which the gas mixture is vented into the surrounding environment. The corrugated tube is attached to the apparatus body with an elbow.

For informational purposes, a description of the operating principles of the IDA-71 apparatus during descent is provided

Breathing in the apparatus is done on a closed circuit. The diver, connecting the valve box to the dry suit or mask fitting, exhales. Then, when the gas mixture circulates through the breathing system, the diver inhales "from the apparatus" and exhales "into the atmosphere." This should be done until the lung automatic device operates and supplies oxygen to the breathing bag. Next, the diver starts the three-fold rinsing: inhale "from the apparatus" - exhale "into the apparatus"; inhale "from the apparatus" - exhale "into the apparatus"; inhale "from the apparatus" - exhale "into the atmosphere." This completes one rinsing cycle. It should be repeated two more times. The goal of the three-fold rinsing is to maximize the removal of atmospheric air from the breathing system. Conducting 4-5 rinses is impractical. After switching to "the apparatus" on the surface, the diver should breathe for 2-3 minutes and adapt to the gas mixture in the breathing system. During inhalation, the gas mixture passes through the regenerative cartridges and short inhalation tubes, reaching the breathing bag. During the diver's descent to depth, a portion of oxygen from the oxygen cylinder, through the lung automatic device, which automatically equalizes the pressure during the diver's inhalation with the ambient pressure (absolute pressure), enters the breathing bag. Thanks to the lung automatic device, the diver will not experience tension during inhalation. During exhalation, the gas mixture passes through the left exhalation tube through the inhalation valve and reaches the triangle, where the flow is distributed to two regenerative cartridges. In the cartridges, the mixture is regenerated (carbon dioxide is absorbed, and oxygen is released). During the diver's ascent to the surface, the breathing system operates on the principle of reducing absolute pressure on the breathing bag, and accordingly, the amount of gas mixture in the bag increases. To prevent damage (rupture), excess gas mixture is vented into the surrounding environment through the relief valve with a compensator. It is important to remember that the valve box of the rebreather should not be removed from the mouth underwater as easily as the second stage of the regulator. First, the shut-off valve must be closed. Otherwise, water will enter the breathing circuit, and the chemical absorbent will be damaged.

The operational check of the IDA-71 apparatus is performed by visually inspecting all components and parts, checking: the presence of components, the strength of the cylinder attachment, inhalation and exhalation tubes, chest strap, and waist belt; integrity of rubber parts; correct connection of regenerative cartridges, valve box, presence of gaskets, and the condition, ease of opening and closing of the valve box valve; presence of dents and damage to parts and assemblies; the degree of tightening of threaded connections, wing nuts, screws, and clamps. When tightening wing nuts, excessive force should not be applied.

To check the oxygen pressure in the apparatus cylinder, it is necessary to slowly open the oxygen apparatus valve and record the pressure gauge readings. Subsequently, close the cylinder valve and verify the drop in oxygen pressure in the system. Check for the presence of regenerative substance in the

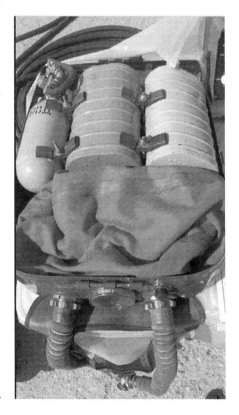

Fig. 107. Rebreather IDA-71

181

cartridges and their condition. Remove the cover from the apparatus, unscrew the cap nut plug, ensure the presence of the chemical substance, and tighten the cap nut plug to its initial position. Then, close the box for the plate substance with the cover (the O3 substance in the cartridges should be underfilled by 10-12 mm).

Check the airtightness of the inhalation and exhalation valve box valves by setting the valve box handle to the "On the apparatus" position and squeezing the corrugated inhalation tube. Inhale through the valve box (if there is no inhalation, the exhalation valve is airtight), then squeeze the corrugated exhalation tube and exhale through the valve box (if there is no exhalation, it means the inhalation valve is airtight). The inhalation and exhalation valves must be airtight; otherwise, there is a risk of diver poisoning with carbon dioxide.

Check the airtightness of the exhalation lines as follows: first, disconnect the exhalation tube from the apparatus valve box, then plug the exhalation ports of the breathing bag with plugs (Pr-217 from the NKU-1 kit), create maximum possible pressure in the exhalation tube with the lungs (if pressure is created, the exhalation line is considered airtight). Then, connect the cartridge (cartridges) and the box to the breathing bag and secure the cartridge and box to the apparatus body. Afterward, connect the exhalation tube to the apparatus valve box.

Check the lung automatic device operation as follows: first, open the oxygen cylinder valve and set the valve box handle to the "on the apparatus" position. Then, perform several inhalations through the valve box until the lung automatic device starts delivering oxygen. If the lung automatic device provides oxygen supply during inhalation without significant difficulties, the lung automatic device is considered normal. To check the resistance of inhalation and exhalation, open the oxygen cylinder valve and set the valve box handle to the "on the apparatus" position. Then, perform 2-3 inhalations and exhalations through the valve box. If inhalation and exhalation occur without complications, the apparatus resistance is considered normal.

To check the operation of the breathing bag safety valve, remove the apparatus cover and fill the breathing bag with exhaled air through the valve box until air starts to escape from the breathing bag through its safety valve. Then, set the valve box handle to the "on air" position and press the breathing bag with the palm. If air escapes through the safety valve during bag filling or with slight pressure, the valve is working correctly.

To check the apparatus for airtightness, set the valve box handle to the "on the apparatus" position, then remove the apparatus cover and open the oxygen cylinder valve. Place a plug (Pr-392 device included in the ZIP-1 set) in the outlet hole of the breathing bag safety valve. Fill the breathing bag with air through the valve box from the lungs, set the valve box handle to the "on air" position, then immerse the apparatus in a bathtub until all its parts are fully submerged below the water level by 10-20 cm, with the breathing bag upwards. The absence of air bubbles indicates the airtightness of the apparatus. After that, remove the apparatus from the water, remove the plug from the outlet hole of the breathing bag safety valve, turn the valve box handle to the "on the apparatus" position, then close the oxygen cylinder valve and release the system pressure by pressing the lung automatic device membrane while simultaneously pressing the breathing bag with the palm. If leaks are found, tighten the nuts or replace the gaskets.

If the IDA-71 apparatus is intended for use in currents, a cap nut must be screwed onto the lung automatic device to prevent the dynamic water pressure from affecting the lung automatic device membrane. The operational check of the IDA-71 apparatus before descending to a depth greater than 20 meters is performed using the same parameters as before descending to 20 meters. Additionally, the presence and supply of the nitrogen-oxygen mixture through the rinsing automatic device are checked.

Semi-closed rebreathers

SCR differ from closed ones in that the breathing mixture is removed even during constant-depth swimming, but the amount of removed mixture is much less than with a regular scuba. The removal of part of the mixture is necessary because, to maintain the required oxygen level in the breathing mixture, artificial breathing mixtures such as Nitrox, Trimix, and Heliox are used here. Therefore, it is necessary to remove excess nitrogen and helium neutral gases. Closed and semi-closed rebreathers, in turn, can be of several types according to the principle by which the optimal composition of the breathing mixture is maintained.

Manual closed circuit rebreathers (MCCR)

The design of manual closed circuit rebreathers generally mirrors that of electronically controlled closed circuit rebreathers, except for the

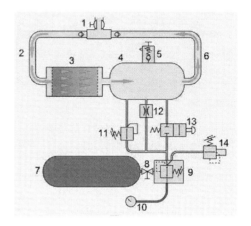

Fig. 108. Semi-closed rebreather diagram semi-closed rebreather diagram: (1) valve box with one-way valves and a manual valve to close the circuit; (2) exhalation hose; (3) chemical absorbent canisters (also called absorbent cartridges or scrubbers); (4) counterlung (gas mixing bag); (5) buoyancy control valve; (6) inhalation hose; (7) oxygen cylinder; (8) valve; (9) isolated reducer (maintains constant pressure regardless of depth); (10) pressure gauge; (11) automatic gas supply valve (lung automatic device); (12) nozzle or throttle for constant gas supply; (13) manual gas supply valve; (14) relief valve.

absence of an electronic control unit with an electromagnetic valve. Instead, oxygen supply is manually regulated by the diver using a manual oxygen supply console. To facilitate this task, a calibrated nozzle or throttle (a valve where the supply can be adjusted) is installed in the rebreather, delivering oxygen at

Fig. 109. Manual valve

a constant rate slightly lower than the hydrogen oxygen consumption rate (approximately 0.8 liters per minute). Some MCCR units lack both a nozzle and throttle, and oxygen is supplied solely through frequent diver-triggered presses on the manual oxygen supply console.

Closed circuit mixed gas rebreathers (CCMGR)

Fully closed circuit rebreathers with electronic automatic gas mixture control (CCMGR - Closed Circuit Mixed Gas Rebreather). This type of rebreather features an electronic control system that includes an oxygen partial pressure sensor, an electronic circuit analyzing the oxygen content in the mixture, and signals an electric solenoid valve to add pure O_2 to the breathing circuit to the optimal level. The advantages of this system include the ability to work with gas mixtures (not just pure oxygen), allowing dives to almost any depth, always maintaining optimal oxygen partial pressure at any depth, no bubbles during swimming, maximum breathing mixture economy, and greater autonomy. On the other hand, it is a complex structure prone to electronic failure, and it

Fig. 110. Automatic valve

is costly to maintain. Sensors operating on an electrochemical principle have a limited lifespan with high costs and typically require replacement at least once a year.

Fig. 111. Location of the cylinders relative to the chamber with the sorbent

These devices always have two cylinders, one filled with pure oxygen and the other with diluent, a gas mixture diluting agent (air or Trimix or HeliOx), an electronic unit with a solenoid electromechanical valve, and a battery. The electronics constantly receive current partial pressure values from three identical sensors placed in the breathing circuit. In the event of one sensor failure, indicating a deviation of its readings from the other two by more than a few percent, the electronics issue a warning signal to the diver and start rejecting the readings of the faulty sensor. Two displays serve for visual control of partial pressure levels: a primary display and a redundant one. The primary display, which is smaller, usually shows only basic parameters, often in the form of simple mnemonic signals. The additional display typically has three digital panels showing oxygen partial pressure readings from each sensor, battery charge level indicator, and some other parameters. Some rebreather electronic units also have additional decompression meter functions. However, most commonly used types do not have an integrated decompression meter and require separate computers to optimize decompression parameters. Calculations when using this type of rebreathers are minimized since the electronics always maintain oxygen partial pressure values in the breathing circuit set by the user. Therefore, critical is only the selection of the optimal partial pressure level depending on the planned dive time.

In the event of a sensor failure, i.e., a deviation of its readings from the readings of the other two by more than a few percent, the electronics issue a warning signal to the diver and start rejecting the readings of the faulty sensor. For visual control

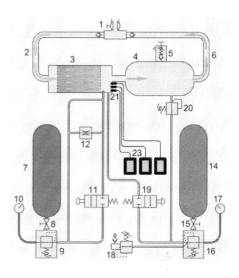

Fig. 112. Manual closed circuit rebreathers (MCCR): (1) valve box with one-way valves and a manual valve to close the circuit; (2) exhalation hose; (3) absorbent canister (also called absorbent cartridge or scrubber); (4) counterlung (gas mixing bag); (5) digestive valve; (6) inhalation hose; (7) oxygen cylinder; (8) oxygen valve; (9) oxygen regulator; (10) oxygen pressure gauge; (11) oxygen manual valve; (12) nozzle or throttle for constant oxygen supply; (14) diluent cylinder (air or trimix or heliox or nitrox); (15) diluent valve; (16) isolated diluent reducer; (17) diluent pressure gauge; (18) relief valve; (19) manual diluent supply valve; (20) automatic diluent supply valve (lung automatic device); (21) oxygen partial pressure sensors; (23) three independent displays for each sensor.

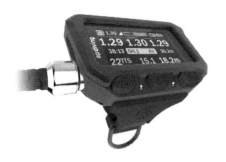

Fig. 113. The main display

of the partial pressure level, two displays are used: the main and the redundant ones. The main display, which is smaller, usually shows only basic parameters, often in the form of simple mnemonic signals. The additional display typically has three digital panels showing oxygen partial pressure readings from each sensor, a battery charge level indicator, and some other parameters. Some rebreather electronic units also have additional decompression meter functions. However, most commonly used types do not have an integrated decompression meter and require separate computers to optimize decompression parameters. Calculations when using this type of rebreathers are minimized since the electronics always maintain oxygen partial pressure values in the breathing circuit set by the user. Therefore, critical is only the selection of the optimal partial pressure level depending on the planned dive time.

Inspiration is a closed-circuit rebreather with electronic control. The very first device of this type in history was invented by Walter Stark and was called Electrolung.

(1) valve box with one-

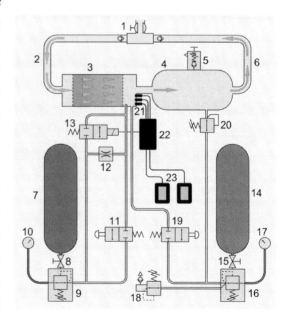

Fig. 114. Diagram of closed-circuit rebreather with electronic control

way valves and a manual valve to close the circuit; (2) exhale hose; (3) absorbent canister (also known as an absorbent cartridge or scrubber); (4) counterlungs (bag for gas mixing); (5) buoyancy control valve; (6) inhale hose; (7) oxygen cylinder; (8) oxygen cylinder valve; (9) oxygen regulator; (10) oxygen pressure gauge; (11) manual oxygen supply valve; (13) solenoid (electromagnetic oxygen valve); (14) diluent cylinder (air or Trimix or HeliOx or Troxtrimix or GelliOx or Trox); (15) diluent valve; (16) diluent regulator; (17) diluent pressure gauge; (19) manual diluent supply valve; (20) automatic diluent supply valve (lung demand valve); (21) oxygen partial pressure sensors; (22) rebreather controller; (23) primary and backup displays (headsets).

The operating principle is that the diluent gas is supplied by a manual or automatic bypass valve to compensate for the compression of the breathing bag during descent, while oxygen is supplied through an electromagnetic valve controlled by a microprocessor. The microprocessor polls three oxygen sensors, compares their readings, and, averaging the two closest values, sends a signal to the solenoid valve. The readings of the third sensor, differing the most from the other two, are ignored. Typically, the solenoid valve operates every 3-6 seconds depending on the diver's oxygen consumption. The dive process looks approximately like this: the diver enters two oxygen partial pressure values into the processor, which the electronics will maintain at different stages of the dive. Usually, this is 0.7 bar for surfacing to a working depth and 1.3 bar for being at depth, passing decompression, and ascending to 3 meters.

Switching is done by a toggle switch on the rebreather console. During the dive, the diver must monitor the operation of the microprocessor to identify possible problems with electronics and sensors. Structurally, closed-circuit rebreathers with electronic control have almost no depth limitations, and the real depth at which they can be used is mainly determined by the accuracy of the oxygen sensors and the strength of the microprocessor housing. Typically, the maximum depth is 150-200 meters. There are no other limitations in electronic closed-circuit rebreathers. The main drawback of these rebreathers, significantly limiting their prevalence, is the high cost of the device itself and consumables. Regular dive computers and decompression tables are not suitable for dives with electronic rebreathers since the oxygen partial pressure consumed by the diver remains constant throughout the dive. With rebreathers of this type, either special computers (VR-3, HS Explorer, Buddy Nexus calculates dives up to 60 meters and only when using air as a diluent) should be used, or the dive should be precalculated using programs such as Z-Plan or V-Planner. Both programs are free and recommended for use by the manufacturers of all electronic rebreathers.

Among the most well-known closed-circuit rebreathers with electronic control are Buddy Inspiration (England), IST Megalodon (USA), and CIS Lunar. These devices have all the necessary safety certificates and are sold only to divers certified for the use of these rebreather models, upon presentation of a certificate, or to training centers licensed to train with these rebreathers. It should be noted that there are many fully homemade rebreather systems in the world. For example, there is information about a German device in which air-zinc batteries for hearing aids were used instead of electrolytic oxygen sensors.

Another constructor of a homemade closed-circuit rebreather with electronic control used a controller from a wired telephone with an automatic number identifier. The well-known Mk-15 rebreather, which was in service with the US Navy, had electronic control but no microprocessor at all. All electronics were analog and based on comparing the voltage of the sensors with its reference values, and instead of a liquid crystal display, a needle indicator was installed, similar to those used in household audio equipment in the mid-80s. A similar indicator is now installed on the backup console of the Steam Machines Prism Topas rebreather. It should also be noted that the efficiency of chemical scrubbers used for homemade rebreathers depends on the ambient temperature. The scrubber resource at water temperatures from 0 to 25°C may decrease by a factor of 2; this fact is not reported in training courses, and chemical manufacturers do not always specify the temperature at which the gas capacity of the scrubber was determined. Before diving with a rebreather, in addition to analyzing the gas mixture, it is necessary to conduct a series of additional tests and calculations, which take a certain amount of time and require special knowledge and skills.

Semi-closed circuit rebreathers

Semi-closed circuit rebreathers with electronic control (ESCR - Electronic Semi-Closed Rebreather). To understand the principle of their operation, imagine a (MCCR) rebreather in which both cylinders are filled with 40% trimix. Such a rebreather will work. The solenoid will activate more frequently than with oxygen, ensuring a constant composition of the mixture in the circuit. Excess mixture will be vented through the valve; all that's left is to keep only one cylinder (since the gases in the cylinders of our imaginary rebreather are the same), and we get ESCR. The first rebreather of this type was the Hollis Explorer Sport.

Fig. 115. Hollis explorer sport

Semi-closed rebreathers are divided into two main operating principles: active gas delivery and passive gas delivery.

Semi-closed circuit rebreather with active gas delivery

CMF SCR - constant mass flow semi-closed rebreathers, the principle of active delivery is based on opening the valve of the cylinder containing the breathing mixture (air or Nitrox), and the gas mixture starts to be continuously delivered through a calibrated nozzle into the breathing circuit.

The delivery rate depends only on the oxygen concentration in the mixture but is independent of the dive depth and physical exertion. Thus, the oxygen concentration in the breathing circuit remains constant under constant physical load.

The oxygen partial pressure is maintained by removing the same amount of used mixture into the water. An excess of the gas mixture accumulates in the circuit, which is vented into the water through a relief valve.

Approximately 1/5 of the exhaled gas is vented. Deflector caps, similar to those used in closed-circuit oxygen rebreathers, can be installed on the relief valves for stealth.

Inhalation occurs through a non-return valve from the inhalation bag. Exhalation occurs through another non-return valve into the exhalation bag. The mixture is cleaned of carbon dioxide in the chemical scrubber cartridge and returns to the inhalation bag. Since the exhalation of the diver contains up to 75% of the initial oxygen quantity, a certain amount of fresh gas mixture is added to the inhalation bag through a dosing device to compensate for oxygen consumption in the breathing circuit.

When the valve (12) of the cylinder (11) with Nitrox breathing mixture is opened, it passes through the regulator (13) into the inlet valve of the counterlung (8) and through the calibrated nozzle at a constant rate into the breathing bag (7). After filling the bag, the mixture begins to vent out through the relief valve (6) at the same rate (whether the diver is using the apparatus or not). During inhalation, the mixture from the

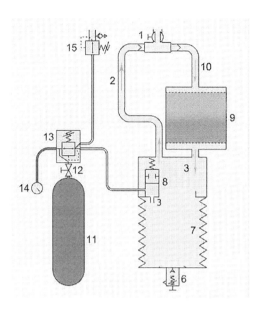

Fig. 116. CMF SCR Scheme: (1) valve box with one-way valves and a manual valve to shut off the circuit; (2) inhalation hose; (3) calibrated nozzle; (6) relief valve; (7) counterlung; (8) breathing gas delivery valve; (9) absorbent canister (breathing cartridge, also known as scrubber); (10) exhalation hose; (11) cylinder with breathing gas (nitrox, trimix, oxygen); (12) valve; (13) regulator (first stage regulator); (14) pressure gauge; (15) second stage regulator.

breathing bag (7) through the inhalation hose (2) and the non-return valve enters the mouthpiece box (1) and further into the diver's lungs. During exhalation, the mixture through the non-return valve of the mouthpiece box (1) and the exhalation hose (10) enters the absorbent canister (9), where it is purified from carbon dioxide and then returns to the breathing bag (7). The mouthpiece box has a special valve that allows closing the mixture supply to the muffler (and water into the breathing circuit). To monitor the oxygen pressure in the cylinder, a pressure gauge (14) is connected to the regulator. During ascent, excess mixture from the breathing bag is vented into the water through the relief valve (6).

Depending on the oxygen concentration in the Nitrox breathing mixture, the delivery rate may vary from 7 to 17 liters per minute. Thus, the duration of the dive (based on the breathing mixture reserves) practically does not depend on the depth because the consumption of the mixture from the cylinder changes very insignificantly at all depths. On the other hand, the oxygen partial pressure in the breathing circuit depends very strongly (even more than with a regular scuba) on two factors: dive depth and diver's physical activity (i.e., oxygen consumption). The dive depth is limited by the oxygen partial pressure in the breathing bag (should not exceed 1.6 bar) and the setting pressure of the regulator. The point is that gas flowing through the calibrated nozzle has supersonic speed, allowing to maintain constant delivery until the regulator setting pressure exceeds the ambient pressure by two or more times.

Decompression calculation

Since the oxygen concentration in the semi-closed circuit rebreather's breathing bag remains constant with constant physical exertion, decompression tables and computers that use calculations based on Nitrox breathing gas are used for diving planning with such devices. Specifically designed for use with semi-closed circuit rebreathers with active gas delivery, computers such as Uwatec Aladdin Air Z O_2 and Cochran LifeGuard have been released, equipped with oxygen sensors, allowing them to calculate the decompression status based on the actual oxygen content in the breathing bag. The oxygen content in the breathing circuit of devices with active gas delivery is calculated by the formula:

$$FiO_2=((VsFsO_2)-ViO_2)/(Vs-ViO_2)$$

where: FiO_2 — (Fraction Inhaled O_2) oxygen content in the circuit < % / 100;

Vs - (Volume supplied) gas supply through the nozzle (liters per minute);

FsO_2 - (Fraction supplied O_2) oxygen content in the supplied mixture < % / 100;

ViO$_2$ - (Volume Inhaled O$_2$) oxygen consumption by the diver (liters per minute) depends on the load, ranging from 0.5 to 3 liters per minute.

Maximum operating depth:

$$\mathbf{MOD = (MaxPO_2 / FiO_2 - 1) \times 10}$$

where: MOD - (Maximal Operation Depth) maximum operating depth (meters);

MaxPO$_2$ - maximum permissible value of oxygen partial pressure (bars) (usually taken as 1.6 for very short time intervals - several minutes or 1.4 for longer periods);

FiO$_2$ - oxygen content in the circuit < % / 100.

Since breathing in these types of apparatus occurs not with pure oxygen but with a breathing mixture containing inert gases, decompression parameters must be calculated for this type of rebreather. Since the oxygen content in the mixture depends on the diver's consumption and not just the percentage of this gas in the mixture, when calculating decompression parameters, both the maximum planned diving depth and the diver's load (oxygen consumption) must be taken into account. When using a Nitrox diver's computer without an oxygen partial pressure sensor or planning dives based on tables, it should be noted that decompression parameters are calculated for the maximum possible content of inert gases in the breathing circuit, i.e., the calculated values of oxygen content in the breathing circuit at maximum consumption, for example, 2.5 liters per minute, are substituted into the computer or used with the table. At the same time, the CNS and OTU levels are calculated at minimum oxygen consumption, i.e., at maximum oxygen content in the breathing circuit. While these calculations are not optimal, they provide additional assurance against decompression sickness and oxygen toxicity. Optimal real-time decompression parameter calculations are obtained when using rebreather computers that can connect to the built-in oxygen partial pressure sensor in the breathing circuit, such as Cochran Lifeguard, Uwatec OXY_2, or VR3. Also, the apparatus's scrubber duration (STL — Scrubber Time Limit) should be considered, calculated by the formula:

$$STL\ (min) = SC \times SCV\ /\ ViO_2$$

where: SC — (Scrubber Coefficient) absorbent capacity of 1 kg of absorbent (XPI ~ 80 l/kg, for Draeger Sorb and SodaLime from 120 to 150 l/kg);

SCV — (Scrubber Canister Volume) amount of absorbent in the canister in kg;

ViO_2 — (Volume Inhaled O_2) minute volume of oxygen consumption by the diver in liters per minute (oxygen consumption volume is approximately equal to the volume of exhaled carbon dioxide).

Semi-closed circuit rebreather with passive delivery of breathing mixture

PA SCR - Passive Addition Semi Closed Rebreather. In this type of rebreather, the partial pressure of oxygen is maintained by forcibly venting a portion of the used mixture into the water. The amount of mixture removed from the breathing circuit is determined by design (the venting coefficient defines the ratio of volumes of the internal and external breathing bags) and ranges from 8 to 25% of the exhalation volume with each exhalation (usually from 1/7 to 1/5 of the exhalation volume with each breath). The volume of the breathing bag is intentionally less than the diver's lung volume. This allows a fresh portion of breathing gas to enter the breathing circuit with each inhalation through the lung regulator.

Since breathing gas delivery occurs only during inhalation and not continuously, the rebreather with passive delivery is limited in depth only by the oxygen partial pressure in the breathing circuit.

This principle allows the use of any gases as breathing mixtures, except for air, and accurately maintains the oxygen concentration in the breathing circuit (regardless of physical exertion and depth).

Due to venting the used gas mixture into the water, the semi-closed circuit rebreather releases several bubbles of breathing mixture not only during descent and ascent but with every exhalation of the diver. During descent, to compensate for the surrounding pressure, the breathing gas mixture is additionally supplied to the breathing circuit through an automatic valve triggered by the pressure difference between the bag and the outside. Although more complex in design, this type is simpler to handle because its operational principle is closest to open-circuit apparatus (SCUBA).

When the cylinder valve (12) is opened, the mixture through the regulator (13) is supplied to the automatic breathing gas mixture supply valve (8). During inhalation, when there is no mixture in the external breathing bag (7), the mechanical linkage opens the breathing gas mixture

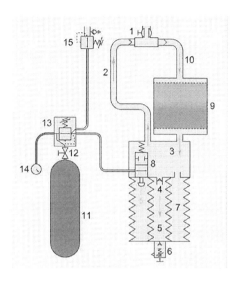

Fig. 117. PSCR scheme: (1) valve box with one-way valves and a manual valve to shut off the circuit; (2) inhalation hose; (3) counterlung pre-chamber; (4) inlet valve of the internal counterlung chamber; (5) internal counterlung chamber; (6) swimmer's valve; (7) external counterlung chamber; (8) breathing gas mixture supply valve; (9) absorbent canister (breathing cartridge, also called scrubber); (10) exhalation hose; (11) cylinder with breathing gas mixture (nitrox, trimix, oxygen); (12) valve; (13) regulator (first stage regulator); (14) pressure gauge; (15) second stage regulator.

supply valve (8), and the mixture is supplied through the inhalation hose (2) via the valve box (1) with one-way valves into the diver's lungs. During exhalation, the mixture through the valve box (1) and the exhalation hose (10) is directed to the pollution intake device (9), and then to the internal (3) and external breathing bags (7). The internal bag (5) receives the mixture through a non-return valve, and the external bag freely. During inhalation, the mixture from the external bag (7) is supplied to the diver's inhalation, and from the internal one (5), mechanically linked to the external one, is vented into the water through the designated valve (6). Since a portion of the mixture is forcibly removed from the breathing circuit, at the end of the inhalation phase, the volume of the mixture in the apparatus's breathing circuit is insufficient, and both bags are fully compressed.

Fig. 118. Semi-closed circuit rebreather

Currently, the mechanical linkage forcibly opens the bypass, and the missing amount of fresh mixture is supplied from the cylinder. During descent, to compensate for ambient pressure, the breathing gas mixture is additionally supplied to the breathing circuit through an automatic valve that operates based on pressure differences in the bag and outside. The most well-known representatives of this type are Halcyon RB-80, K-2 Advantage, DC-55, Interspiro, and CoRa. Since the delivery of breathing gas occurs only during inhalation, not continuously as in rebreathers with active delivery, semi-closed circuit rebreathers with passive delivery are limited in depth only by the partial pressure of oxygen in the breathing circuit. A significant drawback in the design of semi-closed circuit rebreathers with passive delivery is that the mechanism is activated by the diver's breathing movements, and also, with decreasing depth, the concentration of oxygen in the mixture drops significantly. For example, Nitrox32 on the surface transforms into a mixture with 17% oxygen.

Decompression calculation

When diving with this type of semi-closed circuit rebreather, the diver uses all calculations associated with the use of gas mixtures in a standard scuba, but carries a gas reserve that is 4-10 times (depending on the venting coefficient) greater than the actual cylinder volume. In the case of using Trimix mixtures, HS Explorer and VR-3 computers can be used. In the simplest case, regular nitrox computers and decompression tables can be used, similar to rebreathers with active delivery. The oxygen content in the breathing circuit (approximate formula):

$$FiO_2 = ((Pamb \times Kdump \times Ke + 1) \times FsO_2 - 1) / (Pamb \times Kdump \times Ke)$$

where:

FiO_2 - (Fraction Inhaled O_2) oxygen content in the circuit <%/100;

Pamb - (Pressure ambient) ambient pressure (bar);

Kdump = Vinner / Vouter - the ratio of the volumes of the internal (venting bag) to the external, or in other words, the venting coefficient of the rebreather <%/100 (for DC-55 ~ 9%, for Halcyon RB80 ~ 12%);

Ke = Ve/VO2 — the oxygen extraction coefficient by the diver, i.e., the ratio of minute lung ventilation to the volume of consumed oxygen. This value is practically constant for each individual. Its value is individual and depends on the level of fitness and physical health. This value varies from 25 in a poorly conditioned person to 17 in athletes; the average value for a healthy person is set to 20.

FsO_2 - (Fraction Supplied O_2) oxygen content in the cylinder <%/100.

The formula for calculating the required oxygen content in the cylinder for a given depth is derived from the previous formula:

$$FmO_2 = (FiO_2 \times Pamb \times Kdump \times Ke+1) / (Pamb \times Kdump \times Ke+1)$$

where: the designations are the same as in the previous formula.

Mechanical self-mixer

The mechanical self-mixer is a relatively rare design of a semi-closed circuit rebreather. The first such device was created and tested by Draeger in 1914. The principle of operation involves two gases (oxygen and diluent) supplied through calibrated nozzles into the breathing bag, as in a semi-closed circuit rebreather with active delivery. Oxygen is supplied at a constant volumetric rate, as in a closed-circuit rebreather with manual (semi-automatic) delivery, and the diluent enters through a nozzle with subsonic discharge speed, with the amount of diluent supplied increasing with depth. Compression compensation (Carleton SIVA+) of the breathing bag is carried out by supplying diluent through an automatic bypass valve, and excess breathing mixture is vented into the water, similar to a semi-closed circuit rebreather with active delivery. Thus, only the change in water pressure during the descent affects the parameters of the breathing mixture, reducing the oxygen concentration with increasing depth. Mechanical self-mixers are characterized by a change in the oxygen concentration in the breathing bag with changing physical exertion, and this is a direct consequence of their operational principle, which is very similar to the principle of semi-closed rebreathers with active delivery. Depth limitations for a mechanical self-mixer are the same as for a semi-closed circuit rebreather with active delivery, with the exception that only the setting pressure of the oxygen regulator must exceed ambient pressure by 2 or more times. In terms of time, the self-mixer is mainly limited by the volume of diluent gas, the delivery rate of which increases with depth. Air, Trimix, and HeliOx can be used as diluent gases. Calculating dives with self-mixers is very complicated because the partial pressure of oxygen and its concentration in the breathing bag change significantly with diving depth, causing problems both when using tables and when using computers. In this case, the above-mentioned Uwatec Aladdin Air Z O_2 and Cochran LifeGuard computers can help if air is used as a diluent or VR-3 and HS Explorer if the diluent is Trimix or HeliOx. However, simple calculations show that during deep dives, the self-mixer does not provide accelerated decompression, as electronic closed-circuit rebreathers do, which significantly limits the application of the self-mixer. Mechanical self-mixers are the oldest rebreathers after closed-circuit oxygen apparatuses, and they are mainly used in naval forces. This is apparently due to the specifics of military approaches to diving when not a technical masterpiece like an electronic rebreather is required, but the simplest and least maintainable device. The long decompression time is usually not a concern for military divers as they employ a "delayed decompression" approach. There are 4 models of mechanical self-mixers, all of which are designed for underwater mine clearance:

Draeger SM-1 (diving depth 40 meters);

Draeger M-100M (diving depth 100 meters);

Draeger SM-T (diving depth 60 meters);

Carleton SIVA+ (diving depth 98 meters).

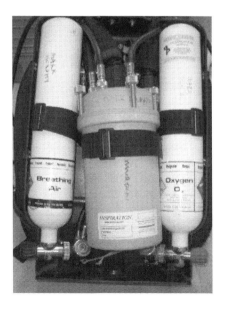

Fig. 119. Mechanical self-mixer

Pros and cons of using a rebreather for diving descents

The rebreather is more physiological compared to scuba diving. When using scuba, we inhale dry and cold air. In the lungs, the air becomes humidified and warmed, and upon exhaling, it is expelled into the water, taking away our warmth and moisture. In the case of a rebreather, the diver breathes a warm and humidified mixture. Additionally, the reaction of carbon dioxide absorption in the scrubber cartridge generates heat, providing the diver with additional thermal protection or heating.

The rebreather ensures a constant and predictable gas consumption, regardless of the depth of the dive, the physical exertion, and the emotional state of the diver. When using scuba, due to increased ambient pressure with depth, the diver consumes progressively more gas, compensating for the water column pressure with each inhalation. This does not happen with a rebreather; the volume of the breathing bag is compensated for once, remaining unchanged until the start of ascent. With a rebreather, the unchanged volume of the breathing system—breathing bag and

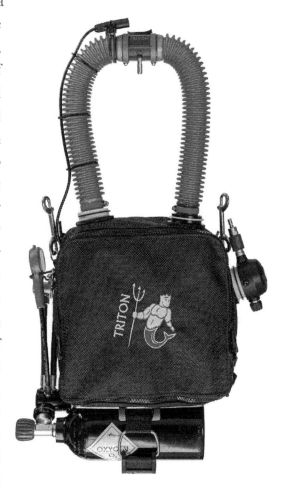

Fig. 120. Rebreather

lungs (as long as the depth remains constant)—means that neither a deep inhalation nor a deep exhalation will change the depth. Buoyancy is perfectly controlled in any conditions, and breath control can simply be forgotten.

A rebreather is much lighter and more compact than scuba equipment (open-circuit gear). Despite venting some amount of gas mixture into the water, a semi-closed circuit rebreather is much stealthier and quieter than scuba. This provides certain advantages to military divers and relieves photographers and videographers from the need to approach skittish fish while holding their breath. **Fig. 120. Rebreather**

Rebreathers use gas mixtures that significantly extend the time spent at depth and are inherently safer than breathing air. As for the drawbacks of rebreathers, they include the following:

When descending to greater depths with scuba, you may descend at a considerable speed. With a rebreather, this is not recommended, as the automatic valve may struggle to supply the gas mixture at rapidly increasing pressure. Breathing may become very difficult for a short time (10-15 seconds).

When diving with a semi-closed circuit rebreather, it is important to remember that the concentration of oxygen in the breathing circuit of the apparatus changes not with the gas consumption but with the physical exertion of the diver. Therefore, dive planning needs to be more meticulous compared to scuba diving, where you consistently receive a mixture with a fixed oxygen concentration. Consequently, errors in determining one's decompression status are possible if the dive is not planned correctly (e.g., if strong opposing currents are not taken into account).

There are also considerations during ascent: when ascending with scuba, you must monitor the speed and vent air from the buoyancy compensator. If you are using a rebreather, you also need to remember that not only the compensator chamber but also the breathing bag of the apparatus expands. While the venting valve will release excess gas into the water, if you have set it for slow venting and poorly control the ascent rate, there is a chance of experiencing pulmonary barotrauma.

K.I.S.S.

Rebreathers (Keep It Simple Stupid or Keep It Simple & Safe, depending on interpretation) are closed-circuit rebreathers for breathing mixtures with semi-automatic control (with manual oxygen delivery). The design of K.I.S.S. rebreathers differs from the previous type in only one aspect, significantly simplifying the structure and enhancing safety (provided the diver is properly trained). The key distinction lies in the fact that sensors and the electronic circuit are solely responsible for monitoring the partial pressure of oxygen, while the diver manually adds oxygen to the breathing circuit when necessary. The electronic block serves only for monitoring the partial pressure of oxygen and displaying it on the screen. The oxygen delivery system is semi-automatic but is not connected to the electronic block, and there is no solenoid valve in this apparatus. Oxygen is continually supplied to the breathing circuit through a calibrated nozzle (similar to semi-closed systems with active delivery), but in an amount insufficient for normal breathing (less than 1 liter per minute). During the dive, the oxygen level in the breathing circuit gradually decreases. Due to the constant oxygen supply through the nozzle, its delivery decreases rather slowly. Therefore, the diver needs to periodically monitor the partial pressure in the circuit, manually add oxygen to the circuit using a bypass, and regularly flush the "apparatus-lungs" system. Flushing the "apparatus-lungs" system is performed by the diver to remove nitrogen from the rebreather system and replace it with breathable oxygen. The diver takes a deep breath through the mouth from the breathing bag to remove all the air it contains. Then, holding the breath, the diver fills the bag with oxygen in one deep inhalation. Afterward, the diver exhales through the nose into the mask space, holding the mask with a hand or helmet. The diver then flushes the system by taking two to three breaths into the breathing bag and exhaling.

Fig. 121. K.I.S.S. Spirit rebreather

After that, the diver takes another deep breath from the bag, holds the exhale, fills the bag with oxygen in one deep inhalation, and exhales through the nose under the helmet or into the mask space while holding the mask with the hand. This concludes a single flush of the "apparatus-lungs" system. Devices of this type are not produced industrially and do not have certification according to European and American safety standards. The material is provided solely for informational purposes. The K.I.S.S. (Keep It Simple Stupid) system was invented by Canadian Gordon Smith.

The closed-circuit rebreather of the K.I.S.S. type is a self-mixer with the most straightforward design. The principle of operation involves the use of two gases. The first, called diluent, is supplied to the breathing bag of the apparatus through an automatic bypass valve to compensate for the compression of the breathing bag during the descent. The second gas (oxygen) is supplied to the breathing bag through a calibrated nozzle at a constant rate, albeit lower than the rate of oxygen consumption by the diver (approximately 0.8 to 1.0 liters per minute).

During the dive, the diver must manually control the partial pressure of oxygen in the breathing bag based on the readings of the partial pressure electrolytic oxygen sensors and add the required amount of oxygen using a manual valve. In practice, this looks like this: before the dive, the diver adds a certain amount of oxygen to the breathing bag, setting the required partial pressure of oxygen (within 0.4-0.7 bar) based on the sensors. During the descent, to compensate for depth changes, a diluent gas is automatically added to the breathing bag, reducing the oxygen concentration in the bag, but the partial pressure of oxygen remains relatively stable due to the increasing pressure of the water column.

Upon reaching the planned depth, the diver, using a manual valve, sets another partial pressure of oxygen (usually 1.3) and operates on the bottom, checking the readings of the oxygen partial pressure sensors every 10-15 minutes. The diver adds oxygen as needed to maintain the required partial pressure. Typically, over 10-15 minutes, the partial pressure of oxygen decreases by 0.2-0.5 bar, depending on the physical workload.

In theory, not only air but also Trimix can be used as a diluent gas, allowing dives to significant depths with such a device. However, the relative instability of the partial pressure of oxygen in the breathing circuit complicates precise decompression calculations. Usually, these devices are used for dives no deeper than 40 meters, although there are cases of successful use of Trimix as a diluent gas for dives to depths of 50-70 meters.

The deepest dive with such a device is considered to be the underwater descent of Matthias Pfizer in Hurghada to 160 meters. In addition to the oxygen partial pressure sensors in the apparatus, Matthias used a VR-3 computer with an oxygen sensor, which monitored the partial pressure of oxygen in the mixture and calculated decompression, taking into account all changes in breathing gas. Standard computers and decompression tables are not applicable to such rebreathers because the partial pressure of oxygen remains relatively constant during the dive but can still vary from the planned value. Due to this, calculating the dive using tables or computer programs will underestimate the time at depth and increase decompression time for safety.

For use with K.I.S.S. rebreathers, VR-3 and HS Explorer computers are best suited, capable of controlling the partial pressure of oxygen in the breathing mixture using an oxygen sensor. There are numerous modifications of commercial, military, and sports rebreathers for the K.I.S.S. system, but all this is done unofficially, under the personal responsibility of the modifier and user. The main drawback of this system is the increased workload on the diver, who must constantly control the partial pressure of oxygen in the breathing gas and adjust it. In industrially produced closed-circuit rebreathers with automatic gas mixing, this task is entrusted to the microprocessor. However, the inventor of the most popular device of this type (Buddy Inspiration) Dave Thompson says the following about the K.I.S.S. rebreather: "The downside of manually controlled rebreathers is that the diver needs to constantly manage them, and these additional actions somewhat burden him, distracting him from the main underwater task."

§ 9. Diver's suits

A wetsuit is specialized clothing designed for underwater dives and other water sports. Every diving professional must distinguish wetsuits based on their intended use. Suits designed for technical diving, scuba diving, free diving, spearfishing, surfing, windsurfing, and kiteboarding can be used by divers for underwater activities to accomplish various tasks. It should be understood that the primary purpose of a wetsuit is to reduce heat loss from the human body in an aquatic environment. In addition to providing thermal insulation, wetsuits can offer protection against potential injuries to body areas and, under specific circumstances, compensate for the buoyancy of the diver.

Fig. 122. Wetsuits

Wetsuits are classified into types

Drysuits: As the name suggests, suits of this class hardly let water in. This effect is achieved by using sealing cuffs (seals) on the hands and neck and waterproof closures - zippers.

Earlier drysuits consisted of two parts, upper and lower; rubber glue, rubber belts, and various methods of connecting suit parts were used for sealing. They can be made from trilaminate (membrane) or neoprene. They are used for dives in cold water. The principle of operation is simple: the suit is airtight (ideally), and with the help of an additional hose connected to the regulator, air is introduced inside. Using the exhaust valve, the amount of air in the suit can be regulated, which helps the diver easily float in the water column.

Wetsuits: Made from neoprene (foamed rubber). As the name implies, water can enter the suit, but once inside, it hardly exits. Thermal insulation is provided by the suit material, thanks to the presence of air bubbles.

It is important to understand that water under the suit cannot be a thermal insulator. The better the suit "fits," the less water circulation beneath it, and the less body heat is spent on heating new, cold water portions. Wetsuits provide good thermal insulation in water temperatures ranging from 10°C to 30°C.

Semidry suits: An intermediate class of suits: despite the presence of seals, water may penetrate into the undersuit space, but in smaller quantities. With a snug fit of the suit, water practically does not enter,

Fig. 123. Trilaminate dry suit

increasing thermal insulation properties. A semidry suit differs from a wet suit in improved sealing of the neck seal (protective collar), wrist, and ankle cuffs. This significantly reduces water circulation inside the wetsuit. Double cuffs are sewn into the wetsuit on the wrists and ankles - one cuff is inside the boot, the other fastens outside. In addition, such wetsuits have a watertight zipper. All this is done to improve thermal insulation. Usually, semidry suits are produced with a thickness of 6.5 mm. An approximate correlation between the temperature of the immersion water and the physical thickness of the wetsuit: 28°C and above - 2 mm; 20 - 27°C - 2-3 mm; 16 - 21°C - 5-6 mm; 12 - 15°C - 6-7 mm; 10 - 12°C - 7-9 mm - monosuit, or a five-millimeter suit with an attached jacket; 10°C and below - a drysuit is already required.

Materials from which wetsuits are made

Most wetsuits are made from neoprene. The thickness of the chosen suit depends directly on the water temperature in which the diver will be submerged. It should be noted that a neoprene wetsuit has positive buoyancy due to the air bubbles contained in the neoprene. For example, a 3mm thick sleeveless wetsuit may provide only 1 kilogram of positive buoyancy in fresh water, while a thick, two-piece wetsuit of 9-10mm can add more than 10 kilograms.

Types of neoprene

Neoprene is produced in two ways: through chemical treatment or by foaming with gas. The properties and durability of neoprene depend on the type of production. Gas-foamed neoprene is stronger and more durable. Chemically foamed neoprene is cheaper, softer, but it compresses and wears out faster. Smooth neoprene ("Dolphin Skin") fits well on the body but can be challenging to put on. Often, inserts in wetsuits, such as armpits, sleeve edges, and the inner part of the

Fig. 124. Monosuit

hood, are made from this type of neoprene. To reinforce the structure of the suit, neoprene is laminated with fabrics such as nylon, plush, or stretch.

Titanium coating

Titanium, which reflects heat, is woven into threads or covers the suit from the outside. It is a composite material that increases the thermal insulation of the wetsuit and prevents heat from leaving your body. A suit with this coating increases thermal protection by more than 15%.

Open cell

Since the inner part of the suit is made of neoprene, the wetsuit literally adheres to your skin, thanks to microscopic bubbles. Therefore, it is called an open cell. Wetsuits are classified based on design:

Monosuit: A jumpsuit that covers the entire length of the legs, arms, body, and even, if it has a built-in hood, the head. Common, reliable, and a convenient option. It just needs to be selected correctly, considering your main goals.

Shorty: A modification of the monosuit without a hood, with short sleeves (just above the elbow), and shortened pants to mid-thigh. Suitable for water temperatures above 25°C. These suits are not suitable for dives to sunken objects, caves, or any other places where there is a significant risk of serious injury to exposed body areas.

Fig. 125. Shorty

211

Two-Piece Suit: A wetsuit consisting of two parts, one of which is a jumpsuit with suspenders ("Long John"), and the other is a jacket with a built-in hood and long sleeves, ending with a crotch piece that can be detached.

Fig. 126. Two-piece suit

A combination suit utilizes separate elements from those mentioned above. Combinations can include a monosuit with or without a hood, paired with a jacket with or without a hood; a sleeveless monosuit with a shorty but with long sleeves; and even three-piece suits like a hoodless monosuit with a separate hood and a shorty with a hood, among other variations tailored for different temperatures and conditions. Convenient combinations are selected based on the complexity of the dive and water temperature. Any of these types of wetsuits may come with either a separate hood or one integrated into the jacket or sleeveless suit. The best suit made from expensive materials will be useless if it doesn't fit properly.

Additional details

Knee pads are essential regardless of the type of water you are diving into. You may have to climb a ladder on a boat, crawl onto a beach, or navigate rocky terrain. They are also crucial for windsurfing or kitesurfing. It's much cheaper to wear a suit with knee pads than to treat abrasions on your legs. Suits with a zipper on the back have a higher collar, which helps retain heat. However, if you feel tight in a high collar, opt for a suit with a front zipper and a deep neckline. Regardless of zipper placement, their presence and greater length positively affect the convenience of putting on/taking off the wetsuit but simultaneously reduce the thermal insulation. Zippers on ankles and wrists, these assist in putting on and taking off the suit but may let water in. Ensure that the zippers are covered with rubber to minimize water ingress.

Diving helmet made of neoprene and gloves

A neoprene diving helmet helps retain head warmth. The body compensates for lost heat by consuming more oxygen, causing the diver to breathe more frequently. Therefore, a good underwater helmet, even in warm water, can reduce gas consumption. The helmet should fit snugly to avoid disrupting blood circulation due to excessive squeezing. It should also not be too loose to prevent excessive water entry. Helmets with special valve designs allow air to escape from under the helmet, preventing water from entering.

Fig. 127. Diving helmet and gloves

Additional elements

Fig. 128. Zipper

Manufacturers add specific elements to meet diverse needs. For example, a chest pad for loading a spear gun in wetsuits for spearfishing, or a pocket for keys in many models. The fit of the diving suit to the diver's body is crucial. Zipper: If you have to hold the zipper from both sides while closing it, choose a larger size. If it closes too easily, opt for a smaller size.

Waistline

Due to the curvature of the spine, there will be a small gap between the diver's body and the wetsuit when putting it on, which will be eliminated during the dive due to water pressure.

Fig. 129. Wrist seals and neck seal

Cuffs

The neck cuff should fit snugly around the diver's neck but not be too tight. Cuffs on the wrists and ankles should also fit snugly against the body.

Fig. 130. Cuffs

Armpits

There will also be small gaps in the armpit area, facilitating the free movement of the diver's arms.

Crotch area

The snugness depends on the diver's comfort. Each wetsuit can be tailored to the diver's body in specialized tailoring workshops or custom-made to accommodate individual preferences and the specifics of diving. Note that many divers prefer to re-glue helmets and replace seals with those made of neoprene. Neoprene is sufficient to provide the required level of thermal insulation. For hand protection, 8mm three-finger gloves with a unique sealing system are used. All seams on the gloves are glued, and double seals on the cuff and back of the sleeve leave no chance for water to seep inside. This dry connection system of a neoprene mitt and neoprene cuff, without using rings, provides much more effective thermal protection than the classic ring system. Note the convenience of quick-release connections for self-replacement of cuffs. The cuff on the ring. The sleeve cuff is replaced within 5 minutes. To replace it, take a flat metal object that is inserted between the inner and outer rings. Then take out the inner ring with the torn cuff, and replace it with a new one. Put it on the ring and insert it back in reverse order. With a spare cuff, you can perform this manipulation without removing the suit. The cuff on the rings is held only by friction, no glue or latches. Latex cuffs have no size differences; any size can be taken and trimmed to the required size. For this purpose, there are rings on the cuffs. The neck cuff is replaced a bit more complicated, but the principle is the same.

Purpose

Wetsuits of varying thickness are used for underwater dives, depending on the diving conditions. In warm water, suits with a thickness of 3–5 mm are used, while in cold water, suits with a thickness of up to 11 mm are employed. However, it is essential to consider that as the depth increases, neoprene suits, under the influence of external pressure, become thinner, resulting in decreased thermal insulation and diminished buoyancy. The latter needs compensation through the inflation of the vest. Dry suits eliminate the mentioned drawbacks but require air (or another gas, typically argon) inflation in the undersuit space to compensate for compression. For spearfishing, open-cell wet suits are used, featuring many small suction cups on the inner side that adhere to the swimmer's body, becoming a second skin. The material of these suits is neoprene foam, with isolated bubbles containing nitrogen or air, acting as effective thermal insulators and providing positive buoyancy.

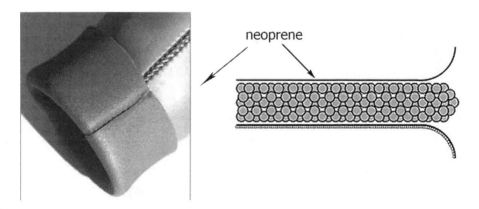

Fig. 131. Neoprene

Hunting suits consist of two parts, high pants (Long John) and a jacket worn over the pants and fastened with special clips. The suit's thickness is chosen based on water temperature, as incorrect selection may lead to freezing or overheating, both dangerous outcomes. An approximate correlation between water temperature and suit thickness for comfortable diving is as follows: 4–12 °C: 9 mm; 10–18 °C: 7 mm; 17–23 °C: 5 mm; 24 °C and above: 3 mm. This table is indicative because individuals have varying sensitivity to temperature. A person comfortable in a 5 mm suit at 15°C might feel cold in a 7 mm suit. For freediving, open-cell suits with an external coating to minimize water friction are used, typically made of polished neoprene or sharkskin. The shoulder area of the cut should allow free arm movement, with a typical thickness of 3–5 mm. For windsurfing, wet or semi-dry suits with thicknesses of 1–5 mm are commonly used. The most widespread are 2 mm short arms and legs or 3/4 mm short arms and long legs. In some cases, thickness may be combined, with inserts of thinner material in areas with active movement, such as under the knees, in the armpits, on the elbows, and the inner part of the thigh.

Dry suits can be made from different materials, including neoprene, trilaminate, or rubberized fabric. Unlike traditional wet suits, dry suits have air inlet and exhaust valves, zipper placement, and a different cut. They usually have built-in boots or socks instead of seals. The Blizzard or similar dry suits, made of non-compressive 4 mm or 7 mm neoprene, are suitable for comfortable dives in water ranging from 8 to 15°C or for extended dives in warmer water from 15 to 20°C. Most of them feature a detachable hood, inflation and deflation valves, and integrated boots or socks. The wrist and neck seals are typically neoprene, but rubber (bottle-neck and conical types) and silicone (conical type with quick-release fasteners) seals are also used. The neck seal is rolled up to create an air lock. The helmet attachment method is practically the same for all types of dry suits. The helmet flange is inserted between the neck seal and the collar. The collar has

Velcro fasteners that securely press the helmet flange to the neck seal. Since the helmet flange and neck seal contact each other with smooth neoprene surfaces, additional sealing is created, preventing water from entering the helmet under the flange. Water that penetrates under the neoprene collar drains through drainage holes. Many dry suits have a waterproof metal zipper on the back over the shoulders, the length of which increases from size to size. The high-strength YKK/BDM zipper is protected from belt wear by a neoprene buoyancy compensator valve. The shoulder area also has a special wear-resistant coating to protect the suit from abrasion by the shoulder straps of the

Fig. 132. Dry suit

buoyancy compensator. Additionally, rubber coating is applied where the compensator straps contact the suit, preventing them from sliding over the shoulders. The knee area is protected by molded thermoplastic kneepads. Inside the suit, there are adjustable suspenders that not only help the suit sit better on the diver's body but also allow easy movement in the suit when the upper part is removed, for example, before or after the dive. In areas of joint flexion in the elbows and under the knees, as well as in the lumbar region, there are inserts made of ultra-elastic AquaFlex neoprene, providing comfortable movement in the dry suit.

Fig. 133. Valves drysuit

The 360° rotating inflation valve, located on the chest, has a neoprene lining on the inside, protecting the diver's chest in case of strong pressure on the inflation button.

Bleed valve, located on the left sleeve, is convenient for use even with thick neoprene gloves. To fully tighten the valve, only one turn is required. Recall that under standard diving conditions, the bleed (stripping) valve should be completely tightened during descent to prevent water from entering the dry suit through the valve. Upon reaching the maximum dive depth, the stripping valve should be turned a quarter turn and left in that position until the end of the dive.

The Ammonite system heats up the gas entering the drysuit through the inlet valve. The principle of operation is based on the functioning of the accumulator and the heating electrical element, which is activated at the moment of the diver's drysuit inflation.

Fig. 134. Valve - ammonite

The close-fitting cut of these suits dictates the availability of both male and female models. Male sizes 7 range from XS to XXL, while female sizes 6 range from XS to XL. Since these wetsuits have a close-fitting cut, insulation from Thinsulate is not suitable for them. To retain warmth, divers use a special undergarment called a skin suit. This undergarment resembles thin 1 mm neoprene suits, equipped with straps on the ankles and loops for the thumbs, preventing sleeves and pant legs from rolling up when putting on a dry suit. The Skin Suit can be used as a standalone wetsuit for dives in warm water. For dives in water below 8°C and near-freezing water temperatures, other types of dry suits are designed, featuring a loose cut, allowing for the use of thick insulators such as Thinsulate or Polar or woolen thermal underwear. Examples of such dry suits include Aqualung's Northland, Tri-Light, and Fusion models. The Northland dry suit is made of compressed neoprene, while the Tri-Light suit is a "membrane" suit made of lightweight, durable trilaminate (nylon-polyester-butyl). Both suits, like all similar ones, have all the attributes of a modern dry suit – adjustable suspenders,

kneepads, protection in areas prone to abrasion, YKK/BDM watertight zipper protected from wear by a valve, latex neck and cuff seals for hands. The main feature of the "Fusion" dry suit is the presence of two layers. The inner layer is directly waterproof, and the outer layer is compressive. The outer shell wraps around the suit like a second skin, preventing the formation of wrinkles. The inner layer is gray, feels like rubberized plastic.

Undergarment

Passive thermal protection for the human body in a dry suit. To protect the diver from hypothermia during dives into cold water, special thermal underwear made of modern synthetic materials is used. Thinsulate-based jumpsuits are sufficiently warm; the

Fig. 135. Undergarment

microfiber structure maintains insulating qualities even when water enters the dry suit, thanks to the material's ability to repel water. This property also allows water vapor, generated on the diver's body, to evaporate freely, enabling the body to "breathe through the skin." Depending on the water temperature, divers also use linen, cotton, and woolen thermal underwear.

Fig. 136. Socks for different types of wetsuits

As for active thermal protection for a diver's body, it includes undergarments with electric heating and suits with water heating. In this case, heating elements are distributed in sections and evenly placed throughout the diver's body.

HISTORICAL DIVING SUITS

Such suits are currently produced and actively used in China and some other countries, as well as in historical dive clubs worldwide. One of the manufacturers is UNITED STERLING (HK).

These suits are made from a three-layered rubberized fabric

Fig. 137. Production of wetsuits

(typhonic, domestic, and shallowest rubber). They are designed for use with three-bolt or twelve-bolt diving helmets. To facilitate this, a rubber flange with three or twelve corresponding holes is placed in the upper part of the drysuit. These holes are intended for the bolts and spindles of the helmet, which are then secured onto the diving suit. At the chest level, in the front and back of the suit, disc-shaped air release valves are installed. They provide ventilation inside the suit and serve as safety valves in case of an uncontrolled ascent of the diver.

Rubber cuffs, adhered to the sleeves, snugly fit around the diver's hands, allowing them to perform tasks in warm water without gloves.

In Figure 138, you can see the standard set of diving equipment, which includes a diving helmet with twelve bolt fastenings, diving chest weights, and diving boots for the legs with a lead sole and brass toe.

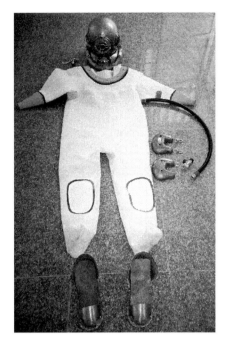

Fig. 138. Set of historical diving equipment

Operation of a dry suit

Before use, spread the dry suit in front of you on a flat surface, unzip the protective zipper and watertight zipper. If the zippers are located semi-circularly on the chest or on the chest side, they can be easily unzipped and zipped independently. In case the zipper is on the back in the shoulder area, assistance is required. Flipping the flap with the neck seal backward, you can start getting into the suit. For greater convenience, take a plastic bag, put it on like a sock, and insert your foot. With practice, getting into the suit can be done quite quickly. Once the pants are on, put on the suspenders on the shoulders and tighten them. Then, using the bag, you can slide into the sleeves. After tightening the suspenders, stretch the neck cuff with your hands and insert your head, as in a regular suit. After straightening the cuff, zip it up. The wetsuit has socks on the feet, over which you can put diving boots with laces or zip-up diving boots. If necessary, any shoes with laces can be worn. At the bottom of the pocket, there is a large drainage valve for water discharge, which is needed when exiting the water. In terms of sensation, dry suits practically have no thermal insulation. If the water is cool and the undergarment is thin, it creates the feeling that the suit is leaking, but in reality, it is not. Upon entering the water, air should be vented. Descending to 3-5 meters can be done without inflating, and as the depth increases, the dry suit is

Fig. 139. Cleaning the drysuit after a dive

inflated. When ascending, air automatically vents from the valve on the forearm. Tilting the body slightly to the right allows air to escape from the valve towards the surface. After completing a dive, when exiting the water, wait for the water between the two layers to drain through the previously mentioned valve.

Caring for the dry suit

To ensure maximum service life, preventive maintenance of the dry suit should be carried out before and after dives. After completing dives, it is necessary to:

Check the suit for damage, look for tears (especially along the seams), check the integrity of the kneepads and elbow pads. The elasticity of neoprene and the stiffness of zippers, together, subject the seams in these areas to very high stresses. Discovering damage early is much easier to fix.

Rinse the suit in clean fresh water. If possible, after diving in saltwater or heavily polluted water, rinse the dry suit in warm fresh water with a mild shampoo or a weak solution of baking soda. Then thoroughly rinse the fabric inside and out.

Clean the zippers and Velcro fasteners with a small brush (a toothbrush will work). After that, treat the zippers with silicone spray. For watertight zippers of dry and semi-dry suits, it is recommended to treat the zippers with wax.

To clean all types of equipment from salt and chlorine, it is recommended to use special cleaning agents, such as Equipment Wash (Trident). After diving in saltwater or a pool, dissolve the agent in water at a ratio of 50 grams of the agent to 10 liters of water. Place the equipment in the solution for 10 minutes, then rinse it in clean fresh water. The solution will remove dirt, salt, organic deposits from the dry suit, and eliminate unpleasant odors.

Hang the suit during drying. Dry the suit in a dark place away from heaters. Use a hanger with padded shoulders to avoid creases. Turn the suit inside out to dry it thoroughly. Lubricate the zippers; it is convenient to use stearin, beeswax, or synthetic silicone. Lubricate, close, and open the zipper when the suit is dry. Dust the rubber cuffs inside and outside of dry suits with talcum powder. It is recommended to store the suit in a hanging position, hanging it on a padded hanger, stretched along a flat surface, or rolled up. In this case, place old newspapers or a T-shirt inside to give the material some shape. This will prevent sharp bends and constant wrinkles. Do not leave the dry suit twisted or stretched. Protect the dry suit from direct sunlight, high temperatures, petroleum products, ozone, and CO carbon monoxide. Pack it in a large plastic bag. Do not place heavy items, such as weight

Fig. 140. Suit during drying

belts and cylinders, on top of the suit. Dents can become permanent and lead to a loss of thermal insulation and faster neoprene wear.

Minor repairs to dry suits

Small tears and cuts in dry suits are inevitable during dives. Once they occur, they should be sealed with any neoprene adhesive. When using a special adhesive for dry suits, such as AQUASURE adhesive produced by SeemannSub, consider some features. For example, it is recommended to store this adhesive in the freezer, and before use, heat the tube in warm water. The adhesive comes with detailed instructions for all bonding and sealing procedures. This adhesive is even stronger than regular neoprene adhesive. Moreover, it becomes elastic after drying, acquiring a silicone-like appearance. A bonded neoprene joint will no longer break at this point, so it can be used not only for bonding neoprene and rubber but also for sealing seams on dry suits. Clean the tear or cut, degrease, and let it dry. Then apply a thin layer of adhesive to both surfaces of the tear and press the glued surfaces tightly together for 15 seconds. The adhesive can be applied in a thin layer (using a spatula) to areas of heavy neoprene wear (for example, seals on the hands and feet), restoring the strength of the neoprene while maintaining its elasticity. Do not use the repaired item within 24 hours of application.

§ 10. Diver's equipment

Diving mask

Diving masks, half masks, swim goggles, and diving helmets are used to protect the eyes and ensure clear vision underwater. The human eye is unable to reproduce information about objects in a denser, optically speaking, medium such as water. Air space between the eye and water is required. The simplest device for ensuring visibility underwater is swim goggles. However, diving with goggles to a depth of more than 1-2 meters is not

Fig. 141. Diving mask with a single-piece glass

recommended. The pressure under the goggles at this depth becomes significantly less than the surrounding environment, and the goggles

226

begin to act like suction cups. As a result, there is a risk of retinal hemorrhage. Therefore, for underwater swimming, a mask is necessary, allowing pressure equalization in the sub-mask space with the pressure of the surrounding environment through exhalation. According to common opinion, the mask is the main item in a diver's equipment. Any mask consists of a soft body, a rigid frame into which one or more windows are inserted, and a fastening strap. The frame is made of metal or impact-resistant plastic. The mask strap can be made of rubber or silicone. Many manufacturers produce masks with a convenient quick adjustment mechanism for the fastening straps and with rotating buckles. This mechanism allows you to tighten or loosen the strap without removing the mask and quickly find the optimal angle for the strap's position.

Diving mask technology

Since the clarity of underwater visibility is achieved through an air layer between the human eye and the water, this air layer is separated from the external environment by glass or transparent plastic. The window must be mechanically strong, not produce shards with sharp edges when shattered, and withstand the chemical impact of seawater. Some types of plastics (although expensive and mainly used by professionals) and tempered glass meet these requirements. The window must be marked

Fig. 142. Diving mask with separate eyepieces

"TEMPERED" for glass and "SAFETY" for plastic.

The introduction of a new material, plexisol, has revolutionized the world of diving masks. Plexisol has an optical refractive index similar to that of water. This material allows the creation of large curved lenses that prevent distortion of proportions and sizes underwater, providing a maximum field of view. Plexisol is ten times lighter and twenty times stronger than glass, allowing the creation of the world's lightest masks. Plexisol lenses are fog-resistant, and they are virtually impossible to scratch. They block ultraviolet sunlight and ensure maximum eye safety.

Most modern masks have a silicone frame (although rubber masks are still produced). Silicone is softer and more elastic than rubber (although less sturdy), more durable, and less susceptible to water and sunlight damage. Silicone can be either black or transparent. Modern engineers design masks that perfectly fit various face shapes. An anatomical design reduces stress on facial bones and muscles, eliminating the need to tighten the strap tightly.

The mask's shape now follows the contours of the face, acquiring a streamlined, curved form that provides low resistance when swimming in water. This significantly reduces the sub-mask volume, and the maximum snug fit to the face ensures a field of view of one hundred eighty degrees, compared to the seventy degrees in standard masks. The presence of a wide and flat seal is usually made of hypoallergenic, elastic, and wear-resistant medical silicone, and the mask's supporting frame is made of high-strength polycarbonate. It should be noted that a transparent silicone frame increases the field of vision but may create slight reflections on the viewing glass.

Choosing a diving mask

From numerous colors and shapes, the best masks are considered those that provide maximum visibility with minimal sub-mask volume, assuming a perfect fit to the oval of the face. To check the mask for tightness and a snug fit, press it to the face without the strap and take a light breath through the nose. If the mask "sucks in" and stays on the face, its shape is suitable for the diver. If there are mustaches, it is necessary to either get rid of them or accept slow but inevitable water leakage. During swimming, water may enter the sub-mask space. This can be caused by hair getting under the mask flange or by laughing, speaking, or yawning. To remove the water, tilt your head back, press the top of the mask (if your mask has a valve, there is no need to press the top edge), and exhale through the nose. Water should be expelled through the bottom flange of the mask. This procedure can be repeated until all water is removed from the sub-mask space.

The space limited by the mask on one side and the diver's face on the other is called the sub-mask space. This space is filled with air. Naturally, the larger it is, the greater the buoyancy and the harder it is to keep the body horizontal or head down. Therefore, it is better to choose a mask with a small volume (about 200 cm3). The wider the field of view, the better. The field of view depends on the size and shape of the window. The hydrodynamic resistance depends on the size and shape of the mask, and the smaller this value, the more convenient the mask. To clear the ears underwater, it is necessary to pinch the nose. When diving with a snorkel, this can be done with one hand. If there is a breathing regulator mouthpiece, it is difficult to perform this procedure with one hand. Here, a mask with a separately designed nose pocket comes to the rescue. This design allows clearing with one hand, reduces the sub-mask space, increases the field of view by bringing the window closer to the eyes, and reduces hydrodynamic resistance.

To compensate for human vision deficiencies, two-lens masks with replaceable lenses have been developed and released. Diopter lenses are selected individually for each eye. At the manufacturing plant, all masks are equipped with regular lenses, which can be replaced with

229

diopter lenses in a few minutes. There is no need to look for special contact lenses with micro-perforations to compensate for pressure. For masks with interchangeable lenses, anti-fog-coated lenses are available. A layer of material applied to the inside of the glass prevents individual water droplets from falling, but does not affect the clarity of the image.

Diving mask care and discomfort relief

When diving, the mask glass may fog up. To prevent fogging, simply wipe the inner part of the glass with a special anti-fog lubricant (a dedicated anti-fog solution). In the absence of such a solution, divers use a natural anti-fog – saliva. The procedure is straightforward. On dry mask lenses, apply a few drops of anti-fog solution and evenly rub it with your finger across the entire lens surface. After 5-10 seconds, rinse the mask in water, and it's ready to wear. This procedure prevents fogging. It should be noted that anti-fog is more effective than saliva; it is designed not only to prevent fogging but also to clean the lens. To clean the mask (e.g., to remove factory coatings), apply a small amount of detergent to the lenses and leave it on longer before rinsing.

During submersion, the increase in water pressure on the mask may cause discomfort for the diver due to the pressure difference outside and inside the mask. To equalize these pressures, a slow exhale through the nose into the mask is necessary.

Another unpleasant result of increased pressure can be discomfort in the diver's ears. This occurs due to the pressure difference on the eardrum between water on one side and air on the other. To equalize these pressures, it is necessary to "clear" the ears, i.e., pinch the nose with the fingers and exhale through the nose. It is convenient to clear the mask with a nose pocket. Full-face masks feature a rubber pocket in the shape of a concave triangle for clearing. To clear, the diver presses the mask to the face with one hand, and the nostrils press against the rubber triangle, simulating pinching the nose with fingers.

Exhaling through the pinched nose allows the diver to compensate for and equalize the pressure.

Full-face diving mask

Fig. 143. Full-face diving mask with built-in breathing tube and attachable mini scuba tank

With the evolution of technology, including advancements in underwater submersions, modern diving masks undergo modifications depending on the tasks at hand. For example, for enthusiasts exploring the underwater world or engaging in short and shallow dives, many manufacturers have started mass-producing full-face masks with an integrated snorkel tube. Some even incorporate connection nodes for a mini scuba tank, as depicted in Figure 143.

Manufacturers of diving equipment also produce full-face masks for divers equipped with scuba tanks or rebreathers. Such masks allow divers to use their own regulators. The simple way to install a personal regulator on the mask involves removing the attachment from the full-face mask and assembling the personal regulator with the rest of the facial system. This enables these divers

Fig. 144. Full-face mask with scuba connection option

to benefit from the superior features of professional full-face masks: no jaw fatigue, no mouth dryness, double sealing for better fit, four or five-point safety straps, and the option to connect a diving communication device.

Fig. 144. Full face mask with built-in speaking device

A full-face mask with a built-in lung automatic provides the diver with the ability to breathe through the nose. The mask has inhale and exhale valves connected to corresponding channels in the lung automatic. These channels are separated, preventing the mixing of inhale and exhale gas mixtures. During inhalation, the gas mixture rises through the valve into the sub-mask space to the window, then passing through another valve, the gas mixture enters the diver's respiratory organs. The constant circulation of the gas mixture prevents fogging of the window. On the frontal side of the mask, there is a compartment for placing a microphone directly in front of the diver's mouth. The earphone is attached to the mask strap. With the use of special attachments, these full-face masks can be equipped with darkened lenses, allowing divers to perform underwater welding work.

Diving masks and helmets for commercial divers

Divers in need of a lightweight and durable commercial diving mask should consider the Surface Supplied MOD-1, produced by Kirby Morgan. This mask is crafted from high-quality materials, including titanium and special polymers, enhancing durability and preventing corrosion. The mask features a side block with two inlet ports – one for the main gas supply and another for delivering breathing gas mixtures from independent equipment. Optionally, this mask model can be equipped with a modular communication system, commonly used with Kirby Morgan diving helmets, and comes with a 4-pin waterproof connector KMDSI.

Fig. 145. Surface Supplied MOD-1 Kirby Morgan

Fig. 146. The diving hood

Fig. 147. Kirby Morgan 18 BandMask with 455 regulator

It is worth noting that standard constructions of neoprene diving hoods are used for these types of full-face masks, while in the masks of the 17th and 18th series of the KMB, the constructions of neoprene diving hoods have been modified to prevent the hood from detaching from the main part of the mask.

The KM BandMask can be used for mixed gas dives as well as in shallow waters. It incorporates the second stage of the SuperFlow 455 regulator. The standard configuration includes the exhaust valve Tri-Valve. The Air Train distributes breathable air along the visor to prevent fogging and provide ventilation. The mask is equipped with an Emergency Gas System (EGS) valve and a check valve. Stainless steel clips are provided for hood attachment, and an azalea blocker is included for hearing compensation. Additionally, there is a silicone seal for the mouth/nose cavity.

The evolution of the design of full-face masks is represented by the diving helmets produced by Kirby Morgan. The most popular model is the Super Lite helmet, designed for professional use by commercial divers. Breathing in the helmet is facilitated by a demand regulator, significantly reducing air consumption and internal noise, thereby enhancing communication quality. Extensive underwater dives have proven the reliability, comfort, and safety of these helmets.

Fig. 148. Kirby Morgan 27 with 350 regulator

Each helmet consists of two parts: a stainless steel neck ring and the helmet itself, made of composite materials in models (17, 27, 47) and stainless steel in models (37SS, 77, 97). The diver wears the neck ring with a neck lock, then attaches the helmet, securing them together. The convenient fastening system ensures waterproofing, preventing accidental detachment of the helmet from the neck ring. Providing complete head protection, the helmet is easy to put on and take off. The gas delivery system allows hoses to be connected to the helmet from the front or over the diver's shoulder.

The SuperLite 17B helmet differs from the SuperLite 17A in the configuration of the valve block. In the SuperLite 17B, the hoses for the main and reserve air supply are connected on the side above the diver's shoulder, while in the SuperLite 17A, the main air supply hose is connected from the front. The 17B valve block is also equipped with a threaded fitting for connecting a hose for inflating a drysuit.

The SuperLite 27 helmet is one of the smallest-volume diving helmets developed by Diving System International. It features a unique locking mechanism for attaching the helmet to the neck ring. Divers can adjust the position of the chin support, neck protection, and hood, ensuring a comfortable and secure fit. The helmet is equipped with the SuperFlow 350 load regulator. The defogging valve has a gas exhaust deflector cover. The valve block design is the same as that of the SuperLite 17B.

The SuperFlow diving helmet consists of the balanced SuperFlow 455 regulator, typically integrated into the SuperLite 18 and 28 helmets. This regulator boasts improved characteristics. While most regulators function satisfactorily at a breathing rate of around 22.5 liters per minute (average nominal value) and at relatively shallow depths, this regulator operates at a breathing rate of 62.5 liters per minute at greater depths.

One of the most technologically advanced diving helmets available today is the Kirby Morgan Diamond. This helmet incorporates all the achievements of the company taken from previous models. It features a fully enclosed circuit that can redirect divers' exhaust gases directly to the surface. By turning the handle, the helmet can instantly transform into an open or closed circuit.

Fig. 149. Kirby Morgan 97 Diamond Closed Circuit Helmet

Mask maintenance

After submersion, the mask should be rinsed with clean fresh water. The mask should not be left in direct sunlight, and care should be taken to avoid the glass coming into contact with hard objects, and the casing from excessive deformation. It is advisable to use special plastic boxes for storage and transportation. According to international codes of all underwater federations, swimming without a mask signals distress.

Breathing tube

The breathing tube is designed to provide breathing while swimming on the water's surface without the need to lift the head for inhalation. The use of a breathing tube is necessary for a diver when swimming on the surface with an empty scuba tank. Breathing through the tube is comfortable and safe when the swimmer is on the water's surface. Even a dive of 20-30 cm makes breathing difficult, as the increasing water pressure affects the lungs, while the pressure of the inhaled air remains atmospheric. Therefore, the length of the tubes is calculated for swimming near the surface. The length and diameter of the tubes can vary. The longer the tube, the less it fills with water and splashes, but the more water needs to be expelled when resurfacing. A larger

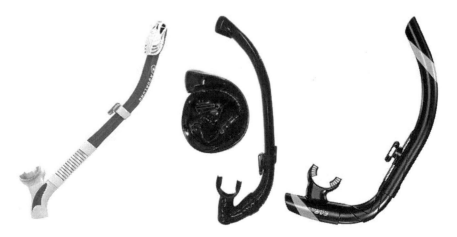

Fig. 150. Breathing tube

tube diameter provides less resistance to the airflow but also increases the volume of water that needs to be blown out. Moreover, a large tube volume retains some of the exhaled air, increasing carbon dioxide content. The optimal length of the tube is considered to be around 40 cm (from the bend to the upper edge), with a diameter of about 2.5 cm.

The main components of the tube are the mouthpiece and the tube, with additional elements being the exhale valve and the inhale valve. The mouthpiece is made of soft silicone, the anatomical shape of which allows holding the tube in the mouth. For divers using scuba tanks, tubes with flexible segments that allow quick switching from the lung automatic to the tube are convenient. Often, special one-way valves are placed in the lower or middle part of the tube, releasing water and air into the water. Such valves significantly ease the effort required to clear the tube. In some designs of diving tubes, a inhale valve is placed at the top to prevent water from entering the tube during submersion. Each tube has a special fastening system in the form of a plastic clip or a rubber ring that attaches to the mask strap. In the absence of fastening, the tube is threaded under the mask strap.

Fins

Fins are attached to the diver's feet and aid in underwater movement, enhancing the efficiency of swimming motions. Two main parameters are highlighted to assess the suitability of fins: the comfort of attachment to the foot and effectiveness in swimming. The comfort of attachment is determined by the design of the foot pocket, while effectiveness depends on the construction and shape of the fin blade.

There are three main variations in foot pocket design: fins with closed heels, fins with open heels, and monofins. Fins with closed heels are used when worn on bare feet or feet in neoprene socks, providing the tightest connection of the fin to the foot. For stronger retention, some divers use special fasteners or lacing. Fins with open heels, equipped with a strap, are more convenient for use with boots. Modern models of adjustable fins allow tightening and loosening the strap directly on the foot. Adjustable straps allow the use of the same fins for divers with different foot sizes, although a spring strap is preferable. A monofin resembles a fish tail and consists of two fins joined together. There is a wide variety of fin blade constructions. For each fin blade, the ratio of useful work to expended energy, in other words, the efficiency coefficient, is crucial.

Fig. 151. Fins

During the stroke, a zone of increased pressure is created on one side of the fin blade's surface, and a zone of decreased pressure on the other side. Vortex flows created at the edges of the fin blade generate additional resistance. Slots at the base of the fin blade allow water to pass through, reducing the pressure difference and thereby weakening the vortex flows. This design does not increase the speed imparted by the fins but reduces the effort during the stroke. As the duration of being underwater is measured by the reserve and consumption of the breathing gas mixture, the more vigorous the physical work of the diver, the more air (or other respiratory gas mixture) is consumed. The more efficient the fins, the less air is needed for the diver's necessary movement. Under equal conditions of immersion, the efficiency of properly selected fins, based on the individual characteristics of the diver, can change the air consumption rate by up to 30%, directly affecting the duration of the dive. Fins with a tunnel effect have excellent hydrodynamic properties. During the stroke, some water inevitably rolls off to the sides, not participating in creating a propelling effect in the diver's movements. If the inner part of the fin blade is made of a softer material than the side parts, then during the stroke, the fin bends, forming a groove that directs the flow of water in the right direction, reducing the amount of water rolling off in vain.

A variation of the tunnel effect is the spoon effect, achieved by a wedge-shaped insert of softer material or longitudinal rubber grooves of different lengths, allowing lateral bending. Fin models like the Mares Volo belong to this type.

Divers who need to cover long distances use fins with long closed-heel blades, which, in terms of speed characteristics, surpass the vast majority of other models and are optimal for swimming without scuba gear. Not coincidentally, underwater hunters worldwide prefer fins of this construction. Rigid plastic or carbon is used for the fin blades. Divers diving on sunken ships or other overhead environments use fins with medium or short blades, made of thin, elastic, and sufficiently rigid plastic, with open-heel rubber pockets.

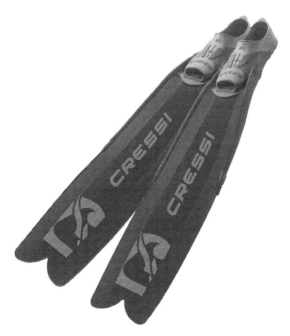

The most popular fins for deep-sea diving are the Scubapro Jet Fin model, introduced in 1965. Choosing fins (a specific model) based on the

Fig. 152. Flippers for deep or long underwater dives

individual characteristics of the diver. Design, color variations, and standard hydrodynamic properties of fins are significant, but it is much more important to consider the individuality of the diver's physical abilities and body type, as well as the particular style of swimming familiar to them, where the fins will be most comfortable. To choose optimally comfortable fins, the diver needs to test several models in a swimming pool or open water. To do this, you need to put on a mask and fins, calm your breathing, and dive on one breath a fixed distance close to the diver's physiological limits. For each diver, this will be a different distance, ranging from 15 to 50 meters.

After a brief rest, it is necessary to repeat the dive with different fins. Attention should be paid to models in which the diver achieves maximum speed, thus reducing the time of the dive. However, the final choice should be made based on the model of fins in which the diver finds this exercise easiest. Such fins will alleviate a significant portion of the diver's fatigue during the dive, and therefore, they will best conserve air. After each dive, it is essential to rinse the fins with fresh water. Do not leave the fins in direct sunlight, and do not dry them on heating devices. Prevent deformation of the fins during transportation and storage, using plastic or other inserts in the foot pocket.

Diving weights

Weights are designed to offset positive buoyancy and provide the necessary stability to a diver during underwater descents. The optimal selection of weights is considered to achieve neutral buoyancy, which is attained by selecting the necessary weights with "empty" diving cylinders

Fig.153. Diving weights

(with residual pressure of 30-50 bar). To select weights for a specific wetsuit thickness, you can use the general formula:

$$A = (B / 5) \times (C / 10)$$

where: A is the weight of the weights; B is the wetsuit thickness; C is the weight of the diver's body.

This formula is general, and in the case of each diver, the selection of weights should be based on individual factors, including: the physiology of the diver's body; wetsuit thickness; fresh or saltwater for immersion; the weight of diving equipment and additional gear attached to the diver's body. The selection of the necessary weights is always determined experimentally. When selecting weights, the diver should ensure that while in the water in full gear with the buoyancy compensator fully deflated, at an average inhalation, the diver submerges to approximately eye level in a vertical position. To this weight, add the weight equal to the air volume in the fully inflated buoyancy compensator. Every 1000 liters of compressed air is equivalent to 1200 grams added to the weight system. Proper weight selection affects comfort during descent.

For example, a diver has a scuba tank with a full 10-liter cylinder with a working pressure of 200 bar. The residual pressure in the cylinder after the dive will be no less than 30 bar. Determine the weight of additional weights for proper "trimming" of the diver?

$10 \times 200 = 2000$ liters

$10 \times 30 = 300$ liters

$2000 - 300 = 1700$ liters

$1700 / 1000 \times 1200 = 2040$ grams

Answer: The weight of the air that the diver will consume during the descent is equal to 2 kilograms 40 grams. Therefore, for proper "trimming," add weights equal to 2 kilograms 40 grams to the main weight when neutral buoyancy is achieved.

Fig. 154. Diving weights for belt

Weights are curved lead plates, each with a specific weight, and are hung on a special belt. The plates are evenly distributed on the belt and usually weigh between 0.5 and 4 kilograms each. There are uncoated weights and rubber-coated weights.

Fig. 155. Diving leg weights

A belt made of soft rubber with a metal buckle with an insertable pin in the holes on the belt is called a "Marseille belt." The rubber belt with a Marseille buckle is considered reliable because it will never unfasten on its own. A nylon strap, 4-5 centimeters wide, with a plastic or stainless steel buckle equipped with a quick-release mechanism is called a "diver's belt." The use of a rubber or nylon belt depends on the diver's preferences. The rubber belt stretches more, restricts the body less, allowing the diver to breathe. At depth, when the neoprene wetsuit is compressed by water pressure, the rubber belt also settles, ensuring a snug fit on the diver's body. In contrast, the nylon belt does not compress, and at depth, it needs to be tightened to prevent the weights from shifting on the diver's body. When many weights are hung on the belt, it begins to exert strong pressure on the lumbar spine. Even in a 5mm wetsuit, the belt with weights inevitably bends the back in this area, causing the diver to swim in the shape of the letter "U," losing hydrodynamics and consuming a lot of energy.

Fig. 156. Special weight pockets for cargo pockets

Depending on the use of diving equipment, divers may use integrated diving weights (usually soft pouches with small lead pellets up to 1 centimeter in diameter, weighing up to 6 kilograms) that fit into the weight pockets of buoyancy compensators. Divers using hose-supplied air and those engaging in breath-hold diving often prefer a weight system called a "tray," which is worn on the back like a backpack. An advantage of this type of weight distribution is that it unloads the lumbar section of the diver's back, but a drawback can be the fixed weight (4, 5, 6, 7, 8, 10 kilograms). Additionally, many divers use weight belts for weighting. They are worn over the wetsuit and have built-in pockets into which lead plates weighing from 0.5 to 2 kilograms are inserted. The weight belt allows for even distribution of the load on the diver's back, and the load can be adjusted by removing or adding the necessary amount of weights, shifting them from the belt or back. Diving experts recommend distributing 40% of the weight on the vest and leaving 60% on the belt, but the distribution should be done considering the diver's comfort. Extra equipment can be attached to the weight vest using special loops provided on many vests. A neoprene vest provides additional thermal protection, although it is not as durable as those made of high-strength nylon or Cordura.

Fig. 157. Diving leg weights

Depending on the type of diving, divers use attachable leg weights. These are rubber straps to which lead weights are attached. Thanks to these leg weights, a diver's legs, clad in thick neoprene socks and fins, are more submerged and less likely to float. The diver exerts less effort to keep them in line with the body. For underwater descents where the diver needs to stand and move along the bottom without using fins, divers use metal backplates or metal boots as leg weights. They are designed to offset part of the buoyancy.

Fig. 158. Diving leg weights

Knives and tools

The essential diving gear includes a diving knife, which every diver must have with them during underwater immersion. Other cutting tools such as diving shears or line cutters can provide additional safety during underwater descents and when performing various tasks underwater. In case a diver gets entangled or to free fish or other living beings, the diver uses their cutting tool to cut through plant ropes, signal lines, telephone cables, hoses, rope loops and cords, or fishing nets.

Fig. 159. Diving knife

The diving knife consists of two parts: a steel blade and a sheath. The blade is secured in the sheath by a special locking mechanism. A cutout for water drainage is provided at the bottom of the sheath. The knife is attached to the diving gear using special rubber straps with buckles or Velcro straps. Carabiners and plastic ties can also be used for attachment.

Indispensable cutting tools in technical diving, cave diving, and for water rescue teams are diving shears, which make it much easier to cut through any entanglement in thin lines and fishing nets.

Also worth mentioning is the line cutter. This part of diving gear is the safest for both the diver and the surroundings. The safe shielded blade prevents accidental cuts and ensures safety. Thanks to universal attachment options and small sizes, the diving line cutter can be placed on any part of diving gear. Its importance should not be underestimated, as such a cutting tool

Fig. 160. Diving line cutter

easily cuts through lines, braided nylon, bungees, neoprene, and a 2-inch strap, as well as almost any other entanglement hazard a diver may encounter at the dive site.

NOTE: After each dive, all cutting tools along with other used gear should be rinsed with a little soapy water, then fresh water, and allowed to dry in the air to prevent blade corrosion.

Handheld underwater flashlight

Underwater flashlights are used to illuminate the underwater environment, especially during dives in dark or poorly lit areas. They allow the diver to see surrounding objects and provide safety and comfort during night or deep-sea dives. The sole parameter by which underwater flashlights compete with each other is the intensity of the light beam.

Fig. 161. Underwater flashlight

Classic handheld and head-mounted underwater flashlights are made of anodized aluminum or robust and heat-resistant plastic. The illuminating heads are protected from the environment by tempered glass. The sealing of battery packs and light heads is achieved using multiple O-rings. Some flashlight blocks are equipped with pressure relief valves to remove gases that may form during the charging of the built-in battery. The rotational magnetic switch on and off feature of flashlights allows avoiding the use of standard switches, which are always weak points in lighting device systems. Some underwater flashlights do not have a switch at all; to turn on such a flashlight, it is sufficient to tighten the light head all the way.

Advanced lighting systems use high-intensity discharge (HID) lamps and light-emitting diodes (LEDs). HID lamps significantly lag behind LEDs due to the need for constant cooling; most of them cannot operate in the air, and they consume significantly more energy (reducing the overall operating time of the flashlight). The bulbs themselves require careful handling, deteriorate over time, and need replacement, whereas LEDs are virtually eternal. Depending on the number and power of LEDs, the heads provide a brightness illumination output.

Portable underwater lighting devices can include chemical light sticks. A diver should remove such a stick from its packaging and bend it in their hands, breaking the inner capsule in the process. By shaking it, the diver accelerates the mixing of chemical components inside the stick, resulting in a sufficiently bright glow that lasts from 8 to 12 hours, depending on the manufacturer. Chemical light sticks are ideal for marking the diver's position or any objects both underwater and on land.

Fig. 162. Chemical light signaling stick

Underwater communications

Conventionally, underwater communication means can be divided into wired and wireless communication. The wired communication setup consists of a control unit located on the surface and specialized headsets worn by divers inside their helmets. The principle of operation is based on telephone communication between the calling surface subscriber and one or more divers underwater, with telephone

Fig. 163. Wired communications

cables (usually along with signal ropes and air supply hoses) leading to them. The underwater communication control unit is a device powered by an external or internal 12-volt battery, also capable of recording conversations and connecting a headset and microphone for the surface operator. Some manufacturers' units can be connected to video recording systems. Thanks to the 4-wire communication, divers can communicate with each other. Microphone modules are placed in the diver's helmet or mask, positioned opposite the diver's mouth, and headphones are attached behind the mask's rubber strap or placed inside the helmet opposite the ears.

In the case of wireless communication, instead of a cable leading to the surface, a transceiver is added to the modules located in the diver's helmet or mask, usually attached to the diver's side. The principle of operation remains the same, as the surface control unit is located on the surface, and only the sensor conducting reception and transmission

**Fig. 164. Single-band multi-channel acoustic
communication system**

on the cable connected to the station is submerged in water. The sensor
operates on the same frequency as the transceivers attached to the
divers, allowing communication with multiple divers or groups of
divers simultaneously. In this case, the underwater unit functions as a
single-band multi-channel acoustic communication system. The
functionality of many modern underwater communication systems
usually includes: automatic electronic connection, voice menu,
multiple channels, separate volume controls for reception and audio
monitoring, voice activation (VOX), and push-to-talk (PTT).

Fig. 165. Underwater ultrasonic and VHF radio

Some communication control units combine underwater ultrasonic and
VHF radio communication with divers on the surface. Typically, the
range of such wireless communication is up to 1000 meters underwater
and up to 10,000 meters via radio channel.

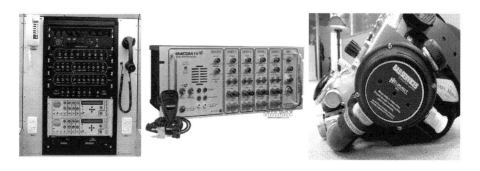

Fig. 166. Gel voice correctors

It is worth noting separately the communication with divers who use gas mixtures containing helium for breathing. As you already know from the previous material, a person breathing with this gas as a component of the gas mixture changes their voice. In this case, gel voice correctors are used for communication with divers, communication for dive management, communication in hyperbaric rescue chambers, as well as communication with the diving bell.

Signal line

The signal line is designed for the descent and ascent of the diver, as well as for underwater communication in the absence of a phone. The signal line is made of four-strand canvas, sisal, or nylon rope and has a length of 50 meters. A loop is tied at one end of the rope, and a button or a becket is applied or tied at the other end. A slip knot is tied at the end with a loop, which is placed around the diver's waist, and the end with the becket is securely fastened to the dinghy or the ship's deck.

Fig. 167. Signal line

During underwater descents in currents or into overhead environments, divers must utilize a lifeline wound on a reel. Such dives include cave exploration, under-ice dives, or rescue missions in enclosed spaces like flooded ship compartments. To ensure the diver's return to the entry point in an overhead environment, the diver uses a main reel with a braided rope up to 150 feet (45 meters) long, which is an essential part of diving gear. A small reel with a wound rope conveniently fits into a diver's gear pocket or attaches to a D-ring in a diver-friendly location.

Divers should note that expanded edges on reel spools facilitate rope grip during winding, keeping fingers free. Typically, these reels are wound with 16-strand bright yellow, orange, red, or white nylon line, with a breaking strength of at least 132 pounds (60 kg). To prevent twisting of the main line, the rope is attached to a stainless steel or brass carabiner swivel, with a breaking strength of at least 400 pounds (181 kg). Having a continuous ascent line is crucial for safe overhead diving. For this purpose, compact reels with a clamp, only 2.3 inches (5.8 cm) long, are used, wound with braided nylon rope up to 50 feet (15 m) long, easily packed in a pocket and deployed when needed. Some of these reels have notches resembling those on an arrow, which secure the reel on a thin line without the need for extra equipment. Such reels with ropes are widely used for connecting gaps between exploration lines, setting up surface signal buoys, marking underwater search grids, and during dives with limited visibility, at night, or in murky waters, or when transitioning from one line to another, where intermediate line is needed to connect two lines or to reach the main lifeline from the entry point into an overhead environment. For more information on using such reels and lifelines, refer to the chapter "Practical Exercises in Extreme Diving".

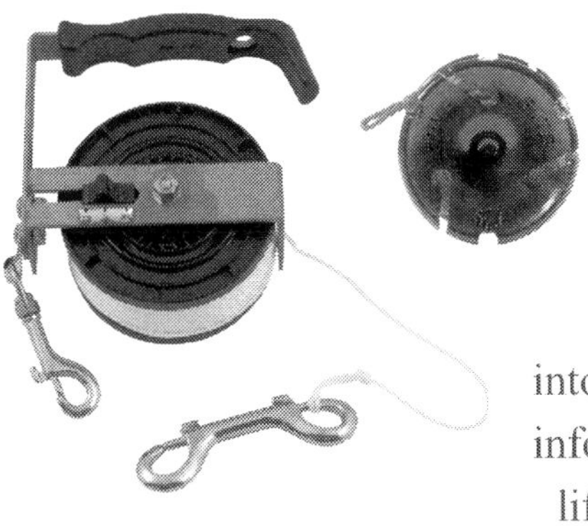

Fig. 168. The small reels

Checkpoint questions for chapter three:

1. What is the purpose of a wetsuit?

2. What types of wetsuits do you know?

3. Name four types of underwater breathing supply for divers.

4. Name the three main components of a scuba set.

5. What is the working principle of a rebreather?

6. What types of rebreathers do you know?

7. How is a high-pressure cylinder constructed?

8. What is the weight of air in a filled 18-liter cylinder at a working pressure of 230 bars?

9. How to remove fog from the glass of a mask?

10. How to remove water from the mask's airspace?

11. What are the purposes of diver's weights?

12. How is the demand valve (second stage) constructed?

13. How is the first stage of a diving regulator (reducer) constructed?

14. Name the differences between membrane and piston first stages.

15. What are the differences between downstream and upstream second stage systems?

16. How do cold-water regulators differ from warm-water regulators?

17. How is an underwater compass designed?

18. How does a pressure gauge differ from a transmitter?

19. What is the difference between scuba and rebreathers?

20. What is the purpose and structure of a scrubber?

21. How does a regenerative rebreather differ from an injector-regenerative setup?

22. How do semi-closed circuit rebreathers differ from closed circuit rebreathers?

23. What are the differences between K.I.S.S. rebreathers and closed circuit rebreathers?

24. What are the differences between rebreathers with active and passive gas delivery?

25. What types of buoyancy compensators do you know?

26. How is a buoyancy compensator constructed?

27. Explain the designs of different types of fins and their operating principles.

28. How is a diving mask and diving helmet constructed?

IV CHAPTER
DIVING EQUIPMENT

The fourth chapter of the textbook is dedicated to various devices and equipment essential for underwater operations. Each paragraph focuses on a specific topic: describing mechanisms for lowering and raising divers, means of underwater propulsion, and tools and methods used for underwater work.

This chapter extensively covers the construction and principles of operation of various types of diving compressors. It explains the structure of oxygen diving compressors, along with the fundamental safety rules for their operation. The means for air purification during the filling of breathing gas cylinders are discussed, and the chapter outlines the basic principles of preparing gas mixtures with gas distribution devices for various diving depths.

In one of the paragraphs, the fundamental principles and structure of hyperbaric chambers for guiding divers through decompression processes, preventing diving-related illnesses, are detailed. The chapter also includes information on the construction of monitoring instruments for gas breathing mixtures and the principles of their operation.

§ 11. Devices used for underwater operations

Additional equipment and special diving devices

As mentioned earlier, mandatory equipment for underwater dives includes a wetsuit, diving mask and snorkel, fins, a weight belt with weights, a diving knife, underwater flashlight, whistle, and a diver's buoy, as well as scuba gear (or another gas delivery system). Depending on the tasks and depth of the dive, the mandatory diving equipment is additionally equipped with items necessary for performing tasks in each specific underwater descent. Such equipment includes devices like watches, depth gauges, compasses, pressure gauges, and dive computers, as well as special underwater devices designed for specific underwater tasks. Examples of such items include welding apparatus, metal detectors, sonar equipment, underwater communication and photo-video recording devices, underwater parachutes, ropes, carabiners, and more.

Underwater video surveillance systems

Video Systems. Video recording and surveillance systems can conventionally be divided into three categories: stationary, portable, and wearable. Stationary video surveillance systems have a control post accessible to the responsible monitoring personnel, which can be located thousands of kilometers away from where the corresponding equipment is installed. These systems include control units, stationary underwater and surface observation cameras.

Fig. 169. Underwater video systems

Portable systems consist of a remotely operated underwater vehicle with a video camera, which transmits the image in real-time via cable to a portable monitor on the surface. Such systems are often used for inspecting unexplored seabeds or assessing the condition of hydraulic structures as a preliminary inspection before a diver's descent.

Wearable cameras are typically mounted on divers' helmets along with an underwater flashlight and also transmit the image in real-time to a portable monitor on the surface, enabling the supervisor to observe and adjust the diver's work. Some video cameras do not provide direct image transmission but instead record video, functioning as underwater video recorders.

Modern underwater video cameras differ in their housing materials, dimensions, and maximum allowable diving depths; otherwise, they share the same distinctions as non-underwater cameras. The choice of a video camera depends on the diver's preferences and specific filming tasks, with attention given to maximum operational depth, size, housing material, lens wide-angle capability, fixed focus or zoom, image stabilization, and the quality of the recording matrix allowing for high-quality recording in low-light conditions. Special attention should be paid to underwater lighting, as higher light intensity accompanying video capture results in a brighter and higher-quality image on the screen.

Fig. 170. Underwater video surveillance systems

Underwater robots (Drones}

Underwater robots are multifunctional tools for enhancing various underwater missions and operations, often used for a preliminary survey of dive sites. An underwater robot can be equipped with an above-water power system, providing optimal diving characteristics and operating time.

These mini-ROV-sized robots possess all the basic functions inherited from larger underwater systems. By using robots as underwater transport vehicles, in addition to the video recorder that they have in

Fig. 171. Qysea underwater robots

each model, depending on the dive tasks, sensors for water quality, sonar sensors, metal detectors, a device with laser pointers having two parallel beams, additional lighting devices, or any other module designed for underwater descent tasks can be installed on the robot.

Underwater Spotlight

Underwater lighting installations and fixtures are designed to illuminate the diver's workplace underwater. Various types of underwater lighting installations and fixtures are used in diver practice, providing general illumination of underwater objects at great depths. The underwater spotlight is designed for use in various situations where intense illumination is required for both above-water and underwater objects, transitioning seamlessly from air to water and vice versa when switched on and warmed up. Examples of applications include illuminating a diver's station, underwater gazebo during descent and ascent, submerged objects, partially flooded compartments, etc., as well as for underwater film and video recording.

The dual-medium underwater spotlight is intended for use as a general lighting source in the air or underwater, integrated into diver equipment (diver gazebos and bells) in both stationary and portable mounting options. It is also part of equipment used in underwater operations zones and for illuminating objects during lifting operations.

The underwater spotlight can be used in the following modes: manual portable, stationary, hanging, including on a float. Its high mechanical strength and modern anti-corrosion protection ensure its durability in the most challenging operating conditions. The spotlight is powered by an above-water transformer unit.

The underwater spotlight kit includes a power transformer unit, power cable from the grid, lighting fixture power cables, and four HT120 fixtures. Additionally, the underwater spotlight can be equipped with a tripod with a magnetic fixator, a tripod with a clamp, a "float-anchor" set for suspended operation, and a cable reel.

The underwater spotlight can be used in manual, portable, stationary, and hanging modes, including on a float. Its high mechanical strength and modern anti-corrosion protection ensure its durability in the most challenging operating conditions.

The standard package includes a 64-meter power cable, four HT120 fixtures, and a spare parts kit.

Additional items available for purchase include a power transformer unit, power cable up to 100 meters long, a tripod with a magnetic fixator or a tripod with a clamp, a "float-anchor" set for suspended operation, and a cable reel for the power cable.

Depending on the installed lamps, the total power of the spotlight is 1800, 10000, or 20000 lumens.

Another one of these installations used by divers in deep-sea dives (over 100 m) is the SGK-57 deep-sea lighting installation. The installation includes: a stationary and portable luminaire; resistance SD-4 to maintain the normal voltage on the lamps of the luminaires when the cable length changes; a cable hank with cable RShM 3X4, 350 m long. The stationary luminaire is movably attached to the platform of the diver's bell, the portable one is placed on the bell platform, has a handle for convenience underwater, and a cable RShM 2X2,5, 25 m long, allowing the luminaire to be moved away from the platform. Both luminaires are of the open type, with a sealed socket for

Fig. 172. Underwater lighting

the incandescent lamp SC-82 at 110 V with a power of 1000 W. The lamp is placed in an ellipsoidal reflector. The reflector has a grid to protect the lamp from damage. The power supply of the installation is provided from the ship's network with a voltage of 220 V using extinguishing resistances. Luminaire SGK-57 has a mass of 12 kg, fits into a box with dimensions of 620X610X564 mm, and has a total mass of 70 kg. Luminaire SGP-57 has a mass of 7 kg, fits into a box (dimensions 412X410X410 mm), and has a total mass of 35 kg. The total weight of the entire installation is about 350 kg. The PPS-1000 lighting installation provides general illumination of underwater objects at depths up to 100 m. The installation includes: a portable luminaire; a cable hank with cable RShM 2X2,5 on a common frame with a laying box; resistance for switching to power from a 220 or 110 V network. The portable luminaire is of the open type with a sealed socket for the incandescent lamp SC-82 at 110 V with a power of 1000 W. The lamp is placed in a reflector with a tube to reduce the angle of dispersion. The tube has a mesh to protect the lamp from damage. The luminaire is equipped with a handle for carrying and mounting on a bracket-holder. Luminaire weight 7 kg. Dimensions of the laying box with a cable coil 1068X600X645mm. Resistance dimensions 510X320X315mm. The total weight of the installation is about 120 kg.

For additional individual lighting at great depths, divers use the VS-1 helmet luminaire, which provides underwater lighting for the diver while working in confined spaces (compartments) at depths up to 75 m. The luminaire includes: a cable RShM 2X2,5 with a cable coil and resistance. The VS-1 luminaire is attached to the diver's helmet. The light source is an incandescent lamp SM-18 at 26 V with a power of 25 W. Power through the cable from the ship's network at 110 V through a resistance or from a 26 V battery. Luminaire weight 2.1 kg. Dimensions of the box with a cable coil and resistance 470X770X660 mm, battery dimensions 610X345X265, box with spare parts 360X215X315. The total weight of the entire installation is about 120 kg. Additionally, for additional individual lighting, divers use handheld underwater flashlights, which provide individual underwater lighting at depths of up to 100 meters depending on the manufacturer.

Dive sonar

A dive sonar, underwater sonar, or handheld underwater echo sounder is a compact portable device that provides divers with information about the underwater topography in their environment. Such devices belong to the category of search equipment. They are designed to detect underwater objects and obstacles during dives, especially when performing tasks in conditions of limited visibility. The handheld sonar operates on the principle of sound reflection from underwater objects. The device emits a sound signal that travels through the water and reflects off the bottom or other objects. The sonar then receives the reflected signal, analyzes it, determines the depth and distance to the measured underwater objects

Fig. 173. Dive sonar

259

Fig. 174. Multibeam Sonar Gemini

and obstacles. The information helps the diver avoid unwanted collisions and maintain a safe distance. Handheld sonars usually have a built-in display that shows information about depth and detected objects. This can be a numerical depth value and a graphical representation of the bottom and other objects. Handheld sonars are typically compact, lightweight, and easy to use. They can be easily held in the hand or attached to the diver's equipment.

Underwater metal detector

·Various metal detectors are used to detect iron and steel targets located underwater. For detecting iron and steel targets such as pipelines, anchors, chains, cannons, dredges, and other submerged metallic objects, especially when they are situated on the seabed covered with layers of silt or sand, making them impossible to detect with sonar or video, towed proton magnetometers are employed.

Let's consider the basic principles of their operation using the example of a magnetometer from JW Fishers company. The marine magnetometer sensor is submerged in water and towed behind a vessel on a cable, while the control and monitoring unit is onboard the ship. An operator monitors deviations in magnetic fields. Typically, the detection range for magnetic objects extends to 1500 feet (450 meters) on each side of the sensor, with an overall scanning swath of 3000 feet, allowing for rapid coverage of large areas. However, the detection range is not affected by the medium between the magnetometer and the metallic target. Performance remains unchanged when searching in mud, sand, or hard corals. A two-second cycle provides a strong feedback signal and is fast enough to detect even small iron/steel targets. The system is fully digitized, displaying current digital measurements, and graphical changes. On the monitor, the operator sees a normogram axis and deviations of each magnetic anomaly, resembling a cardiologist's apparatus for altering heart rhythm. The difference lies in the information reading area where the regularity and frequency of spikes, intervals, and amplitudes belong not to humans but to the seafloor. Adjustable sound alerts enable the operator to determine how significant a change in baseline readings will trigger an alarm. The towed underwater magnetometer sensor boasts excellent hydrodynamic characteristics, smoothly gliding through the water and allowing towing speeds of up to 10 knots. For detecting small targets, towing speeds of 2-3 knots are recommended.

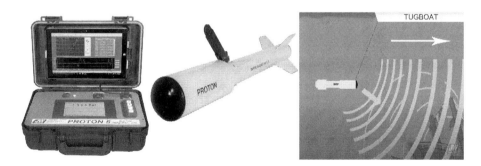

Fig. 175. Magnetometer from JW Fishers company

It is worth noting separately devices such as underwater metal detectors, which can be classified as a diver's handheld tool. The purpose of this device is evident from its name. Each underwater metal detector has a powerful watertight casing characterized by reliable hydroisolation, allowing it to be submerged to specific diving depths (usually up to 60 meters). Some metal detector models lack a screen, relying entirely on headphones, LED, or vibration signals for object detection. To detect metal, the device's coil sends and receives reflected impulses at one or multiple frequencies. Some devices have a discriminator in their settings, allowing the differentiation between ferrous and non-ferrous targets.

Fig. 176. Minelab Excalibur II underwater metal detector

The detection depth of metal-containing objects depends on the size of the target. For instance, a small coin can be detected underwater in the seabed up to 25 centimeters deep, an object the size of a fist can be detected up to 50 centimeters deep, and an object the size of a 200-liter barrel can be detected lying beneath a layer of mud or soil up to 1 meter deep.

Models of metal detectors from different manufacturers do not significantly differ in their detection depth characteristics.

§ 12. Devices for lowering and lifting divers

To facilitate the descent and ascent of divers underwater, various equipment such as diving traps, descent baskets, descent and keel ropes, and keel traps are employed.

A diving trap serves the purpose of lowering divers from the deck of a vessel with low freeboard, a boat, descent platform, another watercraft with low freeboard, or the shore into the water, and subsequently hoisting them back to the surface. These traps can be constructed from either wood or metal.

The trap's width should be a minimum of

Fig. 177. Diving trap

400 mm, with a distance between steps (balusters) of 250 mm.

Metallic traps are designed to fold, typically in two parts, allowing the section entering the water to be raised (tilted) without necessitating removal from its position. They are commonly manufactured in three sizes: 3010, 2720, and 1975 millimeters in length. When deployed, the trap is securely affixed at the diver's descent point, inclined at approximately 70–80° to the horizon, ensuring that the lowest step of the trap is at least 1500 mm below the water's surface. Wooden traps are weighted at the base to prevent buoyancy.

A descent basket is used to lower divers from the decks of high-freeboard vessels or other high-freeboard watercraft or pier walls when the distance from the water surface to the deck (platform) is more than 1.5 m. It is also used to lower a diver to the work site and lift them while conducting decompression. The basket can be made by the ship's personnel using improvised means, such as ropes and a wooden pallet and ballast to give the basket negative buoyancy. Baskets for frequent use are made of metal rods. The descent basket is lowered and raised by a boom or boat beam using a winch mechanism. The descent rope is attached to the top of the basket.

To ensure the safety of divers from marine predators, metallic cage baskets or baskets made of exceptionally strong transparent plastic are manufactured. The safety of the diver working on the descent basket is ensured by a standby boat or boat, so that assistance can be provided if the diver, for any reason, cannot independently return to the descent basket.

Fig. 178. Diver descent and ascent device (DDAD)

Fig.179 Descent basket for shark protection

The decompression basket is designed to accommodate divers during decompression stops specified by the decompression schedule. Baskets come in two-threaded, consisting of two ropes, and single-threaded using a single rope. The balusters (steps) are attached one above the other at a distance of 3 m from each other. The count of balusters is done from the bottom. A ballast weighing about 30 kg is attached to the lower part of the basket, and a sliding bracket is used to connect it to the descent rope.

Fig.180 Decompression basket

Descent rope

After the diver descends into the water via the trap or descent basket, and after checking the tightness of the equipment, they switch to the descent rope, which is intended to direct the movement of the diver during descent to the bottom and return to the surface. Holding onto the descent rope prevents the diver from sinking to the depth or being thrown to the surface. The descent rope is made of hemp, sisal, or nylon rope with a diameter of 50–75 mm. A ballast weighing 30–50 kg is attached to one end of such a rope, which is lowered to the ground.

The second end of the rope is attached to the place where the diver enters the water (at the trap on the deck, at the boat beam used to lower the basket). The descent rope is twice the length of the immersion depth. Thus, for a diving depth of 50 meters, a descent rope with a length of 100 meters is used. Before lowering the ballast, directly on the descent rope, a running rope (guide) is attached, which serves as a guide for the diver to return to the descent rope. If the descent rope is not

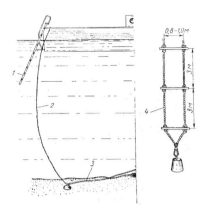

Fig. 181. Devices for lowering, lifting, and moving divers: (1) - trap; (2) - descent rope; (3) - running rope; (4) - keel basket.

Fig. 182. Diver descent for underwater inspection of the ship's hull: (1) - keel rope; (2) - storm trap; (3) - signal rope

265

Fig. 183. Keel basket

lowered to the ground but is attached to the diver's work site under the hull of the vessel, the ballast is not attached. Such a rope will simultaneously serve as a descent and running rope. When lowering divers into a flooded compartment of a vessel, the first descending diver attaches the running rope. Subsequent divers move to the work site using this running rope.

The keel rope is used to hold the diver during short-term work under the ship's hull. Steel and hemp ropes are used to make keel ropes.

The keel trap or keel basket is designed for underwater work that requires a lot of time (repairing damage to the ship's hull, fixing side devices, and other tasks). The keel trap allows the diver to work with both hands and move from one side to the other as quickly as on the keel rope. The keel trap is made on board from improvised means. It looks similar to a regular storm trap, but its width is greater, and the balusters are spaced farther apart. Sometimes a storm trap is used as a keel trap, to which ballast and side guys are attached. The keel trap is made of two ropes and balusters with distances between balusters of 400–600 mm. Ballast is attached to the middle of the keel trap with the calculation that after winding the trap under the ship's hull, the ballast is under the keel. The keel trap has side guys to move it from bow to stern and back.

Diver descent and ascent device (DDAD) – is used for deep-water dives (more than 60 meters) of divers and their accelerated ascent from depth in a diving bell. The bell raised to the ship's deck is connected to the decompression chamber to continue the decompression of divers.

Depending on the location on the ship and the method of transferring the bell to the decompression chamber, stern and side diver descent devices are distinguished. The descent device includes: a diving bell with a platform; a device for moving the bell behind the stern and overboard; a winch; rope equipment for the bell; side diver baskets with descent and ascent mechanisms; hangers for hoses and cables to the diving bell and divers; deep-sea lighting installation.

The diving bell is a steel cylinder with a bottom entrance hatch with a closing lid from the inside and a platform. The platform of the diving bell consists of a welded structure, including a metal platform hinged or bolted to the bell body, with eyelets for guide ropes, seats, a device for attaching lights, stops for diver hoses, and a railing. The platform is designed to accommodate divers during descent and ascent until they transfer to the bell, as well as to accommodate a certain number of diver hoses, tools, and accessories needed for underwater work. The platform has a ballast compartment to

Fig. 184. Side diver bell

give the bell negative buoyancy. Air is supplied to the bell through a diver hose. Hoses and cables are placed on hangers, and their descent and ascent are mechanized. All bell descent mechanisms operate synchronously. Stern diver bell. Technical specifications: length 2665 mm; diameter 1400 mm; internal volume is 3.5 m3; mass in the air with equipment is 1470 kg; mass of the bell with the diver platform and traverse is 4325 kg; negative buoyancy in the water from 200 to 250 kg; diameter of the entrance hatch 700 mm; capacity for equipped divers 2 people; capacity for divers without equipment 5 people; working pressure up to 10 bar. The descent of the stern diver bell is carried out by a two-drum electric winch with a rope layer. Traction force on each drum is not less than 3 tons. The drum capacity is up to 440 meters of 17.5 mm diameter rope. Each drum has a cam engagement and a belt brake. The descent and ascent speed of the stern diver bell is from 5 to 20 meters per minute.

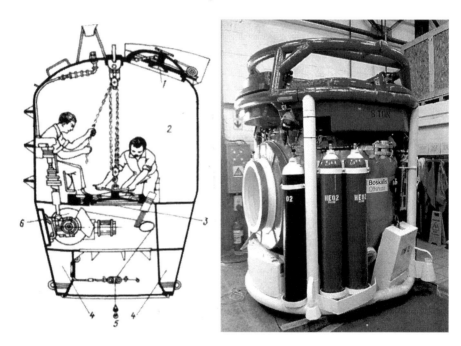

Fig. 185. Momsen McKenna rescue capsule and modern diving bell

Side diver bell. Technical specifications: length 2770 mm; diameter 1544 mm; internal volume is 4.4 m3; mass in the air with equipment is 3000 kg; mass of the bell with the diver platform and traverse is 5420 kg; negative buoyancy in the water from 200 to 250 kg; diameter of the entrance hatch 770 mm; capacity for equipped divers 3 people;

capacity for divers without equipment 7 people; working pressure up to 10 bar. The descent of the side bell is carried out at a speed of 7 to 24 meters per minute, and ascent from 5 to 20 meters per minute. The lifting winch has a traction force of 5 tons on each drum, using a 25 mm diameter steel rope, with a total length of 600 m, a breaking force of about 35 tons, and a drum capacity of 270 m. Steel guide ropes, 18.5 mm in diameter and 300 m in length each, pass through wedge rope stops, traverses, and serve as a means of emergency lifting of the diver bell.

§ 13. Devices for underwater locomotion

During the search for sunken objects, ground inspection, in large water areas, inspection of the underwater part of ships and hydraulic structures, as well as in the search for bottom and anchor mines, divers with autonomous breathing equipment use special towed devices for underwater movement.

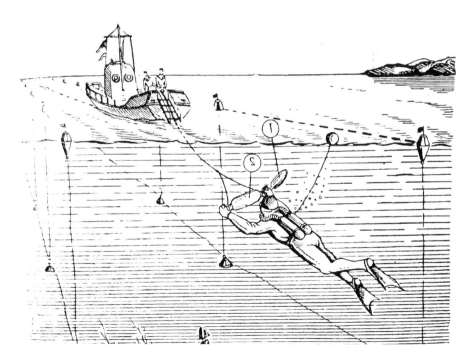

Fig. 186. Towed manual diver's rudder

Fig. 187. Towed manual diver's rudder

Devices for underwater movement are divided into self-propelled and non-self-propelled. Non-self-propelled towing means include: a towing rope with a ballast attached to the end, a manual diver's rudder, a suspended towed basket, and a towed wing-sled-type device.

Self-propelled devices include towed vehicles equipped. Before using any means of underwater movement, it is necessary to adjust the buoyancy of this means. A towing rope with a ballast attached to the end, weighing up to 16 kg, is paid out overboard of the surface vehicle to a depth with a distance of about one meter from the ground. The diver, descending to the ballast, holds onto it and signals the surface vehicle to start moving. The boat moves at a speed not exceeding 3 knots (approximately 1.5 m/s). Depending on visibility, the ground observation range is from 1.5 to 5 meters on either side of the diver.

The manual diver's rudder consists of a blade, handles, and towing blades. The rudder blade is usually made of oak and has positive buoyancy (up to +1 kg). The manual rudder is attached to the surface vehicle by a rope from 25 to 50 meters long. The towing speed of the diver should not exceed 3 knots. The immersion of the diver is carried out to depths of up to 15 meters. In this case, the diver, holding onto the rudder handles, remains in a horizontal position and can make maneuvers to ascend or descend within 2 meters. If necessary to surface, the diver releases the rudder and resurfaces in a normal mode.

The suspended towed basket differs from the towing rope in that it has a seat-basket with ballast attached to it. Such a basket is made of a short board and hemp rope. It is also lowered from the surface vehicle to a depth (from one to one and a half meters from the ground) and towed by the sitting diver, who observes. To increase the observation range from one surface vehicle, two divers can be lowered, each on its own basket. The baskets are suspended from towing ropes, attaching them to a wooden beam 6 meters long, which is fastened across the stern.

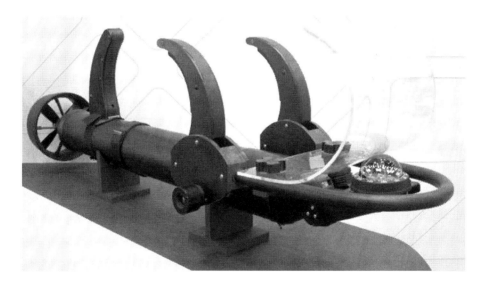

Fig. 188. Towing vehicle with a ballast tank

A towed wing-sled-type device consists of a hull with a ballast tank. Runners and wings are attached to the hull. The cabin, in which the diver lies, is protected from the oncoming water flow by a front windshield made of durable transparent plastic and an opening cowl. The diver in the cabin observes the ground through the front glass.

On the front panel are: a depth gauge, a clock, a control panel for the apparatus, which consists of control levers and a ballast tank blow button. Vertical and horizontal rudder control is done with one lever. Two 1000-watt lights are placed under the sled wings. By moving the light beams in horizontal and vertical planes, the diver also controls them with a lever. The electrical equipment is powered from the tow by cable and in the absence of the tow cable, power is supplied from the built-in battery. Many modern models of underwater towboats are equipped with propellers or water jets powered by electric motors in the stern, which provides an advantage for autonomous movement when necessary. Older models lack autonomous propulsion and rely directly on a towline and the towing vessel for movement. Winged sleds with a diver on board follow the towline, which can range from 30 to 100 meters in length, at speeds of up to 5 knots at depths ranging from 12 to 30 meters. The width of the observed strip depends on the water transparency and the time of day. On a sunny day, it can reach 15 meters, and at night up to 3 meters. When an object is detected on the ground, the diver informs the towing vehicle using an electric signal and releases a buoy-marker. On its board, the sled has four marker buoys. The ballast tank blow system consists of a three-liter air tank compressed to 200 bar, a reducing valve, a compressed air starter, and a ventilation valve. By pressing the starter button, the diver blows the tank and, together with the apparatus, floats to the surface.

A self-propelled underwater tow (Diver Propulsion Vehicle, DPV) is a device powered by a propeller from an electric motor. Underwater tugs come in various sizes, shapes, and technical specifications. Conventionally, diver tow vehicles can be divided into two types: compact hand-controlled tow vehicles and capsule devices for carrying divers. For a long time, the Sea Doo campaign was the leading manufacturer of light and compact tow vehicles. After the Canadian brand switched to the production of jet skis, the Japanese Yamaha became the leader in the production of tow vehicles for amateur diver immersions.

With each passing year, underwater tow vehicle manufacturers upgrade, offering users new advantages of diver tow vehicles. Better control, speed, acceleration, compact size, longer operating time, and more.

Fig. 189. Yamaha tug

Manual tow vehicles (DPV) are mainly made of plastic in the form of a cigar-shaped buoy. The hull is divided into three compartments: propeller, electric motor, and power battery. Handles are placed on the sides of the hull, arranged like bicycle handlebars, with start and stop buttons for the engine, as well as speed control. The buttons are made in the form of plates, allowing them to be pressed even with thick gloves. The diver assumes a horizontal position in the water, grabs the handles with outstretched arms, then starts the engine by pressing the button, and the device begins to move, pulling the diver behind.

New technologies allow tow vehicles to acquire new features. Thus, the smallest (300x300x160mm) tow vehicle "Leefet S1 PRO" to date, weighing 2.5 kg in the equipped state, allows the diver to develop a speed of 4 knots underwater. The modularity of the construction of this device makes it versatile for use. If you want to increase speed or power,

Fig. 190. Underwater tow vehicle "Leefet S1 PRO"

you can assemble the tow vehicle structure from several motors with a single control. Manual control can be replaced with remote control. After that, attach the tow vehicle fuselage to the diver's buoy with special straps, thereby freeing the diver's hands.

Fig. 191. "Pegasus Thruster"

A remote-controlled underwater tow vehicle is attached to the diver's back to his tank with a separate buoyancy strap or to the diver's feet or hands. The tow vehicle control panel is portable and held in the diver's

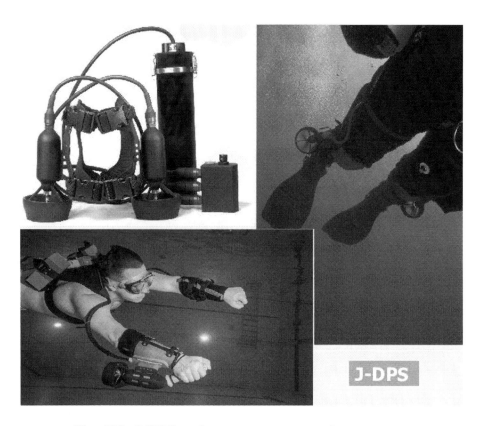

Fig. 192. J-DPS underwater tug mounting systems.

hand. When connected to the tow vehicle with a special wire, the control panel is a handle with a single button. Pressing the button starts the engine and propeller, and when the diver releases the button, the engine turns off. Such a tow vehicle allows the diver to free and use both hands at any time. The streamlined hull of the tow vehicle is made of anodized aluminum, which allowed achieving the lightness of the device – 4.6 kg dry weight to use it at depths of up to 100 meters. The tow vehicle reaches a speed of up to 3 knots if the diver uses fins exclusively for maneuvering. To increase power, it is possible to use 2 paired tow vehicles controlled from one remote. Each part of the device is made as separate sealed modules, so if necessary, the diver can connect and disconnect the motor block, battery block, and control panel while underwater.

Capsule-type underwater tow vehicles are used to transport from one to a group of divers over relatively long distances, 8 to 20 nautical miles. In this case, the diver or group of divers with full equipment sets are accommodated inside the hull of such tow vehicles.

Some modern tow vehicles have ejector thrust, the principle of which is based on water flow control. It is similar to the principle of operation

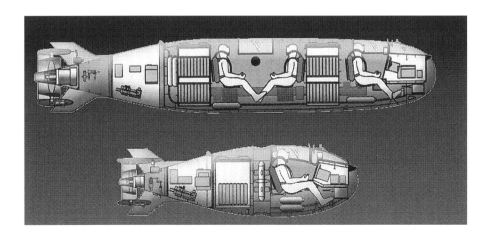

Fig. 193. Scheme of capsule-type underwater tow vehicles

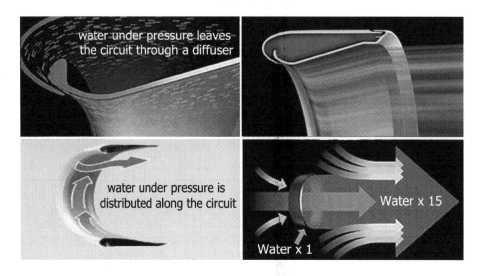

Fig. 194. Diagram of the power plant circuit of a tow vehicle operating on the ejector principle

of bladeless Dyson fans. These tow vehicles have the shape of a rigid backpack, inside which a large through slightly narrowing opening is located from top to bottom. Through the receiving opening, water from the surrounding environment enters the hydraulic compressor, after which, under pressure, it is distributed along the contour of the flat nozzle and exits through the diffuser into the inner part of the contour, transferring the kinetic energy of its flow into the general water stream. Thanks to the Coanda effect, the water coming out from the narrower side creates an area of low pressure on the opposite side, providing more active pulling of water into the tow vehicle's through hole, thereby creating powerful thrust and a water jet behind the tow vehicle.

Diving descents in the observation chamber (bathyscaphe)

Let's talk about a specific means of underwater transportation, namely the bathyscaphe. Roughly, they can be divided into small submarines and deep-sea observation chambers. What sets them apart from underwater tow vehicles is that while inside the capsule of the submersible, divers don't need to wear diving gear.Specialists with

Fig. 195. C-Explorer 3 observation bathyscaphe

diving qualifications, having studied the chamber and passed the exam as a diver-operator, are allowed for descents in the observation chamber. The entry of operators into the chambers should occur with them securely fastened on board or at the ship's side. Closing the hatch cover is allowed only after complete confidence in the proper functioning of communication means and the regeneration system. Chambers must be thoroughly inspected before submersion, and their systems, instruments, and mechanisms tested in action. Their descent means must have shock-absorbing devices. Observation chambers must have reliable regeneration facilities. The time spent by operators in the chambers should not exceed the reliable operation time of their regeneration system. Emergency ascent of chambers should only be performed when there is no possibility of raising them to the surface using shipboard means. Strict fire safety measures must be observed in the chamber. For painting the internal surfaces of the chambers, paints and paint solvents containing no harmful volatile substances should be used. The use of lead-based paints is prohibited.

Underwater observation tools

Special cameras are used for observing the progress of underwater work, visually searching and inspecting underwater objects, directing the diving bell to the work site, as well as underwater photo and video shooting. Technical data for observation cameras vary. For example, the NK-300 observation chamber is a sealed vessel designed for external water pressure at a depth of three hundred meters. It consists of a steel body with welded construction, equipment, and a detachable emergency ballast. The top of the body has a hatch with a spherical cover that closes from the outside using hinged bolts with nuts. For observation, video shooting, and obtaining geodata of the surrounding underwater environment, illuminators are installed in the lower and upper hemispheres, as well as in the hatch cover. They have easily removable protective glasses to reduce fogging of the illuminators. The chamber is equipped with a telephone, ballast discharge and release devices from the lifting cable and cable for emergency ascent. The observer is placed in the chamber on a rotating chair. To control the dive depth, a depth gauge is installed in the chamber. The NK-300 chamber has a convection-type regeneration system, consisting of three regenerative boxes with a total capacity of 2.3 kg of regenerative substance. The system's duration of action is 6 hours. The Galeazzi observation chamber is structurally similar to the domestic NK-300 chamber and serves a similar purpose. Unlike the NK-300 chamber, it has a forced regeneration system. Oxygen replenishment is provided from two oxygen cylinders at a constant supply of 3-4 liters per minute. The Galeazzi observation chamber, with a dive depth of 600 meters, has an autonomous lighting installation, placed either below the chamber or above it. The lighting installation is operated by the observer from the chamber.

§ 14. Diving compressors

To supply divers with air, other gases, or gas mixtures, compressors are used. Diving compressors are classified as follows:

By purpose: for compressing atmospheric air and supplying it to divers; for transferring and compressing gas mixtures or gases.

By installation method: stationary, mobile, and portable.

By type of compressed gases: air, oxygen, and others.

By final pressure of gases created by the compressor: low pressure up to 4 kgf/cm²; medium pressure 20-30 kgf/cm²; and high pressure 150-500 kgf/cm².

By performance: low performance up to 120 l/min; medium performance from 100 to 160 l/min; high performance over 200 l/min.

By type of drive: manual, electric, or internal combustion engine.

By number of compression stages: single-stage, two-stage, three-stage, and multi-stage compressors.

Fig. 196. Diving compressor

Low pressure air diving compressors

A three-cylinder diving pump is used for divers equipped with ventilated gear at depths up to 15 meters.

Technical data for the air pump: internal cylinder diameter 82 mm, piston stroke 216 mm; performance per revolution 3 liters, weight 250 kg. Working pressure 4 kgf/cm². The pump consists of two frames, a crankshaft, two flywheels, a foundation, three cylinders, an air receiver, a pressure gauge, and a cooler. The pump is installed in a wooden case to protect it from damage and weather conditions. The frames are designed to attach the main parts of the pump and are made of cast iron. Frame bearings support the three-crankshaft, which drives connecting rods with pistons. Suction valves are placed in the pistons.

Cylinders and air receiver are installed on rubber gaskets and fastened to the foundation with bolts. A diving pressure gauge of the plunger type is designed to show the pressure of air supplied to the diver. The pump operates as follows: when the crankshaft rotates, the pistons move up and down. Guide rods and plates ensure their correct movement in the cylinders. When the piston moves up, a vacuum is created under it in the cylinder, causing the suction valve to open, and the cylinder fills with atmospheric air. When the piston reaches the top dead center, the vacuum in the cylinder ceases, and the suction valve closes. Then

Fig. 197. Three-cylinder diving pump

the piston descends, compressing the air in the cylinder. As soon as the air pressure in the cylinder exceeds the force of the spring of the discharge valve, it opens and lets air into the air channels of the foundation and further to the diver. During pump operation, the piston, in its extreme lower position, does not touch the bottom of the cylinder, as there is

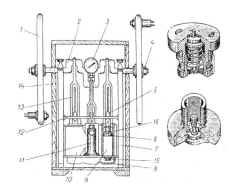

Fig. 198. Schema three-cylinder diving pump

a gap of 1-2 mm between them. The space formed due to this gap is called the harmful space of the pump cylinder. In the harmful space, compressed air remains with each downward movement of the piston. As the piston moves upward, this air expands, occupying part of the cylinder's volume, thereby reducing the volume of the new portion of air entering the cylinder through the suction valve. The pump's performance depends on the number of revolutions of the crankshaft per minute. For example, at 16 revolutions per minute, the performance is about 45 liters of air, at 25 revolutions - 70 liters, at 35 - 95 liters, and at 45 - 120 liters. In places where electrical power can be connected, a pump with an electric drive is used, allowing the diver to dive to a depth of 20 meters. The lightweight diving pump (LDP) is designed to supply air to the diver at a depth of 10-15 meters. The pump is an air pump of simple action with horizontally arranged cylinders. Technical characteristics of the pump: internal cylinder diameter - 97 mm, piston stroke 128 mm, working cylinder volume - 0.95 liters, production per swing period 1.7-1.8 liters, receiver capacity 9 liters, working pressure 5 kgf/cm², weight 55 kilograms. The pump is operated by handles mounted on the lever fork, moving the rod in one direction or the other. In one cylinder, air compression occurs, which, through the pressure valve via the air duct, is supplied to the receiver. In the opposite cylinder at this time, rarefaction occurs, as a result of which the suction valve opens, and atmospheric air begins to enter the cylinder. When the rod moves in the opposite direction, the processes that occurred in the opposite cylinder take place in this cylinder.

The membrane compressor UK40 2M is used by DIY enthusiasts for Hook systems and dives to depths of up to 15 meters. It is designed to obtain compressed air free from oils and other friction and

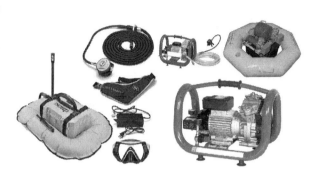

Fig. 199. Hook systems

lubrication products. A two-cylinder compressor V-shaped block is connected to a 7-liter receiver, and a 20-30-meter air supply hose is connected to the diver, at the end of which a second stage with manual air supply control is installed. Nominal working pressure 2.2 bar, maximum 3.5 bar. Productivity is 75 liters per minute. It is used with an electric drive BLDC 550 watts and a 20-ampere battery.

Fig. 200. Air supply hose

Hook systems are used by divers provided there is an emergency air supply system, such as a Spare Air reserve breathing source.

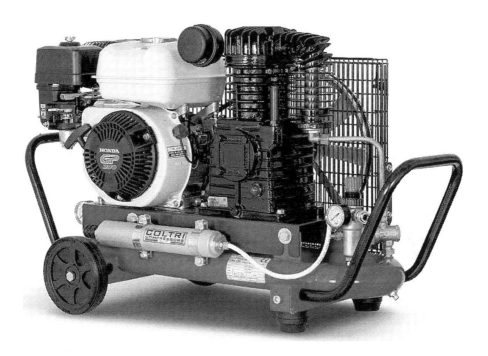

Fig. 201. Low pressure compressor for hose air supply

Professional diving equipment includes low-pressure compressors similar to the Coltri Eolo, which are utilized for delivering air through a hose from the surface to the diver's helmet during prolonged tasks at moderate depths. These compressors are equipped with either a gasoline or electric motor ranging from 2 to 5 kW in power. A receiver is installed at the compressor block outlet to regulate airflow smoothly at different depths, preventing abrupt changes in air supply. A carbon filter safeguards the diver's breathing gas mixture from unwanted impurities. This type of compressor also features a pressure gauge for pressure monitoring and a pressure regulator at the outlet, capable of maintaining pressure up to 10 bars.

Medium-pressure air diving compressors

Medium-pressure compressors are used at diving stations for various underwater technical operations with ventilated equipment. Typically, these are two-stage compressors equipped with electric motors or internal combustion engines. Suction and discharge valves are located in the low and high-pressure cylinders. Atmospheric air enters through the intake pipe with a filter. After compression in the low-pressure cylinder and cooling in the first stage, the air enters the high-pressure cylinder, where it is compressed to 25 bar. Cooled in the second stage refrigerator, the air passes through an oil separator and is pumped through a pipeline into the air cylinders. Diving stations have several air cylinders of different capacities (usually 140 or 280 liters) with a working pressure of at least 25 bar. These cylinders must be kept clean, free from rust and dirt, and require annual flushing and alkalinization. Accumulated water in the cylinders, settling from compressed air, needs to be periodically removed through blowdown valves installed on the cylinders. Compressed air from the cylinders is directed to the

air distribution panel located near the diver's descent point. The panel consists of panels on which air ducts, branches with valves for connecting diving hoses, diving pressure gauges, and a gauge showing the residual pressure in the cylinders are mounted. Panels can be two or three-horned (for two or three divers, respectively), right or left execution.

High-pressure air diving compressors

High-pressure compressors are used to fill air into transport or small-volume cylinders with working pressures ranging from 150 to 350 bar. The simplest of high-pressure compressors is a manual compressor, in the form of a hand pump, built on the principle of multiple compression of atmospheric air by the muscular force of a person.

Fig. 202. Hand pump compressor

Typically used for filling small air cylinders up to 500 milliliters. The high-pressure pump is a system of three cylindrical pistons of different sections (large, medium, and small) inserted into each other (similar to a hydraulic lift). When the pump handle is lifted, the piston-cylinders extend from each other. Then, by pressing the pump handle vertically down, excess pressure is created inside the cylinder. The pressure, created by the effort of the human muscle mass (80 kg), with a piston area of about 5 cm², is about 16 bar, but the air starts to compress the next smaller-section piston-cylinder, with an area 5 times smaller (1 cm²), and the pressure increases proportionally, with the same mass of 0.5. When connecting the third stage, which is 2.5 times smaller in area than the second, the output from the manual compressor reaches a pressure of about 200 bars. The productivity of such a compressor is very low; it takes at least 20 minutes of active physical work to fill a 0.5-liter cylinder.

5 minutes

10 minutes

Fig. 203. Spaire air

An essential characteristic of compressors is productivity—the number of liters of atmospheric air a compressor can compress in one minute. The productivity of high-pressure compressors varies widely—from 100 to 3900 l/min. However, for producing compressed breathing air, the productivity typically ranges from 100 to 500 l/min. Such compressors can be equipped with electric or internal combustion engine drives. Weight and dimensions classify compressors as portable or stationary. The electric drive type is usually 220V or 380V. Compressors with an electric motor can be operated in well-ventilated areas and installed at least 0.5 m away from the wall. Compressors with a gasoline or diesel engine are prohibited from being used indoors.

High-pressure compressors

High-pressure compressors are designed to compress atmospheric air to working pressures of 150, 200, 230, or 300 bars. Simultaneously, they ensure the purification of air from oil vapors and harmful impurities, as well as its drying. The compressed air becomes suitable for breathing in diving equipment. Compressors are based on several basic compressor blocks of various capacities and modifications. Different configurations of units, external appearances, detachable charging panels, and various options contribute to the versatility of these compressors. Additional devices include extra charging units (for up to 4 simultaneous cylinders), devices for simultaneous charging of cylinders at two different pressures, automatic condensate drain systems, additional pressure gauges, high-resilience filtering sections, and electronic control systems for monitoring the cartridge condition.

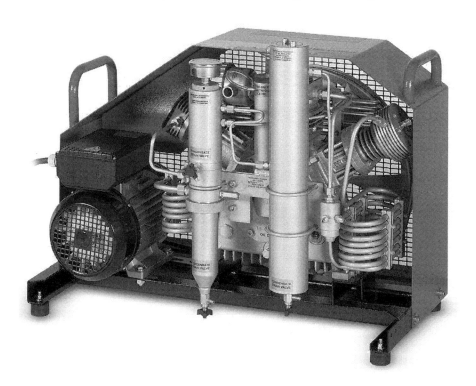

Fig. 204. High pressure compressor

The continuous operation time of compressors with various capacities (l/min) for producing a specific volume of air compressed to a working pressure of 230 bars is as follows:

Compressor Productivity (l/min)	Volume (l) of air compressed to 230 bars			
	10	100	250	500
100	23 min	3 h 45 min	9 h 20 min	18 h 45 min
150	15 min	2 h 30 min	6 h 15 min	12 h 30 min
200	11min	1 h 50 min	4 h 45	9 h 30
250	9 min	1 h 30 min	3 h 45	7 h 30
320	7 min	1 h 10 min	3 h	6 h
500	4-5 min	45 min	1 h 50	3 h 45

Note: When increasing the working pressure (from 230 to 300 bars), the time indicated in the table should be proportionally increased.

The minimum compressor productivity of 100 l/min (0.1 m³/min) ensures filling a 10-liter breathing cylinder to a working pressure of 230 bars in 23 minutes. Consequently, the same cylinder will be charged to 300 bars within 30 minutes.

Compressor block

The foundation of the compressor ensures the compression of atmospheric air to the working pressure. The compressor's lifespan depends mainly on the reliability of the compressor block components, leading many manufacturers to employ various engineering solutions to extend the service life of the produced equipment. These solutions include an effective system for cooling the compressed air through

Fig. 205. Compressor block

carefully calculated cooling areas. Some compressors feature a "floating" piston in the final stage, unconnected to the crankshaft via a connecting rod, thus experiencing no radial loads. Additionally, the piston-cylinder group in the final stage may be manufactured without piston rings (sealing occurs through an oil film). Consequently, the lifespan of the most loaded component increases several times due to minimized friction losses. The application of a pressured lubrication system with a gear pump using a high-pressure oil filter ensures the highest quality lubrication of rubbing parts. Cast iron crank mechanisms increase the compressor's mass and reduce vibrational phenomena, while the use of ball sliding bearings minimizes friction losses.

The fundamental principle of any compressor is gas compression. During the compression of any gas, its temperature increases, and the higher the compression ratio, the more the initial temperature rises. Air heats up during compression because the distance between molecules decreases, and molecules "rub" against each other, releasing a considerable amount of heat. While theoretically, single-stage compression is possible, it is not practical since the air temperature in the cylinder would rise to 400°C. The piston would need to be equipped with 20-25 piston rings, oil and valves would need to be changed after each cylinder charge, etc. To maintain the air temperature in the cylinders within 80-120°C, the compression process in high-pressure compressors is technologically divided into stages with intermediate air cooling and drying. The principle of staged air compression is inherent in all compressors, regardless of design features and performance. Intermediate coolers between stages cool the air from 80-120°C to values only slightly (10-15°C) exceeding the ambient air temperature. Cooling the air, in particular, prevents oil evaporation and coke formation in the compressor block. Therefore, compressors typically have 3-4 compression stages (cylinders). Safety valves are installed between stages to release compressed air into the atmosphere if the fixed pressure level is exceeded in one of the compressor stages. These valves are set to a specific activation pressure and protect the compressor block from overloads.

A three-stage compressor block has approximate activation values as follows: 1 stage – 8 bar; 2 stage – 60-80 bar; 3-4 stage – 230 or 300 bar.

The final stage – 230 or 300 bars (valve on the filtering system). Intermediate coolers are designed as air pipelines between the compressor stages. They aim to cool the hot air (80-120°C) coming from the cylinders to a temperature approximately 10-20°C higher than the ambient temperature. Intermediate separators are devices installed between the 2-3 and 3-4 stages (cylinders) of the compressor, intended for removing condensate (water+oil) accumulated in the intermediate coolers due to the rapid cooling of preheated, moist air in the compressor cylinders. Condensate drainage should be performed every 15 minutes. In most modern compressor models, an automatic drainage system is used instead of manual.

In a 4-stage block, the pressure in stages is distributed as follows: 1st stage – 2-3 bars. Then comes the intermediate cooler. For regions with a very humid and hot climate, an additional separator for condensate drainage is installed after the first compression stage. 2nd stage – 15-20 bars. After the second stage, moist air forms condensate during cooling, so an intermediate separator for condensate drainage is essential. Failure to remove condensate would lead to compressing water in the last stage, which is practically incompressible. The engine power would be insufficient, and the compressor would stall. The centrifuge principle is used in the intermediate separator - air is spiraled, water droplets settle on the inner walls, and flow down. The condensate has a milky shade, as it consists of a fine-dispersion mixture of water and oil droplets.

The 3rd stage delivers 45-75 bars depending on the compressor block model and the final working pressure (230/300 bars). After the intermediate separator for condensate drainage, the fourth stage follows, where air is compressed to the final working pressure of 230 or 300 bars and supplied to the filtration system.

From the last compression stage, air under pressure of 230 or 300 bars enters the final cooler. It is a long tube of small diameter (about 10 mm), easily bendable in the required direction, and can be compactly laid in limited space. To increase heat dissipation, the final cooler has a

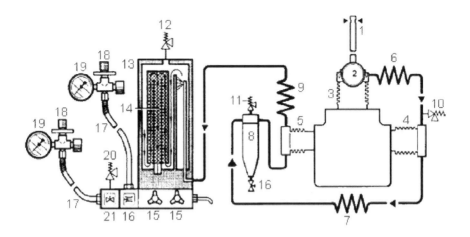

Fig. 206. Compressor scheme: (1) telescopic intake pipe; (2) air filter; (3) cylinder 1st stage; (4) cylinder 2nd stage; (5) cylinder 3rd stage; (6) intermediate cooler 1-2 stages; (7) intermediate cooler 2-3 stages; (8) intermediate separator; (9) final cooler; (10) safety valve 1st stage (8 bar); (11) safety valve 2nd stage (60-80 bar); (12) safety valve (230 or 300 bar); (13) filtering section P21; (14) removable cartridge; (15) manual condensate drain valves; (16) pressure maintenance valve (150 bar) – non-return valve; (17) high-pressure hoses; (18) charging valve; (19) pressure gauge; (20) safety valve (230 or 300 bar); (21) working pressure switch (additional option).

ribbed profile. The air cools from 80-120°C to values slightly (10-15°C) above the ambient air temperature. Cooled air enters the filtering section, where it undergoes final drying and cleaning from the oil/water dispersion. The filtering section consists of a housing with a safety valve and a replaceable cartridge inside the housing. Due to the design features of the filtering section housing, charging cylinders without the installed cartridge is impossible. The pressure in the filtering section housing is maintained at no less than 150±10 bars. This slows down the passage of compressed air through the cartridge, thereby increasing the cleaning efficiency and reducing the load on the last stage compression cylinder. Filling cylinders with compressed air is done through the charging device. For portable compressors, it consists of a high-pressure hose about 1-2 meters long and a valve with a mounting system for Din or Yoke cylinders (G 5/8 or stub thread). The charging device for stationary compressors is the so-called "flag valve," which provides either direct (without using a charging hose) or remote (with a charging hose) connection of cylinders to the compressor. Both devices allow disconnecting or connecting cylinders without turning off the compressor.

Disconnection of a properly functioning compressor and cessation of the process of charging cylinders with compressed air can be done either manually or automatically after reaching the required final pressure in the cylinders. To prevent overcharging cylinders beyond the standard pressure, the compressor is equipped with a final safety valve, which is installed on the filtering section and is set to a trigger pressure, usually 20-30 bars higher than the final pressure. Depending on the compressor model, the safety valve can be set (by prior order) to operate within a working pressure range of 155-420 bars. In practice, in the vast majority of cases, a working pressure of 230 or 300 bars is in demand. When the valve opens due to reaching the trigger pressure, the supply of compressed air to the cylinders stops. The compressor continues to operate, but the air is vented into the atmosphere.

If there is a need for frequent compressor transportation, attention should be paid to portable compressor stations. The most compact diving air compressors weigh around 50 kilograms. They deliver compressed air to cylinders at a rate of up to 100 liters per minute. These include Italian models like Coltri Sub MSN 6/EM (EM for electric type, SH for petrol type), Nardi Pacific 100, German models like Bauer Junior II, Poseidon Edition 100, I.D.E. Bavaria Fun 100, and others.

These compressors are compact with small dimensions and weight, simple and reliable in operation, and have a high degree of cleaning compressed air from harmful breathing impurities. They are equipped with a single-phase electric motor with a power of 2.2 kW and achieve a capacity of about 100 liters of air per hour. They deliver pressure at 225, 250, 275, or 300 bars, depending on the installed air release valve exceeding the pressure of this valve. The operating principles of all these compressors are the same, with minor variations. The working part of such compressors consists of three or four double-acting cylinders with a crank-connecting rod mechanism. It is not uncommon to encounter a three-stage, two-cylinder V-type air compressor based on the AK-150. The first and second stages are in the first cylinder, and the third is in the second cylinder. The working pressure of such a compressor is 150 bars. Portable compressors usually consist of a tubular steel frame on which the compressor, engine, air purification system, pressure gauge, emergency air release valve, and charging device are installed. Compressor cylinders and air in the intercooler are cooled by an air flow created by an axial-type fan pulley mounted on the compressor's crankshaft.

Using an air compressor

Each compressor comes with an operating manual that should be reviewed before use. The principles of preparation and startup for all compressors are almost the same with slight variations. Before starting the compressor, carefully inspect it, check the fastenings of the units, the oil level in the crankcase, and the reducer. On coolers and filters, open the blowdown valves. For water-cooled compressors, check the level and presence of cooling liquid. Then, start the engine and let the compressor run idle for 10 minutes, checking the operation of cooling and lubrication systems. In the absence of signs of incorrect operation, connect the cylinder intake valves and the compressor relief valve (if the compressor has a clutch, engage the clutch). Then close the relief valve and check the overall operation of the compressor. For the next few minutes, purge the entire system with air, close the blowdown valves, and start pumping air into the cylinders. During operation, monitor the oil level and pressure gauge readings. Before stopping the compressor, open the blowdown valves on the coolers and oil separator. Release the pressure in the compressor with the relief valve (and disengage the clutch, bringing the engine to idle). The compressor system is considered airtight if the readings on the control pressure gauge do not change significantly within five minutes after the engine stops. IMPORTANT TO REMEMBER!

When the compressor starts operating, the supply of compressed air to the cylinder does not happen immediately after switching on but is delayed by 1-2 minutes. During this time, the housing of the filtering section is charged with compressed air to a pressure of approximately 150 bars. Before filling air into the cylinder, before opening the cylinder valve, make sure that the pressure in the compressor system exceeds the residual air pressure in the cylinder being filled. For filling the cylinder, first open the valve of the compressor's charging device, then the valve of the cylinder. After the filling is complete, close the valves in reverse order – first, the cylinder valve, then the compressor valve. The air temperature in the cylinder is directly proportional to the pressure, and during the cylinder filling process, the cylinder heats up. After stopping the compressor, the air in the cylinder cools down, and its pressure drops slightly. Therefore, you can restart the compressor and "top up" the cylinder to the working pressure. Note: the "top-up" operation is allowed only once.

Always leave the compressor pressurized. Static pressure is not dangerous. If the compressor is not used often, it is recommended to run it for preventive maintenance for 30-40 minutes once a week.

Maintenance of the compressor and some types of routine work

For the reliable operation of a functioning compressor, its routine maintenance must be performed after a strictly defined number of operating hours. Such maintenance includes: checking the drive belt;

servicing the inlet air filter; checking for tightness; checking valves; replacing mineral oil or synthetic oil; cleaning filter compartments and replacing replaceable filtering elements; flushing intermediate separators; replacing valves; replacing pistons and rings.

The frequency of compressor oil replacement

The compressor crankcase is filled with oil ranging from 0.4 to 4.0 liters, depending on the model of the compressor block. The oil lubricates moving parts, improves friction, anti-corrosion, and anti-seizure properties. In a working compressor, the oil heats up to a temperature of 80°C. Mineral oil (catalog number N22138) requires planned replacement every 1000 hours of compressor operation but no less than once a year. Synthetic oil (catalog number N19745) requires planned replacement every 2000 hours of compressor operation but no less than once every 2 years. It is possible to switch from mineral oil N22138 to synthetic oil N19745 (or vice versa). Changing the oil type is recommended as follows: after completely draining the old type of oil and the initial filling of the new type of oil, let the compressor run for 100 hours, after which completely drain the oil and replace it with fresh oil of the same type. During further compressor operation, perform planned oil replacement according to the compressor manual. Ambient temperatures at which the compressor can be operated. High-pressure compressors are designed and guaranteed to operate at ambient temperatures from +5°C to 45°C. At these temperature conditions, the non-freezing of compressor oil N22138 in the compressor crankcase, the non-freezing of water condensate in intermediate separators, and the filtering section are ensured. Also, the overheating of the compressor is excluded (provided it is correctly installed). In conditions of elevated ambient temperatures (above +45°C), the use of compressors is possible but requires forced ventilation (cooling) of the working area - the room. In conditions of reduced ambient temperatures (below +5°C), the use of compressors is possible but requires an individual approach to each specific case. Compressor oil does not solidify up to -35°C, and therefore, it does not cause problems with starting the compressor in the cold. The problem arises with the freezing of water condensate, and there are two ways to solve this problem. The first way is to start the compressor in a heated room at +5°C, followed by taking the compressor outside, or ordering and purchasing a special modification of the compressor with electric heating and an insulated casing. Such modifications of compressors are adapted to operate at temperatures down to -40°C.

The oxygen compressor can be used to charge small air cylinders. Such a compressor is painted black, and an appropriate inscription is made. Using the compressor for alternating pumping of air and oxygen is prohibited!

Conservation of the compressor

If a prolonged interruption in operation is required, compressors can be stored under polyethylene film in a dry, warm, and dust-free room for 6-24 months without special conservation measures. The ten commandments for conserving the compressor or before conserving the compressor, it is necessary to:

1. Start the compressor for 10 minutes, ensure there are no leaks, and check and tighten all connections if necessary.
2. Drain the condensate from intermediate separators and the filtering section, without removing the filtering cartridges.
3. Release the pressure in the compressor through the charging device.
4. Disconnect the supply air pipes from the suction valves of all stages.
5. Start the compressor and inject a small amount (about 10 cm3) of compressor oil into the suction valves of all stages.
6. Shut down the compressor, remove the replaceable element of the air suction filter, close the suction throat of the filter with a cork or crumpled paper.
7. Close all valves.

8. Run the compressor for 10 minutes every 6 months of storage.

9. Replace mineral oil every year of storage, and synthetic oil every 2 years.

10. Before putting the compressor into operation, fill it with fresh oil.

§ 15. Air filters

As is known, for underwater breathing, a diver can only use clean and dried air. The content of harmful impurities in it at normal pressure should not exceed: carbon monoxide 0.02 mg/l, nitrogen oxides 0.04 mg/l, and total hydrocarbons 0.3 mg/l. An excess of carbon monoxide in the breathing air alters the hemoglobin level in the blood and is hazardous to the health and life of the diver. Therefore, one of the most critical components of any breathing air compressor is the oil-water separation and filtration system, denoted as 'P' (from English 'purification'). Inlet air filter. Air intake from the atmosphere is usually done at some distance from the compressor. Before entering the compressor block, an air filter is installed, which traps large particles and dust. The replaceable filter element should be visually checked at least once a week. If the filter element is contaminated, it can be rotated 90 degrees clockwise and reused, with a total allowance of 3 rotations. The replaceable element must be replaced no less than every 500 working hours or once a year.

During the compression of air, additional processes of air filtration and drying take place. The filtration process is preceded by intermediate and final moisture-oil separation. The intermediate oil-water separator is designed as a separate unit and operates on the principle of a centrifuge, effectively separating impurities from the air. The atmospheric air filtration system is based on the use of multi-stage oil-water separators and special replaceable filtering cartridges. Each replaceable cartridge is layered with special materials that absorb residual moisture, oil, and other impurities before supplying compressed air to the breathing cylinders. The layers are separated by felt gaskets. The main fillers of the cartridges are molecular sieve (MS), activated carbon (AC), hopcalite (HP).

MS is a fine-grained substance of light beige color with increased absorbent properties, absorbing water molecules in large quantities (up to 20% of its own weight). Unlike water molecules, oil molecules do not penetrate the granules of MS and settle on their surfaces, gradually forming an impermeable shell for water molecules, thereby reducing the cartridge's absorption properties. AC is granulated activated carbon. The size of the granules is optimally selected. Activated carbon cleans the air from oil vapors that have passed through MS, aerosols, organic substances, hydrocarbons, volatile impurities, and gases such as chlorine, etc. HP is a necessary filler for cartridges used in compressors with internal combustion engines. It has an oxidizing ability to convert carbon monoxide molecules into carbon dioxide molecules ($CO > CO_2$).

Air from the last stage of the compressor enters a pipe closed from above, located between the concentric walls of the filter. Through an opening in the wall of the pipe, air is blown onto the inner wall of the filter. Thanks to this, the air is brought into a rotational motion. Water and oil microdroplets are dispersed by centrifugal force, settling on the inner wall of the filter and draining into the condensate collector, which is removed by the drainage system. After that, the air enters directly into the filtering section of the cartridge, consisting of several sequentially filtering elements. The first of which is the oil-water separator, which cleans the air from oils and moisture by an adsorbent called the 'molecular sieve.' After the molecular sieve, activated carbon is placed, which absorbs oil vapors and harmful gaseous substances, or purification is carried out by the method of catalytic combustion of harmful impurities (oil vapors, hydrocarbons, and carbon monoxide) in elements consisting of silica gel and hopcalite. The hopcalite layer, located after activated carbon, converts carbon monoxide into carbon dioxide. The layers of activated carbon and hopcalite are separated by a layer of molecular sieve. The filtration is completed by purifying the air from solid microparticles, which is provided by the molecular sieve or lime chemical absorbent and hygroscopic cotton. These elements purify the air from carbon dioxide and nitrogen oxides. Carefully selected components of the filtering section, the size of their granules, and their mutual arrangement ensure maximum air purification and a long service life of the filtering section.

Depending on the compressor's performance and the divers' needs, the following types of filtering cartridges are used: P21, P31, P41, P61, etc. When using original filter cartridges, it ensures reliable air preparation for breathing according to the international standard EN 12021-61. With proper maintenance and installation of filtering elements, according to the operating manual of the compressor used, if the concentration of CO_2 in the intake air does not exceed the specified regulatory values for breathing air, the amount of air that can be charged into the cylinders is as follows:

Filter Section Type	Compressor Performance, l/min	Nominal Pressure, bar	Cartridge Service Life, m3	Number of 10L Cylinders (Ambient Temp=10°C) at 200 bar and 300 bar
P21	Up to 250	140 - 350	160	80
P31	Up to 350	140 - 350	725	360
P41	Up to 450	90 - 420	1900	950
P61	Up to 680	90 - 420	2950	1470

Section P21 is the most compact and simple. It is installed on compressors with a capacity of up to 250 l/min. The cartridge is designed for charging up to 80 standard 10L cylinders at a pressure of

200 bar. Section P31 has a cartridge life of up to 360 standard cylinders. The P31 system can be installed on compressors with a capacity of up to 350 l/min. Section P41 is used for stationary compressors with a capacity of up to 450 l/min. Cartridge life is up to 950 standard cylinders. Section P61 is designed for compressors with a capacity of up to 680 l/min. Charging up to 1470 standard cylinders is possible. The cartridge is a replaceable element, and its operational life (volume of purified atmospheric air) is limited.

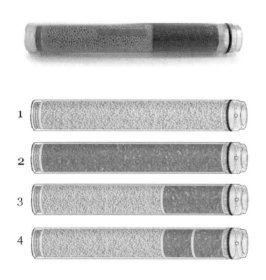

Fig. 207. Section P21

To monitor the condition of the cartridge, various methods can be used, namely:

Regularly weigh the working cartridge. The critical weight of a fully depleted cartridge is indicated on its packaging. If the weight exceeds the allowed limit, the cartridge should be replaced.

Keep a record of the compressor's working time and count the number of charged cylinders. Considering the compressor's performance, approximately estimate the volume of atmospheric air passed through the cartridge.

Install a control sensor B-TIMER on compressors with P21, P31, P41 filter sections, which counts the total compressor operating time and reminds you in a timely manner of the need for urgent cartridge replacement.

Install the electronic control system ECOSAFE / SECURUS on P41, P61 filtering sections, which will warn in advance about the need to replace the cartridge and will shut down the compressor only when it is fully saturated with harmful substances. This system allows using the cartridge's resource to 100%.

Use the air quality control system and gas analyzer Aerotest or its analog. The cleaning ability of the filtering section components largely depends on the degree of saturation with water. Therefore, control over the moisture of the filtering section is required.

Air filters for old-model compressor installations

Special air filter FBS-55 is used at air pressure not exceeding 55 bar. It is designed to purify air from oil, dust, and other harmful substances, and is a small cylinder with spherical bottoms. The removable upper bottom houses a pressure gauge, safety valve, and a tee with two outlets for hoses. Inside the casing, there are two metal grates, and the space between them is filled with metal steel shavings that separate solid particles and moisture from the air. In the upper cavity of the casing, there are four gas-proof boxes BSMO-2, which trap harmful gaseous and fine mechanical inclusions. The lower bottom has an air outlet horn ending inside the casing with a reflector and outside with a valve. At the bottom, there is a drain valve for purging the filter and releasing accumulated moisture. Air enters the filter through a hose, and the pressure in the filter is regulated by the valve. The assembled filter weighs 35.5 kg.

High-pressure filter FVD-200 is designed to purify air from harmful impurities during cylinder filling and is designed for pressures up to 200 bar. Inside the casing, there are two cartridges with filtering substances connected in a common disassembled block. The lower cartridge is filled with a layer of small aluminum rings (8 cm), vegetable fibers (5 cm), and silica gel (30 cm). The upper cartridge consists of a layer of silica gel (10 cm), activated carbon (20 cm), lime chemical absorbent (10 cm), and vegetable fibers (5 cm). For discharging condensate, oil, and moisture to the lower part of the filter,

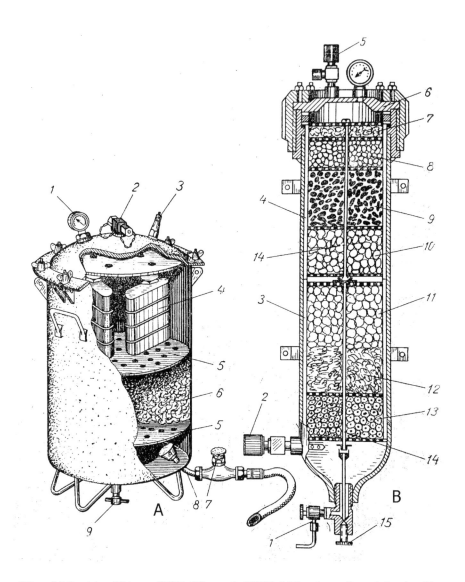

Fig. 208. Air filters PFS-55 and FVT-200. A – Special air filter PFS-55: (1) – pressure gauge; (2) – tee; (3) – safety valve; (4) – gas-proof box; (5) – play 6 iron shavings; (7) – valve; (8) – horn; (9) – drain valve; B – High-pressure filter FVT-200: (1) – drain device; (2) – intake valve; (3) – lower cassette; (4) – upper cassette; (5) – exhaust valve; (6) filter cover; (7) – vegetable fiber; (8) – chemical absorbent; (9) – activated carbon; (10), (11) – silica gel; (12) – vegetable fiber; (13) – aluminum rings; (13) – aluminum rings.

a drainage device is provided. The control valve is intended to determine contamination of silica gel with oil, which, when the layer is heavily saturated, flows down the pipe. To release accumulated condensate, it is necessary to open the valves of the drainage device, blow the lower part of the filter with compressed air. To prevent blowing out the filler from the cassettes and improve the condensation of oil and water vapors in the filtering layers, the filter's inlet connector is equipped with a throttling washer. The filter can operate without recharging for up to 300 hours, and the weight of the loaded filter is 170 kg.

The high-pressure air purification block (PB 200) includes FVD-200 and an attachment to the filter that includes: hopcalite cartridge, air heater, receiver, refrigerator, connecting fittings, and control-measuring instruments. The throughput capacity of the cleaning block is 1700 l/min, working pressure is 200 bar, and the weight is 420 kg.

The portable high-pressure air cleaning block (PB 200) consists of an air heater, fittings, a panel with control-measuring instruments, and cartridges of HPI chemical absorbent and hopcalite. All units are attached to a common frame and placed in a metal case, the front and rear covers of which are hinged for ease of maintenance. The weight of the block in the loaded state is 30 kg. The HPI cartridge is used to purify air from carbon dioxide (CO_2). The hopcalite cartridge serves to purify air from carbon monoxide (CO) and some other impurities (oil vapors, certain hydrocarbons, and other harmful chemicals). Hopcalite, at high temperatures, has sorption properties. Cartridges for sorbents are steel cylindrical vessels, the lower part of which has connectors for filling, and the upper part has tees for supplying and discharging purified air. The air heater heats the air to a temperature of 100-120°C for subsequent heating of hopcalite to the working temperature. It consists of a flat coil through which air passes and two tubular heating elements placed between two aluminum plates in special grooves. The panel with control-measuring instruments. It includes a pressure gauge for monitoring air pressure in the apparatus's filled cylinders, two shut-off valves for admitting air to the portable block and releasing purified air to the charged apparatus cylinders, a signal lamp for monitoring the operation of the air heater, a plug socket for connecting the block to the electrical network.

Operation of PB-200

Before starting the cleaning block, open the rear and front covers. Then, using a connecting tube, connect the block to the compressor and plug it into the electrical network. When the heater is switched on, simultaneously open the air inlet valve and slightly open the exhaust valve to allow hot air to pass through the cartridge during hopcalite warming. The end of hopcalite warming is determined by the first turning off of the control lamp on the panel. It is connected to the network in series with the heating elements of the air heater and subsequently serves to monitor their operation. After the hopcalite is heated, the filled cylinder is connected to the nozzle using a charging tube, the air outlet valve is fully opened, and charging is carried out. The pressure is monitored by the pressure gauge installed on the panel. The air passes sequentially through the cartridge with lime chemical absorbent, the air heater, and the cartridge with hopcalite.

After completing the filling, close the air outlet valve and disconnect the filled cylinder. Then release the air from the filling tube, disconnect the filter from the power source, and blow it with air. Afterward, close the air inlet and outlet valves. Remove the filling and connecting tubes, and close the connectors with blind nuts. After the block cools down, close the covers of its casing. To change the contents of the cartridges, open the rear cover, remove the half-ring securing the cartridges, disconnect the tubes. Remove the plugs' nuts from the cartridge connectors and empty the used chemical substances. Then flush the internal spaces with warm water and blow with compressed air until all moisture is removed. To fill the cartridges, HPI is used – 1.4 kg and hopcalite – 1.8 kg, which should be sifted through a fine sieve before filling to remove dust. During operation, keep track of the cartridge resource, based on the volume of filtered air in filled cylinders. Cartridge replacement is required after processing 300 m^3.

§ 16. Oxygen compressors

Oxygen compressors are designed to fill small-capacity cylinders of diving apparatuses to pressures of 15-200 bar by bypassing and subsequently transferring oxygen from transport cylinders.

These compressors are produced in two types: with manual drive and electric drive. All of them are two-cylinder, single-stage, plunger compressors with a toggle mechanism.

In terms of construction, oxygen compressors consist of a cast-iron frame mounted on a wooden base, two horizontally arranged cylinders, pipelines, and a lever. Inside the cylinders, there is a plunger rod, and valve boxes are screwed onto the external ends. In the valve boxes, which are connected by suction and pressure pipelines,

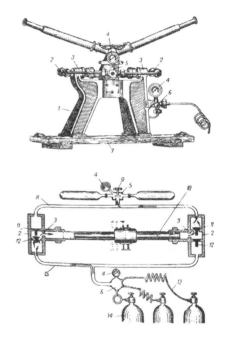

Fig. 209. Oxygen compressor operating diagram:(1) – frame; (2) – valve boxes; (3) – cylinders; (4) – pressure gauges; (5) – manifold; (6) – star; (7) – base; (8) – pressure pipe; (9) – manifold shut-off valve; (10) – plunger rod; (11) – compression valves; (12) – suction valves; (13) – coil; (14) – transport cylinders with oxygen; (15) – suction pipe.

suction and compression valves are paired and placed. At the entrance to the valve box, there is a mesh filter that traps solid particles. The connections of the valve boxes are sealed with fiber gaskets. The suction pipe is connected to the intake star, which has five outlets. A pipe connecting the star to the suction pipe is connected to the lower outlet, and a pressure gauge showing the pressure in the transport cylinder is connected to the upper one.

The remaining outlets are intended for connecting transport cylinders using coil hoses with nuts. The pressure pipeline is connected to the manifold, which has a valve and three outlets (for a pressure gauge and two small-capacity cylinders). The plunger rod is made of stainless steel and sealed with three leather cuffs. These cuffs are put on brass rings and compressed with sealing bushings and lock nuts. The suction and compression valves are of the disc type, arranged to allow oxygen to pass only in the direction of the manifold. The compressor is operated by a rocking (toggle) mechanism. During rocking, the plunger rod performs reciprocating movements. Compression of oxygen occurs in one cylinder or the other, and it is pumped through the manifold into the cylinders.

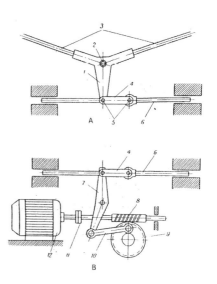

Fig. 210. Oxygen compressor drive schemes:
A – manual drive; B – electric drive; (1) – lever; (2) – lever axis; (3) – handle; (4) – rings; (5) – ring axes; (6) – plunger rod; (7) – lever; (8) – worm gear; (9) – gear wheel; (10) – connecting rod; (11) – elastic coupling; (12) – electric motor.

Using the oxygen compressor

Before starting the compressor, it is necessary to wash, degrease, and wipe with a clean rag all its fittings, as well as tools. The compressor is carefully inspected, and its operation is checked. To check the tightness of the entire system, open the valve of the transport cylinder connected to the star. The free outlets and the manifold valve should be closed. (It is recommended to use at least three transport cylinders). Wet the system connections with soapy water and, by gas bubbles, identify areas of poor sealing. All detected malfunctions must be corrected. Before starting work and during oxygen pumping, every hour of intensive work, the plunger rod must be lubricated with a water-glycerin mixture. A mixture of 50% glycerin and 50% distilled water is used for lubricating the compressor. Due to the explosiveness and rapid combustion of oxygen, the use of any other lubricant is not allowed. Small cylinders are filled in the following order. After the entire system is connected and checked for serviceability and tightness, proceed to pump oxygen. To do this, sequentially open the valves of the transport cylinder with the lowest pressure, the compressor manifold, and the cylinders being filled. In this case, gas from the transport cylinder will flow into the small cylinders by gravity until the pressure is equalized between them. Then, they pump them with the compressor until the pressure in the filled cylinders exceeds the pressure in the used transport cylinder by two times. After that, close the valve of the first transport cylinder and open the valve of the second transport cylinder, where the pressure of oxygen should be higher than in the cylinders being filled, and continue pumping as in the first case. If the pressure in the small cylinders has not reached 200 bar, connect the third transport cylinder to the work, and the pumping process is repeated in the same order until the pressure in the filled cylinders rises to the norm. After that, close all the valves. In the absence of a compressor or its malfunction, small cylinders can only be charged by bypassing oxygen from the battery of transport cylinders. It is recommended to make a battery of three cylinders with a pressure of 200 bar or five with a pressure of 150 bar. After charging, disconnect the coil hoses, wipe all accessories and the compressor with a clean rag, and place the cylinders with capped outlets back in their places.

§ 17. Equipment for preparing breathing gas mixtures

Pressure-reducing devices are designed to reduce pressure and ensure a constant flow (or pressure) of the supplied gas. The main technical data for reducers used in diving gas systems.

Fig. 211. Equipment for gas mix preparation

Gas distribution devices are devices designed to regulate the supply of air to divers based on quantity and specified pressure, as well as to control gas consumption during diver descents. Gas distribution devices include: air distribution diving panels; control panels for deep-sea stations; control panels for decompression (recompression) chambers.

Mixing devices are designed for the preparation of two- and three-component gas mixtures supplied to divers. Air (previously purified from harmful breathing impurities), helium, medical oxygen, and nitrogen are used to prepare gas mixtures. In diving practice, the method of preliminary preparation by mixing single-component gases in containers (cylinders) and the method of dynamic gas mixing in special gas mixers during diver descents are applied. Typical diagrams of installations for preparing gas mixtures are shown in the figure.

This scheme is used for preparing heliox-oxygen mixtures (HOM) with a low oxygen content (3-7%) and air-helium mixtures (AHM). To prepare HOM, oxygen is transferred from an oxygen cylinder into a helium-filled cylinder to a specified pressure. The advantages of the scheme include the absence of complex devices and ease of installation. However, drawbacks include: the extended gas mixing duration (up to 48 hours); the need for special cylinders for mixing, as contaminating helium cylinders with oxygen is prohibited; inability to alter the mixture composition without purging the previously prepared mixture, resulting in significant gas losses; a large number of oxygen cylinders is required for high-pressure mixtures due to high residual pressure in the cylinders. The second option is more costly and is used to prepare heliox-oxygen, air-helium, and nitrogen-heliox-oxygen mixtures with various ratios of single-component gases. To prepare a mixture in a high-pressure transport cylinder, gases constituting the desired gas mixture are sequentially introduced until the calculated pressure is reached. When preparing gas mixtures, it is essential to follow the sequence of gas supply: air-helium: helium + air; heliox-oxygen: helium + oxygen; nitrogen-heliox-oxygen: helium + oxygen + nitrogen. This gas mixture creation method has significant advantages: gas mixing time in the transport cylinder is about 20 minutes; contamination of transport helium cylinders is eliminated; residual gas pressure in transport cylinders is 15-20 kgf/cm^2, increasing gas utilization efficiency to 0.9-0.94; allows storing single-component gases in stationary containers, avoiding labor-intensive loading and unloading of transport cylinders; enables changing gas mixtures in the transport cylinder without purging a previously prepared mixture of specific composition. Drawbacks include: inability to change the mixture composition during a diver's descent; the presence of large volumes and dimensions of cylinders for gas mixing. The third gas mixing option is used to prepare two- and three-component gas mixtures and includes booster compressors in the scheme, ensuring high gas utilization efficiency (0.90-0.94). The gas mixer allows preparation and alteration of mixtures during descent, and gas analyzers provide continuous monitoring of the oxygen and helium composition in the gas mixture. The system provides: preparation and supply of one-, two-, and three-component gas mixtures to two divers at pressures of 1-35 kgf/cm²; supply of an emergency (pre-prepared) mixture to two divers at pressures of 1-35 kgf/cm²; supply of air to two divers at pressures of 1-30 kgf/cm² from the ship's medium-pressure air network (30 kgf/cm²). When preparing gas mixtures, strict compliance with oxygen handling requirements is essential, primarily periodic degreasing of oxygen pipelines, and when transferring oxygen, slowly and smoothly opening the valves; the oxygen flow rate in pipelines should not exceed permissible values.

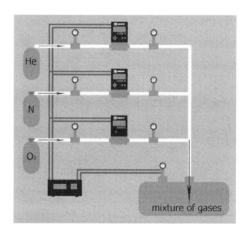

Fig. 212. Scheme for gas mix preparation

§ 18. Decompression and recompression chambers (Barochambers)

Decompression and recompression chambers are designed for conducting therapeutic recompression for specific diver-related illnesses and decompression for divers at the surface. By purpose, chambers are classified as decompression, flow-decompression, and therapeutic recompression. However, since they do not have significant differences, these chambers are commonly referred to with the general term "barochambers". Each underwater dive carries the risk

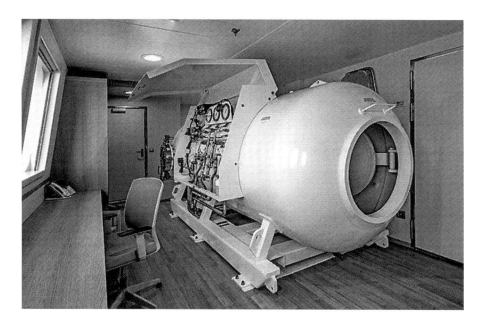

Fig. 213. Decompression chamber

of decompression sickness. Although numerous decompression tables and algorithms for calculating tissue saturation with various gases have been developed today, and underwater computers monitor divers' adherence to these calculations during their dives, the risk of decompression illness exists due to the physiological peculiarities of each individual.

The "Unified Rules of Occupational Safety in Diving Operations" require the presence of a decompression chamber at the dive site when diving exceeds a depth of 12 meters or the ability to transport the affected individual to it within an hour.

Structurally, a decompression chamber must satisfy the following requirements: internal working pressure of at least 10 bar; the doctor's ability to enter and exit the chamber without disrupting the recompression regime; pressure ascent rate of 4-5 bar within one minute; the capability to perform various therapeutic procedures; the ability for the patient and doctor to breathe in the chamber with various gas mixtures.

Barochambers differ in size, the number of compartments, hatches, and volume. In most cases, barochambers are closed cylindrical steel vessels with spherical bottoms, with one or two compartments connected by hatches for divers' entry and exit. Each chamber must have windows for observing the patient and be equipped with a system to increase the air pressure in the chamber to 10 bar and decrease it to atmospheric pressure. Barochambers are also equipped with communication devices and instruments for monitoring gas environment parameters (pressure gauges, gas analyzers, and other equipment).

Conventionally, barochambers are divided into two types: stationary and transport. Stationary barochambers have a diameter of 1 to 3 meters, 2-3 compartments, and their weight can reach several tons. Transport barochambers are intended for the temporary placement of the affected individual and transporting them to a stationary barochamber for a complete course of treatment. In modern barochambers, a transport barochamber is connected to a stationary one using a special bayonet-type docking node, one part of which is located on the stationary barochamber, and the other on the transport one. This type of connection is used for docking spacecraft, submarines, and diving bells.

Fig. 214. Barochamber

The main difference between these two types of barochambers lies in their mass-dimensional parameters. The diameter of transport barochambers does not exceed 1200 mm, and the weight is 1200 kg, and these dimensions apply to chambers mounted on chassis. Folding transport barochambers, made of lightweight high-strength materials, are also considered transport barochambers. Such chambers do not have docking nodes for attachment to stationary barochambers, as their small diameter allows them to be introduced through standard hatches of stationary barochambers.

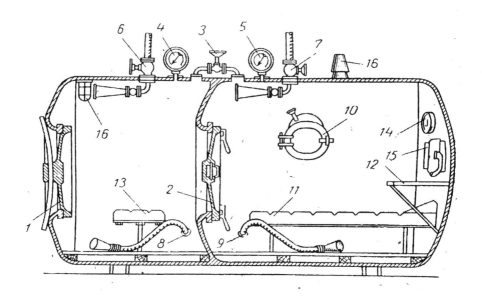

Fig. 215. Large recompression chamber device: (1), (2) - hatches; (3) - pressure equalization valve; (4), (5) - pressure gauges; (6), (7) - upper nipples; (8), (9) - lower nipples; (10) - airlock; (11) - bunk; (12) - table; (13) - seat; (14) - internal pressure gauge; (15) - telephone; (16) - external electric light.

A large recompression chamber is a robust steel cylinder with spherical bottoms. Illuminators for observation and external lighting are installed in the housing. Inside the cylinder, a spherical partition divides it into two unequal compartments, which are hermetically isolated from each other and can be under different pressures. For entry, the compartments are equipped with two hatches with airtight covers that open inward. The small compartment (ante-chamber) is for the transfer of divers or a doctor when transitioning to the large compartment, where pressure exists. The large compartment is a chamber where therapeutic recompression and decompression of divers are carried out. To transition from the ante-chamber to the large compartment and vice versa, the pressure in the ante-chamber is equalized with the main compartment. A pressure relief device is used to equalize pressure in the compartments. Pressure in the compartments is monitored by pressure gauges. Safety valves on the external part of the chamber automatically release pressure. Gas analyzers for oxygen and carbon dioxide continuously monitor the gas environment parameters in the barochamber. An emergency signal is triggered if the oxygen and carbon dioxide content exceeds permissible limits. Advanced gas analyzers include temperature and humidity sensors.

The breathing gas mixture enters the barochamber compartments through special nipples located on the chamber's ceiling. For periodic ventilation of the compartments, the breathing gas mixture is discharged through other nipples located at the bottom of the compartments. In some chambers, additional hatches for transferring medicines, food, and other items to the chamber without reducing the pressure in the compartment are installed in the side or bottom of the large compartment. Inside the barochamber, there is a removable flooring, a bunk, a table, one or two seats, an internal pressure gauge, a telephone, and external lighting devices. In older model chambers, the lights were inside the barochamber. On the external surface of the barochamber, there was a cable entry housing for electric lighting with a control device for the tightness of the lights. Steam heaters and sealed electric heaters up to 500W are used to heat divers in cold weather. All electrical equipment is spark-explosion-fireproof, and the power supply voltage does not exceed 24 volts. During breathing in a closed space like a barochamber, the concentration of carbon dioxide increases, and the percentage of oxygen in the breathing gas mixture decreases. To remove harmful substances from the breathing gas mixture and increase the percentage of oxygen in the breathing gas mixture, barochamber ventilation is conducted. The air volume required for ventilation depends not on the chamber's volume but only on the intensity of breathing (lung ventilation rate) and the number of people inside the barochamber (approximately 45 liters/min per person at rest). Ventilation in an open system is carried out approximately every 12 minutes. Such processes require significant air reserves and powerful compressors. Thus, about 1200 cubic meters of air are consumed in total for one treatment cycle (under the longest recompression treatment regimen lasting about 61 hours).

Some barochambers use semi-closed ventilation systems. When using such systems, air is constantly supplied to the barochamber through special nozzles based on the number of people inside. Passing through the nozzles, air goes through cartridges with a chemical absorbent called HPI, which absorbs carbon dioxide. The cartridge designs act as injectors facilitating the circulation of the gas environment in the barochamber. To prevent pressure buildup in the barochamber, there is an automatic pressure relief valve that maintains constant pressure. The advantages of the semi-closed ventilation system include automatic operation during one stage of decompression, and the patient uses significantly less air consumption (12 l/min). The closed ventilation system of the barochamber is based on the removal of carbon dioxide by special air purification units (scrubbers) equipped with HPI chemical absorbent (sodalime, sodasorb, or similar). Oxygen is supplied to the barochamber through a flowmeter strictly in quantities necessary for normal breathing. Thus, there is no air consumption for barochamber ventilation. This is crucial for transport barochambers as it eliminates the need for a large number of heavy air cylinders, reduces the system's weight significantly, and increases autonomy. Since pure oxygen is supplied to the barochamber's gas environment, there are increased safety requirements for all barochamber equipment, including the telephone station, electric motors, lights, and other equipment.

Using the barochamber

During underwater operations, the barochamber must be ready for use. Preparing the barochamber for work involves a thorough check of its devices, including checking the tightness of the barochamber and its instruments. To perform such a check, first, open the entrance hatch, turn on the lights and telephone, and, if necessary, turn on the heating. Inventory is introduced simultaneously, opening the air supply valves to the compartments, and the functionality of the air supply system is checked. Then, close the hatches of the barochamber, and increase its internal pressure to 2-3 bars. Possible leaks are visually identified by listening for the sound of escaping air or by applying soapy water and checking for bubbles. Check the operation of the pressure relief valve and bypass valve. In chambers where ventilation is conducted in an open system, the operation of air compressors and filters is checked. In the absence of malfunctions, the chamber is considered ready for recompression (decompression) procedures.

Conducting recompression (decompression) is carried out in the following order. Divers are brought up from a certain depth, their gear is removed, and they are placed in the barochamber. The pressure of the air mixture in the chamber is increased to the pressure corresponding to the depth from which the diver was raised. During recompression, the compartment with the diver in the barochamber is periodically ventilated. During the procedure, divers are strictly prohibited from smoking or igniting a fire. If something needs to be introduced into the chamber during operation, a special airlock or front compartment of the chamber is used. To do this, the pressure in the airlock is equalized with atmospheric pressure by opening the valve, and the required item is placed in the airlock. After that, the external hatch and the airlock valve are closed, the pressure is raised to the

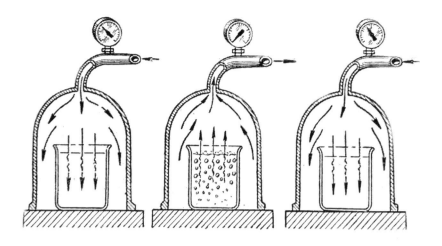

Fig. 216. Decompression and recompression processes

pressure of the compartment with the diver, and the valve equalizing the internal pressure between the compartments is opened. After pressure equalization, the internal hatch between the compartments is opened, and the delivered item is removed. The internal hatch and the valve are closed again, and the air from the airlock is released into the atmosphere. As the diver undergoes recompression, the pressure in the chamber is gradually reduced to atmospheric pressure (using data from decompression tables). Then the diver exits the barochamber. Oxygen decompression in the barochamber is carried out using isolating breathing apparatus. In some cases, when the diver's condition is severe during recompression in the chamber, a doctor may be present, and the inhalation method of oxygen recompression is applied using a medical inhaler. With this method of oxygen recompression, oxygen is exhaled into the chamber and accumulates in it, so the chamber is ventilated to ensure that the oxygen content in the air does not exceed 25%.

During the operation of the hyperbaric chamber, fire safety rules must be observed. Individuals inside the hyperbaric chamber are strictly prohibited from: lighting an open flame and having sources of fire; smoking and having any smoking mixtures; signaling by striking steel objects against the chamber's body; wearing shoes with metallic soles and toes; using the telephone inductor for call signals; using and having any electronic devices and gadgets, including radios, fitness trackers, watches, headphones, mobile phones, tablets, and laptops; having flammable liquids or items soaked in petroleum products. Hyperbaric chambers are tested in action once a year with the maximum working pressure of air, and every ten years, they undergo hydraulic tests at one and a half times the working pressure with an examination of the body's condition. Under test pressure, the chamber is held for five minutes, then the pressure is reduced to the working pressure, during which an inspection and tapping of welded seams with a hammer is carried out. If condensation and small drops appear in the welded seams, the chamber is not allowed to operate until welding defects are rectified and retesting is done.

§ 19. Monitoring and measuring devices

Monitoring and measuring devices are designed to determine the technical parameters of diving equipment during routine work, measure gas pressures in tanks and gas system pipelines, determine the composition of gas mixtures, control the quality of chemical absorbents and regenerative substances, and provide underwater orientation for divers.

The verification and control setup is intended for checking all parameters of breathing apparatus, anti-gas suit check valves, and injector-regenerative equipment. The testing setup allows determining: the tightness of low and high-pressure apparatus cavities; the breathing resistance of the apparatus system; the supply (passing capacity) of the manual starter (bypass); the resistance and opening pressure of anti-gas suit check valves; the tightness of regenerative cartridge bodies; the tightness of the inlet and outlet valves; the setting pressure of the reducer; the start of the breathing apparatus opening (automatic bypass); the resistance of the breathing apparatus; the opening pressure of the reducer's relief valve; the constant supply and setting pressure of the reducer; the amount of injection and the resistance of the injector-regenerative system of diving equipment.

The verification setup includes: (1) oxygen mechanism of the breathing apparatus; (2) control manometer; (3) rubber tube; (4) rheometer-manometer; (5) scale for oxygen delivery rate.

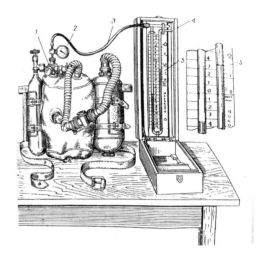

Fig. 217. Determination of the oxygen delivery rate by a rheometer-manometer

The three-scale rheometer-manometer includes: (1) large-diameter capillary; (2) two-way valve; (3) small-diameter capillary; (4) connecting tube; (5) oxygen delivery scale ranging from zero to four liters per minute; (6) oxygen delivery scale ranging from zero to four hundred cubic centimeters per minute; (7) resistance scale; (8) V-shaped tube; (9) glass reservoir; (10) rubber tube. The rheometer-manometer is designed for measuring small gas flows and pressures with an accuracy of ±2%. Measurement limits for gas flow rate: 0.5–3.0 l/min, pressure: 1–30 mm water column. Dimensions: 300x150x510 mm; weight approximately 2 kg.

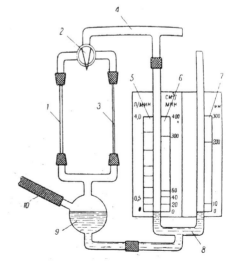

Fig. 218. Three scale rheometer manometer

Fig. 219. Gas analyzer

The Hempel gas analyzer is the simplest volumetric gas analysis device designed to measure the concentration of oxygen in gas mixtures with an accuracy of ±0.1%. The device operates based on the principle of absorbing oxygen from the analyzed gas mixture into an absorbent solution and comparing the final volume of this mixture with the initial volume. Dimensions: 250x100x135 mm; weight approximately 1 kg.

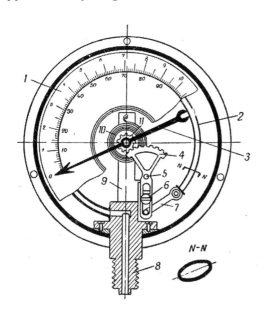

Fig. 220. Diver's pressure gauge

Gauge structure: (1) scales; (2) tube; (3) arrow; (4) toothed sector; (5) toothed sector axis; (6) screw; (7) rod; (8) nipple; (9) stand; (10) spiral spring; (11) gear.

Diver's pressure gauges are intended for determining the pressure of air, oxygen, and gas mixtures in cylinders, pipelines, and diving hoses, in decompression chambers, and other diving devices. The working measurement range of diving pressure gauges equals the upper limit of measurement. Gauges are manufactured for operation in the air environment with temperatures from 0 to +30°C, excluding the possibility of access inside the device. All gauges designed to work with oxygen have the inscription "Oxygen - Oil Hazard" on the dial. Wrist diving depth gauges (depth indicators) are designed to determine the diver's depth underwater with independent equipment.

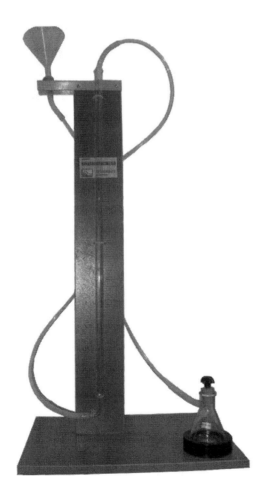

The calorimeter is a volumetric gas analysis device used to determine the saturation level and ultimate absorption capacity of the chemical substance (HPI) and regenerative substance. The method is based on measuring the volume of carbon dioxide released from the chemical substance by hydrochloric acid solution. The released carbon dioxide is collected in a graduated burette, and its volume is determined using a liquid-filled vessel. Dimensions: 360x200x120 mm; weight approximately 2.5 kg.

Fig. 221. Calorimeter

Checkpoint questions for chapter four:

1. What devices exist for lowering and raising divers?

2. What devices do you know for moving divers underwater?

3. How is an underwater tow vehicle constructed?

4. What types of tow vehicles do you know?

5. In what ways do divers move underwater using underwater tow vehicles, in other words, how is diver towing carried out?

6. What types of diving compressors are used in diving?

7. How is an oxygen diving compressor constructed?

8. What are the basic safety rules when working with an oxygen compressor?

9. What means are used to purify air for filling its cylinders?

10. How is a high-pressure air compressor constructed?

11. What is the frequency of changing compressor oil in high-pressure compressors, and how is the switch from synthetic to mineral oils, or vice versa, carried out?

12. How is a low-pressure air compressor constructed?

13. How is a medium-pressure air compressor constructed?

14. How is a lightweight diving pump constructed?

15. How is an air filter constructed?

16. What means are used for underwater lighting on ships and vessels?

17. What does underwater visibility depend on?

18. What are hyperbaric chambers used for?

19. How is a hyperbaric chamber constructed?

20. Name the principles of operation of reducing, mixing, and gas distribution devices.

V CHAPTER
DIVING DESCENTS

Chapter fiveth of this manual delves into the intricate aspects of organizing and executing diving descents. The chapter details types of diving signals, encompassing visual signals and those communicated through rope pulls. Basic knowledge will teach you how to use decompression tables, following principles standard across international diving schools. Practical considerations, such as the assembly of scuba gear, proper weight belt usage, and techniques for clearing a diver's mask, are addressed. Guidelines for achieving neutral buoyancy are provided, enhancing divers' proficiency in fundamental skills. Techniques for diving in various challenging environments, such as narrow spaces, under distressed ships, in swift currents, smoke-filled ship compartments, and under ice, are also discussed. The information contained in this chapter equips divers with a comprehensive understanding of the procedures, equipment, and safety measures essential for successful and safe underwater descents.

§ 20. Organization of diving descents

Diving descent is a set of actions ensuring the safe immersion of a diver to depth, the execution of underwater work, and the ascent of the diver to the surface. Diving descents are an integral part of various diving operations and are carried out according to a general plan of work execution. Proper and clear organization of diving descents is a guarantee of diver safety.

The organization of diving descents should be carried out following the sequence of actions (10 commandments), during which one should:

1. Study the nature of the work and the conditions in which they are to be performed.

2. Familiarize oneself with the weather forecast.

3. Develop a plan of organizational activities.

4. Determine the necessary personnel, specifying performers, deadlines, and individuals overseeing the execution and distribution of responsibilities of those involved in the dive, as well as technical support personnel.

5. Select, prepare, and equip the location for the diving descent. To do this, measure the depth, current speed, and water temperature.

6. Establish the composition of the diving equipment, descent support and gas supply means, necessary tools, devices, and equipment, taking into account calculations of consumables such as the required amount of air (gas), chemicals, and others.

7. Conduct a working check of the diving equipment, tools, and diving gear. This includes checking the serviceability and completeness of the main and backup diving equipment and tools, descent and gas supply means.

8. Ensure safety measures for the diving descent, check the completeness of medical supplies, and the operability of the decompression chamber.

9. At the diving descent site, arrange a place for the diver to dress.

10. Ensure the diver's safe descent to depth, with proper communication support from the surface team during the diver's underwater stay. In case of necessity, supply the diver with everything necessary to perform the planned underwater work. Followed by the diver's ascent to the surface, undressing, and cleaning of the diving equipment.

By their nature, descents can be shallow - up to 12 meters, medium - up to 40 meters, and deep - over 40 meters. Descents to depths exceeding 20 meters and training descents in regenerative equipment must be equipped with a decompression chamber located at the descent site or in the nearest area. In the latter case, it is necessary to know the location of the chamber, establish visual, telephone, or radio communication with it, and have transportation (car, boat) ready to transport the affected diver. If the chamber is single-compartment, the descent of the next diver is allowed only after the previous diver has exited it.

Approval and supervision of diving descents

Diving descents are carried out under the supervision of the senior diving instructor, appointed from the senior personnel of the stations or senior diving groups, or diving specialists, with overall guidance from the head of the diving service or the ship's captain. Diving stations that are to conduct diving descents must be fully equipped with personnel (divers and support staff), as well as diving and medical equipment. According to general rules of the diving service, only individuals who have undergone special training, are trained in the use of the corresponding diving equipment and equipment, are familiar with safety measures for diving work, and are deemed fit for underwater work based on their health, are allowed to participate in underwater descents.

Apprentice divers are allowed to practical descents at training diving stations under the guidance of instructor-divers after passing an examination to test their knowledge of the curriculum and obtaining approval by order. All diving descents, including training, practice, and sports descents, must be provided with the necessary serviceable and complete diving equipment. A diving station is a designated group of a minimum of three people created to perform any tasks during diving descents. The station's senior must allocate responsibilities among the divers before each descent, assign someone responsible for dressing the descending diver, and distribute other responsibilities depending on the specific conditions of the descent. Specify the range of duties for each participant and establish interchangeability. In cases where there are two divers at the station, underwater descents under normal conditions are only permitted with the permission of a diving specialist or a person responsible for diving work. In such cases, one or more individuals specially trained in servicing divers should be assigned to assist the divers. Descents underwater with only two divers, without prepared supporting personnel, are allowed in exceptional cases, such as during rescue operations or other emergencies. All personnel at the diving station must be pre-instructed and have a clear understanding of the tasks, nature, and conditions of upcoming descents and the scope of work. During the briefing, prototypes of devices or their models, which divers will have to deal with underwater, should be widely used. Individuals from the diving or support staff who do not know their duties are not allowed to participate in descents and descent servicing.

Diving station for descents to depths up to 40 meters is equipped with a minimum of three divers. One of them is appointed as the senior diver. Among the diving station, responsibilities are distributed as follows: one of the divers makes the diving descent to perform work. The second ensures the work of the first underwater, maintaining communication with him through a signal rope. The third, maintaining communication with the diver working underwater (via radio or telephone), regulates the supply of breathing mixture to the diver if it is supplied to him through a hose and is ready to descend if necessary. Thus, the first diver is called the descending one, the second - the providing one, the third - the securing one. During underwater work, divers can interchange positions.

On small vessels, a diving station is created with two divers, with the second diver simultaneously serving as both providing and securing. The diving station for descents to depths exceeding 40 meters is equipped with a minimum of four divers and is led by the senior instructor diver of this group. Descents in bolt equipment are allowed with at least six divers. The deep-sea diving station for descents to depths exceeding 60 meters is equipped with deep-sea divers in the quantity provided by the ship's staff. Deep-sea descents are carried out under the guidance of a diving specialist and a specialized physiologist doctor.

Large diving groups are created for the simultaneous descent of several divers underwater with the aim of urgently performing work, surveying large areas, and carrying out special tasks. The leader of the descent is responsible for the safety of the descending divers. No one, except for them, has the right to give any instructions to the diving and servicing descent team. In case of incorrect actions by the leader of the descent that may lead to an accident, they can be relieved of their duties by the direct immediate supervisor of the diving service or the ship's captain. In this case, the head of the diving service (or the ship's captain) takes over the command, and if he is not authorized to lead descents, he appoints another leader who has such authorization. The transfer of leadership in the diving descent can only be done after the descent is completed. The assumption of the position of the descent leader and the reverse transfer of leadership is recorded in the diving work journal.

Fig. 222. Travel end in the overhead environment

During descents of diving groups with a distance from the descent site at such a distance where maintaining communication with the surface via a signal line or radiophone is impossible, divers are connected to each other by a line that simultaneously serves as a signal and guide from one diver to another.

Diving station - a place for the descent of divers equipped with everything necessary. The place for the diving descent should be chosen with the calculation to accommodate diving equipment and gear, as well as the personnel servicing the descent, and should also be a place allowing the dressing and undressing of divers. The place for the diving descent should be located as close as possible to the conduct of diving work, at a height not exceeding two meters from the water surface. Descents can be made from the deck of self-propelled and non-self-propelled watercraft, as well as from quay walls, shores, floating cars, from ice, or from helicopters. In all these cases, the place for the diver's descent must be equipped with means for the diver to enter the water and exit it.

To descend divers from the shore, a platform must be constructed, elevated above the water at its highest level (during high tide). Diving descents without a platform are allowed only in diving gear that does not have a hose supply of breathing gas mixture to the diver. Also, descents in such gear are permitted from helicopters, which are conducted in a special basket or using a storm ladder with the helicopter securely hovering above the descent site. Descents from high-board ships, piers, or other structures higher than two meters above the water are made using a gantry with cargo handling equipment (crane-beams). A boat or cutter should be present at the location of diving operations in these cases.

On ships, the locations for diving descents are established based on the availability of free areas and the convenience of supplying air from the ship's air system, the location of lifting ship mechanisms that can be used for descent and ascent of the diving gantry. The captain of the ship approves the location of diving descents. In all cases when divers are descended from a ship, a standby boat must be at the side, ready to accept the diver if necessary. The most convenient and reliable means of entering the water is the diving ladder. It provides a descent into the water until a sensation of buoyancy appears and, upon ascent, allows standing on its lower step without feeling the weight of the gear. The diving ladder is installed and securely fastened for the diver's descent into the water and exit from it. For descending a diver to the seabed near the ladder, a descent line is attached. If work is carried out by a diver under the ship's hull, the descent is organized and carried out from the keel ladder or end. With the beginning of the underwater descent, a command is announced on the ship, after which it is prohibited to turn the propellers and activate mechanisms related to onboard devices until the end of the underwater descent.

In cases where the underwater descent is conducted away from the location of underwater work, a travel end is laid from the descent location in the direction to the site of underwater work, along which the diver moves on the ground in the desired direction.

Preparation of the descent location at the standard diving station involves checking the presence and serviceability of all diving and medical equipment, conducting necessary repairs and completion, replenishing supplies of compressed air, breathing gases, and consumables to the calculated quantity. All diving equipment of the station must be delivered to the descent location, protected from adverse weather conditions, and maintained in a condition ensuring reliable operation. The descent location must have a heated room for the preparation, inspection, and drying of equipment, as well as for dressing divers and their rest before and after the descent.

In accordance with the 'Rules for the Operation of Descent and Lifting Devices,' descent devices such as diving bells, diving bells, arrows, trusses, and descent-lifting winches must be tested in action - by a control descent (without divers) before the start of each diving descent every day. The decompression chambers are checked once a day before the descent of the first diver (first pair of divers). In this case, the presence of a sufficient supply of compressed air in the cylinders, the tightness of the mains and valves on the mains and chambers, the quality of the rubber seals on the covers of the entry hatches and gates (the hatches are pressed with air from the inside at a pressure in the chamber equal to 0.2 kgf/cm2), the serviceability of pressure gauges on chamber compartments (needle position, expiration date, presence of a seal), the operation of the telephone device, lighting, and heating, meeting fire safety requirements, completeness of chamber compartments with accessories and tools necessary for descents, are checked. The results of the check are recorded in the diving work log.

At the underwater descent location, signaling devices must be prepared to warn passing ships, vessels, and other watercraft of the underwater work being conducted.

Signals indicating the presence of a diver underwater, during daylight and under conditions of normal visibility, are two special flags: the "Diver's flag" and the "ALPHA flag", according to the international code of signals (One according to the naval code of signals), or light signals at night and in conditions of insufficient visibility, which consist of three lights - upper and lower in red, and the middle one in

white, arranged on the mast one below the other. On ships, these signals are hoisted on the gaff of the side from which divers are lowered. On the shore or on watercraft without standard masts for raising signals, a temporary, well-visible mast should be installed. The flags must be on a rigid base to prevent sagging in calm weather.

The "Diver's flag" - a red cloth with a white diagonal stripe from the upper left corner to the lower right.

Fig. 223. Diver's flag

Fig. 224. ALPHA flag

The "ALPHA flag" has a cloth with vertical division in half into two colors. One half in white is closer to the mast, and the other half in blue includes a white triangle, the long side of which is located opposite to the mast. The peak of the white triangle is directed towards the center of the flag and is located in the center of its blue half. Thus, the effect of writing the blue letter 'k' on a white background is created. The Diver Down ALPHA flag indicates: 'I have a diver down, keep clear of me, and proceed at reduced speed.' The internal laws of each country establish how far vessels must pass from the supporting vessel and how far divers can move away from the flag. If there are no such laws, divers are advised to stay away from the flag at a distance of up to 15 meters, and vessels should stay at a distance of at least 30-60 meters. Mooring to ships conducting diving operations is prohibited without the permission of the diving supervisor. After the diver has surfaced, and the command to finish the dives is given, a warning signal is lowered from the mast.

Preparation of diving equipment for descent is carried out on the day of upcoming underwater descents. All items of prepared equipment for descents should be taken out and laid out at the diving station in a position convenient for conducting a working check and dressing divers. Equipment preparation involves putting it in working condition. Attention is paid to the completeness and serviceability of the main and backup diving equipment. Depending on the type of equipment, preparation includes: charging oxygen cylinders or other breathing gas mixtures; charging boxes with a chemical absorbent, charging cartridges with a regenerative substance; checking parts and assemblies of breathing apparatuses and equipment as a whole. In cases where divers descend in equipment with hose delivery of breathing gas (from manual pumps, pumps driven by internal combustion engines, or electrically driven pumps), pumps are installed at the descent location, securely fastened, and diving hoses are connected to them. The diving pump is installed so that the air it draws is clean, without gas impurities from working units. Tools intended for underwater work are checked by visual inspection, brought to the descent location, and ropes are prepared for delivering the tool to the diver.

During the equipment check, means of descent support, tools, materials, the quality of the chemical absorbent or regenerative substance, the presence and composition of gas mixtures in cylinders, and the correctness of their connection should be prepared and verified. Cylinders with medical oxygen and helium must have a factory passport with the results of laboratory analysis.

Also, during the preparation of diving equipment, communication devices with divers, underwater lighting devices, and other means of supporting diving operations are checked in action. When preparing for descents in ventilated or injector-regenerative gear, bubbling relief valves must be installed on the diving suits, which need to be checked for a tight connection to the suit, as a loose connection can cause the suit or diving suit to be non-watertight. The sizes of the suits are selected according to the height of the descending divers. The diving suit should allow squatting freely (checked when putting it on); otherwise, during prolonged underwater work, significant abrasions on the knees may occur. A telephone headset is installed in the helmet, if it was removed for drying, and it is checked. The threaded parts of the helmet are carefully checked, as well as the functionality of the sealing gaskets. The pressure in the air supply system cylinders is brought to the working pressure. If air is to be supplied by a diving pump (manual or electrically driven), it is put into working order: unfastened, lubricated, the cover is slightly opened, and its action is checked. When descending in injector-regenerative gear, the preparation includes: charging regenerative chemical boxes and checking the devices for supplying the gas mixture from the cylinders, as well as checking the functionality of the injector device. Regenerative cartridges of rechargeable boxes must be well-dried, and regenerative boxes, after charging, must be well-sealed. High-pressure cylinders are charged with a breathing gas mixture suitable for human breathing at the depth of the upcoming work. When descending in regenerative types of equipment, the preparation mainly involves charging breathing apparatuses with gas mixtures and regenerative substances, as well as selecting hydro suits of the required size. When charging the apparatus, attention should be paid to the accuracy of matching the selected mixture with the technical description of this equipment and the depth of the upcoming work. The use of gas mixtures not provided for in the technical description is unacceptable and dangerous. Apparatus cylinders must be charged to the working pressure, taking into account the cooling to the water temperature.

When descending in equipment with an open-circuit breathing system (scuba), the preparation includes charging the cylinders of the compressed air apparatus, choosing the sizes of fins and wetsuits, fitting and adjusting the weight belt, shoulder and waist straps of the apparatus. In the hose variant, checks are performed on the operation of the air supply means. The cylinders of the apparatus must be charged with clean air. The quality of the air supplied to divers by compressors, for

Fig. 225. Checking the waterproof seal of a dry-type wetsuit.

the absence of harmful impurities, should be checked every three months in chemical laboratories. The same check should be performed when newly installed or repaired compressors are put into operation. The use of air for the breathing of divers from compressors without the specified checks is prohibited. The results of the air analysis are recorded in the compressor log and in the diving work journal. All gauges installed on air and gas pipelines must be carefully checked and functional. Checking and sealing of pressure gauges should be done at least once a year, and verification of working gauges with a control gauge should be performed at least once a quarter. The results of these checks are recorded in the diving work journal. The watertightness of the equipment and the tightness of the connections in general are checked on the diver when immersed in water. Both the diver and the diver on the signal line, ensuring the descent, must carefully monitor all equipment connections. If air bubbles appear from non-sealing points on the diver, the non-sealing must be addressed and eliminated. The descent of the diver is not allowed in case of equipment non-sealing. During the inspection of diving weights, galoshes, fins, masks, and half-masks, attention should be paid to the functionality of the devices by which they are attached to the diver. Malfunctioning fastening devices can lead to emergencies.

Any malfunctions found in the equipment and measures taken to eliminate them are recorded in the equipment log. The results of the operational check are reported to the descent commander, recorded in the diving work journal, and signed by the person checking the equipment.

§ 21. Diving signals

Signals between divers include: using a signal line, sound, light, tactile, and signals can also be given by hands. Means for signaling and communication include: buoy; whistle; gesture alphabet; slate (plastic board for inscriptions); means of voice communication, including underwater radios and wired telephones. When working at shallow depths, especially when preparing divers, short signal lines attached to buoys on the water surface are used. Buoys are monitored from the diving station, and if necessary, divers are provided with the necessary equipment or assistance. In autonomous equipment, divers are released in pairs without a signal line. In this case, they must not lose sight of each other and should always be ready to assist each other. In poor visibility, diver pairs are connected by a signal line 10-15 meters long. The transmission of conditional signals to the diver through the signal line is carried out in accordance with general rules. To transmit conditional signals, first choose the slack of the signal line, and only then clearly send signals by pulling the line. The supporting and securing divers must loudly convey the content of all signals received from the descending diver. To avoid misunderstandings, each signal must be repeated to the person to whom it is addressed. An exception is the alarm signal from the diver, which should be raised immediately.

Fig. 226. Transmission of conditional signals using a signal line

Signals to the diver using a signal line:

Pull once – "How do you feel?"; "Repeat"; "Choose a signal towards you".

Pull twice – "Stop"; "Do not go further"; "Stop the descent!"

Pull three times – "Descend".

Pull four times – "Ascend."

Shake once – "Danger"; "Ascending to the surface".

Shake twice – "Continue descent"; "Go straight".

Shake three times – "Stay in place"; "Lowering the second diver".

Pull once and shake – "Go right".

Pull twice and shake – "Go left".

Pull, shake, and pull – "Emergency signal".

Diver's signals:

Pull once – "Feeling good"; "Repeat".

Pull twice – "I have stopped".

Pull three times – "I am descending".

Pull four times – "I am ascending".

Frequent tugs more than four times – "Alarm"; "I am not feeling well"; "Ascend quickly".

Shake once – "Stop"; "Halt descent (ascent)"

Shake twice – "Continue descent (ascent)"; "Bleed hose signal".

Shake three times – "Entangled"; "Cannot free myself without the help of the second diver".

Pull once and tug – "Pass the tool".

Pull twice and tug – "Pass the line".

Pull, shake, and pull – "Emergency signal", the meaning of which divers must indicate before the descent.

Sound signals

In cases where divers are released without a signal line, signals are given by sound. To convey signals underwater, a diver can use any solid objects that come into his hand, which, when struck, produce a sound. Stones or pieces of metal can be used for this purpose. Due to the higher density of water than air, sound travels further and faster in water. Thus, two solid bodies, when struck, produce a loud and distinct sound. For example, you can tap a stone against another stone underwater or use special rattles. In the worst case, a diver can use a knife and scuba cylinders. In this case, by hitting the metal cylinder underwater with a metal rod or knife, divers use conditional signals to convey the necessary information. For example, the signal 'Go left' (pull twice and shake) is transmitted by two single and one double hit.

Tactile signals

These signals are used by diving partners in case of poor visibility or if one of the partners loses the mask. The diver who lost the mask becomes passive, controlled by the partner who grabs the suspension element of the buoyancy compensator.

A jerk forward – "Forward".

A jerk backward – "Stop".

Several jerks backward – "Moving backward".

A jerk to the left – "Left".

A jerk to the right – "Right".

During night dives or at great depths, signals given by hands may be poorly visible, so a flashlight is used to convey signals, directed at the bottom in front of the partner.

Fig. 227. Light signals (laser pointer signals)

337

"Drawing" a circle on the ground in front of the partner – "Are you okay?"

"Response, everything is okay!"

Wavy movements of the beam or simply frequent chaotic movements in the field of view of your partner – "Attention!" or "Pay attention to me!"

Hand signals

Fist clenched with the thumb pointing upward: 'Ascend.'

Fist clenched with the thumb pointing downward: 'Descend.'

Fist clenched with the thumb indicating a direction: 'Swim in that direction.'

Forming the letter 'O' or a circle with the thumb and index finger, while the other fingers are straightened: 'I'm okay' or 'Are you okay?'

Fist clenched into a tube: Equivalent to the signal meaning 'I'm okay' or 'Are you okay?' Used when working with mittens (gloves with undivided fingers).

Both hands raised and joined above the head to form the letter 'O'; if one hand is occupied, the signal is performed with one hand, forming a semicircle. The fingertips touch the crown of the head: Equivalent to the signal meaning 'I'm okay' or 'Are you okay?' Used at a greater distance or on the surface.

Neck cut with an open palm: 'I'm out of air,' 'No air to breathe.'

Swinging the wrist up and down with an open palm: 'I have problems.'

When on the surface, the diver makes sharp up-and-down hand movements, hitting the water with the hand: 'Diver in danger!' or 'Help!'

Hugging oneself with both hands: 'I'm freezing.'

Repeatedly clenching and unclenching the fist: 'I have cramps.'

Index fingers pressed together and pointed towards the partner: 'Let's go together,' 'We are buddies.' Indicates that they should stay close to

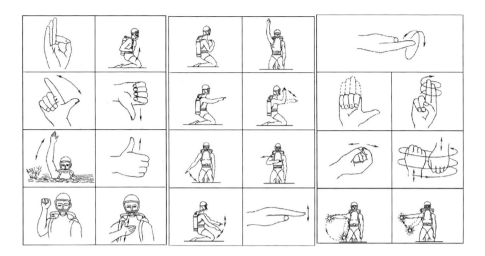

Fig. 228. Hand signals

each other, within a meter to a meter and a half, to help each other in case of need.

Left and right handshake: Equivalent to the signal meaning 'Let's go together,' 'We are buddies.' Indicates that they should stay close to each other, within a meter to a meter and a half, to help each other in case of need.

Palms folded into a boat shape: 'Boat,' 'Ship,' 'Barge.' Can be used as a question: 'Where is the boat, ship, barge?'

Fist clenched on an outstretched arm: 'Danger.' The hand points in the direction of the danger.

Index and middle fingers folded in a V-shape, moving towards one's eyes as if pointing to one's own eyes: 'Look!' If the speaker wants to show something, the second gesture should indicate the direction. If the goal is to attract attention to oneself, then the hand should be placed on the chest afterward.

Open palm, fingers pointing vertically upward, palm facing the direction of the signal recipient: 'Stop,' 'Halt.'

Swinging an open palm towards and away from oneself horizontally: 'Stay at this depth,' 'Need neutral buoyancy.'

Cutting motion across the wrist: One hand simulates a grip, and the other, with the index and middle fingers straight, represents a knife. 'Cut,' 'Slice.'

One hand's index and middle fingers simulate the movements of a diver's legs, while the semi-open palm of the other hand represents the 'diver,' creating the signal for 'diver in the tube' – a signal for penetration into overhead environments (wrecks, caves, etc.).

Hand movements simulating the expansion and contraction of the chest (inhale and exhale): 'I'm out of breath (exhausted).'

Index fingers of both hands describing a circle: 'Repeat' (last movement, gesture, etc.).

Index finger bent like a hook: 'I have a question,' 'What are we going to do?' 'What was that?' etc.

Index and middle fingers of one hand folded together and applied to the palm of the other: 'How much gas is left?' or 'Show the pressure gauge.'

One finger pointed upward indicates the number '10.' (Can be used with other gestures to indicate the desired number.)

Two fingers shown, or more, as agreed upon by the divers before the descent.

Open palms of both hands forming the upper angle of a triangle, connected by the fingertips: 'I want to go home,' 'Shall we return?'

Clenched fist with the palm facing away: 'First backup signal, the meaning of which divers must indicate before the descent.'

Hand formed into the letter 'T,' with the fingertips of the second hand covering the tips of the fingers: 'Second backup signal, the meaning of which divers must indicate before the descent.'

These signals should be memorized by all divers involved in the descent and those supporting the descent.

Signals between divers indicating marine fauna

Depending on the dive location (e.g., in the Red Sea or the Maldives), different instructors and local dive guides may use different variations of signals to denote specific marine inhabitants. Divers also sometimes invent signals themselves for use in a particular situation. Often, these signals coincide, are repeated, and are used in the same variations.

Here are some examples:

Fists on both sides of the head: Hammerhead shark.

Open palms of both hands together, with fingers spread like a 'fan': Fire coral.

Wiggling index fingers on both sides of the head: Lobster.

Clenched hand so that the thumb is opposed to all other fingers. Movements imitating the opening and closing of tentacles are performed with the fingers of the other hand, which is placed above the first one: Octopus.

Hands clenched into fists, with thumbs spread apart. The hands are placed one on top of the other. Circular movements of the thumbs: Sea turtle.

Hand clenched in a fist, pressed to the forehead: Napoleon wrasse.

Hand held vertically above the head with clenched fingers pointing upwards, imitating a fin: Shark.

§ 22. Decompression and non-decompression dives

As known, with the increase in external pressure during a dive, nitrogen begins to dissolve in the diver's body. The longer the diver stays under pressure, the more gas dissolves in their body. To avoid detrimental effects of decompression sickness, it is essential to ascend in a way that allows all nitrogen dissolved in the blood and tissues to exit naturally through the lungs, without forming bubbles that could disrupt blood flow. Therefore, the recommended ascent speed for a diver should not exceed 10 meters per minute.

Non-decompression dive is a scuba dive where the ascent to the surface can be done continuously without harm to the diver's health. The non-decompression limit is the moment after which ascending from depth to the surface requires stops to eliminate inert gas accumulated in the diver's tissues. The non-decompression limit depends on factors such as the dive depth, time spent at a given depth, duration of surface intervals after the last dive, accumulated inert gas after a series of dives, water temperature during the dive, wave height on the surface, and altitude during mountain dives.

Decompression dive is a scuba dive where, upon surfacing, mandatory stops at specific depths and for a certain duration are required. During these stops, nitrogen, helium, or other gases accumulated in the diver's tissues naturally exit through the lungs. Ascending to the surface without observing decompression stops can lead to decompression sickness or death.

For safety in diving, divers calculate, using decompression tables, the number, depth, and duration of stops, or they use specialized dive computers. Decompression tables indicate the time until reaching the non-decompression limit based on the dive depth, and they specify conditions under which performing a safety stop becomes advisable. Safety stops are not decompression stops and are carried out even during non-decompression dives.

'Deep stop' is conducted for one minute at a depth equal to half the maximum dive depth. 'Safety stop' is carried out for three minutes at a depth ranging from three to six meters.

Modes of non-decompression dives and staged decompression stops are built as a result of experiments and mathematical modeling. These models are continually refined by various individual scientists and research groups. All these tables share a common function; each decompression table, with varying levels of conservatism, reflects the dependence of the absorbed inert gas on the duration of the dive, depth, and breathing gas composition.

diving depth in feet																					
10		20		30		40		60		80		100		120		140					
	15		25		35		50		70		90		110		130		150				
3		6		9		12		18		24		30		36		42					
	4.5		7.5		10.5		15		21		27		33		39		45				

diver's time at the bottom:

60	35	25	20	15	5	5											A
120	70	50	35	30	15	15	10	10	5	5	5	5					B
210	110	75	55	45	25	25	15	15	10	10	10	7	5	5	5	5	C
300	160	100	75	60	40	30	25	20	15	15	12	10	10	10	8	7	D
	225	135	100	75	50	40	30	25	20	15	15	13	12	10	10		E
	350	180	125	95	60	50	40	30	30	25	20	20	15	15			F
		240	160	120	80	70	50	40	35	30	25	22	20				G
		325	195	145	100	80	60	50	40	35	30	25					H
			245	170	120	100	70	55	45	40							I
			315	205	140	110	80	60	50								J
				250	160	130	90										K
				310	190	150	100										L
					220	170											M
					270	200											N
					310												O

tissue nitrogen saturation level

maximum time without decompression

depth when the diver dives again

surface interval

time before re-dive

Fig. 229. Non-decompression limits table for air

The foundation of the theory of inert gas elimination from the human body was laid by French physiologist Paul Bert in 1880 when he formulated the cause of nitrogen bubble formation. Building on these calculations, English physiologist John Scott Haldane developed the first decompression tables in 1908. Since around 1960, Swiss medical doctor Albert Bühlmann has been developing decompression algorithms, which served as the basis for modern dive computers. With a Ph.D. in elementary particle physics, American scientist Bruce Wienke began working on two-phase algorithms for decompression models, gas transport, and phase mechanics around 1990. Subsequently, he developed a new algorithm allowing the use of helium in breathing mixtures, employing reduced gradient bubble models (RGBM), which introduced a new approach to gas absorption and elimination in dive planning and diver preparation.

Despite minor differences, practically all decompression tables have three main components:

The first table shows the amount of nitrogen saturation in the diver's body during the dive, the non-decompression limit, and the duration and depth of decompression stops, if necessary.

The second table indicates the excess nitrogen that the diver's body needs to eliminate naturally through the lungs during ascent to the surface and during the interval between dives. It also shows the residual nitrogen level in the body before a repeated dive.

The third table specifies parameters for a repeated dive, such as the amount of residual nitrogen at the beginning of the dive and non-decompression limits for various depth values.

The degree of nitrogen saturation in the tissues is expressed with alphabetical Latin indices from A to Z — the further the letter from the beginning of the alphabet, the stronger the nitrogen saturation. During one cycle of diving, one cannot switch from one table to another. All tables have conditional parameters indicating the amount of nitrogen in the body and the time of its saturation or elimination:

Residual Nitrogen Time (RNT) is the hypothetical time at the beginning of a repeated dive as if the diver were already at a specified depth, assuming this dive were the first.

Actual Bottom Time (ABT) is the time spent during a repeated dive.

Total Bottom Time (TBT) is the sum of Actual Bottom Time and Residual Nitrogen Time, indicating the hypothetical time of a dive at a specific depth during the first dive. The No-Decompression Limit (NDL) is the maximum allowable dive time that does not require decompression during ascent. The Adjusted No Decompression Limit

(ANDL) is the maximum allowable time for a repeated dive without decompression during ascent.

As evident from the tables above, the non-decompression time limit varies for different gas mixtures. Dives at high altitudes, 300 meters and above, require adherence to special rules that adjust for the dive depth. The most common modern decompression tables, such as NAUI, PADI, DCIEM, Max Hanna, Bühlmann, BSAC, Huggins, and Basset, are available in the public domain.

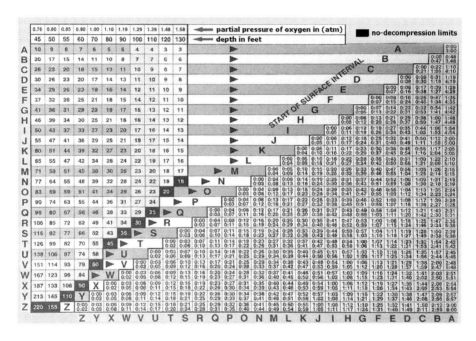

Fig. 230. Non-decompression limits table for Nitrox (EANx32)

Various decompression tables differ not only in their creation date and authorship but also in their intended use. For instance, PADI tables are designed for recreational divers making non-decompression and repeated dives with short intervals. DCIEM tables underwent testing in cold water during active physical exertion, making them more conservative than others.

345

Since each human body has individual characteristics, it is recommended for each diver to choose the table that best suits their body's capabilities. It is advisable to start with the most lenient non-decompression dive profiles and always keep in mind that no decompression table completely eliminates the risk of decompression sickness.

A table is considered applicable if the risk of illness resulting from its use during long deep dives does not exceed 6%. There are special tables for dives in water bodies above sea level and for dives using breathing gas mixtures enriched or depleted with oxygen, containing various inert gases.

Decompression tables for planning dives exist not only in tabular form but also in the form of a so-called 'wheel.' One advantage of the 'wheel' is that it allows divers to calculate multi-level dive profiles, where the diver plans to dive to different depth levels. While time calculations from a table are based on the maximum depth reached, using the 'wheel,' the diver simultaneously considers all shallower levels, significantly increasing their underwater stay.

NAUI (National Association of Underwater Instructors) tables are designed for a wide range of recreational divers. The first table shows non-decompression time in minutes at depths up to 40 meters (in circles), and if the limit is exceeded, it shows the duration of decompression stops in minutes at a depth of 5 meters (in black cells). The actual depth value is always rounded to the nearest table value.

Example: A diver spent 33 minutes at a depth of 17 meters. After surfacing, they fall into the 'G' group, where decompression is not needed. However, after 45 minutes, the diver needs to dive again. In the second table, find the interval in the cell from 41 minutes to 1 hour 15 minutes. Since during the surface interval, some nitrogen has left the body and some nitrogen remains, the diver is now in the 'F' group, and a correction is needed for the repeated dive.

Each cell in the third table contains two numbers: the upper one, reflecting the level of residual nitrogen, indicates the time already spent at that depth (RNT — residual nitrogen time), and the lower one shows the allowable non-decompression time at that depth (ADT — actual dive time). When in the 'F' group, a diver dives to 15 meters, and table 3 shows that the residual nitrogen level corresponds to 47 minutes already spent at this depth. Therefore, the diver has 33 minutes remaining until the non-decompression limit. Spending half an hour at the given depth, the diver approaches the limit of allowable non-decompression time. After surfacing, they belong to the 'J' group according to the first table. If the diver had to stay at the bottom for an additional 10 minutes, a five-minute decompression stop at a depth of 5 meters would be required, transitioning to the 'L' group.

PADI's Recreational Dive Planner (RDP) decompression table is designed for a wide range of recreational divers making shallow and frequent multiple dives during vacations.

PADI planners in diving tables, alongside the no-decompression limit, specify the time for decompression stops during ascent if the diver exceeds the no-decompression limit. The diver needs to perform an emergency decompression stop. If the no-decompression limit is exceeded by less than 5 minutes, PADI tables prescribe an emergency decompression stop of 8 minutes at a depth of 5 meters, and all dives should be postponed for 6 hours after surfacing. If the no-decompression limit is exceeded by more than 5 minutes, the emergency decompression stop at 5 meters should last at least 15 minutes, and the next dive is recommended no earlier than 24 hours later. More details on bottom time and decompression time can be obtained from the tables.

For example, according to the first table, after a 33-minute dive to 17 meters, the diver belongs to the 'M' group. After spending 45 minutes on the surface, they transition to the 'F' group (according to Table 2).

Following the table instructions (Table 3), the diver can spend an additional 49 minutes at a depth of 15 meters without decompression. If they dive for 40 minutes for the second time, summing it with the 23 minutes of Residual Nitrogen Time (RNT) and referring back to the first table, the diver is classified as belonging to the 'U' group after the repeated dive. The first planner table is color-coded non-uniformly. Black cells contain the no-decompression limit, and gray cells represent bottom time, after which a safety stop is strongly recommended. If the diver's residual nitrogen group at the end of the dive is 'X' or 'W,' the next dive can be made no earlier than one hour later. Being in groups 'Z' or 'Y' allows the next dive only after three hours.

DCIEM (Canada's Defence and Civil Institute of Environmental Medicine) diving tables are among the most popular worldwide. They differ from other tables by including depth adjustments 'D' for dives in mountain lakes and rivers. For those interested in underwater activities in high-altitude lakes, this is a crucial addition to standard tables. For example, according to Table A, a 33-minute dive to 17 meters places the diver in the 'E' group. After 45 minutes, the residual nitrogen level corresponds to 1.6 (Table B). This means that at a depth of 15 meters, the diver can spend a maximum of 38 minutes without decompression. If, after a repeated 30-minute dive, the diver plans another dive, they must multiply their 'bottom time' by the residual nitrogen level, resulting in 'effective bottom time' equal to 48 minutes. With this value, they should return to Table A (where the number 50 corresponds to them) and classify themselves as belonging to the 'E' group. If the residual nitrogen value did not exceed one after the first dive, the diver could start calculations for the repeated dive from the first table. With residual nitrogen exceeding 2, the diver is recommended to refrain from repeated diving.

Max Hanna's dive tables are user-friendly during dives thanks to their rational design. Their algorithm is embedded in the memory of many dive computers. The first part of the table is divided into 19 sections by depths from 9 meters to 63 meters. Each section shows the duration and depths of decompression stops. In the left column below the diving depth, the no-decompression limit time is separately listed. The next column indicates the actual dive time, and the far-right column shows nitrogen saturation groups. The second table not only includes surface rest intervals but also shows the allowable time interval before flying for each repeated group. Thus, divers in the 'B' group can board a plane as early as 6 hours after surfacing, 'E' group divers after 24 hours, and 'G' group divers after 36 hours. The second column from the right shows for each group the time after which nitrogen tissue off-gassing is such that the second dive becomes the first. In this case, for repeated dive calculations, the first table should be used. For example, 'B' group divers can dive again according to the first table after just 1.5 hours, while 'G' group divers only after 6 hours. The third table takes into account the level of nitrogen in the body before starting a repeated dive. It is conditionally expressed in time spent at a certain depth. To determine the ascent mode, one needs to add this conditional value to the actual time spent at that depth during the repeated dive and place this value in the first table.

Buhlmann's dive tables closely resemble Max Hana's tables. Moreover, the initial tables of both researchers were released collaboratively (Buhlmann-Hahn dive tables). The first table determines the Residual Group (R.G.) of the diver after the first dive. It is essential to note the figures to the right of the bottom time, separated by a slash '/'. This indicates the time for a decompression stop at a depth of 3 meters in cases where no-decompression limits are exceeded. For instance, the figures 25/5 in the 30-meter column signify that spending 25 minutes at a depth of 30 meters will require a five-minute decompression stop at a depth of 3 meters. The second table provides a new R.G. after the surface interval. For example, if the diver finishes the first dive and transitions to the 'C' group, staying on the surface for a duration of 10 to 25 minutes will move them to the 'B' group. The third table determines the Residual Nitrogen Time (RNT). The RNT value, indicated in minutes, is found at the intersection of the R.G. after the surface interval and the planned depth of the next dive. Knowing the RNT, the diver refers to the first table. In the case of a planned decompression dive, the diver should add the RNT to the bottom time of the next dive. Thus, the diver obtains the Total Bottom Time (TBT). If it is necessary to determine the no-decompression limit for a repeated dive, the RNT should be subtracted from the maximum time specified in the first table.

§ 23. Diving descents

Working in diving gear with scuba tanks provides the diver with greater maneuverability compared to using surface-supplied diving equipment. The use of scuba tanks as the working diving gear is an optimal solution, associated with the simplicity and safety of diving descents. For diving work, the diver must have at least two sets of diving gear. The preparation of diving gear includes

Fig. 231. Diving descent

filling the breathing gas cylinders, calculating the permissible time underwater, and a functional check of all equipment parts.

In most cases, scuba tanks are filled with compressed air using a high-pressure compressor. Additionally, filling scuba tanks can be done through transfer or topping off from transport tanks. Quite often, for underwater dives, breathing gas mixtures based on oxygen are used, and the tanks are filled with gases other than air in these breathing gas mixtures. During the filling process, there is a risk of fire due to the use of oxygen and an explosion risk due to the use of gases under high pressure. The mixture's composition must be safe for the depth and duration of the planned dive. If the oxygen concentration is too low, the diver may lose consciousness due to hypoxia, and if it is too high, the diver may suffer from oxygen toxicity. The concentration of inert gases, such as nitrogen and helium, is planned and verified to avoid nitrogen narcosis and decompression sickness. Standard decompression tables designed for safe open-water dives are not applicable to dives using oxygen-enriched mixes.

Checking diving equipment

Before each dive, the descending diver must perform a functional check of their diving equipment. The pressure in the tank is measured with a pressure gauge, and its value is recorded in the diver's logbook. Visual inspection determines the integrity of the scuba knots, the reliability of attachments, the strength of shoulder, waist, and chest straps, and the external condition of the buoyancy compensator for any ruptures and secure valve attachments. The airtightness of the working parts of the scuba gear, the proper operation of the buoyancy compensator's inflator and air release valves, as well as the correct operation of the diving regulator and its stages, is checked with the tank valve open. Before opening the tank valve, the diver should press and hold the bypass button on the second stage regulator, simultaneously with opening the tank valve. Upon hearing the hiss of air coming out of the second stage, the button should be released, and the tank valve should be further opened by turning the handle to the stop, followed by making half a turn in the opposite direction. Then, the scuba is immersed in water with the second stage mouthpiece down. If the scuba is airtight, no air bubbles should escape to the surface. To check the regulator's functionality, the tank valve of the scuba is opened using the method described above. After that, with the mouthpiece of the second stage in the mouth, the diver takes several even deep breaths. A properly functioning and correctly adjusted second-stage regulator should not create resistance during inhalation or exhalation. It is important to note that after inhalation, the second stage should sharply cut off the airflow. The proper operation of the buoyancy compensator is checked for airtightness of the air-filled bag and the functionality of the inflator and air release valves. Connected to the regulator, the buoyancy compensator, with the tank valve open, is filled with air by pressing the corresponding button on the inflator console. After that, the compensator should be immersed in water; if the compensator bag is airtight and the air release valves fit tightly, no air bubbles should escape to the surface. By sequentially pulling the cord of each air release valve, the appearance of bubbles can be observed, and returning the valve to its original position should stop the air bubbles. It is not recommended to check the functionality of the air release valves with the buoyancy compensator fully inflated. With increased pressure inside the buoyancy compensator's air bag, the air pressure on the air release valves reaches a point where these

Fig. 232. Checking

352

valves start to release air automatically. Checking dry-type wetsuits is done visually for any tears and cracks in the fabric, as well as the neck and wrist cuffs. The proper operation of zippers is also checked by opening and closing them. Airtightness is checked directly on the diver just before immersion when entering from a shallow shore or a diving ladder. The diver enters the water up to the chest and squats. At this time, the assistant checks the airtightness of the diving equipment. If the dry-type wetsuit is airtight, no air bubbles should escape to the surface. The functionality of the inflation and air release valves is tested by pressing the inflation button on one and rotating the valve 900 clockwise on the other valve.

Briefing before a diving descent

Before the divers start putting on their gear, they must be briefed by the dive supervisor about the nature, methods, and sequence of underwater tasks, safety measures, as well as informed about the underwater descent conditions (presence of currents, depth and duration of underwater stay, and task execution conditions).

Calculations of the time spent underwater with scuba using an air breathing gas mixture

Example:

Diving depth ....30 meters.

Air pressure in the tank ....230 bar.

Tank capacity ....15 liters.

Minimum pressure that should remain after the dive ...50 bar.

Air temperature ....…... +25°C

Water temperature .... +10°C

Determining the amount of air in the tank

When determining the amount of air in the tank (in liters), the total pressure in the tank is converted to atmospheric pressure by multiplying the tank's capacity by the pressure:

$15 \times 230 = 3450$ litres

With a temperature change of 10°C, the volume of air per 1 liter of tank capacity changes by 0.5 liters. Therefore, the correction factor for the temperature difference for this scuba apparatus is determined:

$15 \times 0.5 = 7.5$ litres

In this example, the temperature difference correction is calculated accordingly:

$7.5 \times (25 - 10) = 112.5$ litres

Thus, the air volume in the tank, taking into account the temperature difference, will be:

$3450 - 112.5 = 3337.5$ liters.

From this obtained air volume in the tank, the non-reducible air reserve, which must remain in the tank after the dive, needs to be excluded.

$3337.5 - (50 \times 15) = 2587.5$ liters.

Determination of air consumption

Air consumption is determined by lung ventilation and the diver's diving depth. The lung ventilation value is taken from a table that provides the amount of consumed air in liters per minute.

Air consumption for breathing per minute, converted to one atmosphere, will be equal to the lung ventilation value taken from the table, multiplied by one-tenth of the diving depth in meters plus one:

$40 \times (0.1 \times 30 + 1) = 160$ liters.

To determine the allowable dive time, the total air volume should be divided by its consumption per minute:

2587.5 / 160 = 16 minutes.

Therefore, the calculated allowable dive time for a diver underwater is 16 minutes. When diving with scuba apparatus with an air breathing mixture at depths exceeding 12 meters, the final time at depth must take into account the time for decompression stops.

Temperature	Wetsuit type	Characteristics of work		
		light	moderate severity	heavy
To 10	Dry-type wetsuit with insulation liner Neoprene wetsuit 9-10	30	40	60
10-15	Dry-type wetsuit with insulation liner Neoprene wetsuit 7-9	25	35	55
15-19	Dry-type wetsuit with insulation liner Neoprene wetsuit 5-7	20	30	50
20-25	Dry suit with cotton liner	20	30	50

Diver's dressing

Depending on the type of wetsuit, the assistant may be needed during the dressing and undressing of the diver. If the wet suit has an open-cell structure, the diver can put it on independently, having previously moistened the parts close to the body with a soap solution or special

355

oil. However, assistance from another person is required to remove it after the dive. The dressing procedure depends on the type of equipment. If dives are conducted in warm water, it is not necessary to wear warm thermal underwear. However, it is recommended to wear thin cotton underwear to prevent chafing in certain areas of the body and ensure a snug fit of dry-type wetsuit parts to the skin.

The assistant is needed when dressing and removing a dry-type wetsuit with a shoulder zipper and when putting on a GK-4 wetsuit. To seal the connection of the jacket and pants, the outer waist cuff of the jacket is rolled up, and the sealing ring is put on the inner waist cuff, which is then wrapped around the ring. The outer waist cuff of the jacket is then lowered. When putting on the wetsuit, attention should be paid to avoid folds, as air accumulated in folds will create excessive positive buoyancy. Next, the diver puts on the ankle weights and weight belt. When putting on the scuba apparatus, it is important to ensure that all straps are adjusted so that the scuba tank is comfortably positioned on the diver's back, and the first stage of the regulator is located precisely between the diver's shoulder blades. When putting on the mask, adjust the strap to ensure that it does not slip off and does not cause discomfort to the diver from excessive tension. A diver's knife and underwater flashlight are secured in a convenient location on the diver's body or buoyancy compensator. Check for the presence of a diver's buoy for emergency ascent.

In some cases, divers may need to independently don self-contained underwater breathing apparatus (SCUBA) equipment while on the water surface. Important and useful skills in this scenario include independently donning the scuba or rebreather using the buoyancy compensator. To a diver on the water surface, the supporting diver provides the underwater gear with an inflated buoyancy compensator. Before starting to don the diving gear, the diver must fasten and loosen the shoulder straps to the maximum, unfasten the waist and chest buckles. Turn the scuba tank with the bottom facing towards oneself, the diver should sit on the buoyancy compensator and insert arms into the shoulder straps. Then, in a vertical position, tighten the shoulder and waist straps and fasten the waist and chest buckles. Putting on the weight belt in the water requires the diver to inflate the buoyancy compensator. Inserting the mouthpiece of the demand valve into the mouth, lying on the back, and continuing to breathe through the regulator. Take the new weight belt from the supporting diver, holding it with both hands so that the free end is in the right hand and the buckle is in the left hand. Then, with the right hand, transfer the belt to the abdomen so that the free end is on the left and the buckle is on the right. At this moment, without twisting the belt, the diver must grab it where the weights end with the right hand. After that, the diver turns over the left shoulder, lying face down in the water, while the belt with weights remains in place, ending up on the diver's back. After that, the diver should tighten the belt at the waist and fasten its buckle. Before the diver descends, the apparatus is turned on, and the diver checks the functionality of the scuba once again with their breath. A signal line is attached to the waist of the descending diver, and then the breathing apparatus is put on and secured. From the moment the signal line is put on, the diver is continuously in the hands of the supporting diver throughout the descent and until the descending diver finishes undressing. It is not allowed to tie the signal line to any objects, except for the main end, which must be securely fastened before the descent. If the descent of divers is carried out without a signal line, to prevent accidents, a control line is put on the diver, which is attached to the float, or the divers are descended in pairs, connected by a connecting line. The descent of a pair of divers without a connecting line is allowed only in clear water and for performing simple tasks at shallow depths.

Diver descent

Diver descents for underwater swimming differ somewhat from descents for performing tasks on the bottom. At the beginning of the diver's descent, along with checking the tightness of the diving gear, the diver's buoyancy is adjusted. To do this, the diver, holding onto the diving ladder with one hand, lies horizontally (if descents are made from a shallow shore, this is done at a shallow depth), observing his descent or ascent. By adding or reducing the number of weights on the weight belt, the diver achieves a position where his buoyancy is close to zero. In this case, the diver, taking a deep breath, should feel a lifting of his body in the area of positive buoyancy, and upon exhalation, his body should submerge, acquiring negative buoyancy. Buoyancy is adjusted at the minimum residual pressure of the gas breathing mixture in the scuba tank. It should be noted that a tank filled with a breathing gas to the working pressure is several kilograms heavier than an empty one.

The time of the start of the diver's descent underwater (which is marked in the diver's logbook) is considered the moment of turning on the breathing apparatus or connecting the inhalation tube from the regulator to the inhalation port in the equipment with exhalation into the water.

Dressed and equipped with the diving apparatus, the diver descends onto the diving ladder and slowly descends along it until their head is submerged in the water. In this position, the diver must remain to allow the supporting diver to check the tightness of the gear. It is prohibited to submerge the diver underwater upon the slightest equipment malfunction detected at the beginning of the descent. Further descent of the diver can only be carried out after completing the gear tightness check, upon the command from the surface. After checking the tightness and functionality of the diving gear and adjusting buoyancy, the diver lifts their head above water. Upon receiving the approving signal from the supporting diver, the descending diver transitions from the ladder to the descent line, holding onto it and descending to the bottom. Underwater, the diver should breathe calmly and steadily, avoiding breath-holding. During the descent, the surrounding environment exerts pressure on the diver's body, so, as needed (anticipating the onset of ear pain), the diver should equalize. (The more frequently the diver equalizes the pressure in the Eustachian tubes with the surrounding environment, the better for their body).

The initial descent speed of the diver to a depth of 8–10 m should not exceed 6–8 m/min, then it is allowed to increase to 20 m/min depending on the diver's training and well-being.

The supporting diver during the descent of the descending diver pays out the signal line (and the air hose), keeping it taut all the time. If the descending diver signals to stop the descent, the supporting diver holds the line and raises it by approximately 0.5 meters. Further descent can only continue upon the command of the descending diver. If there is no response from the diver to the signal transmitted twice via the signal line or another communication method, the supporting diver immediately starts lifting the diver to the surface. If communication with the diver is restored during the ascent, and they report feeling well, they are descended again to the bottom to continue underwater work.

The diver's stay underwater

Upon reaching the bottom, the descending diver must check the degree of inflation of the breathing bag (when using oxygen equipment) or the supply of air in autonomous diving gear such as scuba. Upon reaching the bottom, the diver needs to look around, determine the type of bottom (hard or muddy, and perhaps encountering a type with a sinking layer of peat or hydrogen sulfide). After that, they need to ensure the cleanliness of the signal line and hose, and the absence of excessive slack and side effects that could negatively affect the descent, and signal, 'I'm on the bottom, feel good!' The diver's actions underwater should be deliberate, cautious, and thoughtfully sequential. While performing the task, it is necessary to constantly monitor one's well-being, the operation of the diving equipment, and changes in the surrounding environment. Periodically, the diver should check the signal line and hose for tension and freedom from entanglement. During underwater movements in conditions of limited visibility, the diver should swim cautiously to avoid entanglement in fishing gear, debris, and other objects underwater, with which collisions are possible. The diver should not experience difficulties and shortness of breath, heat, sweating, or other discomfort while working underwater. Swimming underwater places a significant physical burden on the diver, so they must regulate the speed of their movements based on their breathing, and in case of noticeable acceleration, the diver should reduce muscle activity, slowing down the movement speed or taking short breaks. While on the bottom and performing underwater tasks, the diver must monitor the equipment's functionality and the reserve of the breathing gas mixture in the scuba tanks (using a pressure gauge or the transmitter of a dive computer). In all cases of equipment malfunctions or feeling unwell, work should be stopped, the state should be reported to the descent commander, and, maintaining composure, act according to their instructions. Divers working in pairs or groups must mutually monitor the condition of the equipment and well-being, and assist each other if necessary. During the diver's stay underwater, the supporting diver must carefully monitor the movement of the diver using the signal line. The direction of the diver's movement can be determined from the surface by the direction of the signal line, and bubbles emerging from the water during descents with exhalation into the water. On the diver's demand, the supporting diver must promptly pay out or reel in the hose and signal line, maintaining a certain slack to avoid hindering the diver's movements at the workplace. Throwing the signal line is prohibited. Passing the signal line to other individuals is only allowed with the permission of the descent commander. In this case, the person passing the line must make a conditional signal through the signal line about the diver's well-being and, after receiving a response, pass the signal line into the hands of the recipient. The recipient must report to the descent commander about assuming responsibilities.

The ascent of the diver to the surface is carried out upon completion of the task or after the allotted time underwater has elapsed. The supporting diver must strictly monitor that the established time underwater is not exceeded. The ascent is announced with a signal two minutes in advance. Responding to the signal, the diver approaches the descent line, takes hold of it with their hands, passes it between their legs, ensures the cleanliness of the signal line, and signals for ascent. Upon this signal, the supporting diver starts reeling in the signal line, issues a command to mark the start time of the ascent, and raises the diver at a speed not exceeding 10 meters per minute. Uncontrolled ascent of the diver (except for ascents in autonomous gear) from any depth is prohibited. During their ascent, the diver should not hold their breath; it is recommended to take short inhalations and slightly prolonged exhalations

After work at depths up to 12 meters, divers are brought to the surface without stops, and from greater depths – with decompression stops. The duration of stops at corresponding depths is determined from tables based on the maximum depth and the time the diver spent underwater. Factors such as the time spent underwater (which is the sum of half the time spent on descent and the total time the diver stays on the bottom) are taken into account.

In the case of an unplanned ascent, a diver in autonomous gear must, before starting the ascent, fill the gas and release the emergency buoy attached to their equipment to the surface with a line. Emergency ascent is carried out in case of water ingress into a dry-type diving suit (the diver pinches the water entry point with their hand and ascends to the surface), as well as in case of malfunctions in diving hoses or the regulator. In case of continuous air supply from the second stage, the diver must remove the mouthpiece and, holding it near the mouth, take breaths, controlling the flow of inhaled air by adjusting the tightness of their lips. In this case, the diver must stop the descent, and immediately ascend to the surface. If the demand valve does not supply air at all, the diver, holding their breath, should release the weight belt and, if necessary, the scuba, or, in case of free ascent, exhale continuously, expelling expanding air from the lungs. If a decompression chamber is installed at the worksite, divers are brought to the surface using surface decompression (or mixed decompression) to reduce time spent on in-water stops. In this case, from the stop indicated in the decompression tables, divers are quickly brought to the surface and placed in the decompression chamber, where the pressure is raised to the level corresponding to the depth of the last underwater stop. The pressure in the chamber is then reduced according to the decompression table.

The undressing of a diver in hose equipment begins on the ladder, while in autonomous gear, undressing occurs after exiting the water. First, the heavy parts of the equipment are removed from the diver, followed by the rest. The signal line is removed before removing the drysuit. In cases where a diver needs to remove diving gear while remaining in the water, they must start by inflating the buoyancy compensator. If necessary, this can be done with the mouth. Then, the gear should be removed, starting with its heavy parts, beginning with the weight belt. To do this, unbuckle the belt buckle, take the weight belt off, thread the free end into the buckle, and buckle the belt again. After that, the weight belt is passed to the supporting diver. Next, the diver should lie on their back, undo all the fastenings and straps holding the autonomous equipment (scuba or rebreather) on the body, remove the buoyancy compensator, and, holding it in their hand, pass it to the supporting diver. After that, the fins are removed one by one and passed to the supporting diver. After this, the diver can climb the ladder onto the deck. The removed equipment is cleaned from dirt, rinsed in clean fresh water, wiped, and dried in the shade. After this, the equipment is packed for storage in standard bags and boxes. Tools used by divers underwater are cleaned, rinsed, wiped, lubricated with special grease, covered, and packed into storage boxes.

§ 24. Practical exercises, mastering basic diver skills

Students who have completed theoretical training and passed the examination for admission to diving are allowed to make underwater descents.

The organization and conduct of training descents require additional safety measures. Training descents should only be conducted in specially equipped locations, open water bodies, or pools. A mandatory condition for ensuring training descents to depths exceeding 12 meters is the availability of a barochamber ready to receive casualties immediately. During diving training from the shore or pier, the underwater bottom in the descent area must be thoroughly inspected and cleared of foreign objects that a diver could catch on or get entangled in. There should be no sources of water pollution near the descents. The results of the bottom inspection must be documented.

Fig. 233. Diving locations

The area of the water allocated for descents must be marked with special signals to warn floating vehicles against entering it during descents.

Diving training for divers is provided by: a diving descent supervisor, a doctor (in case medical assistance is needed), and diving instructors. The provision of descents is ensured by the readiness of a backup diver from the instructors' team to descend immediately. The backup diver must be ready for an immediate descent. During warm-water descents, the backup diver may descend without a wetsuit. When practicing tasks related to moving on the bottom, each instructor can provide descent for no more than three trainees. Before the diving descent, trainees are divided into groups of three, forming diving stations. All training tasks are practiced by each trainee, and they take turns performing duties.

Before the descent, trainees independently conduct a working check of the diving equipment under the supervision of a diving instructor. After that, the diving equipment must be thoroughly rechecked by the diving instructor before the descent begins. During diving descents from the ladder, no more than two trainees can descend simultaneously from each ladder. When a trainee is in the water, continuous monitoring with periodic inquiries about well-being (every 2-3 minutes) is maintained. If a trainee does not respond to the well-being inquiry twice, they are immediately started to be brought to the surface with a backup diver sent simultaneously. A mandatory condition for conducting training descents is the sequence of practicing tasks. A trainee who has not completed the next training task is not allowed to practice the next one.

Assembling the scuba

The first step is a visual inspection of the scuba components. The date of the last hydro test of the cylinder is checked, then the protective threaded cap is removed from the exhaust valve, and the threaded connections of the cylinder are checked for contamination. In case of contamination of the threads, the contamination is removed with water using a small brush and a rag.

Then, by turning the handle of the cylinder shut-off valve, a brief (one second) opening and closing of the cylinder valve are performed. In this case, the compressed air, when exiting the cylinder, will dry and finally remove minor contaminants remaining on the valve. Next, the condition of the buoyancy compensator is inspected, the reliability of its fastenings, clasps, and carabiners of shoulder, waist, and breast straps. After that, the integrity of the air bladder is checked, and the tightness of the buoyancy compensator valves, the correct operation of the inflator, and air release valves are verified. To do this, press the inflator button and inflate the air bladder of the buoyancy compensator with the mouth. After releasing the button and squeezing the air bladder with hands, listen to whether the compensator makes hissing sounds of outgoing air; in the absence of such sounds, the compensator is considered airtight. (The airtightness of the buoyancy compensator can be checked by immersing it in water in an inflated state; in the absence of visible bubbles of air, the compensator is considered airtight.) After that, release the air from the bladder, checking the operability of the air release valves. To do this, pull on the special cords leading to the valves one by one, and the hose leading to the inflator, inside which there is usually a control cord for the air release valve.

When the air release valves work correctly, the buoyancy compensator is deflated. In conclusion, a visual inspection of the regulator's condition, the integrity of the hoses for microcracks and twists at the connection points inside the metal sleeves, is carried out. The inspection includes checking the glass of the pressure gauge or the integrity of the dive computer, second stages. The regulator is checked by removing the protective cap from the thread to check the integrity of the thread, the presence of a sealing ring in Din systems. (In Yoke system regulators, the sealing ring should be on the cylinder valve). In the absence of malfunctions, proceed to the assembly of the scuba. To bring the disassembled scuba into working condition, it is necessary to place the cylinder in a vertical position. Then take the buoyancy compensator, turning its back to the valve outlet, put it on the cylinder through one or two straps attaching it to the cylinder. Tighten the cylinder attachment strap, fastening the buckle in a way that the cylinder is securely (firmly) attached to the buoyancy compensator. (To check the reliability of the cylinder attachment, take the buoyancy compensator by the shoulder straps and try to shake the cylinder out of the strap with one or two sharp movements). If the cylinder moves even slightly, tighten the cylinder attachment strap more, and repeat the check. Before attaching the regulator to the cylinder valve, it is necessary to lubricate the sealing ring on the regulator (or cylinder) with a special lubricant. It should be noted that in regulators with two second stages, in single-valve single-cylinder systems, the hoses leading to the lung regulators are on one side (for right-handed - in the right hand, respectively for left-handed - in the left hand), and the hose leading to the inflator and pressure gauge is on the other side (for right-handed in the left hand, and for left-handed - in the right hand). When attaching the regulator to the cylinder, it should be taken into account that the hose leading to the inflator control panel on the buoyancy compensator is on the side of the left shoulder (standard) for right-handed people. For left-handed people, it is necessary to change the position of the hose on the buoyancy compensator, and if left-handed people cannot do this, one of the second stages can be located on the left side next to the hoses leading to the pressure gauge and buoyancy compensator. When attaching the regulator to the cylinder, hold the reducer at an angle of 30-45^0 clockwise, screwing the fastening without effort, feeling that the thread of the reducer has reached the moment when the sealing ring touches the valve (or the reducer for Yoke systems), clamping the sealing ring should be carried out not by tightening the fastening but by turning the reducer itself by

$30\text{-}45^0$ in the opposite direction (a quarter turn counterclockwise), aligning it to the zero degree mark relative to the vertical axis of the cylinder valve. Excessive clamping of the sealing ring is not recommended. After attaching the reducer to the cylinder, connect the quick-release mechanism of the inflator hose to the connector of the control panel. To do this, remove the protective cap from the inflator connector, then, taking the hose in the palm of your hand, use two fingers of the same hand to move the metal casing of the quick-release mechanism in the direction of the rubber hose, and with the other hand, hold the inflator, directing the metal connector into the hole of the quick-release mechanism of the air supply hose from the regulator. After putting the hose on the connector to the stop, release the casing of the quick-release mechanism, which will fix the hose on the inflator control panel. After checking the fixation of the hose on the inflator control panel, you can proceed to open the shut-off valve of the cylinder. Before opening the shut-off valve of the cylinder, turn the pressure gauge glass in the opposite direction. Then press and hold the bypass button on the second stage of the regulator, simultaneously starting to open the shut-off valve, hearing the hissing of air coming out through the second stage, release the bypass button, and continue to open the shut-off valve, unscrewing the handle to the stop, after which make a half turn of the rotating handle in the opposite direction. After that, place the assembled scuba on the cylinder in a horizontal position and, removing all hoses and devices inside the buoyancy compensator, secure the scuba in a stable vertical or horizontal position.

The disassembly of the scuba should be carried out in reverse order. First, it is necessary to place the scuba in a stable vertical or horizontal position. Before disassembling the scuba, close the shut-off valve of the cylinder. By pressing the bypass button on the second stage, bleed the air from the regulator system. Disconnect the air supply hose from the inflator control panel. Disconnect the regulator from the cylinder.

Remove the buoyancy compensator from the cylinder. Put protective caps on the regulator, cylinder valve, and inflator connector on the buoyancy compensator. Vent the air from the air bladder of the buoyancy compensator (if available).

Diver's entry into the water can be conditionally divided into three methods. The first method is entering the water from the shore, the second is entering the water with a wide step from a boat, ramp, or pier, and the third is entering the water backward from the side of a boat.

The first method

In the presence of a shallow shore with a solid bottom, divers, in full gear, supporting each other, enter the water backward until the depth allows swimming. After that, they should lie on the water and swim, sequentially executing the plan for further descent. If the water is calm and the bottom is firm enough for the diver to enter the water up to the waist, the diver, having donned the scuba and weight belt on the shore, wearing the mask around the neck with fins in hand, can enter the water up to the waist, then put on the fins and mask, and continue the scuba descent.

Fig. 234. Diver's entry with a wide step

The second method

Entering the water with a wide step is used when entering the water in full diving gear from a platform or a ship with a water entry area. The novice diver, in full diving gear with an inflated buoyancy compensator, should stand on the edge of the platform facing the water. With the palm of the right hand, press the mask and the second stage of the regulator to the face, and with the left hand, grab the back of the head, pressing the mask strap to the head. Pushing off, take a wide step forward. The step should be large and confident enough so that the cylinder, located on the back, does not catch on the edge of the platform. In the water, the novice diver must show the "OK" sign to the supporting diver.

The third method

The novice diver, in full diving gear (mouthpiece of the second stage in the mouth, mask on the face, fins on the feet), should sit on the edge of the boat with his back to the water. With the palm of the right hand, press the mask and the second stage of the regulator to the face, and with the left hand, grab the back of the head, pressing the mask strap to the head. Pushing off from the bottom of the boat with the feet, falling out of the boat, the diver should fall into the water backward.

Fig. 235. Diver's entry into the water backward

Changing the second-stage regulator underwater

Every diver, while underwater, should be able to switch from the main air supply to the reserve system by changing the second stages used for breathing. This exercise is fundamental and essential for all divers. In the event of removing (falling out) the mouthpiece of the second-stage regulator from the diver's mouth, the housing of the second stage instantly fills with water. To continue breathing underwater, it is necessary to clear the second-stage regulator's chamber of water. This can be done in two ways: by clearing it with a deep and sharp exhale or by using the forced air supply valve.

To practice the skill of removing the second-stage regulator from the mouth and continuing to breathe underwater, the diver should, while breathing from the scuba, immerse to a shallow depth. The depth for practicing the skill of changing the second-stage regulator should correspond to the diver's height so that the diver's head can be above the water if they wish to stand on the ground. Having reached the appropriate depth, the diver should deflate the buoyancy compensator. For convenience, stand on the bottom by kneeling or assuming a comfortable squatting position and holding onto the ladder (or lifeline) for stability with one hand. Taking a deep breath, the diver should hold their breath and remove the second stage of the regulator from their mouth with the other hand, directing the mouthpiece of the second-stage regulator towards the bottom. After that, the diver should slowly push the second stage away from them at arm's length and return the regulator to its original position by inserting the mouthpiece back into their mouth. With a sharp and deep exhale into the mouthpiece, the diver clears the chamber of the second stage of water, allowing them to continue breathing calmly.

The second method is practiced almost the same way as described in the previous section, with one small difference. Having reached the depth for practicing the skill of clearing the second stage of the regulator from water inside its housing, the diver must deflate the buoyancy compensator. For convenience, stand on the bottom by kneeling or assume a comfortable squatting position and hold onto the ladder with one hand. Taking a deep breath, the diver should hold their breath and remove the second stage of the regulator from their mouth with the other hand, directing the mouthpiece of the second-stage regulator towards the bottom. Then, the diver should slowly push the second stage away from them at arm's length and return the regulator to its original position. Inserting the mouthpiece into their mouth and blocking the air supply hole with their tongue, the diver should press the button responsible for the forced air supply to the regulator. In less than a second, the chamber of the regulator will be cleared of water by air, and the diver can continue peaceful breathing through the regulator. When changing the primary regulator to the reserve regulator, the exercise is performed with one additional difference.

Having reached the depth for practicing the initial skills, the diver must deflate the buoyancy compensator. For convenience, stand on the bottom, leaning on the knees, or assume a comfortable squatting position and hold onto the ladder with one hand. Taking a deep breath, the diver should hold their breath and remove the mouthpiece of the second stage of the regulator from their mouth, releasing the second stage from their hand. While the diver is underwater on breath-hold without an air-supplying regulator in their mouth, they should slightly tilt in the direction where the regulators of their regulator set are located (right for right-handed and left for left-handed, respectively). Tilting their right (left) arm backward, the diver should slowly make a circular motion to find the hoses leading to the second stages. Selecting the necessary regulator and inserting the mouthpiece into their mouth, the diver should clear the chamber of the regulator of water using one of the two methods described above and continue breathing through the selected regulator.

Practicing skills where the diver breathes from the partner's octopus. This skill may be useful for a diver in case of a sudden cessation of air supply for breathing from their own diving equipment. Such an emergency situation may arise due to equipment malfunction or in cases where air runs out underwater, or it is necessary to switch to an alternative source of breathing gas supply. The practice of this skill is conducted as follows: Both divers participating in the training should descend to a depth that should correspond to the height of the shorter diver so that, if desired, the shorter diver can stand on the ground with their head (which is shorter) above the water. Both divers sit on the bottom, leaning on their knees, facing each other at arm's length. The diver practicing the skill takes a deep breath, removes the regulator from their mouth, and releases it, after which they signal to their partner, 'I'm out of air.' Then, they find the partner's octopus, take it in their hand, and insert it into their mouth. After that, by holding the partner's right elbow with their right hand and taking the inflator with their left hand, the diver lifts themselves above, venting air from their buoyancy compensator (these movements indicate the simulation of an emergency controlled ascent). After breathing for 30 seconds, the skill of this exercise can be repeated. To consolidate this skill, the exercise with changing the primary regulator to the partner's octopus should be performed with both divers swimming at the bottom at a training depth. After practicing the skills of changing the primary regulator, the exercise with the reserve octopus can be reinforced by breathing in pairs from the same second stage of one regulator.

Practicing this skill proceeds as follows: After the student diver signals to the partner, 'I'm out of air,' the partner takes a deep breath, holds their breath, removes their regulator from their mouth with one hand, and hands it to the diver who ran out of air. At the same time, with the other hand, they grab the buoyancy compensator or the shoulder of their partner. After clearing the chamber of the regulator of water using one of the two methods, the student diver who ran out of air takes two deep breaths and returns the regulator to the partner. In turn, the partner takes the same two deep breaths and passes their regulator to the student diver. Holding onto the partner's shoulder or buoyancy compensator with their left hand, they take the inflator with their right hand and lift it above, venting air, simulating an emergency controlled ascent.

Removing water from under the mask

Quite often, water can get under a diver's mask. Depending on the situation, the diver may need to clear the mask underwater to prevent fogging of the viewing glass or put on a mask underwater in case of an emergency situation. To practice this skill, the diver needs to descend to a training depth that corresponds to their height, allowing the student diver to stand up in full height, supporting themselves with their feet on the ground if necessary, while keeping their head above water. Having reached the appropriate depth, the diver must deflate the buoyancy compensator. For convenience, kneel on the bottom or assume a comfortable squatting position. To avoid eye irritation from dirty water, the exercise can be performed with closed eyes.

The practice of this skill is as follows: being in a vertical position relative to the bottom, the diver should tilt their head slightly forward and, using their fingers, lift the lower part of the mask seal to allow a small amount of water to enter the space under the mask. Then, holding the mask with both hands, gently move it to allow the water inside to wash the mask lenses. After that, the diver should return their head to a vertical position, press the mask to their face around the forehead area, and smoothly make one (or several) deep exhalations through the nose while slightly lifting the lower part of the mask with the thumbs. Nose exhalation should be carried out until all the water is completely removed from the space under the mask. If defogging the mask was not successful on the first attempt, the exercise should be repeated. In case water accidentally enters the space under the mask, it is necessary to check the possibility of hair getting under the mask seal or the tension of the retaining strap.

After practicing this skill, the exercise of removing water from the mask space should be reinforced by changing masks underwater. To do this, the diver needs to completely remove one mask from their head, replace it with another mask, and then remove the water from the mask space.

Purging

During descent, the pressure from the surrounding environment increases on the diver's body, so it is necessary to equalize the pressure, anticipating the onset of pain in the ears.

Fig. 236. Purging

The more often the diver equalizes the pressure in the Eustachian tubes with the surrounding environment, the less painful the descent will be. The exercise is conducted jointly with the instructor. This exercise can be started at the surface. To do this, the diver should close their nostrils through the mask with the thumb and index finger in such a way that when attempting to exhale air from the lungs through the nose, there is a sensation of filling the inside of both ears with air, without the air from the nose coming out. Feeling the complete filling of both ears with exhaled air from the inside, you can start descending underwater. Literally every half meter of descent, the instructor must check the condition of the student diver and perform another equalization. If the ear has not equalized, it is necessary to ascend half a meter higher and equalize again. If equalization is still unsuccessful, the diving descent should be stopped, and the diver should ascend to the surface.

It is recommended to practice this skill with a descent along a line with depth markings, initially not exceeding 12 meters. During ascent from the bottom to the surface, breath-holding should be avoided, and the ascent rate should be at least two times slower than the rate of bubble ascent from exhaled air (no more than 10 meters per minute).

Neutral buoyancy

The hover of a diver in a horizontal position and the hover of a diver in a vertical position within the water column are practiced by student divers at the bottom. These skills are recommended for refining the neutral buoyancy of a diver at depth. To achieve neutral buoyancy at the bottom in a horizontal position, the student diver, descending to the bottom, must completely vent the air from the buoyancy compensator. Upon reaching the bottom, they should lie face down on the substrate, avoiding bending the knees. After assuming a horizontal position, the diver gradually inflates the buoyancy compensator using the inflator (or, in case of inflator malfunction, by orally inflating the buoyancy compensator) until the body is lifted about $300-400$ millimeters above the substrate, with the tips of the fins barely touching the ground. While exhaling, the diver should feel their body settling onto the substrate, and during inhalation, the body should slightly rise. In this position, the diver should remain for at least 30 seconds, controlling buoyancy with their breathing.

Afterward (without holding the breath or taking deep breaths), the diver should swim a distance of 10-15 meters above the substrate. Then, they should stop and, without moving their legs or arms, hover over the substrate for at least 30 seconds, adjusting buoyancy if necessary through breathing.

To practice the skill of vertical hovering in the water column, the student diver should sit on the bottom and completely vent the air from the buoyancy compensator. This exercise should be divided into two stages: first, practicing neutral buoyancy skills with a seated position, and second, practicing the skill in the lotus position. For the first stage, the student should gradually inflate the buoyancy compensator until their body detaches from the bottom by about half a meter. Then, the diver should assume a seated position, resembling someone sitting on a chair, and if necessary, they are allowed to adjust buoyancy only with their breath, without using hand or leg movements. The student should maintain this position for at least one minute.

For the second stage, the student diver should kneel on the bottom, fully vent the air from the buoyancy compensator, and, by gradually inflating the compensator, achieve a weightless state where the knees lift about 15-20 cm above the substrate with straightened legs. After that, take a deep breath and cross the legs, sitting in the lotus position about half a meter above the substrate. Buoyancy can only be adjusted through breathing. The student should maintain a state of neutral buoyancy for at least one minute.

Exchanging diving equipment with another diver on the bottom

The practice of this skill can be conditionally divided into two stages. The first stage involves removing, exchanging, and donning the weight belt, and the second stage involves removing, exchanging, and donning the scuba unit with the buoyancy compensator.

First stage

During their descent, the student diver, reaching the bottom, must completely vent the air from the buoyancy compensator. Then, they need to sit on the bottom so that their spread legs and the tank behind serve as points of support. After that, using both hands, unbuckle the weight belt. Holding the buckle with the left hand and the free end with the right hand, press the weight belt against the back and transfer the strap to the abdomen in such a way that the buckle is on the right and the free end is on the left. Fasten the belt and pass it to the assisting diver. Receive the weight belt from the assisting diver. Sit in the same position as when removing the weight belt. Place the weighted belt on the abdomen, unbuckle the buckle, use the right hand to grab the belt by the free end where the weights end, and use the left hand to lean against the bottom. Then, the diver should flip over onto the abdomen over the left shoulder, simultaneously grabbing the belt buckle with the left hand, placing the weighted belt on the back. After that, tighten the belt to size, fasten the buckle, and flip back to the original position.

Second stage

During the diving descent, while on the bottom, the student diver and assisting divers must completely vent the air from their buoyancy compensators, positioning themselves opposite each other on the substrate and leaning on their knees. The distance between the divers should allow for easy placement of the equipment set between them, and each diver should be able to reach it with their hand. After that, each diver should loosen the shoulder straps and unbuckle the waist and chest straps. If necessary, the student diver should open the left shoulder buckle, remove the buoyancy compensator from their shoulders, and place the scuba unit in front of them while holding it with one hand. The student should continue breathing from the regulator of their scuba unit during this process. When the scuba unit of the assisting diver is next to their own scuba unit, the student diver should slightly lean toward the side where the spare second stage of the assisting diver's regulator is located. Holding their scuba unit by the shoulder straps of the buoyancy compensator with one hand, the diver should use the other hand to take the octopus from the other scuba unit. After taking a deep breath and holding their breath, the diver should remove the second stage of their own regulator from their mouth, insert the octopus from the other scuba unit into their mouth. Then, using one of two methods, the diver should clear the water from the octopus and continue breathing through the regulator of the second scuba unit. Once it is ensured that the assisting diver has made the same replacement of the second stage and is breathing from the second stage of the student diver's regulator, the divers can exchange scuba units. After receiving the scuba unit from the assisting diver, the student diver should, if necessary, buckle the shoulder buckles and loosen the shoulder straps. Insert the right hand into the right shoulder strap of the buoyancy compensator and (with the same right hand) grab the tank by the bottom, move the compensator to the back. With the left hand, find the left shoulder strap and insert the hand into it. Then, release the bottom of the tank, fasten the waist and chest straps, and tighten the shoulder straps of the buoyancy compensator. Continue the diving descent according to the dive plan.

§ 25. Features of diving descents in various conditions

All diving descents must be thoroughly thought out, planned, and executed by experienced divers. The leader of the diving descent must conduct additional safety briefings in each specific case, considering the specifics of the descent in challenging conditions, and record this information in the diving log.

Descents in swift currents

The safety of diving descents largely depends on how well the conditions in which they are performed are taken into account. This is especially true for descents in challenging conditions, such as strong currents or storms. Diving descents from a drifting vessel are not allowed. When changing currents during the tide and ebb, the vessel should not rotate so that the diver's hose and signal line do not get entangled with the anchor chain. Descents in currents of 2 meters per second are prohibited. Diving descents are not allowed in waves exceeding 3 points. In exceptional cases, for the purpose of saving lives, diving descents are allowed in waves up to 5 points. A breaking wave can knock the diver off their feet and drag them across the rocky bottom, leading to a dangerous location with possible underwater obstacles.

If the descent is made from a ship, the diver may be hit by a wave against the ship's side or knocked off the ladder. Floating means are positioned so that after paying out the anchor chain to a depth of 8-10 meters, the diver descends to the work site with the current. For descents from the shore to inspect the riverbed, a guide must be laid in advance from one shore to the other, which is delivered to the opposite shore by a boat or shot with a line thrower. In all cases of descents in swift currents, increased requirements are imposed on diving equipment and descent support means. Due to the impossibility of communication using the signal line in strong currents, only telephone, radio, or sound communication is used. To increase the stability of the diver underwater, a double set of weights is worn. Diving weights and boots are of increased weight. Diving hoses of the spiral type are used. When descending along the descent line, the diver is equipped with additional detachable ballast.

Diving in a diving bell should be carried out using additional ballasting. In the absence of a diving bell, the descent of divers is allowed along the descent line with weighted ballast. In this case, the mass of the ballast on the descent line should be increased to a level where it does not sweep away the descent line (75-100 kg). During descent, it is recommended to use a sliding carabiner, with which the diver holds onto the descent line. To move to the work site, a travel line attached to the ballast of the descent line and a metal rod (on soft bottoms) are used. Releasing the travel line from the hands of the diver is prohibited. When descending in a rebreather, to prevent the inadvertent venting of the gas mixture from the bag through the relief valve, the diver must assume a position where the breathing bag of the rebreather is protected from rapid flow by any large underwater object or the diver's body. Using various devices, experienced divers can perform work in currents with speeds of up to 1 meter per second. Diving descents and ascents are carried out only along the descent line. A strong rope called the 'travel line' with a buoy at the end is attached to the load on the descent line. During ground movement, the diver holds onto the buoy without putting it on their arm. The diver's movement speed on the bottom in strong currents can be very slow, as in some cases, the diver needs to lean forward significantly, crawl if necessary, pressing against the bottom with a metal probe or knife, and simultaneously, pushing off with the toes, move forward. For prolonged and complex tasks (ship lifting, underwater welding and cutting, etc.) and when the current speed exceeds 2 meters per second, protective devices are used: shock shields, deflectors, floodable containers, etc. A standby boat should be present at the descent site. In case of an emergency ascent of the diver to the surface, they must be towed by the boat to the diver's ladder or pulled up on a signal cable, hose, and lifted onto the deck. A repeated descent to depth is only allowed if the diver feels well.

Descents at night

Diving descents at night make it difficult to service the diver and observe them from the surface. For underwater work at night, divers are provided with powerful directional light sources: lamps and spotlights of the diving station and the adjacent water surface to have good visibility of the station's instruments, signal line, hose, and air bubbles rising to the water surface. The workplace underwater and the underwater part of the diver's ladder are illuminated with underwater lights, a portable lamp, and flashlights. Divers should be provided with daytime rest and sleep before night descents.

Diver's work in narrow spaces, such as tubes, trenches, tight compartments of sunken ships, so-called wrecks, and caves, is considered the most complex and requires special training. Before starting the dive, the diver should familiarize themselves with the available information about the location: room drawings and the arrangement of mechanisms and loads, the direction of underwater currents, and others if possible. When descending into a dark flooded compartment of a ship, a permanent light source or beacon is installed opposite the entrance hole, serving as a landmark. For underwater work, a minimum of two divers are directed - a working and a safety diver. After descending into a flooded area, the diver secures the travel line

Fig. 237. Descents at night

at the entrance, attaching the other end of the line at the workplace, so that with its help, divers can return to the exit in case the signal line gets entangled. During this time, communication between divers (in the absence of radio and telephone communication) is carried out either using a connecting line or by sound signals (whistle or blows to the ship's hull § 21). During work in narrow spaces, various devices should be bypassed, and the narrowest sections should be passed forward with the feet, and return forward with the head.

Descents under the hull of a distressed ship

When sealing holes in the ship's hull, the diver must be careful not to be sucked to the hole by the water flow entering the hull. To avoid this, the diver needs to approach the hole cautiously, holding on securely to the bell or ladder, and perform the work in such a way as to be able to quickly change their position and move away from the hole. When placing and securing patches, the diver should ensure that the signal line and hoses and cables are not caught by the patch and keel ends. Lowering a diver under the hull of a grounded ship or rocks is only possible if the ship sits firmly on the bottom, does not move, and does not rock under the influence of waves. The diver should avoid narrow and inaccessible places, as with slight movement of the ship, they may be crushed by the hull, or their exit may be blocked.

Work in smoke-filled compartments of the ship

In the event of shipboard fires, diving breathing apparatus is used as special respiratory devices for entry into smoke-filled compartments. Divers are assigned in pairs for work: one is the working diver, and the other ensures support. For reconnaissance and firefighting, divers wear breathing apparatus with masks or helmets and signal lines. When using oxygen breathing apparatus, they are covered with pieces of wet burlap to protect against sparks and overheating. Thin steel cable should be used as signal lines, and special gloves, if possible, to protect divers' hands from burns when touching hot objects. Communication between divers in smoke-filled compartments is ensured in the same way as when working in a flooded compartment. Diving into aggressive liquid solutions with high density, such as oil and petroleum products, is allowed only in cases of extreme necessity for emergency elimination or human life rescue.

Descents into gasoline and other volatile and toxic liquids are prohibited

When descending into muddy water or clayey mine solutions with a density significantly higher than that of water, additional weight should be added to the descending diver, evenly distributed over various parts of the equipment. The total mass of additional weight is determined by trial descents depending on the density of the muddy water or solution. Special diving equipment should be used for descents. When descending into aggressive liquids, special dry-type diving suits made of special materials are used. To prevent corrosion, suits should be thoroughly moistened with fresh water before each descent, and a layer of liquid soap should be applied to the surface. After each descent, corrosive and inflating valves should be cleaned of petroleum products, wiped with waste, and metal parts lubricated with special silicone grease. The duration of a diving descent should be limited to 30 to 60 minutes, depending on the diver's condition and working conditions. The duration of work in one diving equipment should not exceed 3 hours.

Diving descents in winter and under ice

Winter dives for divers are carried out at air temperatures not lower than -15 °C. In cases of extreme necessity, such as fighting for the survival of the vessel or rescuing individuals, dives are allowed at lower temperatures with mandatory implementation of safety measures depending on specific conditions. The duration of ice dives depends on the specific tasks assigned to the diving group and is generally limited to a diving time of 10 to 15 minutes, especially if divers are wearing

Fig. 238. Diving descents under ice

wet diving suits. Dives are halted with a growing sensation of cold, as there is a risk of slow attention loss and inadequate responsiveness. General weakness arises, leading to erroneous reactions in case of accidents.

Fig. 239. The heated tent set up near the dive site

During underwater dives in reduced temperature conditions, measures are taken to prevent the divers from hypothermia and the freezing of diving equipment. Steps must be taken to preserve the strength of the ice cover at dive locations. It is prohibited to discard on the ice combustible and lubricating materials that degrade the strength of the ice. Divers dress and check their equipment in a warm facility located as close as possible to the dive site. Hot water should always be available at the dive site if possible. For extended work on mines, a booth on skis is installed for direct dives. Diving hoses must be well purged with compressed air before and after immersion to remove moisture. Air in the air system cylinders should be pumped the day before so that its temperature decreases to the ambient temperature, and the water in it has time to condense and be removed by blowing.

Requirements for diving equipment

Ideally, a diver should be dressed in warm (or woolen) and dry wetsuit with a separate argon inflation system (a gas with low thermal conductivity). It is desirable for the diver to dive in a carbon helmet or a full-face mask. For short dives, regular diving masks, neoprene wet suits with a thickness of at least 7 mm, neoprene diving hoods, gloves, and socks are mandatory. For dives under ice or in cold water, only cold-water regulators should be used. When diving in cold water, each diver should have a backup source of breathing gas. To do this, either pony bottles or independent systems with two independent regulators on a double-valve cylinder, or a spark with two valves and separate breathing gas supply systems for the diver, should be used. It should be understood that any regulator can fail to deliver gas freely or stop gas delivery. In case of any emergency situation, diving should be immediately stopped, and the surface should be returned to.

The procedure for conducting an under-ice diving descent begins with planning. To facilitate team collaboration, the diver group gathers, assigns responsibilities for each participant in the upcoming under-ice immersion, and first determines the descent location. Experienced divers familiar with the local terrain identify a safe spot for ice entry, considering not only the surface conditions, ice thickness, depth, current speed, and direction but also the seabed conditions if the descent is less than 5 meters deep. The under-ice immersion takes place in close proximity to the ice surface with a sufficient depth for submersion, typically considered acceptable between 5 to 10 meters. It is essential to account for the fact that in areas with slushy ice and still water, the first descending diver will stir up a cloud of murky water, limiting visibility during the descent.

Another crucial factor is considering that the farther the descent location is from the transport access point, the more resources and time are required to deliver necessary diving equipment and auxiliary gear, such as an ice auger, chainsaw, under-ice anchor, guiding ropes, and lines. During the planning phase, all preparations for the under-ice immersion must be documented in writing.

Under-ice immersion should be conducted through a specially carved ice hole. Firstly, a sufficient area is prepared to accommodate the cut, equipment, and the diver securing and supporting the diver. The shape and size of the cut depend on the objectives. The hole can be triangular, quadrangular, or rectangular with side dimensions ranging from 1.5 to 3 meters. A triangular cut allows the descending diver to brace against sharp corners with both hands, facilitating easier access to the ice.

Fig. 240. Photo of the ice hole

In a specific location, after clearing the ice of snow, the installation of reliable and clearly visible barriers begins. Typically, wooden logs are frozen into the ice around the immersion area, and red-white or black-yellow strips are stretched along the perimeter. Using a chainsaw or a specialized manual ice saw, the necessary-sized ice hole is cut. To ease the cutting of the ice thickness at the corners of the cut, it is recommended to use an ice auger to make holes.

Fig. 241. Triangular ice hole

After measuring and cutting the openings in the ice, the main ice hole is lined with thick boards on the edges and cleared of fine ice. A diver's ladder is lowered into the hole, and the release end is led out. To secure the ladder or release end and the root part of the signaling line, a second small cut is made nearby, where a log with a pre-attached loop for fastening the ends is frozen or led. The diver's reel with an adequate reserve of rope is also secured to this log. Each diver must have an individual reel secured on the surface near the exit from the cut. It is prohibited to fasten ropes of different divers to one and the same log. For each reel used by different divers, a separate cut with a frozen or led log is required, and all ropes are measured to the required length on-site. Usually, the distance of the under-ice immersion is limited to 25 meters, taking into account the immersion depth.

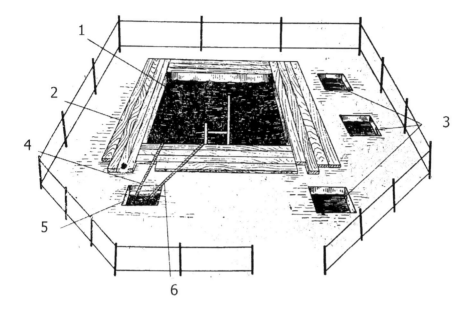

Fig. 242. Ice hole: (1) - ice hole for descending underwater; (2) - boards, (3) - small cutout windows, (4) - small property for the log, (5) - rope for securing the ladder; (6) - descent line.

To ensure the safety of the ice diving descent, safety holes are cut along the shoreline in case of emergency situations. Typically, they are small in size and located at a depth of approximately 1.5 meters. If orientation is lost, the error can be corrected using a compass – divers turn north and head towards the shoreline, in the direction the compass points before submerging under the ice. In case of an orientation mistake (right-left), swimming along the shoreline allows one to reach the designated location where a spare hole is located after some time. After this, preparation for the ice dive is considered complete.

Before submerging, the diver's belt is secured with a safety line, tying the knot to prevent unintentional untying. The line should be positioned under the buoyancy compensator so the diver can remove the scuba gear underwater to address any malfunctions. Divers are grouped in pairs, each connected by a signaling line to the surface support divers. The signaling line serves three functions: creating a line of orientation for the group, assisting in returning, and facilitating communication with simple signals. In case of limited visibility or current, diving pairs are tethered together.

All divers, including support and safety divers remaining on the surface, must undergo safety and emergency procedure training. Immediately before entering the safety hole, a buoy is placed as a reference, and a shield is set up as a reminder of coordinated signals for support and safety divers. The number of divers simultaneously entering through one hole should not exceed two to avoid entangling safety lines. Dives start and end only in the hole where the descent has already taken place.

At the beginning of the dive, the diver must maintain a breathing rhythm: slow inhale, pause, slow exhale. This rhythm reduces the likelihood of regulator freezing. After stabilizing breathing, the diver should check regulators for freezing and possibly switch the second stage to free-flow gas delivery mode. To do this, it is necessary to breathe from the second stages of each regulator in turn.

During ice dives, care should be taken not to cut or damage the edges of the ice, the signal line, or other diving equipment. Every diver going under the ice must possess the following skills: maintaining neutral buoyancy (to avoid collisions with the ice), slowing down ascent in case of losing part of the weight to reduce impact on the ice, and signaling using safety line. During the dive, each submerged diver should periodically send signals according to their condition. When bringing a diver up from the depth under the ice, the diver should use the signaling line to move towards the hole, pushing off the ice with hands and feet. In case of any equipment malfunctions or a sudden feeling of intense cold, the diver should immediately cease underwater work and resurface.

Means of providing ice diving descent

During the descent, a support and safety diver must be on the surface, whose duties include assisting in entering and exiting the safety hole, relaying signals to and from the diver underwater, lifting the diver to the surface in case of an emergency signal, providing first aid if necessary, and ensuring the presence of a rescue diver ready to start the rescue immediately (equipped and tied with a line). It is mandatory for the diver to be dressed and ready for the descent in cold air at low temperatures, posing a threat of freezing of the diving gear. Rubber equipment loses elasticity and becomes brittle; freezing valves in the breathing apparatus and regulators occur, forming ice plugs in the hose connections, obstructing air supply. The chemical absorbent and regenerative substance freeze and cease to work. To avoid this, one should try to minimize the time a diver spends on the surface between leaving the premises and diving into the water. After leaving the water, the diver should quickly return to the premises. To prevent freezing of the diving equipment valves during the diver's transition to the workplace, regulators and apparatuses are insulated with warm materials. In case of freezing, they are poured with hot water or immersed in a hole for thawing and airing.

Emergency situations during diving descents

During diving descents, there is a possibility of situations where there is a danger to the life of the diver. Such situations can be divided into two groups: the first includes cases where the diver finds himself in a position where there is an obstacle to reaching the surface (these include entanglement of the diver, surfacing, sinking into the depth); the second group includes various malfunctions of the diving equipment. In the event of any emergency situation, the descending and securing divers must assess the situation without unnecessary haste and take immediate measures to ensure the safety of the descending diver. When working in narrow and hard-to-reach places, the signal line, telephone cable, or breathing gas supply hose may become entangled.

If entanglement or jamming occurs and it is impossible to untangle them, the sequence of the diver's actions will depend on what is entangled. When only the signal line is entangled, the diver takes it in his hands on both sides of the entanglement and, using a diving knife, first cuts it between himself and the entanglement, then on the other side of it, after which he ties the free ends and signals for ascent.

Fig. 243. Emergency ascent

If the telephone cable becomes entangled, the diver cuts it on both sides of the entanglement and, using the signal line for communication, surfaces. In case of simultaneous entanglement of the signal line and the telephone cable, the diver first cuts and ties the signal line, then cuts the telephone cable. In the event of simultaneous entanglement of the signal line, telephone cable, and breathing gas supply hose, the diver first cuts and ties the signal line, informs the surface about the emergency situation. Upon receiving such a signal on the surface, the securing diver is immediately prepared, and if the diver underwater cannot untangle himself independently, a securing diver is sent to him.

When working in a current or loss of cargo, in cases where the diver gains excessive positive buoyancy, the diver should try to hold onto the work area by grabbing onto some object with his hands. In case of uncontrolled ascent, he should try to make continuous exhalations until surfacing to avoid barotrauma of the lungs. In the event of rapid descent and a sharp increase in pressure, it is possible for the diver to be squeezed. In cases of the diver sinking to the depth (for example, when he is torn off from the platform or from the downline), the diver should make a continuous inhalation, if possible, to fill the lungs as much as possible, simultaneously selecting the signal line and, with frequent pulls on it, signal the securing diver. The securing diver, noticing the sinking working diver or receiving a signal from him, must immediately and as quickly as possible pick up the signal line, hold it, and immediately lift the diver to the surface. Continuous air supply under pressure or a sudden decrease or cessation of air supply should be considered emergency malfunctions of the scuba regulator. In the case of continuous air supply, the diver must release the mouthpiece from his mouth and, holding it with his hand, make careful inhalations through compressed lips, immediately starting to ascend to the surface. The cessation of air supply requires the diver to take more rapid and decisive actions. Sensing a lack of air on inhalation or a failure to supply it, the diver must hold his breath and immediately begin to ascend to the surface, using the free ascent method, discarding weights.

Free ascent

The method of free ascent involves the diver's lung air supply at depth exceeding the surface air supply by a factor equal to the pressure at depth over atmospheric pressure. During forced ascent, the diver should not delay exhalation or accelerate it by compressing the chest. As the diver ascends to the surface, the air in the lungs will expand, and the diver will feel its excess, requiring continuous exhalation.

Simultaneously, this exhalation should be moderate to maintain a sufficient air supply in the lungs. The diver should keep the mouth open, allowing the air to freely exit the lungs. At the same time, to avoid decompression sickness, the ascent speed should not exceed 1 meter per second. The ascent speed should be regulated by following rising air bubbles, moving behind them and not overtaking.

Checkpoint questions for chapter five:

1. What activities are involved in organizing diving descents?

2. How is the descent of divers conducted underwater?

3. How is the diver's ascent performed?

4. How is the three-time flushing of the oxygen system conducted?

5. What is a diving station?

6. What types of diving signals are used in diving?

7. How is the scuba gear arranged?

8. What are the basic safety rules when working in swift currents?

9. What communication tools are used with the diver during immersion?

10. What does the flag on a vessel indicating 'Diver Down' look like?

11. What does the international diving flag look like?

12. What are the types of diving signals?

13. State the meaning of the diving signal where the rope is pulled twice.

14. State the meaning of the diving signal where the rope is pulled with frequent tugs.

15. State the meaning of the visual signal where the diver makes a throat-cutting gesture with the edge of the palm.

16. State the meaning of the visual signal where the diver forms a triangle with the palms of both hands, touching the fingers.

17. State the meaning of the visual signal where the diver clenches the fist and points upward with the thumb.

18. What is the no-decompression limit?

19. How does a no-decompression descent differ from a decompression descent?

20. How does a 'safety stop' differ from a 'deepwater stop'?

21. What are decompression tables intended for?

22. How is the assembly of scuba gear performed?

23. How is the weight belt worn in the water?

24. How is the clearing of a diver's mask conducted?

25. How many weights should a diver have for neutral buoyancy?

26. How many additional weights should a diver have when diving with a full 18-liter air cylinder at an operating pressure of 300 bars?

27. How to remove water from the second stage regulator when changing the demand valve?

28. How to remove water from under the mask space?

29. How is the change of scuba gear performed underwater?

31. How are diving descents conducted in narrow spaces?

32. How are diving descents under the hull of a distressed ship conducted?

33. How are diving descents in swift currents conducted?

34. How are diving descents in smoke-filled compartments of a ship conducted?

35. How are diving descents under ice conducted?

36. Name two groups of emergency situations during diving descents.

37. Describe the method of free ascent.

38. Describe how to check the waterproof integrity of a dry-type wetsuit.

VI CHAPTER
HYDROTECHNICAL STRUCTURES

Chapter sixth of this textbook explores hydraulic engineering and marine structures. The chapter contains useful information about the river structure and geological aspects, defining a shoal and examining factors influencing flow velocity in rivers

The chapter delves into hydraulic structures, which will be useful to divers when inspecting, repairing or constructing overflow canals and spillways, indicating their differences and structural features. The process of lockage is explained, providing insights into its execution. Various types and forms of dams are covered, including the concept of rapids, enhancing understanding of hydraulic structures.

The chapter provides a detailed examination introduce s marine hydraulic structures, unraveling their functionalities, and of the definition of types of hydraulic structures: water intakes, piers and breakwaters, each of which has its own characteristics. Information is given on the dry docks to provide a comprehensive understanding of their design and usefulness in the context of commercial diving.

§ 26. Fundamentals of hydrology

Hydrology is the science of the waters of the Earth and the processes occurring in these waters. River hydrology is one of the branches of hydrology that examines processes occurring specifically in river waters. A river is a watercourse formed by the combination of atmospheric precipitation and groundwater. For rivers located in regions of the Earth with sub-zero temperatures during the winter calendar period, three main periods are characteristic: spring high water; summer-fall period, during which the river is mainly fed by groundwater; winter period, which is divided into three phases: freezing; ice formation; breakup. The period when vessel movement is possible along the river is called navigation. The area from which a river collects water is called the river basin. The place where a river's permanent channel appears is called the river's source or origin. The point where the river flows into the sea, lake, or another river is called the river's mouth. The longitudinal profile of the river is obtained by making a longitudinal section of the river (or its section) along the line of greatest depths. When constructing the longitudinal profile of the river, the vertical scale is taken much larger than the horizontal one, causing the riverbed profile to appear as a serrated line, with peaks corresponding to shallow areas (rapids) and troughs to deep areas (pools).

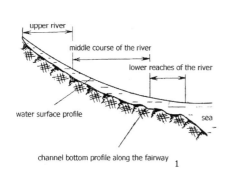

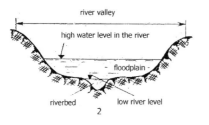

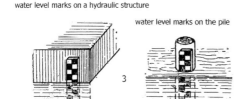

Fig. 244. River profile: (1) – longitudinal river profile, (2) – transverse profile of the river valley, (3) – rail water gauge post: on the wall of a hydraulic structure, on a single column.

The transverse section of the river valley is determined by a vertical plane, in which the following elements are distinguished:

River valley – a trench-like depression in the Earth's crust formed by the long-term activity of the river.

Riverbed – the lowest part of the valley occupied by the river flow at average and low water levels.

Floodplain – the part of the valley bottom filled during high water levels. The river level throughout the calendar year is not constant. Usually, it rises in spring due to snowmelt, during rain floods, glacial melting, and high-altitude snow.

The river level is monitored at certain points – water gauge posts of various types. The flow velocity at all points in the transverse section of the river is not constant. At the bottom, it is less than on the surface, and in the middle, it is greater than at the banks.

The flow rate depends on the slope of the river, depth, and roughness of the channel. In plain rivers, the speed varies from 0.2 to 3 meters per second, while in mountainous ones, it ranges from 6 to 8 meters per second and more. River waters carry solid particles of sediment, called sediments, formed as a result of channel erosion and soil erosion from the basin surface. Part of the eroded products, when the flow rate decreases in the middle and lower reaches, begins to settle at the bottom, forming elevated areas - shoals and riffles. Shoals adjacent to one of the banks are called shoreline, and those in the middle of the river, not connected to the banks, are called midstream. Long and relatively narrow shoals are called bars.

A riffle is a sedimentary formation, usually a slanting transverse wave, crossing the river channel. River mouths flowing into seas and oceans are subject to the action of tides. During high tide, seawater moves upstream, causing a change in the direction and speed of the flow in its estuarine part. The tidal current diminishes with distance. During low tide, seawater begins to move back towards the estuary, and the flow rate increases. The movement and displacement of sediments during high tide occur from the sea upstream, and during low tide - in the opposite direction, with sediments being carried into the sea most intensively at this time.

Types of river hydraulic structures

A dam is a hydraulic structure that is part of a pressure hydrocomplex. A hydrocomplex is a complex of hydraulic structures erected on one section of a river and interconnected by purpose and operation. For example, the "Svetlovodsk hydrocomplex" (on the Dnieper River in Ukraine), consists of a dam, hydroelectric power station, and a navigation lock. The dam obstructs the watercourse and holds water on one side (upstream) at a higher level than on the other (downstream). This difference in water levels is called the head on the structure and is denoted by the Latin letter "H." The part of the reservoir or river located above the dam is called the upper headrace, and the part below the dam is called the lower headrace.

There are many types and designs of dams that differ in construction materials, structural features, and methods of water passage. According to construction materials, dams are divided into the following types:

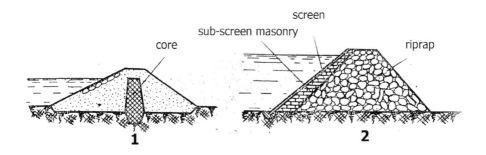

Fig. 245. Dams: (1) - an earthen dam with a clay core; (2) - a dam of stone structure with a reinforced concrete screen

Earth dams. They are constructed from local soils. Such dams adapt well to foundation deformations and do not form dangerous cracks. The dam body can be homogeneous if the soils it consists of are impermeable to water. If the soil filters strongly (e.g., sand), impermeable barriers made of clay, silt, or concrete are created in the dam body.

Stone-fill dams consist of a mound of stones of various weights (from 80 kg to 3 tons and more). Gaps between large stones are filled with smaller stones. To ensure water impermeability, a waterproof screen made of reinforced concrete, clay, etc., is placed in the upper slope zone.

Concrete dams are constructed from hydraulic concrete with the addition of large stones. Reinforced concrete dams are characterized by special strength, provide significant concrete savings, but their construction requires a large amount of metal.

Wooden dams of pile or log type are simple in design but not durable due to the susceptibility of wood to decay.

By design features, dams are classified into the following types:

Gravity dams resist sliding due to their own weight. This category includes earth, stone, concrete, and sometimes wooden dams.

Arch dams resemble an arch in plan. Such dams are built at sturdy banks in narrow gorges. They transfer all the load from the water pressure to the banks.

Buttress dams consist of a series of trapezoidal walls, located at some distance from each other and covered with flat slabs or arches. To prevent the buttresses from bending under the water pressure, they are often connected to each other with horizontal beams of rigidity. In most cases, buttress dams are made of reinforced concrete.

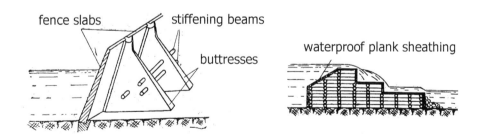

Fig. 246. Diagram of a solid and log-type dam

By the method of water passage, dams are divided into spillway dams, where water drains over the dam body, and impervious dams that do

399

not allow water overflow. In impervious dams, water from the upper headrace to the lower one passes through special water-permeable structures located outside the dam or through openings in its body. These openings are called spillways and have gates. The spillway dam includes impervious and spillway parts called spillways and covered with gates.

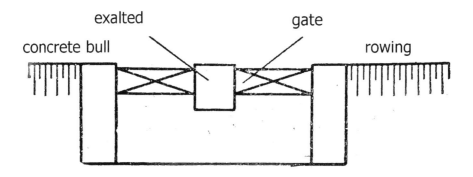

Fig. 247. Scheme of the spillway part of the dam

The main forces acting on the dam are the water pressure from the upper headrace and the filtration pressure of the flow on the base of the structure directed from bottom to top, reducing the stability of the dam. Filtration pressure arises under the action of the head created by the dam when a certain amount of water, moving between the particles of the soil or through cracks, enters the lower headrace, washing away particles of soil from under the structure. The flow overflowing through the spillway falls into the lower headrace from a great height and can cause erosion of the bottom behind the dam if measures are not taken to strengthen it. The foundation part of the dam, through which the water flow passes, is called the flue bed. The body of the dam is the part that perceives the pressure of the water. The plunge is made of impermeable or non-permeable materials. It protects the channel in front of the structure from erosion and serves as an extension of the water filtration path under the structure, reducing filtration pressure. For the same purposes, sheet-piled walls at the base of the dam, made of wood or metal (for a long length), are used. The water breaker is a massive concrete slab that absorbs the impact of water falling through the spillway. The riprap protects the bottom from erosion by the flow at the transition from increased speeds to normal. It is less massive and is usually made of stone rubble or dressed stone, loaded with stone, etc. In rocky soils at the base of the structure, the plunge, riprap, and sometimes the water breaker are absent, and instead of sheet piling, a cementation curtain is installed. For this, holes are drilled under the front edge of the dam, and a cement solution is poured into them, which fills all the cracks in the rock, thereby increasing the water resistance of the dam.

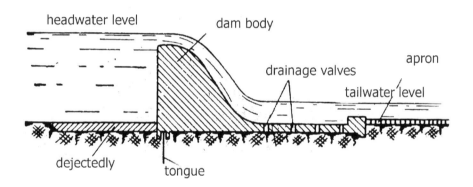

Fig. 248. Elements of the dam's flue

At the lower end of the flue bed and under the water breaker, where the filtrating water exits into the lower headrace, drains of various designs are installed. They provide a free outlet for water, thereby reducing filtration pressure and at the same time preventing the erosion of soil from under the structure. To prevent filtration through the shore bypass of the dam where it attaches to the banks, anti-filtration structures such as sheet-piled walls and screens are also constructed.

The spillway dam usually occupies not the entire width of the river channel but its deeper part. Sections of the dam connecting the spillway part to the banks are constructed from local material. The spillway and impervious sections are connected to each other using so-called piers. If the distance between the piers is large, additional supports (bulls) for bridges and lifting mechanisms of the gates are placed between them. Spillways and spillways at dams serve to discharge floodwaters from the reservoir and are used to drain reservoirs. Spillways are constructed in the banks and are often open. They consist of an inlet channel, a spillway proper with gates or without them, and a discharge part of rapid flow (a channel with a steep slope lined with concrete) or a stepped drop and a discharge channel. Various energy dissipaters are installed at the end of the discharge part. Sometimes closed shaft spillways are used.

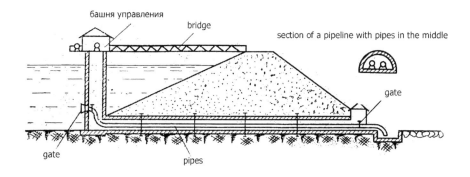

Fig. 249. Scheme of a tubular spillway

Spillways outside the dam body are more often constructed for earth and stone dams, while in concrete and reinforced concrete dams, they are more often placed directly in the dam body. Spillways can be tubular and tunnel types. Tubular spillways are metallic or reinforced concrete pipes laid in the foundation of the dam in a special gallery and covered with gates. Gates are controlled from a tower using special mechanisms. Riverbed fasteners are installed near spillways in the upper and lower headraces. Tunnel spillways, in cross-section, represent a tunnel.

Dam gates are movable bulky structures up to 50 meters long and weighing up to 100 tons, closing openings in dams and serving to allow the passage of water, ice, and sediment from the upper headrace to the lower. Gates close both spillway and bottom openings in dams. They are usually made of metal, less commonly of wood. The main types of gates that close spillway openings include:

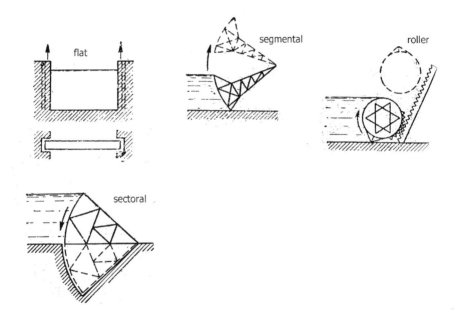

Fig. 250. Schemes of the main types of dam gates

Flat gates have a shield-like shape and move vertically in the slots of bulls or piers.

Segmental gates, rotating around fixed hinges, are attached to bulls or piers.

Roller (cylindrical) gates are used in heavy ice conditions or an abundance of bottom sediments.

Sector gates transfer pressure to the flue bed and, when opened, lower into a special chamber in the body of the dam.

Water intakes (water inlets) are hydraulic structures through which water enters various aqueducts. Water intakes protect aqueducts from the entry of bottom sediments and floating objects (ice, branches, etc.). They also provide for the shutdown of aqueducts. The water intake may include a dam. Open and deep water intakes are distinguished. The open water intake consists of an approach part, a water intake, and a coupling part - a section coupling the water intake opening with the normal channel cross-section. The water intake includes a flue bed - a foundation slab and coupling piers (additional bulls are erected for a wide spillway opening). A threshold is always constructed in the inlet opening, rising above the riverbed by 1-2 meters and designed to protect the channel from sediment infiltration. The water intake is equipped with debris-retaining grates and gates. Often, settling basins - special chambers with a large cross-sectional area, where, due to a decrease in water velocity, suspended sediments settle, are placed behind the water intakes, and then are removed.

A deep water intake is located in the reservoir and represents a recessed opening in the aqueduct, equipped with debris-retaining grates and gates above the upper headrace level. The openings of deep water intakes are located on the slope of the bank and extend into the reservoir. Often, a water intake is combined with the spillway of an impervious dam. In rivers and lakes, water intakes are concrete, stone, or wooden structures into which water enters through special windows with grates. These structures often support and protect the pipe taking water. A pumping station, often combined with a water intake structure, is located near the water intake.

Locks are structures designed to allow the passage of vessels from the upper headrace to the lower and vice versa. A navigation lock is a chamber enclosed by side walls and separated from the upper and

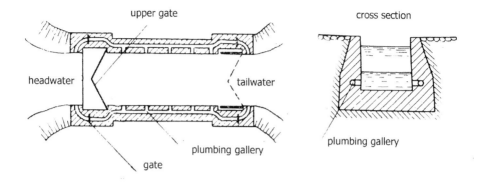

Fig. 251. Scheme of a lock

lower headraces by gates. The gates are located in the thickened walls called "heads". Through special conduits in the heads, walls, or bottom, the lock can be filled with water to the level of the upper headrace. The operation scheme of the lock when a vessel passes from the lower headrace to the upper is as follows: the vessel enters the chamber, the lower gates close behind it, water from the pipelines enters from the upper headrace and fills the chamber until it aligns with the level of the upper headrace, after which the upper gates open, and the vessel exits into the upper headrace. Various lock designs exist. Locks can have one or several consecutive chambers. In areas of intense navigation, chambers can be located side by side, parallel to each other. Lock gates can be hinged or in the form of ordinary dam gates, which are flat panels.

Shoreline reinforcement

In places where structures are erected on rivers, narrowing the width of the flow, such as areas near bridge piers, an increase in flow velocity and the formation of whirlpools can occur, leading to the potential erosion of nearby shore sections. This is also facilitated by currents in channels, near water intake structures, and locks. Due to the fact that riverbeds in erodible soils are subject to changes, with some areas eroding while others accumulate sediments, shorelines and embankments in erosion-prone areas are reinforced with stones dumped along the slope or metal grids filled with stones. In particularly critical areas, shorelines are reinforced with concrete or reinforced concrete facings.

Types of maritime hydraulic structures

A **marine port** is a set of structures and devices providing vessels with a calm anchorage in a water area protected from waves, enabling loading operations, repairs, and other operations.

Protective structures shield the port from waves. These include breakwaters and seawalls. Breakwaters are structures extending into the sea and connected to the shore. Seawalls are structures extending into the sea for a short distance, not connected to the shore. Three types of protective structures are distinguished: sloping, vertical, and combined. Sloping structures have a trapezoidal cross-section, with the side facing the sea being shallower. Materials for sloping structures include broken stone, fragments of rocky soil, and concrete masses of various shapes. Stones for protective structures are usually arranged by size, with smaller stones laid at the bottom and larger stones placed closer to the waterline, as the pressure of waves on the structure is

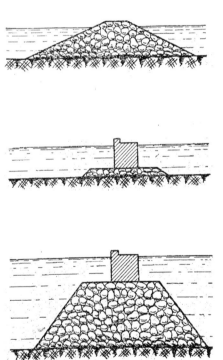

Fig. 252 Types of protective structures

406

maximum in this area. When using concrete masses as a bulkhead, a foundation of stones (stone bed) is usually laid on the bottom first, which more evenly distributes loads on the soil and protects the structure from soil erosion underneath. Vertical-type structures bear less wave load, as the wave, when approaching the vertical wall, does not break but reflects. Vertical protective structures are divided into two types based on their working principle: gravitational (resisting lateral water pressure due to their weight) and pile (resisting displacement due to the attachment of piles to the foundation soil). Gravitational structures made of large (covering the entire length of the breakwater) reinforced concrete boxes weighing up to 100 tons are called giant masses. They are manufactured onshore, floated to the installation site, and then immersed, filled with concrete, stone, or sand.

Gravitational protective structures are divided in height into the foundation, underwater, and above-water parts. The foundation consists of a stone bed. In cases where the seabed soils are weak, excavation of soils for the laying of dense rocks is carried out before laying the stones in the bed. After leveling the bed with the required degree of accuracy, the underwater part of the structures is erected, made of rubble, massive masonry, or giant masses. If the foundation soil is not strong enough, a preliminary laying of masses is sometimes done without careful jointing of seams. Masses are laid above the water level to obtain a load equal to the weight of the entire structure before the final laying of the masses.

Above-water part is a monolithic superstructure made of concrete with a seaward-facing wall, known as a parapet. The superstructure increases the weight of the structure and prevents wave overflow through it during storms. The outer part of the bed, to prevent erosion by waves simultaneously with the construction of the underwater part, is covered with protective masses. The construction sequence of gravitational structures is the same for breakwaters, seawalls, and

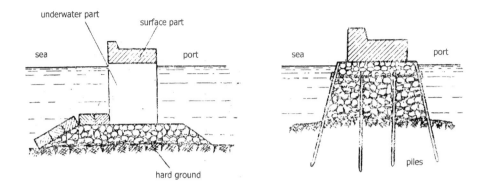

**Fig. 253. Gravitational shielding structure
and pile with a stone core**

docks. Pile-type structures (wooden) are used in seas where the soil allows for driving piles, and the depths do not exceed 5-6 meters. Such structures consist of two continuous rows of piles, reinforced with longitudinal grips made of logs and tightened between them with steel rods spaced 1-2 meters apart. The space between the rows of piles is filled with stones, and a monolithic superstructure of concrete or rubble masonry is built on top. Protective structures made of metal sheet piling (solid walls) are constructed from individual metal beams of a special shape driven into the ground. Sheet piles are connected to each other by special "locks," consisting of protrusions and recesses that interlock. Such connections allow piles to be driven both straight and along curves of small radius. A protective structure made of metal sheet piling contains two parallel sheet-piled walls connected by tie rods with sand between them or forms closed cells of various shapes, adjacent to each other and filled with stone or sand. Mixed-type protective structures are vertical walls erected at a shallow depth on a prism of stone fill. Each breakwater, from the sea side, and breakwater from both ends have small extensions called heads, on which beacon lights are usually installed. Heads are subject to the strongest impacts of waves, so they are carefully constructed. Berthing structures are located along the port territory, either directly adjacent to it (quaysides) or protruding into the water at an angle in the form of piers. These structures either form a continuous embankment wall supporting the backfilled soil, or a through structure consisting of piles or columns supporting the upper platform. In cases where a continuous area along the entire ship is not required for loading operations (e.g., loading bulk goods by conveyors or petroleum products by pipelines), docks consist of individual massive supports, to which ships are moored. The space between them is covered with a light upper structure. Floating docks are erected for significant sea level changes, representing special pontoons connected to the shore by gangways. Such docks are mainly used for passenger boarding and disembarkation.

Solid berthing walls can be gravitational or pile-type. The construction material used is the same as for breakwaters. Embankment walls of gravitational type have much in common with protective structures of the same types. Boards with stone loading, proper masonry of masses, giant masses, and stone bedding at the base are used. Behind the wall, stones are laid to reduce the lateral pressure of the soil. If the foundation soil is weak and cannot support the weight of heavy gravitational walls, pile structures are used.

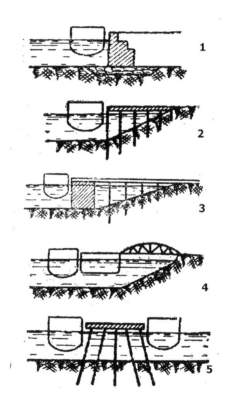

Fig. 254. Types of berthing structures: (1) - solid embankment wall; (2) - pile embankment; (3) - dock with massive supports; (4) - floating dock; (5) - pier on piles.

409

The simplest of them is a bulkhead, consisting of a continuous sheet-piled row of wooden, metal, or reinforced concrete piles. Sheet-piled piles are held by metal anchor rods attached to special anchor piles or plates. The most common bulkheads are made of metal sheet piling. Berthing structures are equipped with fenders in the form of rubber tubes or old car tires that soften the impact of the vessel when approaching the berth and mooring devices – bollards or special rings (bitts).

Hydraulic structures of ship repair and shipbuilding enterprises

Ship repair enterprises are usually located in the port area and include, in addition to repair workshops, repair docks where ships under repair are afloat, as well as ship lifting devices. Shipbuilding enterprises may be located outside the port and, in addition to factory workshops, have facilities for launching completed ships into the water and finishing docks where the final completion and equipment of the ship take place. For lifting and repairing small ships weighing 1-2 thousand tons, cradles and slips are used. A shipyard cradle is a series of inclined ship-lifting tracks extending from the shore underwater. Using winches anchored on the shore, metal trolleys move along the rails, carrying the ship ashore and placing it on special supports (keel blocks) for repair. Cradles can be longitudinal—when the ship is pulled out of the water bow or stern first, and transverse—if the ship is lifted out of the water by the side. Repaired or newly constructed ship hulls are usually launched into the

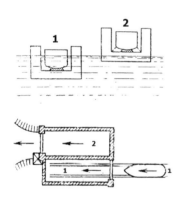
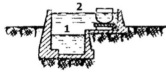

Fig. 255. Schemes of operation for a floating dock and a filling chamber

water using the inclined slipway of the shipyard cradle. Large plants use dry docks. Slips differ from cradles in that, after lifting the ship out of the water on inclined tracks, it can be moved sideways using other special carts and placed on the side platforms called slipway bridges, after which other ships can be lifted. The basis for each inclined rail track is wooden or reinforced concrete piles with transverse beams and decking laid on their heads. Sometimes, low-height wooden boards or long reinforced concrete slabs placed on a stone bed are used as the foundation.

The construction of the underwater part of the foundation (threshold) is reinforced. A dry dock is a chamber submerged below the factory territory mark and surrounded on three sides by retaining walls (concrete or reinforced concrete). The fourth side of this chamber has an inlet opening connecting it to the water area so that the water level in the chamber is the same as in the port's water area. After the ship enters the dock, the inlet opening of the chamber is closed with a special gate, water is pumped out of the chamber, and the ship settles on special supports located at the bottom of the dock—keel blocks. After drying the chamber, the underwater part of the ship's hull is repaired. Upon completion of the repair, water is let in, the ship floats, and is taken out of the dock.

Floating docks operate on the principle of dry docks. Thanks to special compartments (pontoons) filled with water, they can submerge into the water to reach the required depth, at which a ship undergoing repair can enter the dock. A floating dock is convenient because it can be towed from one port to another as needed. The materials used to build docks of this type are metal or reinforced concrete. Surveying. In the construction of hydraulic structures for the temporary fixation of the construction line, surveyors use points on the ground—stakes located at a certain distance from each other. They are marked with stakes or piles, and on the water with beacons, anchored buoys, or floats. The starting point of the route is designated as the zero point of the stake.

On drawings, stakes are indicated by a point with a special sign and number. The concept of "stake" is used when inspecting hydraulic structures. In this case, the structure is divided into sections of 5-10 meters in length. Stake markings are applied to the structure itself with paint or by some other method. The location of detected defects is tied to the nearest stake.

Checkpoint questions for chapter six:

1. How do overflow channels differ from spillways?

2. How is lockage carried out?

3. Name marine hydraulic structures.

4. How is a dry dock arranged?

5. What is a surveying stake?

6. What is a ship repair cradle?

7. How does a scupper differ from a riprap?

8. What is a flute bed?

9. Provide the definition of a shoal.

10. What influences the flow velocity in a river?

11. Say verbally, pointing to any map you have, where is the source, and where is the mouth of a river?

12. What is a river basin?

13. Name the main types and forms of dams.

14. What is a rapid?

15. Name types of dam gates.

16. What is a giant caisson?

17. What is a water intake?

18. How do a mole and a breakwater differ?

19. Name three types of protective structures.

20. Provide the definition of a seaport.

VII CHAPTER
EQUIPMENT AND TOOLS FOR UNDERWATER OPERATIONS

The chapter seventh proceeds to explore various manual, pneumatic, and electric tools details the means employed to seal holes on a ship, elucidating the essential tools for this critical task It includes an in-depth examination of an explosive action tool, delving into the principles governing its operation. Subsequently, the chapter discusses tools used for underwater earthworks, broadening the reader's understanding of their applications.

The chapter provides insights into the intricacies of underwater rigging activities, elaborating on the differences between marine knots used for rigging work, with a step-by-step demonstration for tying is included.

There is also a section concentrates on lifting pontoons, offering a comprehensive understanding of their structure and operational principles.

§ 27. Tools for diving operations

Various tools are used in underwater operations: manual, pneumatic, electric, and explosive action tools.

Manual Diving Tools: These include the same tools used in surface work: hammers, sledgehammers, saws, drills, wrenches, chisels, screwdrivers, and other common tools. Specialized diving tools include an inclinometer-angle gauge, a diving ruler, a fathomstick, and diving scissors.

Diving ruler - this ruler, with a length of 150 centimeters, is used to determine the dimensions of various objects and damage to the underwater part of structures with an accuracy of up to 1 cm. To take measurements, the diver sets the zero of the ruler at the beginning of the measured object, unscrews the fastening bolt, and moves the slider to the other end of the measured length so that the outer edge of the slider touches the end of the measured object. The diver then communicates the result or passes the ruler to the surface.

Inclinometer-angle gauge - this tool measures the angles of inclination of various underwater objects and structures, as well as the list and trim of sunken vessels. To measure angles underwater, the diver places the inclinometer on the inclined surface, clamps the ram clamp holding the pendulum, and when the pendulum takes a new position, clamps it again and communicates the result or passes the inclinometer to the surface for the diver in charge.

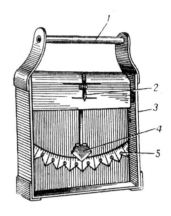

Fig. 256. Inclinometer-angle gauge: (1) handle; (2) wing screw; (3) body; (4) pendulum; (5) scale

Detachable diving fathomstick - this tool is used to accurately determine the depth or height of individual underwater structures. It is made up of four aluminum alloy composite links with a total length of 8 meters. The bottom link has a shoe for support, the two middle links have demarcations in decimeters, and the top link has markings in centimeters. The links are connected by spring locks. For measurements, the fathomstick is assembled from links based on the depth at which work will be carried out. When assembling, the link with markings in centimeters should be on top. The diver sets the fathomstick in place for measurement, and on the surface, using the markings on the top link, determines the depth or height of underwater structures, communicating the results to the diver in charge.

Diving scissors - these are designed for cutting steel cable or individual strands with a diameter of up to 12 millimeters and soft steel wire with a diameter of up to 10 millimeters.

414

Pneumatic diving tools

This category includes drilling machines, pneumatic hammers, chipping hammers, pneumatic wrenches, shears, and saws. These tools are powered by compressed air supplied through a hose.

Working with pneumatic diving tools, only divers trained to use these tools and briefed on safety procedures are allowed to work with pneumatic diving tools. The pneumatic tool is provided to the diver only when at the work site. Before starting the pneumatic tool, access of compressed air to the working hose is closed, and the absence of pressure in the tool is verified.

After the tool is provided to the diver, the freed end is raised. The pneumatic tool must be pre-adjusted and have a mild recoil. Air should only be supplied when the tool is in the working position. Before activating the pneumatic tool, the diver must assume a stable position and signal "turn on the air." After finishing the work, he signals "turn off the air" and releases the air from the working hose.

Electric diving tools

These tools mainly consist of drilling machines, disc saws, drill bits, screwdrivers, and wrenches. These tools can be used at the maximum immersion depth of divers in soft gear, and strict safety precautions must be followed. When using tools with electric drives, it is necessary to ensure the proper insulation of the tool. Divers must hold the electric tools by the handles provided for this purpose and are prohibited from holding the tools by the electric cord. When working with impact and drilling hammers, their start-up is allowed only after installing the impactor (drill). When working with cutting tools, it is forbidden to touch the rotating cutting part of the tool, remove chips or sawdust, or replace drill bits until it has completely stopped. In case the drill bit gets stuck in the hole, the machine should be stopped, and the drill bit and hole cleared only after that.

Fig. 257. Underwater welding

Means for underwater electric welding and cutting of steel

Special electrode holders and electrodes are used for underwater electric welding and cutting of steel. Electric current to the electrode holder and the metal mass (return conductor) is supplied from the surface through a cable with a cross-section of 35-120 mm² from direct current welding units or welding transformers with a nominal voltage of 30 to 70 volts and current adjustment limits from 80 to 1000 amperes.

The electrode holder is used for underwater welding and cutting of steel underwater with a metallic rod electrode, 350-400 millimeters in length and 4-6 millimeters in diameter, with a special coating thickness of 0.5–1.3 millimeters.

The design feature of the holder is the increased insulation of all its current-carrying parts. Welding and cutting of steel underwater occur in a vapor-gas bubble generated by the high temperature of the electric arc's combustion, pushing water away from the welding or cutting site (melting) of the steel.

An electrode-oxygen holder is used only for cutting steel underwater using a special tubular electrode into which oxygen is supplied under pressure through a hose from the surface. The use of oxygen significantly increases cutting efficiency. The tubular electrode, 350 millimeters long, has a cross-section of 7×2.5 millimeters and is externally coated with waterproof insulation. The electrode is powered by current from welding units through a cable from the surface. The principle of steel cutting is based on the burning of molten metal by an electric arc in the oxygen stream, which is supplied to the cutting site through the channel of the tubular electrode. Water is pushed away from the cutting site by the resulting vapor-gas bubble, allowing the cutting process to proceed without hindrance.

Underwater cutting is one of the most frequently performed tasks underwater. Traditionally, for many years, cutting of ferrous metals was carried out using arc or oxyfuel cutting methods. Electrodes for arc cutting EPR-1 and electrodes for exothermic cutting labeled ETS, as well as electrode holders EKD 86/93, have gained wide application in domestic practice.

In recent times, exothermic cutting methods have been gaining increasing popularity. This method is based on the combustion of metal in an oxygen-rich environment. The high temperature of the electrode's combustion allows cutting through practically any materials: ferrous and non-ferrous metals, concrete, stone, wood, plastics, as well as composite materials. Moreover, exothermic cutting proves to be more efficient compared to traditional arc cutting.

For cutting with domestic exothermic electrodes labeled ETS, an essential condition is supplying electrical current to the exothermic cutting process. The current strength should not exceed 150A. A constant welding current source with a falling external characteristic type ASUM-400, ADD-4002TI is required. Drawbacks of cutting with ETS electrodes include the burning of the electrode's side wall when it touches the structure being cut, as well as the large size and weight of the used welding current sources, resulting in low work productivity.

BROCO electrodes, unlike ETS electrodes, ignite without the need for electrical current, which is only necessary for igniting the electrode at the initial stage. Any welding current source can be used for igniting BROCO electrodes, and in its absence, a 12V car battery can be used. The use of a car battery as a power source is recommended for work depths of no more than 20 meters.

Special tubular electrodes are used for exothermic cutting, consisting of an internal heat-releasing element in the form of rods, which are installed in a copper tube covered with insulating material, ensuring the burning of insulation simultaneously with the tubular electrode. The rods are made of low-carbon steel. In BROCO electrodes, the diameter and wall thickness of the tubular electrode, the number and material of heat-releasing rods, as well as the hydro-insulating coating of the electrode, are optimal for increasing productivity and minimizing electrode consumption with maximum cutting ability.

The electrode ignites in an oxygen stream due to the action of the electric arc formed between it and the object being cut (or a special plate of arc contact igniter when cutting composite materials). After the electric arc is formed, the electrode begins to burn independently, reaching a temperature of 5500°C at the tip. The electrode continues to burn as long as oxygen is supplied.

The high temperature at the electrode tip and the oxygen flow lead to the melting or burning of the material being cut. Additionally, the oxygen flow blows away the molten material beyond the cutting line. The efficiency of underwater exothermic cutting largely depends on the oxygen flow rate. Special high-performance oxygen regulators are used to ensure the required flow.

Explosive action tools

Explosive action tools consist of a hole-punching gun that utilizes the energy of an explosive charge to punch holes and drive spikes into metal sheets with a thickness of 9 to 25 millimeters. When working with explosive action tools, they should be treated as firearms. Before using the tool, it is necessary to ensure that there are no explosive materials or people behind the panel being punched. A faulty tool should not be used. Barrels should only be loaded on the surface and provided to the diver in a charged state in some kind of case; handing them over at the end is prohibited. The loaded barrel should only be taken from the side and inserted into the gun body without pressing the safety. When moving underwater, hold the gun with the barrel away from you. Do not press the safety until the gun is in place for firing. In case of misfires, wait for the time specified for such cases in the instructions, and then change the barrel or bring the gun to the surface for reloading.

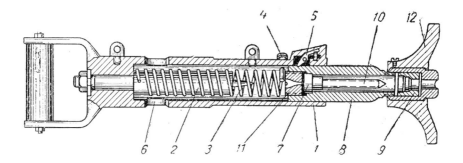

Fig. 258. Underwater hole-punching gun: (1) – body; (2) – drummer; (3) – hammer spring; (4) – fuse; (5) – latch; (6) – hole for gases to escape; (7) – cartridge; (8) – trunk; (9) – spacer bushing; (10) – punch; (11) – breech; (12) – tripod.

The hole-punching gun is a cylindrical body with a handle at one end and an opening for inserting a cylindrical barrel at the other. The barrel is loaded with a charge and a steel spike or punch. Inside the body, there is a fixed striker that pierces the capsule and a spring. At the front of the gun, there is a latch with a spring that serves to hold the barrel from falling out. The safety holds the barrel from moving inside the body and prevents accidental firing. At the bottom of the body, there is a hole for the gas to escape. Two loops are located at the top for hanging the gun on a rope. The catch locks the barrel, preventing explosive gases from entering the gun body. The distance sleeve is inserted into the nipple and adjusts the force of the impact of the ejected spike or punch. The hole-punching gun is supplied to the diver without the barrel at the end. The barrel, which is charged on the surface, is supplied separately. Inserting the barrel into the body, the diver presses its tripod against the place to be punched and presses the safety with his finger. With a sharp press of the handle with the other hand, the gun body is pushed forward, compressing the striker's spring, and the striker's point pierces the cartridge's capsule. As a result of the shot, the spike or punch flies out of the barrel and pierces the hole.

Safety measures when operating a hole-punching gun. When working with a hole-punching gun, the following safety measures should be observed: do not use the hole-punching gun in case of any malfunctions; before starting to punch holes in the ship's hull or panel, check for explosive materials or gases behind them; do not press the gun's safety until it is prepared to fire; do not use a more powerful charge than required for the given sheet thickness (if the metal thickness is less than 8 millimeters, the driven spike will not hold); to avoid ricochets, hold the hole-punching gun perpendicular to the metal sheet being punched; do not aim the barrel towards the diver or the surface; it is prohibited to load and reload the hole-punching gun underwater.

Dredging and ground-suction tools

Special dredging and ground-suction tools assist divers in performing earthworks underwater, eroding and removing soil when raising sunken objects, cleaning pits for hydraulic structures, developing underwater trenches for laying pipelines, and carrying out other labor-intensive tasks.

The hydraulic nozzle is a metal tube with a detachable conical attachment at one end, creating a powerful water jet capable of eroding dense soil. At the other end, there is a pressure hose from a high-pressure pump – a hydromonitor, supplying working water under a pressure of 10-16 atmospheres.

Significant pressures create a large reactive force pushing the hydraulic nozzle backward. A non-reactive nozzle, having reverse holes through which water exits in the opposite direction, balances the reactive force and facilitates the diver's work. To further facilitate the diver's work with a reactive nozzle, a weight and an additional restraining rope are attached to the hose about 1.5 meters from its connection to the nozzle.

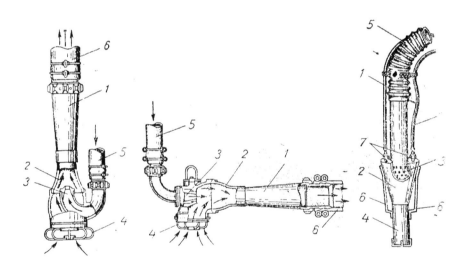

Fig. 259. Water jet ejectors and pneumatic soil suction. Vertical and horizontal ejector: (1) - ejector pipe; (2) – diffuser; (3) – nozzle; (4) – receiving grid; (5) – pressure hose; (6) – discharge hose. Pneumatic soil pump: (1) – air hoses; (2) – air box housing; (3) – holes in the pipe; (4) – soil pump pipe; (5) – discharge hose; (6) – staples; (7) – union nuts.

Water jet ejectors and pneumatic soil suction devices are used to remove loosened soil and suction mud, sand, and gravel. Water jet ejectors come in two types: vertical and horizontal, differing in the location of the receiving opening. In a vertical ejector, the receiving opening is perpendicular to the tube and diffuser, while in a horizontal one, it is on the side.

Ground-cleaning work with water jet ejectors is carried out at depths up to 8 meters. The principle of operation of a water jet ejector is based on the fact that working water, entering under pressure from the power pump through the pressure hose and passing through the nozzle into the diffuser, gains high speed and carries with it a mixture of water and soil (slurry) through the receiving grid. The slurry is ejected through the discharge hose, with the soil content in the slurry being 20-25%.

A pneumatic soil suction device is used for suctioning soil underwater and removing it sideways. The soil suction device is often used in conjunction with water jetting from a power pump. To eliminate the consequences of a collapse, a hydraulic nozzle should be present in tunnels along with the soil suction device.

Compressed air, supplied from compressors via two or three hoses, is used to operate the pneumatic soil suction device. Passing through holes in the soil suction pipe, the air mixes with water, forming a light foamy mass. Under pressure, this mixture moves up the pipe, and water entering the lower part of the pipe sucks in soil particles. Pneumatic soil suction devices have suction pipe diameters of 150-200 millimeters and start working from depths of 10-12 meters.

During soil erosion, one must be cautious of the diver entering the water jet. During soil suction, the intake opening of the pneumatic soil suction can get clogged, leading to additional buoyancy. Upon resurfacing, the soil suction may pull the diver upwards, and after venting air, it may sink to the bottom with the diver. To prevent this, the soil suction must be secured at the workplace. To neutralize the jet reaction when using a hydraulic nozzle with a standard attachment, the nozzle must be fastened with the plant end to a toggle or ballast. When using a pneumatic soil suction, be cautious of ejection in case of inlet blockage, as it may reach the surface and fall back to the ground. Therefore, the soil suction should also be fastened to a toggle or ballast to avoid suction of hands and tearing of gloves and diving suits. Manual cleaning of the soil suction grid is allowed only after stopping the air supply and turning off the soil suction.

Underwater Hydraulic Tool

The hydrodynamic tool is a powerful, reliable, economical, and compact equipment indispensable for emergency-rescue, repair-restorative, and construction hydrotechnical operations underwater. By using manual hydraulic dynamic tools, significant productivity in underwater works can be achieved at a low cost. The principle of operation of hydraulic tools is based on utilizing the energy of the flow of working fluid under excess pressure. Special hydraulic oil is used as the working fluid, pumped into the tool by a pump station (hydro-compressor) through a flexible hose.

Hydraulic tools can be employed at various stages of both underwater and surface construction for the installation and dismantling of underwater structures. For instance, drilling holes for anchoring bolts or explosive charges, cutting metal, wood, and concrete structures, as well as road repair works.

Hydrodynamic tools designed for underwater work include cutting tools (disc and chain saws, grinding machines), drills and hammers, impact wrenches, submersible pumps (drainage and slurry). Unlike pneumatic tools, hydraulic tools have several significant advantages: higher power with smaller dimensions, no air bubbles interfering with the operator's work, reliable operation at low temperatures, low noise, and the ability to use underwater tools for surface operations.

Hydrodynamic tools consume significantly less energy during operation compared to pneumatic tools with comparable impact energy and torque.

Hydrodynamic tools are fire and electrically safe. The risk of accidental ignition is eliminated during operation. The working hydraulic fluid, acting as a dielectric, does not accumulate static electricity. Hydraulic oils based on hydrocarbons (petroleum), biodegradable non-flammable fluids based on vegetable oil, and water-glycol mixtures are used as working fluids for underwater operations.

Key requirements for hydraulic fluids, set by leading hydraulic tool manufacturers: kinematic viscosity at 40°C within 27-46 mm²/s, freezing point not exceeding -23°C, flash point not lower than 170°C. These requirements are met, in particular, by hydraulic oil brands such as "Shell Tellus T32," "Shell Tellus T46," "EnviroLogic 132," and others.

Hydraulic hoses and tools are equipped with normally closed quick-release connections, virtually eliminating the leakage of working fluid during tool replacement or accidental hose disconnection during underwater operations.

The "hydro-compressor - hoses - tool" system forms a closed circuit filled with working fluid, insensitive to contamination, high humidity, and critical temperatures. Thanks to this, underwater hydrodynamic tools serve reliably for a very long time and do not require complex technical maintenance. After working in seawater, it is sufficient to rinse the tool with a stream of fresh water, wipe it dry, and treat it with a moisture-displacing liquid (e.g., WD40), then lubricate it with hydraulic oil.

Underwater hydrodynamic tools have several differences from tools for surface use. Corrosion-resistant materials are used, additional seals and gaskets are installed. The design of handles, start, and control mechanisms is engineered to allow a diver in gear and work gloves to operate easily and safely underwater in confined conditions and limited visibility. Another difference from surface tools is the absence of the need for supplying compressed air or water to cool the tool.

Water supply under pressure is recommended only in specific cases (diamond chain saws, diamond drills, and hammers) to remove abrasive debris from the working area, thus preventing jamming and breakage of expensive chains and drills.

All tools are designed to perform multiple operations. This versatility is achieved through the possibility of changing attachments. For example, for impact wrenches, there is a range of attachments for nuts of various sizes.

Fig. 260. Hydraulic brush

One way to significantly reduce the operational costs of long-distance vessels is by cleaning their hulls from fouling without dry-docking. Well-established equipment for underwater ship cleaning is offered by PHOSMARINE. The equipment systems, MINI-BRUSH KART and BRUSH KART, are mounted on a frame with a crane beam for lowering and lifting.

The core of the equipment is a rotating cleaning machine with a brush, powered by a hydraulic motor. Hydraulic fluid is supplied through a coaxial hose from a hydraulic pump unit located on the surface. The positive buoyancy of the coaxial hose contributes to reducing the diver's effort during operation. Hoses are connected using quick-release couplings.

The brush design ensures its suction to the surface of the cleaned hull and provides linear movement. This allows cleaning both vertical and horizontal surfaces. The diver only needs to control the movement of the cleaning machine. All machines have the ability to reverse the direction of rotation.

The brushes can remove all types of fouling, from algae to mollusk shells. Specially selected brush materials with varying stiffness allow the removal of algae roots without damaging the protective coating of the hull.

Drainage tools

In underwater operations, drainage pumps, water pumps, and hydroturbines are widely used. They are used to pump water from emergency or lifted vessels, coastal trenches and pits, as well as during flooding and draining of large-diameter pipelines. By action principle, centrifugal, piston, and water jet pumps are distinguished, and by the type of engine used – motor pumps and electric pumps. Pumps that supply water to the ground-jetting nozzles are called ground-jetting pumps or hydromonitors.

Means of ensuring ship survivability

Ship survivability is the vessel's ability to withstand accidental damage, restore and maintain its operability. One of the essential elements of ship survivability is its unsinkability, or the ability to stay afloat, maintaining its navigational qualities after flooding one or more compartments.

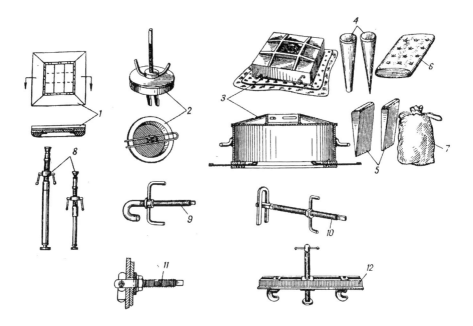

Fig. 261. Emergency and rescue equipment:(1) – hard plaster with soft sides; (2) – metal patch with a clamping bolt; (3) – metal valve patch; (4) – a plug with a typical end and sharp; (5) – a sharp wedge with a blunt end; (6) – pillow with tow; (7) – oiled tow in a bag; (8) – metal sliding stops; (9) – hooked bolt; (10) – bolt with folding bracket; (11) – bolt with a rotating head; (12) – universal clamp.

Each ship is equipped with emergency and rescue equipment placed in compartments. It includes emergency materials, fire-fighting and drainage tools, various devices and equipment, special devices, and tools. For plugging holes on the ship, pre-made patches, shields, beams, plugs, wedges, boards, pillows with hemp, oiled hemp, metal supports, hook bolts, bolts with folding brackets, metal brackets, universal clamps, and others are available. Patches can be soft and hard. In turn, soft patches are divided into canvas and chainmail.

A canvas patch is made from thick canvas. Its edges are covered with canvas tarred rope with loops. It is used to patch small holes and opened seams on the outer plating.

A chainmail patch consists of rings of steel cable with a diameter of 9-10 millimeters, covered on both ends with two layers of canvas. It has considerable strength and can be used to patch larger holes with the installation of false shrouds.

A rigid patch is a shield made of two, three, or four layers of pine boards. Canvas, tied with tow, hemp, or technical lard, is laid between the rows of boards. At the edges of the shield, a cushion made of tarred oakum and canvas is made. Hooks are passed through holes in the patch and fastened to the edges of the hole.

For large holes with protruding torn edges, as well as for holes located in the area of the bow or stern, a box-type patch is applied. To make it, divers first remove a template from the hole. The box-type patch is made of two layers of boards to the size of the hole. The metal clapper patch consists of a metal case — a box with a sealing device on the end in the form of a canvas valve. The patch provides sealing of holes with burrs directed towards it. The metal patch with a clamping bolt is used to plug small holes in the hull. Plugs, wedges, beams, and boards of various sizes are made of dry pine or spruce. Plugs have the shape of a truncated cone with a bevel of 3-50. Large plugs, due to positive buoyancy, hinder the diver's work when plugging holes. Therefore, to neutralize positive buoyancy, they are ballasted with weight. Wooden plugs, wedges, and chocks are used to plug small holes, cracks, and knocked-out rivets. Wedges are used to seal widening seams, detached coamings (a raised border around the cockpit or hatch of a yacht or other boat to keep out water) of hatches, and so on. Chocks are usually supplied to the diver on a rope, in the strands of which they are inserted. Their positive buoyancy is neutralized by hanging a weight on the rope. Bolts are used to fasten rigid patches.

Wooden supports are manufactured from emergency beams. Their dimensions range from 2000 to 4000 millimeters. Metal supports have a length of 600 to 2500 millimeters. They are used to reinforce bulkheads and press the patch for internal compartment placement.

They operate on the principle of a screw jack. A clamp or screw clamp, consisting of a bracket and screws, is used to seal small holes and opened seams. Brackets, plugs, pipe wrenches, and lever tools are used to eliminate pipeline damage. Holes are classified by size as follows: small holes, as well as spygats, illuminators, necks with an area of up to 0.05 m²; medium-sized holes, as well as Kingston grilles and other openings with an area of up to 0.2 m²; large holes, hatches, small hatches, neck doors, and other openings with an area of up to 2 m²; very large holes, hatches, cargo ports, and other openings with an area of over 2 m².

Tackling tools

Ropes. To perform rigging work, ropes made from various organic materials (tow, flax, jute, cotton, etc.), synthetic products (viscose silk, nitro silk, nylon, etc.), and metals (steel, copper, aluminum, etc.) are used. Steel, vegetable, nylon, and composite (tow-steel) ropes are widely used for the manufacture of ship lifting slings, standing and running rigging, mooring lines, tugs; for installing and fastening patches, diving descent and signal lines, etc. Steel ropes are made on special machines. Ropes are classified as rigid, semi-rigid, and flexible based on their particular strength. The thickness of a steel rope is determined by its diameter according to existing standards. In maritime practice, the rope is measured by its circumference. With the same breaking force, a steel rope is 2.5 times lighter and 3 times thinner than a vegetable one. Also, with the same thickness, it is 8-10 times stronger than a vegetable rope. Steel ropes are more durable, unaffected by oil, heat, and humidity. However, they deteriorate from tight bends, easily form kinks, and are difficult to work with underwater. Vegetable ropes are usually 250 meters long, while shipworking ropes are 100 meters. Signal and descent lines, running guides, and straps for diving loads are made from vegetable ropes. Ropes require careful maintenance; soiled vegetable or steel ropes are washed with fresh water after use and dried. A steel rope should be lubricated with oil or grease.

Rigging tools

Swage is used for splitting strands when braiding ropes and making splices. Swage is made of wood or metal in various sizes and shapes.

A mallet is a cylindrical billet made of oak, maple, or beech, fitted on a wooden handle. It is used to align the strands of ropes that have deformed during splicing, as occurs during the weaving of ropes and making splices, etc.

Half-mushroom consists of a wooden billet with a semi-circular cross-section and a handle. The billet has a longitudinal semi-circular groove, with which the half-mushroom is applied to the rope. Shackle or marlinspike, used in making a splice or serving a rope, is applied to

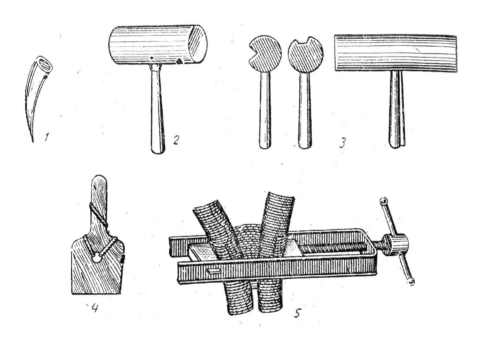

Fig. 262. Rigging tools: (1) – pile; (2) – front sight; (3) – half-muscle; (4) – rigging blade; (5) – machine for bending cables.

the half-mushroom with several wraps and then looped around its handle two or three times. Rigging spatula is used in the same cases as the half-mushroom, i.e., when applying splices and serving ropes. Rope-bending machine is used to bend rigid steel ropes during the manufacture of splices and the application of splices. Rigging accessories and tools used in rigging work.

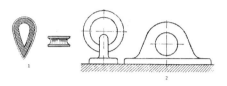

Fig. 263. Rigging accessories: (1) - clevis; (2) - thimble and fathom

Clevis - a metal ring with a groove around the circumference, which is spliced into the splice to prevent the rope from bending sharply. Clevises can be elongated, round, and triangular.

Fathom and thimble

The fathom is called a fixed metal ring used to place blocks of tackles, canvas blocks, connecting brackets, etc. The thimble is a movable ring used for the same purposes.

Brackets are rigging, anchor, and lifting. Rigging brackets are divided into straight and round. Straight brackets are intended for steel ropes, round ones for tow ropes. Anchor brackets are used to connect the anchor chain. In emergency and rescue work, they are used when one bracket needs to connect two or three slings. Lifting brackets are used in lifting operations. They can be

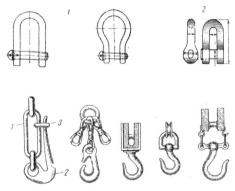

Fig. 264. Rigging brackets and hooks brackets: (1) - straight; (2) - round; (3) - anchor. **Hooks:** (4) - folding hook, (5) - cargo hook; (6) - swivel hooks.

panel and pontoon, designed for a maximum load of 20, 40, 70, 100, 175, and 200 tons. Hooks are forged steel hooks used to fasten ropes and chains when delivering items. Hooks are divided into solid, swivel, folding (snaps), glagol-hooks, and cargo hooks. Talrepes are used to tighten false shrouds on a hole, patches of patches, transverse naves of pontoons, and in other operations.

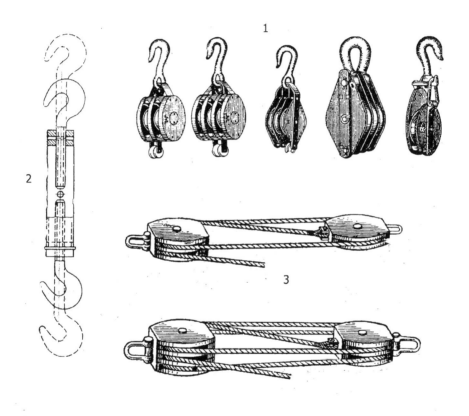

Fig. 265. Blocks, screw talrep, pulley tackles

Blocks (1) are used for basic tackles, as well as for changing the direction of traction. Blocks can be single-sheave, double-sheave, three-sheave, and multi-sheave; by material of manufacture - wooden and metal. Wooden blocks are used for tow ropes, and metal ones are used for steel ropes.

Gurden or screw talrep (2) is a tackle passing through a fixed single-block. It is used where it is necessary to change the direction of traction. In diving, it is used when lifting cargo from the hold of a submerged ship.

Tackles (3) based between two single-blocks are used where a large force gain is not required. Tackles based between a double-sheave and a single-block are used for tensioning slings and keel ends of patches. In ship practice, they are called grip-tackles. Gin blocks are large blocks with a large number of sheaves. They are used for lifting heavy loads. In emergency and rescue work, they are used to pull ships off shoals, pull them ashore, and turn submerged ships on an even keel. The pulling force of gins reaches 40-60 tons. Large floating cranes have gins with a lifting capacity of 100, 150, and 200 tons.

Marine knots, marks, bends, and splices

Every diver must be well-versed in marine knots, tie them correctly, and be able to rig various objects underwater in conditions of poor visibility. The following knots are most commonly used in diving operations:

Clove hitch (1): Tied when it is necessary to quickly secure a rope around a log, pipe, rail, during towing, or lifting onto the ship's deck. For reliability, tie the clove hitch with a half hitch.

Hook knot (2): Used to secure thick ropes on a hook. The doubled end of the rope is laid in the hook, and the core part of the rope is covered from above, after which the working end is secured with a thin line or marlinspike. The hook knot can be tied anywhere along the rope.

Square knot (3): Used when tying two ropes of approximately the same thickness. A piece of wood (cleat) is inserted into the knot's center during strong tightening.

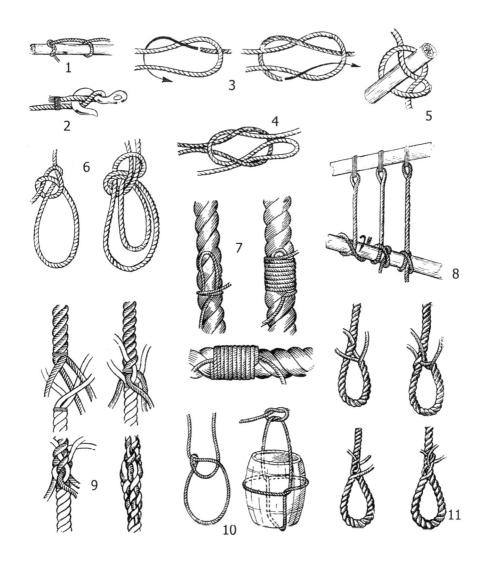

Fig. 266. Marine knots

Reef knot (4): Tied the same way as the square knot in all cases where a reliable but quickly untied knot is needed. One of its working ends is inserted into the corresponding loop, folded in half.

Swivel knot (5): Used to deliver various tools and ends to a diver working underwater. A small peg is made on the rope at the point where the knot is to be tied, into which the folded rope is inserted.

Bowline (6): Used to secure a safety line around a person's waist when work is carried out overboard a ship. A small peg is made on the rope. The rope's end passes into the peg, encircling its core part, and then enters the peg again, but in the opposite direction.

Simple mark (7): Made at the ends of ropes to prevent them from unraveling, at the ends of strands when splicing ropes, making splices, toggles, serving, etc. Used in diving to fasten diving hoses and connectors to corrugated hoses of diving equipment.

Belay hitch (8): Used to tie a rope to objects with smooth surfaces, such as torpedoes or when rigging wood. A short rope is wound around the object, crossed on the applied hitch, wound around the object again in the same direction, and passed under the crossing hitch.

Short splice (9): Temporary marks are placed at some distance from the rope ends intended for splicing. The ropes are untwisted into strands at the marked points, and the ends are also marked. The marked ends of the splicing ropes are shifted close to each other so that each strand of one rope is located between two adjacent strands of the other rope. A marlinspike is used to make the punch, passing the working strands of one rope under the core strands of the other rope according to the "through one under one" rule.

Barrel hitch (10): Used for rigging barrels, cans, bottles, amphorae, etc. A half-hitch knot is tied in the middle of a short (6-7 meters) rope. The half-loops of this knot are spread to the sides and put on the lower part of the object. The free lower part of the knot should pass under the object's base, while the half-loop of the knot should embrace it from the sides.

Simple splice (11): Made on mooring ropes, throwing ends, signaling diving lines, etc. At some distance from the end of the rope, a temporary mark is applied, after which the rope is untwisted into strands, and the ends are also marked. Then the rope is laid out in the form of a splice of the required size, and each of the free strands is

435

passed under the corresponding strand of the undeveloped part of the rope. The strand punches are made according to the "through one under one" rule in the direction opposite to the rope's descent.

Underwater devices for measuring the thickness of various materials

In their work, divers often utilize instruments for measuring metal thickness. These instruments have a wide range of applications, from measuring the thickness of ship hulls to measuring the thickness of pipes in underwater oil pipelines. Handheld ultrasonic thickness gauges typically employ a combined transducer type with a single active piezoelectric element, serving both for emission and reception of ultrasonic waves. Such devices operate on the principle of multiple reflections of sound waves, meaning measurements can be taken without the need to remove protective coatings up to 10 millimeters thick.

Fig. 267. An underwater device to measure metal thickness using ultrasonic waves

The transmitted ultrasonic pulse passes through the coating and metal, reflecting off the metal's back surface. The returning echo then reflects off the nearest metal surface, with only a small portion of the echo returning through the coating each time. The time between these small echo signals gives us the time for the echo signal to travel within the metal, allowing for the determination of metal thickness. The returned echo signals do not necessarily need to be consecutive, as the sensor automatically interprets and calculates the thickness. A minimum of three echo signals is checked each time. This algorithm is embedded in the Automatic Measurement Verification System (AMVS). All ultrasonic thickness gauges can be calibrated based on the speed of sound in the material being measured. The speed of sound in the coating material differs from that in the metal, and it is important that the coating's influence does not distort the measurement of metal thickness.

In conditions of poor underwater visibility, when the diver cannot see the display, the instrument's data can be accessed by another person on the surface. With access to the underwater thickness gauge sensor, the surface operator can remotely adjust settings on the device, including calibration, units of measurement, and resolution.

Lifting pontoons

To raise sunken ships, various objects, and reduce vessel draft when navigating shallow waters, lifting devices utilizing the principles of Archimedes are employed. Such devices include lifting parachutes and underwater pontoons. There are rigid and soft pontoons. Soft pontoons made of rubberized fabric have a lifting capacity of 5 to 10 tons. Rigid steel pontoons have a lifting capacity of 40 to 400 tons.

The rigid lifting pontoon is a watertight floating structure divided inside into two or three compartments. In the compartments' bottoms, there are throats for water inflow and outflow in case of flooding and pontoon blowing. To blow the compartments, the pontoon has nipples with valves at the top to supply and release air. In each compartment's bottom, so-called appendages are installed, serving to release excess air and protect the pontoon from tearing. The throats and appendages allow the internal and external pressure in the pontoon to equalize when surfacing. To reduce weight in the water and facilitate handling during installation, there is an air chamber inside the pontoon where water does not enter during flooding.

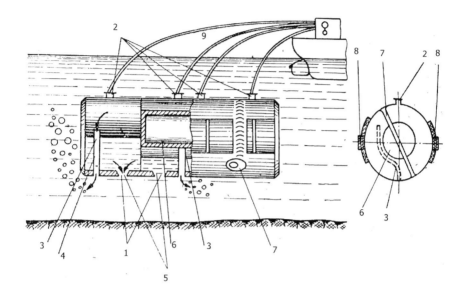

Fig. 268. Scheme of a cylindrical lifting pontoon: (1) - throats; (2) - nipples with valves; (3) - appendages; (4) - air outlet through the appendage; (5) - water outlet through the throats; (6) air chamber; (7) - hatch; (8) - wooden sheathing; (9) - air supply by hoses.

Through the pontoon's hull at an angle of 30 degrees to its diametrical plane, two sluice pipes pass, serving for the passage of lifting slings, which are attached to a stopper located in the middle of the pontoon's upper part. Submerged and surface stability is provided by solid ballast located in the lower part of the pontoon. For lifting and supporting the pontoon in a submerged position, eyelets are welded for mooring and towing the upper part of the pontoon. The principle of the pontoon's operation is based on Archimedes' principle, according to which a floating object displaces an amount of water equal to its weight and the applied load. When water is expelled from it by air supplied through air hoses from the surface, the pontoon acquires positive buoyancy, obtaining lifting force equal to the difference between the weight of the water displaced from the pontoon and the weight of the pontoon itself. This force is used to lift heavy objects, including vessels. For example, a 200-ton steel pontoon has the following characteristics: length - 11.72 meters; width - 5.7 meters; height - 5.7 meters; lifting capacity in fresh water - 200 tons; weight in the submerged position - 3.3 tons; weight in the surface position, including ballast - 67 tons; pontoon draft with closed throats - 1.63 meters; pontoon draft with open throats - 2.01 meters.

Fig. 269. Soft pontoons and lifting parachutes

A soft pontoon consists of two tubes through which an inflation hose passes inside. The pipe simultaneously serves as a throat for water discharge during pontoon inflation as expanded air exits when the pontoon resurfaces. In the upper part of the pontoon, two projections are located, serving for air release during flooding and rigging of the pontoon. They are equipped with plugs that open before inflation. For example, a pontoon with a lifting capacity of 10 tons has the following characteristics: length - 3.8 meters; diameter - 2.02 meters; weight - 125 kilograms. The principle of operation of the underwater parachute is similar to that of pontoons. Lift parachutes are used for raising and moving small objects underwater. In the absence of air supply hoses, a diver can inflate such a parachute from their own scuba regulator, and to control buoyancy in these lifting devices, they install air release valves

Checkpoint questions for chapter seven:

1. Name a manual diving tool.

2. How to use a diving inclinometer-angler?

3. What does a diving footstalk consist of, and what is it used for?

4. What pneumatic diving tool do you know?

5. What electric underwater tool do divers use?

6. What is an electrode holder, what types do you know, and what are they used for?

7. What does an electrode for cutting steel underwater look like?

8. What explosive action tool do you know, explain the principles of its operation?

9. What tools are used for underwater earthworks?

10. What tool belongs to underwater draining means?

11. What is used to seal holes on a ship?

12. What devices and tools are used for rigging work?

13. How does a reef knot differ from a hook knot, show how both knots are tied?

14. Tell us about the structure and operation principles of lifting pontoons?

15. What types of pontoons do you know?

16. Can you explain how hydraulic tools work?

17. What hydraulic tools do you know?

18. How do you measure metal thickness? Explain the basic principle of operation of this tool

VIII CHAPTER
DIVING WORKS

Depending on the purpose and location of diving descents, all diving works are divided into four categories: ship, special, underwater technical, and rescue. The eighth chapter delves into a wealth of information covering both routine and emergency scenarios, revealing the diverse array of tasks undertaken by divers in underwater. It examines methods for underwater hull inspections, the process of propeller removal, addressing stranded ships, special underwater works, searching for sunken objects, lifting submerged vessels, fisheries-related underwater activities, the application of underwater explosives, technical underwater operations, construction and restoration of underwater structures, techniques for underwater concreting, laying pipelines and cable mains, rescue underwater works, and providing assistance for medical conditions such as barotrauma, decompression sickness, and hypothermia.

Each section of this chapter contains valuable information pertaining to its respective topics, eliciting in-depth explanations regarding the methods, procedures, and considerations inherent in each type of underwater work

§ 28. Ship diving works

Ship diving works involve maintaining the underwater part of the ship's hull and on-board devices in working order, as well as eliminating their damage. These works are divided into periodic and emergency. Periodic diving works are carried out to maintain the underwater part of the ship's hull and its on-board devices in accordance with the requirements of operational instructions. Emergency diving works are carried out to correct emergency damage to the hull and on-board devices of the ship. Emergency diving works are divided into works in flooded compartments of the ship and overboard.

Periodic diving works

Periodic diving works include dives for the preventive inspection of the underwater part of the ship's hull and on-board devices, and for cleaning the underwater part of the ship's hull and on-board devices from fouling.

The preventive inspection of the underwater part of the ship's hull and on-board devices is carried out by a diver from the keel end. Moving along it from side to side (when inspecting large ships, the diver moves from one side only to the keel), the diver carefully examines the hull within the visibility limits. Then, the keel end is transferred along the ship's hull towards the stern or bow, and the diver examines the next part of the ship's hull. The keel end is moved until the inspection of the entire planned section of the hull is completed.

During the inspection of the underwater part of the ship's hull, the diver must determine the degree and nature of marine fouling, check for dents and cracks in the hull plating, the deflection of the rudder blade and propeller blades, retractable devices, and assess the degree of clogging of the Kingston grates. The information obtained from the diver is recorded in the hull inspection log for further action to maintain the ship in proper condition.

Fig. 270. Ship hull cleaning and repair

Cleaning the fouling of the underwater part of the ship's hull and on-board devices is carried out from the keel trap or from a gazebo. This work can be performed simultaneously by several divers. To do this, the underwater part of the ship is divided into sections, within which tactile traps are set up or gazebos are lowered. One or two divers can work on each keel trap.

Metal brushes and scrapers, electric or pneumatic tools are used for hull cleaning. Often, cleaning is accompanied by minor repairs, welding or sealing small cracks with a sealant. Cleaning starts from the waterline on both sides and finishes at the keel. Then, the keel trap is moved and secured in a new location, ensuring that there are no gaps and the entire area is cleaned. After completing the cleaning, the most experienced diver performs a final inspection of the entire underwater part of the ship's hull.

For cleaning on-board devices of the ship, diving gazebos are brought directly to the workplace: to the rudder, propeller, Kingston, and other devices. Rudders and propellers are cleaned with scrapers and metal brushes, and retractable devices are cleaned only with steel brushes.

Kingstons are cleaned when clogged with algae, ice, or sediment. The diver on the gazebo locates the Kingston grid, cleans the heads of the screws attaching it to the bulkhead, unscrews them, and removes the grid. Then, using a scraper and brush, they clean the Kingston bulkhead, and the valve plate and its seat are wiped with a cloth. If it is not possible to clean the Kingston in this way, a plug is placed on the hole of its bulkhead, and the Kingston is disassembled from the ship's compartment. Plugs for Kingston bulkheads are also installed when repairing Kingston valves and preparing the ship for wintering in ice, where there is a risk of freezing Kingston. Kingston bulkhead holes are plugged with wooden plugs, rigid plasters, and boards, depending on their size. A wooden plug is selected to fit the size of the Kingston hole so that two-thirds of its length can enter the hole. The plaster with soft edges should cover the Kingston around the contour by at least 100 mm. In the absence of ready-made plugs, patches, or wooden shields of the required sizes on the ship, they are made by their own efforts from emergency wood materials. For a tight fit of the plaster cushion, the skin around the hole and Kingston is carefully cleaned within 100–150 mm.

Plugs and patches, pre-ballasted, are lowered to the diver on a line with a wooden end. He inserts the plug into the hole of the bulkhead and firmly drives it in with hammer blows. The supplied patch is applied to the openings of the bulkhead and pressed to the hull with hook bolts. Filtration of the plug is eliminated by sealing the leaky areas with resin putty. After the repair and assembly of the Kingston, the plugs are removed. Before placing the Kingston gratings back in place, it is necessary to thoroughly inspect the Kingston bulkhead and remove lint, debris, and tools from it, and also lubricate the bolt holes with tallow.

Diving works during the docking of ships and on slips, divers must familiarize themselves with the location of the keel blocks and the areas of damage to the ship's hull before flooding the dock. During the docking of the ship, it is necessary to check the correct placement on the keel blocks and cages, determine the location of damaged areas of the ship's hull. When inspecting cages and keel blocks, it is forbidden to go under the ship's keel.

If the ship is placed on a slip, it is necessary to descend only from a diving boat and only after the ship touches the keel blocks (carriages) with its bow or stern part. Being at a safe distance from the bow or stern, the diver instructs how to move the carriage – slacken it or pull it tight. During the drying of the dock, the grates of the drying system may become clogged. In such cases, it is necessary to stop draining, lower the diver, and clean the grates from foreign objects. When pulling the ship out of the dock, divers inspect its hull and, in case of finding wedges stuck to it, remove them. Repair of slip tracks and release of release devices. To ensure that the slip tracks of the slips are in working order, divers systematically inspect them. During this, they check the strength of rail fastening, the alignment of the rails, and measure the distance between them with a template. Damaged rails are handed over to the diver from the base, they are sharpened, and raised to the surface. When laying new rails, the diver temporarily secures them with nails and drills holes for bolts, which are installed by two divers.

Divers also perform underwater work to clean the slips from deposits and foreign objects and salt the slip tracks. After the ship is launched and moored, the release device is handed over. To free the ship's hull from it, the diver cuts the metal connections of the release device with an electric cutter. Then, with a winch, the diver sharpens the parts of the release device for lifting them from the water.

Emergency rescue diving works

Works carried out on a ship to eliminate an accident and prevent the ship from sinking are called emergency rescue diving works. They are carried out by the ship's crew, and in cases where its forces are insufficient, special rescue vessels equipped with means of providing all kinds of assistance come to the aid of the distressed ship. The part of emergency rescue works performed by regular divers of rescue vessels is called emergency rescue diving works. Emergency rescue works usually begin with a diving inspection of the underwater part of the hull of the emergency ship.

These works are carried out to determine the nature and size of the damage and to determine the necessary underwater work to keep the ship afloat. When diving inspection, the following safety rules must be observed: Diving is not allowed if the ship loses buoyancy or lists. It is forbidden to approach the diver to the hole through which water enters the ship. In the place where the diver is working, water should not be pumped out from flooded compartments, kingston blowouts, cargo loading or unloading, and trash disposal should not be carried out. During the transfer of the keel rope underwater, the diver must be lifted out of the water.

The diver must exercise special caution when working near a torn hole with sharp protruding edges to avoid damaging his equipment and getting injured. When descending into a flooded compartment of the ship, the diver must first study the location of the rooms, devices, and equipment in it according to the drawings and layout. To work in hard-to-reach places of the compartment or in cluttered rooms, divers descend in pairs to assist each other in case of danger. Diving works under the hull of the ship from the ground can be carried out in cases where the distance between the keel and the ground is at least one meter. In the case of especially severe damage, when partial plugging of the holes does not ensure the reliable buoyancy of the ship, the method of supporting ships with ship lifting pontoons is used.

In accidents involving the flooding of ship compartments, the vessel may capsize while retaining some buoyancy reserve. If there are surviving individuals in the flooded compartments of the capsized vessel and further submersion is halted, the primary focus is on rescuing people. For this purpose, divers from the rescue vessel descend below deck, clear passages to the compartments where people are located, lay a lifeline to these compartments, and bring people out one by one, providing them with autonomous underwater breathing apparatuses during the ascent to the surface. Simultaneously with the rescue of people, measures are taken to keep the capsized vessel afloat.

The most effective among the immediate measures is the supply of air to create air cushions in undamaged compartments and tanks of the capsized vessel. Air is supplied through diver's hoses or blowing (pontoon) hoses from the compressors of the rescue vessel. The hoses are led and secured by divers into open hatches, entrances, vestibules, ventilation risers, and "bellows" of fuel and water tank ventilation pipes. If the rescuers have underwater hole-punching guns with special hollow needles, air can be supplied to the emergency compartment through these needles. Diving inspection of flooded compartments can be carried out while the ship is underway, and the inspection of the underwater part of the hull and devices is done at anchor, alongside a pier, or in drift, as well as during grounding. Each diver assigned to work must have a specific task and a designated inspection area. In this regard, the work supervisor must ensure that the diver is well acquainted with the ship's structure in the assigned work area.

The inspection of a flooded ship compartment is carried out by one or two divers. The main task of the inspection is to detect punctures, cracks, separated seams, and deformations of the hull plating, transverse bulkheads, deck planking, platforms, watertight closures, as well as damage to pipelines supplying essential mechanisms and devices. Before the inspection, the diver in the flooded compartment, using a handheld flashlight, quickly surveys his area and determines the cluttering of passages and the possibility of access to the sides, bulkheads, and decks. If the passages are cluttered, they are cleared before the inspection. First and foremost, divers inspect the side plating of the hull, followed by bulkheads, decks, platforms, and watertight closures. If necessary, pipelines and technical means are also inspected. During the work, the diver reports to the surface supervisor about the discovered punctures, cracks, separated seams, and other damages. All identified damages are recorded on a diagram of the underwater inspection of the flooded compartment, with references to stringers and other landmarks in the compartment.

The inspection diagram is signed by the diver who performed the work. For the inspection of a discovered puncture, crack, or separated seam in the hull plating in bulkheads, the diver first clears the damaged area of insulation and, if necessary, removes elements of equipment obstructing access to the damage. When inspecting watertight closures such as doors, hatches, scuttles, etc., the diver checks for bulges, damage to kingstons and rubber seals, as well as the serviceability of standard locks.

The inspection of hull damages and intake devices, when the ship is grounded, is crucial for determining its position on the ground and choosing the most effective method of refloating. Divers determine the areas of contact between the bottom and the ground, the character and relief of the ground under the bottom and at the sides, and the degree of the hull's embedding in the ground. They then establish the locations, character, and sizes of damages to the underwater part of the hull, propellers, rudders, as well as extendable devices of the ship. In the event of compartment flooding, a diver can, by descending into the flooded compartment, discover stones that have entered through a hole in the bottom and determine the sizes of the bottom damages. To choose the safest way to refloat the ship, divers inspect the planned route for taking it to deep water.

After lifting the ship off the ground, a comprehensive underwater inspection of the underwater part of the hull is carried out. First and foremost, areas of the underwater part of the hull within the boundaries of flooded compartments or tanks and out-of-order intake devices are inspected, followed by other areas of the hull. Each diver meticulously examines the plating and intake devices on his designated area as he moves along the keel end. All inspection data are recorded on a diagram of the underwater inspection of the ship's underwater part, with references to stringers and other landmarks in the compartment.

The inspection of punctures, cracks, separated seams, and deformations in the hull plating of the ship is carried out from both the side of flooded compartments and from the outside of the ship. With good lighting, the diver in the flooded compartment and outside the ship can easily detect punctures and dents in the hull plating, determine their shape and sizes. However, it can be challenging to detect pits, cracks, and separated seams, so the diver must conduct a particularly careful inspection to find them. The sizes and shapes of small and medium-sized punctures or dents are determined using a wire template made of thick soft wire, bending it to the shape of the puncture or dent.

The outline and dimensions of a larger breach on the ship's side are determined using plumb bobs. To do this, markings are made on the ship's deck in the area of the breach, with points every half meter. Holding the plumb bob at point one, the weight of the plumb bob is lowered into the water, and the diver places mark one on the plumb bob. Then, the assisting diver moves the plumb bob to point two, and the diver near the breach places two marks on it (at the upper and lower points of the breach). After marking the plumb bob, it is lifted from the water, and corresponding measurements are marked on the sketch according to the marks. The plumb bob is then lowered again into the water, moved to point three according to the deck markings, and the measurement operation is repeated.

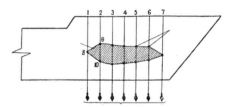

Fig. 271. Measurement of the puncture size using plumb bobs

To measure the curvature of the hull plating together with a large breach, wooden box templates or angle templates are used. The box template is made to such dimensions that the wooden frame covers the edges of the breach or the contour of the dent by 100-200 mm. Mobile planks are attached to the frame with a single nail. The box template is ballasted with a slight negative buoyancy and given to the diver, who positions it on the breach as if applying a patch made according to such a template, diverts the free ends of the bars to the skin, and fastens them to the plank with additional nails. The angle template is made in the same way as the box template. An underwater ruler is used

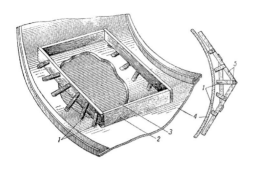

Fig. 272. Template for measuring the curvature of the breach

to measure the breach underwater. The ruler, 150 cm long, is made of duralumin or oak, with a vernier screw securing the slide. Measurement accuracy is up to 1 cm. When measuring the breach, the diver places one end of the ruler against one edge, and the end of the slide - against the other, fixing the slide with the vernier screw. If visibility underwater is good, the diver takes the measurement using the ruler and reports it to the surface by phone; if visibility is poor, the diver measures by touch and sends the ruler with the fixed slide to the surface for reading.

For changing the underwater angle of inclination of any device, as well as the list or differential of a sunken ship, a diver's clinometer is used. When measuring the angle of inclination, the diver places the clinometer on the deck, the inclined structure of the device, and when the pendulum stops swinging, tightens the vernier screw, and sends the clinometer to the surface, where he reports the angle of inclination. In clear water, the diver can determine the angle of inclination himself and communicate the data to the surface by phone. Diving work on inspecting damaged pipelines and technical equipment in flooded compartments is carried out if their restoration and use, or shutdown, is necessary. The diver carefully inspects the damaged areas of pipelines, determines possible places to cut ruptured pipes, and closes valves as instructed by the work supervisor. When inspecting technical equipment, the diver must identify visible external damage, damage to the foundation, the condition of drives, and connections with other mechanisms. Inspections of intake devices (propellers, rudders, and extendable devices) are carried out to determine the possibility of underwater repairs or cleaning them from foreign objects. During the inspection, divers must carefully examine the blades of propellers and rudders, their guards, propeller shafts, and their brackets. It is necessary to find out if there are any breaks or bends in the plating, whether the rudder blade is not bent or torn from the flange or rudder post hinge, whether there are any entangled ropes or chains on the propeller, and whether the fairings of the extendable devices are not bent or damaged. All identified damages or malfunctions are recorded on a diagram of the underwater inspection of intake devices. After the diving inspection, full or partial patching of the breaches is carried out using patches, wedges, and cement boxes.

Emergency diving operations in flooded compartments of the ship

In flooded compartments of the ship, divers can perform the following emergency operations: install submersible drainage devices and clean their intake grids; reinforce the main bulkheads of the deck, platforms, and watertight closures; patch hull damage; repair pipeline damage; facilitate the lifting of cargo from flooded compartments. The installation of submersible drainage devices, for pumping water out of the flooded compartments of the ship, is carried out as follows: Portable jet pumps and ejectors with attached drainage hoses and working water hoses, or submersible electric pumps with suction and drainage hoses, are lowered on hemp ropes, and divers control the descent. If necessary, they guide the drainage devices and install them in the lower, uncontaminated, and convenient locations in the holds. During water pumping, divers clean clogged debris from the intake hose grids, and if lifting them to the surface is difficult, periodically check the position of the hoses inside the ship.

Reinforcement of main bulkheads, decks, platforms, and watertight closures is often performed by divers during the preparation of ship compartments for drying. For reinforcing bulkheads, decks, platforms,

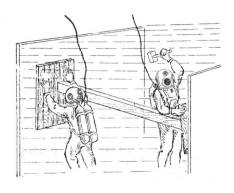

Fig. 273. Installation of supports between bulkheads

and watertight closures, the following materials are used: wooden beams, boards, wedges, construction nails, and staples. The following tools are used: crosscut saws, wood saws, carpenter's axes, crowbars, and hammers. The water pressure is absorbed by the bulkheads, decks, and platforms and transferred to their frame, consisting of vertical and horizontal connections (stanchions and shelves). Therefore, reinforcement is applied not to the panels of these structures but to their rigid frame at the site of damage. When reinforcing bulkheads, supports should be started from the lower parts, considering that the lowest located frame structures will bear the greatest water pressure.

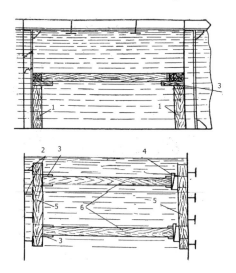

Fig. 274. Placement of two supports between bulkheads: (1) – supporting beam; (2) – damaged stanchions; (3) – board; (4) – wedges; (5) – beam-pad; (6) – support.

The reliability of reinforcing bulkheads, decks, platforms, and watertight closures depends on the ability to distribute loads borne by the supports to a larger number of frame stanchions. For this purpose, a beam is laid on the stanchion, on which one or several supports rest. Supports should be placed so that they preferably take a perpendicular position to the reinforced structure or at an angle close to

452

90 degrees. In such a position, supports will work most reliably. If the stanchion in the reinforced structure is damaged, a short beam is placed at the site of damage, and a support is placed in its middle. If such a wooden beam cannot be laid (due to the cluttering of the mechanism), the support should be placed directly on the damaged stanchion. Placing the support directly on the structure's panel is not allowed. Small gaps between supports and the reinforced structure are filled by driving in wooden paired wedges. The width of the wedges should be equal to the width of the supports. After wedging, supports, beams, and wedges are fastened together with long nails and iron brackets. Wooden supports made from beams are manufactured to

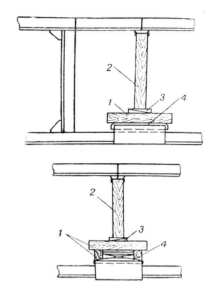

Fig. 275. Reinforcement of smooth hatch covers and hatch with a dog clutch: (1) – support beams; (2) – support, (3) – wedges, (4) – hatch cover.

the dimensions taken on-site by divers, who use underwater rulers, folding steel rulers, and measuring lines for this purpose. Supports intended to be fixed with wedges are cut shorter by 40-50 mm, and those resting on the beams are cut shorter by the thickness of the beams. Examples of reinforcing bulkheads with wooden supports are shown in the figure.

Doors, hatch covers, hatches, and portholes are reinforced with supports to achieve sealing along their coamings and not damage the locking devices (flywheels, latches). For this purpose, supporting beams are used on which supports are installed. Before securing the doors, hatches, hatches, and portholes, divers inspect them, feel the gasket rubber, check the operability of latches, and cleanliness of the coamings for foreign objects. If the doors and closing covers are damaged, they are pressed against the coamings with supports, and the gaps are sealed with putty. In cases where the covers are torn off, patches or wooden shields are applied to the hatches and hatches, and they are secured with supports or hook bolts.

Fig. 276. Placement of a rigid patch on a breach and fastening with hook bolts

Sealing damage to the hull from the inside of flooded compartments is carried out by divers during the preparation of compartments for drying. Emergency property, emergency lumber, and tools are used for patching holes, cracks, and separated seams in the hull plating and watertight closures. Sealing large breaches (with an area from 0.2m² to 2m², dimensions of 1.4×1.4 m) from inside a flooded compartment is quite challenging for divers. Such breaches are patched with wooden patches made on board, with soft edges. The patch, placed on the breach from above into the compartment, should cover the breach evenly, and wooden or metal sliding supports are used to secure it. For fastening the patch with metal supports, they are selected based on measured distances and handed to the diver for installation. If it is decided to secure the patch with hook bolts, they are pre-inserted into the patch along the contour of the breach. After placing the patch over the breaches, divers engage the hook bolts with the edges of the breach and screw the bolt nuts until the patch is tightly pressed against the plating of the hull. In flooded compartments, divers often have to patch medium and small breaches. Sealing medium breaches (with an area from 0.05 m² to 0.2 m², dimensions up to 0.5×0.5 m) can be done with various patches. If a patch is fastened on the breach with a single bolt with a hinged bracket, holes are made in the patch for the bolt. The diver inserts the hinged bracket into the breach so that it catches the edge of the breach, then passes the bolt through the hole in the patch, and screws the nut, tightly pressing the patch to the breach.

Medium-sized breach patches, located between frames, are secured using universal clamps. To do this, the diver starts by placing the clamp above the breach, hooking its grips onto the frames and turning the pressure screw until it stops. Then, the diver inserts the patch under the clamp and tightens it against the breach with the screw. Sealing small breaches (with an area up to $0.05m^2$, dimensions up to $0.22\times0.22m$) is done with small patches using

Fig. 277. Placement of a rigid patch on a breach and fastening it with a universal clamp

the same methods as for medium breaches. Separated seams are patched with wedges wrapped in resin putty. The wedges are driven into the gaps with a hammer until fully inserted, and the gaps between the wedges are filled with twisted resin-putty wraps. Small breaches of round shape are sealed with wooden plugs. The plugs are pre-coated with resin putty and driven into the breaches with a hammer until fully inserted. Holes from fallen rivets or fragments are plugged with small plugs. In the lower part of the hull, small round holes are plugged with bolts with swivel heads for greater reliability. For this, a bolt with a swivel head is inserted into the hole, and after turning the head and securing it against the plating, a rubber gasket with a washer is put on the bolt, and, by tightening the nut with a wrench, the gasket is pressed against the plugged hole. Combating water filtration through various patches of breaches is introduced to divers during the drying of flooded compartments. In case of significant water filtration into the compartment, several divers descend, dressed in hydro costumes without breathing apparatus. Divers inspect patch and other closures located above or at the water level in the compartment, and if leakage points are found, they patch them with twisted resin-putty wraps, greased with thick saturnine red or technical lard. If necessary, they additionally tighten the fastening of the patches. Repairing damaged pipelines in flooded compartments is carried out as follows. Standard emergency property is used to fix pipelines: sheet paronite (a composite of asbestos with natural or synthetic rubber), rubber, lead, red copper, soft steel wire. Typically, damaged sections of pipelines are either shut off or switched to spare bypass sections, and they are repaired by divers only in extreme cases. If valves and clinks are in a flooded compartment, divers perform the shutdown and switching of pipelines. When switching pipelines in a flooded compartment, a diver should always be ready to switch the pipeline back. He can leave the shut-off device on the pipeline after confirming with the head of the diving work about the correctness of completing the task. For significant pipeline damage, the diver finds the nearest flange connections on it or determines the location for cutting out the damaged section. Then, he

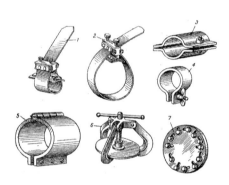

Fig. 278. Emergency equipment for repairing pipeline damage: (1,2) – universal tape clamps; (3) – clamp on bolts with overlays; (4) – clamp-hoop; (5) – hinged clamp; (6) – universal plug with three grips; (7) – universal plug with bolts.

disconnects the flange connections of the pipeline, removes the damaged section of the pipe, and places universal plugs of the corresponding size on the flanges. Before placing the universal plug with bolts on the steam pipeline, its flange is cleaned, and a paronite gasket lubricated with graphite grease is placed on it. At least four bolts are inserted into the holes of the plug, and it is attached to the flange by screwing the nuts until the gasket is tightly pressed against the plugged hole. Placing a universal plug with three grips on the pipeline flange is much easier than placing a plug with bolts.

If there are no flanges on the pipeline, the diver cuts the damaged section of the pipe with a saw, pipe cutter, or electric cutter, cleans the cut area from burrs (metal overflow), and plugs it with wooden plugs or installs a coupling, securing it at the ends of the cut pipe with wire mesh or clamps. To place a

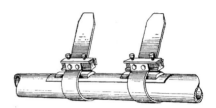

Fig. 279. Two clamps and an elongated overlay

coupling made of rubber hose on the cut section of the pipeline, its inner diameter must be equal to the outer diameter of the pipe, and its length should be 200-300 mm longer than the length of the cut section. The coupling is put on the ends of the pipeline, pre-lubricated with grease, and secured with clamps. Small breaches or cracks in pipelines are patched with clamps, the types and sizes of which are selected based on the diameter of the pipe and the pressure of the working medium. Universal clamps (20-50, 50-100, 100-200) are used when the pressure of the medium in the pipeline is up to 30 atmospheres. To place the clamp, the diver unscrews the bolts, releases the tape, unscrews the pressure bolts, places a paronite gasket lubricated with graphite on the damaged pipe, then puts the tape on the pipe and inserts its end under the clamp. After pulling the tape tightly against the pipe, he secures it with bolts and evenly tightens the pressure bolts.

If the crack is of significant length, several clamps are placed using an extended overlay.

After placing the clamp in the pipeline, slowly increase the pressure to the working one. If the patch significantly leaks, the pressure in the pipeline is released, and the clamp is tightened again by screwing the pressure bolts. Lifting loads from flooded compartments is entrusted to divers when it is necessary to unload compartments or extract valuable property and equipment from them. When performing such work, divers are responsible for rigging underwater loads and monitoring their exit from the flooded compartment. Loads underwater are rigged with slings supplied from above. The diver attaches a pendant to the rigged load, using it to guide the lifted load into the hatch. Before starting unloading operations, the leader instructs the divers about the nature of the lifted loads, their weight, rigging methods, and precautions when lifting particularly valuable and dangerous loads. During rigging of loads and their lifting from the hold, the diver must carefully monitor so that the lifting tackle does not trap the hose or signal end. After rigging the load, the slack of the tackle is taken up. The diver, ensuring the reliability of the rigging, takes the pendant, moves aside from the hatch, informs the leader of the start of the load lift, and, by tensioning the pendant, guides the lifted load into the hatch or other opening. It is prohibited to select or lower the load without the diver's signal. When lifting heavy and bulky objects, it is necessary to exit the water, but not together with the load, and especially not underneath it.

Emergency diving operations outside the ship

Outside the ship, divers can perform the following emergency operations: plugging holes in the underwater part of the ship's hull; cleaning and repairing damaged propellers; cleaning anchors and anchor chains; searching for and lifting sunken objects. Emergency diving operations outside the ship are carried out while it is moored alongside, at anchor, or in some cases, during drifting. In this case, divers participate in the work of the ship's emergency parties.

Plugging holes in the underwater part of the ship's hull

Outside the ship, in the underwater part of the hull, large and medium-sized breaches are usually sealed due to the difficulty of sealing them inside a flooded compartment. To work at the hole from outside the ship, the diver leads the under-keel ends, or divers are lowered on diving umbrellas. Before plugging the hole, divers bend inward (with hammer blows) any protruding burrs (if the plating is of small thickness), remove the shape and dimensions of the hole. Based on the measurements, they select a patch with soft edges from the available ones on the ship (if the hole is in the area of the straight side) or make a special patch according to the contour of the ship's hull (if the hole is in the area of the curved side). The finished patch and other plugging devices are ballasted and delivered to the hole, where divers are lowered. Patches larger than one square meter are delivered to the installation site on under-keel ends, and patches of smaller sizes are delivered on free ends.

The applied patch is attached to the hull with hook bolts, pre-inserted into the patch along the contour of the hole, and is pressed against the hull with nuts (with welded handles). Sealing small holes, cracks, and separated seams outside the hull is no different from sealing the same damage from inside flooded compartments. Water is pumped out of compartments whose waterproofing has been restored. During water pumping and the flooded compartment, divers check the tightness of the patches and other hull sealing outside, and areas where water leaks are patched with tarred oakum, impregnated with thick grease or technical lard.

Cleaning and repairing propellers are entrusted to divers who perform heavy work to clean propellers from tangled ropes and fix the blades of small ships' propellers. Propellers are cleaned from tangled ropes and nets in various ways depending on the material (vegetable or steel), the size of the rope, and the nature of the entanglement. If a vegetable rope or net is wound on the propeller, they cut them with a sharp knife or metal scissors. When a steel rope is wound, it is cut with manual scissors for cutting ropes, a hacksaw for metal, or cut with a blacksmith's chisel and hammer. If the ship has underwater metal cutting tools or underwater gas cutting tools, they are used to clean propellers.

To cut a wound steel rope on the propeller with manual scissors, the diver splits it into strands with a marlinspike and hammer, with a diameter of no more than 10-12 mm. Then, a stationary knife blade is inserted between the marlinspike and the strand, and by pressing on their lever, the strand is cut. In the absence of scissors and other tools, the rope is cut with a saw or chopped with a blacksmith's chisel and hammer. Two divers chop the rope, one holds and guides the blacksmith's chisel, the other strikes it with a hammer. To chop, choose the most tightly tensioned part of the rope or drive a wedge under the loosely tensioned part.

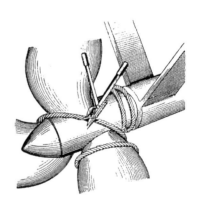

Fig. 280. Splitting a steel rope into strands

If the wound rope has a free end but cannot be unwound, the method of pulling tightly tensioned strands is used. To do this, the diver winds the free end of the rope around the hub in the direction of its unwinding, connects the end to the tackle with a bowline knot or fastens the tackle hook to the strand. Then, the tackle is pulled with a fid or a winch, pulling out the tightly tensioned strand of the rope. These actions are repeated until all the strands are pulled out. If the wound rope does not have a free end, it is cut, and the resulting free

460

end is used to pull out the tightly tensioned strands.

Bent edges of propeller blades are straightened on small ships using a hammer and a metal plate. The plate is suspended on a tackle, and, falling under the water to the damaged blade, it must be 2-3 times heavier than the hammer to prevent the edges of the blade from bending back. For the diver to work under the propeller, a ballasted umbrella is led, and its tackles are secured to the deck. The diver, descended to the umbrella, brings the plate to the blade and straightens the bent edges with hammer blows. If the propeller has removable blades, they can be replaced with spare ones if damaged. To remove such a blade from the propeller hub, first, the nuts of the bolts fastening the flange of the blade are unscrewed with a wrench. Then, the blade is rigged with a tackle supplied from the deck, and after shifting it from its place, the bolts are removed, and it is lifted onto the deck. Placing a spare blade on the propeller hub is done in reverse order.

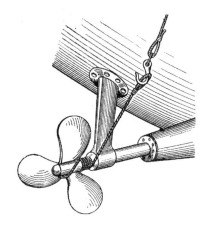

Fig. 281. Pulling tight strands of rope with a tackle

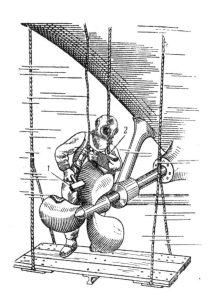

Fig. 282. Straightening bent edges of the propeller

Removing ship propellers afloat is done in various ways depending on the size of the propeller, the design of its attachment to the shaft, and the tightness of its fit on the propeller cone. One of the common constructions for attaching a propeller to the shaft is shown below. To remove such a propeller, the descended diver performs the following actions:

1. Measures clearances between the propeller hub and the deadeye or bracket bushing.

2. Marks the limit seating line of the propeller on the cone of the shaft.

3. Unscrews the nuts securing the fairing and removes it.

4. Unscrews the lock of the thrust nut.

5. For loosening the thrust nut several turns, a diver is provided with a special wrench with an extended lever and a tackle attached to it. The diver places the wrench on the thrust nut and signals to the surface, where the team selects the tackle. The diver watches the rotation of the

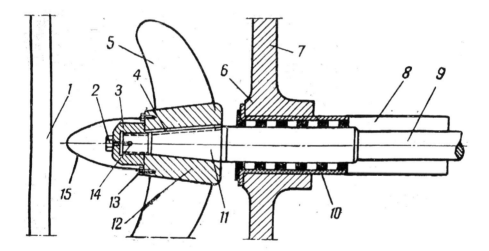

Fig. 283. Diagram of propeller attachment to the shaft: (1) – rudder post of the aft bulkhead; (2) – stopper; (3) – thrust nut; (4) – key; (5) – blade; (6) – apple of the aft bulkhead; (7) - stern post of the aft bulkhead; (8) – deadeye pipe; (9) – propeller shaft; (10) – deadeye pipe; (11) – cone of the shaft; (12) shaft hub; (13) – pin; (14) – threaded tail of the shaft; (15) – fairing.

wrench and shifts it from flat to flat. If the nut does not come off, manual tackles are used to apply force to the wrench handle.

Propellers are shifted from the propeller cone in various ways. Three different methods will be described below.

The first method is shifting the propeller with steel wedges. It is done in the following order: the descended diver is provided with sets of steel wedges; he places them on opposite sides of the propeller shaft between the hub and the deadeye bushing (or bracket) and secures them with hammer blows. Then, a tube with a load inside, suspended on a rope, is brought to the wedges on the propeller. The wedges are driven from the surface using this load, manually moved inside the tube. The diver directs the tube to the

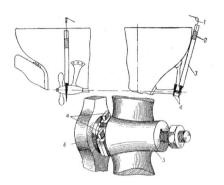

Fig. 284. Shifting the propeller using wedges: (1) – rope; (2) – load; (3) – guide pipe; (4) – steel wedges; (5) – propeller hub; (6) – deadeye bushing.

wedge, shifts it from one wedge to another, and observes the shift of the propeller. For shifting small propellers, the diver drives the wedges with a hammer.

The second method involves shifting the propeller with a puller and clamping bolts installed on the propeller hub and the end of the shaft; it is done as follows: The diver installs a cup-shaped puller with a locking bolt on the hub or installs clamping bolts with a cross plate on the propeller blades. By turning the key of the locking bolt (or nuts of the clamping bolt), he shifts the propeller from the cone of the shaft.

The third method is intended for use by divers who have undergone special training in working with explosives, as it involves shifting the propeller with the explosion of small charges. A charge of dynamite or TNT weighing from 50 to 200 grams, depending on the weight of the propeller, is used for shifting. Two such charges are used for shifting the propeller. The diver, descended to the propeller with charges, places them on the shaft. The charges are placed opposite each other, between the propeller hub and the bracket or deadeye. The charges are placed on copper gaskets to protect the shaft from damage and secured with wires. After coming out of the water, the diver detonates the charges using a blasting machine. Lifting the propeller to the surface is done after shifting it from the cone of the shaft. To do this, the diver sharpens the propeller by its blades, using two lifting ropes.

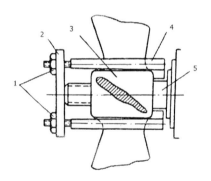

Fig. 285. Shifting the propeller with clamping bolts: (1) – nut; (2) – plank; (3) – propeller hub; (4) – clamping bolt; (5) – propeller cone.

The third rope is a traction rope, attached to the hub to remove it from the shaft. The ropes are led through canvas blocks to winches or windlasses and are tightened. Then, the diver releases the thrust nut, wraps the thread of the shaft with oakum and a wooden block, and shifts the propeller from the shaft using the lever. After lifting the propeller onto the deck, it is thoroughly cleaned and lubricated with grease on the cone of the shaft.

Placing propellers afloat is done in the reverse order of their removal. A new or repaired propeller is lowered to the installation site, with the key on the shaft and the keyway in the hub previously turned into a vertical position. Then, at the signal of the descended diver, the propeller is brought onto the cone of the shaft, and after the thread emerges from the hub, the diver screws on the thrust nut. The propeller is tightened to the thrust nut using a wrench with a lever operated from above. After ensuring the correct seating of the propeller, the diver installs the thrust nut lock on the cone and the fairing.

Cleaning anchors

Cleaning anchors and anchor chains when the anchor is entangled with its or someone else's anchor chain, a steel rope, and other objects usually requires lifting the anchor to the surface. If lifting a stuck anchor or chain is not possible, they are cleaned underwater on the bottom with the help of divers. To do this, the anchor chain of the entangled anchor is chosen on the windlass, and a diver is lowered to the bottom to the entanglement site. When inspecting the anchor or chain, the diver should not go under the anchor chain, as in case of accidental lowering of the anchor, it can press the diver to the bottom.

During inspection, the diver determines what the anchor or chain caught on and their position on the seabed. The diver reports the inspection results to the diving descent supervisor. To clean an anchor caught with one or two flukes in a chain (rope, cable lying on the seabed), a diver is provided with a shackle from the ship's side (or two shackles from different sides). One end of the shackle is pre-attached to the knuckle, and the diver guides the free end under the chain at the entanglement site, pulling it

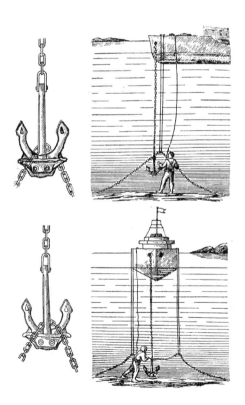

Fig. 286. Cleaning anchors and anchor chains

465

on board. Then, the shackle is slowly hoisted with a winch under the supervision of the diver, and upon his command, it is stopped as soon as the anchor flukes are freed from the chain (the anchor may be slightly lowered during this process). The diver moves the entangled part of the chain away from the anchor flukes, after which the anchor is hoisted until it is above the chain hanging on the shackle. Once assured of this, the diver ascends to the surface via the descent line, the anchor is hoisted to its place, and the shackle holding the chain is released.

Cleaning the anchor chain occurs in cases where it is entangled with foreign objects or the anchors of other ships lying on the seabed. To do this, the anchor chain is chosen on the windlass, a diver is lowered to the seabed from a boat, and a shackle is provided to him. After detecting and examining the chain entanglement, the diver attaches the shackle to it below (2-3meters) from the entanglement site. Then, at the diver's command, the shackle is picked up, and the anchor chain is prepared until a slack is formed. After that, the diver, by diverting it to the side, releases the entangled anchor chain, and it is slowly hoisted to a certain length. To release the shackle, the chain is hoisted up after the diver comes to the surface.

Salvaging a ship aground

Salvaging a ship aground is the most complex and labor-intensive task. Factors determining the severity of the emergency situation include: the nature of the ground at the ship's grounding location; the magnitude of buoyancy loss; the presence of hull damage; the size and longitudinal location of the areas where the ship's bottom contacts the ground. In some cases, in the absence of significant hull damage, soft ground at the grounding location, and minor buoyancy loss, the ship can be salvaged by the ship's crew without external assistance. If it is not possible to independently salvage the ship, powerful salvage tugboats are involved in the operation. Salvage work in these cases

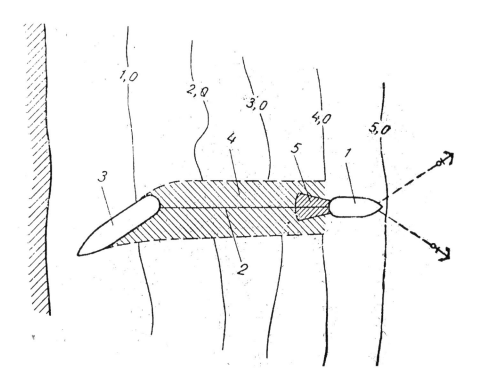

Fig. 287. Canal erosion by the screws of a rescue vessel: (1) – rescue vessel; (2) – tow rope; (3) – emergency ship; (4) – channel route; (5) – area of action of the propeller jet

begins with a thorough underwater examination of the ship and the ground, measuring depths and creating a "depth tablet," and determining the magnitude of lost buoyancy (based on the changed draft of the ship, taking into account the volumes of flooded compartments). The most effective and fast method of salvaging the ship from the ground is then selected based on the results of these works. If the ship has no breaches, the ground at the grounding location is soft, and the magnitude of the lost buoyancy is small, the salvage can be carried out by the traction efforts of one or several rescue vessels (tugs).

One of the effective methods of salvaging ships from the ground with large buoyancy losses and soft grounds is channel erosion by the

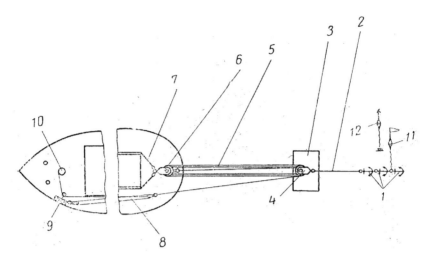

Fig. 288. Lifting the ship off the ground with tackles: (1) – three anchors attached sequentially; (2) – anchor cable; (3) – washboard or float holding the movable block to prevent twisting; (4) – fixed block; (5) - reverse thrust; (6) – movable block; (7) – hawser passed behind the hatch coaming; (8) – tackle (preventers); (9) – canvas block; (10) – anchor spindle; (11) – buoy of the last anchor; (12) – control buoy.

screws of a rescue vessel. This operation is performed as follows: the rescue vessel, at a safe depth, anchors on two spread anchors and provides a towing cable to the emergency vessel. Operating the screws in the forward direction, hoisting the towing cable on the winch, and sequentially tightening the anchor chains, the rescue vessel washes away the ground with the jets of its screws, thus creating a channel of sufficient depth to the emergency vessel. Then, continuing to operate the screws near the emergency vessel, it flushes the ground from under it. After that, the emergency vessel is pulled into the washed channel and taken to deep water. Works according to the described method are carried out with the mandatory participation of divers, who inspect the ground for the absence of large stones every 5-10 meters along the planned canal route.

In case of insufficient pulling forces of rescue vessels or their inability to approach at distances allowing the attachment of a towing cable to the emergency vessel, significant pulling forces can be obtained by using reverse thrust and anchors with substantial holding power. Anchors are set at distances of 200-250 meters from the emergency vessel in the direction of the planned pulling, and they are dropped or laid in a single line (in a row). A fixed block of the reverse thrust is attached to the rope secured to the shackle of the last anchor. The second block is attached to the sturdy structures of the emergency vessel on its deck. By hoisting the running end with a winch or tackles, the required pulling force in the reverse thrust is created to lift the ship off the ground. The end of the reverse thrust attached to the block is called the root end; the end going to the winch or manually tensioned is the running end. When working with blocks, the root end (reverse thrust spar) may be shorter than the running end. The running end is one of the two ends of the rope that is not secured. Divers are involved in checking the position of anchors on the seabed and in deepening them by undermining the ground.

§ 29. Special diving work

Special diving operations include activities related to the underwater inspection of underwater objects and seabed reliefs, searching for and lifting objects submerged in the waters of ports and harbors, shallow roadsteads, and fairways, work on fishing grounds, as well as diving operations for bottom cleaning and explosive works.

Search for sunken objects

When valuable items, instruments, or tools fall overboard, it is necessary to immediately place a buoy (with a buoyant and a ballast) at the location of their submersion. Diving operations are carried out in two stages: first, the search for the sunken object, and then its lifting to the surface. Diver descents are organized from the ship's side or from a boat. The underwater search for sunken objects is carried out by one of two main methods. The diver searches for a marked object, buoyed, by the trawling method, in concentric circles, and an unmarked object by bypassing along the guiding ends and the running rope. For search operations from a boat, at least two divers are appointed, along with a team of rowers led by a supervisor. Having found the sunken object on the seabed, the diver attaches a buoy to it for marking. The lifted sunken objects are raised from a boat or ship after being properly rigged by the divers. To do this, after descending to the place of the object's submersion, the diver is provided with a lifting shackle from the surface. Rigging the object with an appropriate knot, considering its shape and weight, lifting begins after the diver surfaces. The underwater search for sunken objects is carried out by inspecting the seabed using the following methods: bypass along the guiding ends and the running rope; trawling with a twine rope; trawling in concentric circles. The search can be conducted by inspection, metal detector, handheld radar, or echosounder, or by probe with or without the use of means of transportation. The organization of special diving works and safety measures in this case are as follows: only divers who have undergone special training are allowed to carry out search operations; when searching for mines, divers use non-magnetic equipment; for communication with divers, a non-magnetic telephone is used, and in its absence, communication with divers is carried out through a signal line. Before starting the underwater search, divers are briefed on the work area and instructed on the adopted method of work. The search and lifting of explosive objects must be carried out by well-instructed divers, in the presence of experienced specialists. In the case of searching for explosive objects, divers are familiarized with the types, principles of operation, and structure of objects that are expected to be discovered. Immediately before the dive, the dive leader checks whether the descending divers have any objects with magnetic properties and assigns specific tasks to each of them. During the search operations, any explosive object found on the seabed is considered dangerous, so the diver must act extremely carefully and strictly follow the instructions of the supervisor. Explosive objects, in addition to aviation bombs, shells, mines, and torpedoes, include cylinders and special containers filled with liquid or gas.

The search is carried out by direct inspection of the seabed from suspended platforms, dragging with a canvas trawl, examining the seabed with a probe made of non-magnetic metal, and using a non-contact metal detector. When an explosive object is detected, the diver, without touching it, installs a buoy with a canvas rope at that location. After appropriate instructions, the diver begins to lift the dangerous load. Rocket warheads, bombs, and shells are lifted with a canvas rope, tying it with a slipknot with a single turn. Small items are lifted in baskets or special cases.

Diving searches for explosive objects are recommended to be conducted during daylight hours and in sea conditions with a wave height of no more than three points. The lifting of explosive objects is allowed in sea conditions with a wave height of no more than two points. If a torpedo is found, the diver must approach it from the side against the current, apply a stopper to the propellers, and only then proceed to defusing it. For this, a canvas end or a flexible chain is tied in front of the tail plumage with a slipknot.

In the case of detecting mines with "whiskers" or "antennas," it is not allowed to touch the signal end and other equipment items, wash the mine with water under pressure. When a mine is found, which by external signs may be magnetic, it is not allowed to rock and move it on the seabed or allow settling during washing, unscrew bolts, and open hatches.

Diving searches for objects using the bypass method along guide ends and the running line are applied in poor underwater visibility. The designated search area is divided into strips 50-70 meters wide and

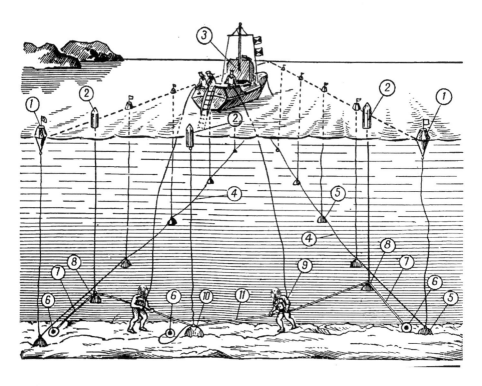

Fig. 289. Diving search for objects by bypass method: (1) – guiding buoy; (2) – control buoy; (3) – diving boat; (4) – guiding rope; (5) – ballast; (6) – small load; (7) – remote end; (8) – extreme ballast; (9) -diver; (10) middle ballast; (11) running line.

150-250 meters long by laying guide ropes on the seabed and placing buoys with ballasts to mark the surface boundaries of the surveyed strip. Across the guide ropes, a running line is laid with a length of 60-80 meters, which has portable ballasts with attached control buoys at the ends and in the middle, as well as remote ends with small loads. From a boat anchored in the middle of the surveyed strip, two divers are lowered, who, along the running line, move along the strip in a certain order. As the divers move, the boat correspondingly moves. In the event of the discovery of mines with "whiskers" or "antennas," it is not allowed to touch the signal end and other equipment items, wash the mine with water under pressure. When a mine is found, which by external signs may be magnetic, it is not allowed to rock and move it on the seabed or allow settling during washing, unscrew bolts, and open hatches.

The movement of divers underwater is shown in the layout diagram.

Diving searches for objects using the bypass method along guide ends and the running line are applied in poor underwater visibility. The designated search area is divided into strips 50-70 meters wide and 150-250 meters long by laying guide ropes on the seabed and placing buoys with ballasts to mark the surface boundaries of the surveyed strip. Across the guide ropes, a running line is laid with a length of 60-80 meters, which has portable ballasts with attached control buoys at the ends and in the middle, as well as remote ends with small loads.

From a boat anchored in the middle of the surveyed strip, two divers are lowered, who, along the running line, move along the strip in a certain order. As the divers move, the boat correspondingly moves. The movement of divers underwater is shown in the layout diagram.

Divers, having reached the seabed, approach the middle ballast and, holding onto the running line, move in different directions. When they reach the extreme ballast, they move them forward along the guide ropes by a distance equal to the length of the remote end (from

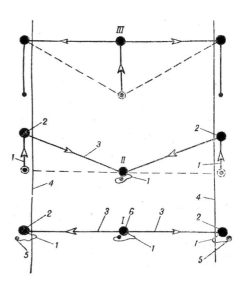

Fig. 290. Scheme of laying the running line along the guides: (1) – remote end; (2) – extreme ballast; (3) – running line; (4) – guiding rope; (5) – small load; (6) – middle ballast

2 to 6 meters depending on underwater visibility), leaving their small loads in the places of the ballast, and return along the running end to the middle ballast. Then they move the middle ballast forward by the distance of the remote end and again move towards the extreme ballasts. After pulling the small loads of the remote ends to the ballasts, they repeat the cycle of movements.

Moving along the running lines, divers carefully inspect the seabed within visibility range, and when moving ballasts, they drag the surveyed strip with the running line. If the diving search is conducted by a single diver, the strip for examination is divided into 30-40 meters. The running line is equipped with only two ballasts, which the diver moves sequentially along the guide ropes. The discovered object on the seabed is marked with numbered marker buoys. The diving search by dragging with a canvas trawl is used to survey small areas with good underwater visibility. The search is carried out by two divers lowered from a boat. Divers, holding small ballasts attached to the ends of a canvas rope, 40-50 meters long, move in different directions along its length and drag the rope along the seabed in the specified direction. Simultaneously, they inspect the ground ahead and sideways. In case the rope gets entangled, divers lower the ballasts to the seabed and converge, with each of them following the direction of the rope, manually going through it to the entanglement point. If the entangled object turns out to be the sought-after one, one of the divers sets a marker buoy, releases the rope, and the survey continues.

Diving search by dragging in concentric circles is applied to small areas in conditions of poor underwater visibility and when the approximate location of the sunken object is known. To survey the seabed in this way, a running end with a ballast and an attached canvas pull (a rope 15-20 meters long) with marks every meter are paid out from the boat. When the diver reaches the seabed, he chooses the pull through the descent end and, depending on visibility and the relief of the seabed, sets the search interval. For this, he takes the pull in his

Fig. 291. Scheme of searching by dragging in concentric circles:
(1) - descent end; (2) - ballast; (3) - knots; (4) - pull; (5) - search
item.

hand, stretches it and moves away from the descent end to a distance
of the first mark. If the descent end ballast is visible, he moves to a
mark where it is convenient for him to conduct the search. After setting
the search interval, the diver moves in a circle, carefully inspecting the
seabed and dragging the pull. After completing a full circle, the diver
moves to the next search interval to the corresponding mark and again
goes in a circle, but in the opposite direction (singing: "I am a little
horse, but I cost a lot of money..."). The survey of the seabed continues
until the diver inspects the ground within a radius equal to the full
length of the pull. If the sought-after item is not found, the descent end
with the ballast and pull is moved to another location, and the search

Fig. 292. Diving search using a metal detector

continues. In muddy soil and poor visibility, the search is conducted in the same way as in good visibility, possibly by touch or using special devices, with the search interval always set to one meter. The diver, moving in a circle, feels the ground with his hands or, using a metal detector, conducts the search coil over the muddy ground in such a way as not to miss any areas in the surveyed area.

Diving search by probe is applied when it is known that the sought-after item is buried in the seabed in the surveyed area, but it has not been possible to detect it by other means. When surveying the seabed with a probe, the diver moves in the same way as when surveying by dragging methods, with a canvas trawl, concentric circles, and bypassing the running line. Moving, the diver plunges the probe into the ground in front of him and on the sides every 0.5 meters or less. For surveying by bypassing the running line, the search area is divided into strips 1 meter wide, and running lines are laid at their boundaries. In places where the probe encounters solid objects, the ground is washed away.

Diving search using means of underwater transportation significantly accelerates search operations. Non-self-propelled and self-propelled means of underwater transportation are used in conditions of good underwater visibility, flat bottom relief, and calm water surfaces, where the use of transportation means is possible. For the search of non-magnetic and non-acoustic mines, self-propelled tow sleds are employed. If there are concerns about encountering anchor mines or mines with "tails" and "antennae" in the search area, the surveyed area is initially trawled to remove them. When using towed underwater sleds or rudders for search, the area to be surveyed is divided into strips 10 meters wide for two divers and 5-6 meters for a single diver. Each diver on the towed sled or controlling the towed rudder observes to the right and left for 3-4 meters. Upon discovering the sought-after object, the diver signals to the boat and releases a buoy marker. Guided by this buoy, divers are lowered for rigging and lifting the found object.

Fig. 293. Diving search using means of transportation

Underwater tow sleds are typically used for searching in large areas. When surveying the seabed, the diver steers the underwater tow sled on a predetermined course, using an underwater compass and a clock to count the time of movement on the course. The speed of the tow sled should be approximately constant. The diver's course of movement is adjusted from the boat, which monitors the movement of the signal buoy towed by the diver. Signals about changes in the diver's course are communicated using sounds (e.g., tapping with a hammer or striking metal objects against a buoy submerged in the water). Upon finding a sunken object, the diver throws a buoy marker and continues the search if multiple items need to be found.

Lifting sunken objects

The lifting of found objects to the surface. A buoy marker is set at the location of the sunken object discovery. Rigging and lifting of the load are carried out according to a pre-selected method based on the results of the underwater survey. Reliable and sturdy steel or fiber ropes, rigging clamps, hooks, as well as special lifting devices and hoisting devices manufactured for the specific load, are used for rigging and lifting. Rigging the load. Before proceeding with the rigging, it is necessary to assess how reliable and safe the chosen method is for the diver. Rigging should ensure a balanced position of the load during lifting. If the load is large, two slings are used for rigging, placing the center of gravity of the load between them so that it does not fall during lifting.

The slings should be secured on the load with a "choke" or by using a circular hitch with a steel or fiber hawser. The lifting hooks of the slings, if the slings are of the same length, are taken on the hook of the lifting rope; if the slings are of different lengths, they are connected with a clamp, and the hook is placed behind the loop formed by the slings. After rigging, the lifting rope must be tightly tensioned under the supervision of the diver in charge of rigging. The lifting of water-

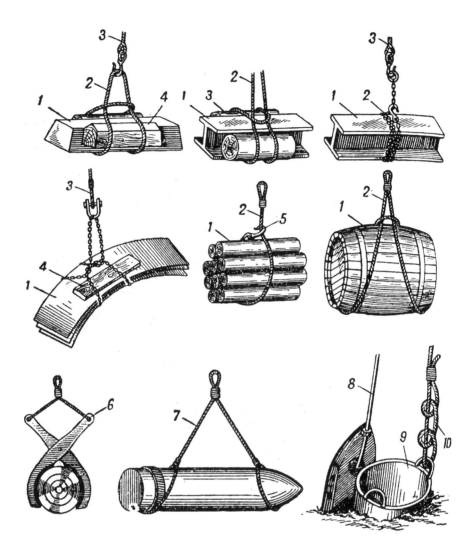

Fig. 294. Rigging and lifting the load: (1) - load; (2) - sling; (3) - shackle; (4) - pads; (5) - sliding hook; (6) - dogs for elongated objects; (7) - special sling; (8) - mine grapple; (9) - anchor; (10) - dumping with a simple pike.

rigged loads should be carried out only with reliable lifting devices and lifting slings. When unloading flooded ships to avoid a dangerous tilt, the rigging and lifting of loads should start from the upper deck. Special devices (grapples or grabs) should be used for lifting sorted iron, barrels, and other cargo in standard packaging. Small loads may be lifted in metal mesh and baskets.

Rigging the load, the diver must tension the lifting sling and ensure the rigging's reliability. After checking the cleanliness of the hose and signal cable, it is necessary to ascend to the surface or decompression stop or move to a safe distance before giving the ascent command. The diver is allowed to return to the rigging site only after being informed that the load has been lifted and placed in the prepared location.

When lifting the load from the cargo hold, after rigging the sling, the diver must go onto the ship's deck and observe the load exiting the hatch opening. When the load aligns with the deck, the diver should move to a safe location.

Rigging various types of explosive items

In case an explosive or another item requiring special handling is found, the appropriate specialist—such as a sapper, chemist, or archaeologist—is called in to guide further rigging, lifting, and towing operations of the found item.

Rigging and lifting the found explosive item are carried out in the following order. The diver's boat is anchored 200 meters from the buoy marker placed at the location of the discovered item. The boat receives a soft pontoon (underwater parachute) with hoses for inflation and a towed end for towing the raised item, as well as a diver in gear and supporting personnel on the dive team. The boat approaches the marker buoy and is positioned near it on a non-magnetic anchor. Then, divers are lowered to the seabed to rig the item as directed by the specialist. After rigging the item, the diver slightly inflates the underwater parachute, attaches the towing end, provided from the boat, to its lifting sling, and attaches a buoy marker to the explosive item (in case it becomes submerged during towing) before surfacing. The boat returns to the diver after picking them up.

Fig. 295. Rigging the torpedo: (1) stopper; (2) rigging with a lifting rope (stopper knot); (3) torpedo.

Subsequently, they start inflating the underwater parachute and observe its ascent. As soon as the underwater parachute surfaces, the towing rope and inflation hose are handed over to the towboat, which tows the explosive item to the place of disarmament or destruction at the slowest speed. The diving boat ensures the continuous inflation of the underwater parachute with air. Typically, small items from the seabed are lifted in baskets and buckets, and the diver does not necessarily need to surface but should be away from the raised load, as it may slip. The anchor mine is rigged using a mine grapple if its anchor is embedded in the seabed. In this case, the diver secures the stopper knot of a chain connected to the lifting rope behind the mine grapple. When the mine's anchor is not embedded in the seabed, the lifting rope is taken behind the anchor with a clamp or two hitches.

481

The aviation magnetic mine is rigged with a hemp rope with a diameter of 50 mm, using a choke with a single hitch. The semi-circular magnetic mine is rigged with a double hemp rope and a choke. To prevent the mine from slipping out of the sling during lifting and towing, the sling must pass between the protruding parts of the mine. To lead the sling under the mine, the diver creates a trench with a wooden or aluminum shovel. Torpedoes are rigged by the tail using a hemp or steel soft rope and a stopper knot. Before rigging the torpedo, it is necessary to close the trigger on its body and apply a stopper to the screws to prevent them from operating.

Large and medium-caliber shells are rigged individually using special devices, brackets, and cases. The bracket is made of thin sheet steel, and after leading it under the projectile, it is tensioned with a lifting shackle.

They make the case from boards. The case nest, where the projectile is placed, is padded with felt. Small-caliber projectiles and artillery mines can be placed by the diver in a basket or a wooden case with compartments matching the sizes of the projectiles.

Fig. 296. Transporting small projectiles

Diving operations for lifting automobiles, tractors, and other machinery start with the search for sunken objects. When an underwater object is discovered, it is marked with buoys and then carefully inspected.

The inspection of sunken objects begins with an external examination and identification. If the object turns out to be searchable, the position and depth in the ground are determined, as well as the possibility of rigging. Unidentified objects should be approached cautiously. If it is an unknown combat vehicle or part of an unexploded missile, an attempt should be made to identify any signs or inscriptions on the surface of the object, and the following information should be relayed to the surface: the shape of the object, dimensions, and external characteristic features.

Diving operations, including dredging, cleaning, and rigging, are prohibited until the object is identified, and approval is obtained from demolition experts. After determining the nature of the sunken object, its position on the ground, the presence of damage, and locations for attaching slings, a method is selected for lifting the sunken machinery. Heavy objects are typically lifted using floating cranes, towed power from the shore, and in winter, from ice.

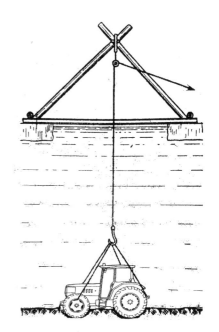

Fig. 297. Lifting equipment

Afterward, divers are tasked with determining the nature and profile of the seabed around the sunken object and the path of the path to pull the sunken object. This path must be inspected by divers and cleared of stones and other obstacles. To facilitate the towing effort, divers often have to dredge the soft ground with a water monitor, washing the seabed to the hard soil layer.

When lifting heavy equipment, which is in an overturned state, the diver washes the ground to create pits in front of and behind the sunken object.

Rigging underwater various objects and means of transportation (cars, tanks, and other machinery) for pulling ashore is done using their standard cargo devices (tow hooks) and robust connections. If the lifted vehicle lacks these standard devices, it should be rigged using a chokehold. In case of the danger of slipping of the lifting sling, it must be secured with a safety line. Regardless of the methods of lifting or pulling sunken machinery, the diver securely rigs it and attaches one end of the towline to the body or hook of this machinery and the other to the tow truck or winch.

Fig. 298. Flipping the sunken tractor: (1) - rope for transformation; (2) - direction of the rope when washing the pit; (3) - washed pit; (4) - log pit; (5) - log

The diver leads two slings, which are supplied to him from the surface, rigging the equipment behind the frame, under the tracks, behind the tow hooks, or slings. After that, he brings the slings up on the sunken object and connects them to the lifting rope with a clip or throws them onto the hook of the lifting rope. On the lifted object, after rigging, a buoy or stake is placed, indicating its movement during extraction. The sunken object is lifted only after the diver surfaces.

All actions with lifting devices during the diver's work are allowed only according to his instructions. The only exception is the "Stop" signal, which is executed immediately, regardless of who issued it. During lifting and lowering of loads, jerks and high speeds are not allowed, as this can cause the load to shift in the slings and fall, as well as the breakage of lifting slings.

Fig. 299. Lifting a sunken vessel

Marine salvage diving operations

All activities carried out during the lifting of a sunken vessel are called marine salvage diving operations. Such operations begin with determining the location of the sunken vessel underwater. The search for the sunken vessel is conducted by ships equipped with hydrolocation means and special electromagnetic devices.

Buoys are placed at the presumed locations of the sunken vessel, and these areas are subsequently surveyed by divers. After discovering the sunken vessel on the seabed, the diver must securely mark it with a buoy by attaching a buoy rope to one of its sturdy structures. If the vessel is to be lifted, the bow and stern of the vessel should be marked with buoys.

Inspection of the sunken vessel

The objectives of the diving survey are to obtain necessary information about the underwater situation for the preparation of a plan or the selection of a method for conducting diving work.

Data on the condition of the vessel and the presence of emergency damages are obtained through a thorough external and internal inspection. This includes determining the presence of anchors in hawseholes; for deployed anchors, determining the direction of anchor chains; the degree of encrustation of the hull with shells; the presence of illuminators (open, closed, broken) in the hull; the presence of objects protruding beyond the side (lifeboats, cranes, ropes, torn parts of the deck, and superstructures, etc.); the presence and condition of propellers; the condition of superstructures, decks, coamings, hatches, guns, torpedo tubes, masts, booms, smokestacks, and other deck devices; the presence of damage to the hull and their dimensions (holes, dents, cracks, wrinkles, etc.) with precise indication of their location relative to the side and approximate landmarks on the deck. The primary diving survey of the sunken vessel requires the diver to establish the nature of hull damage and their location; the depth of the vessel in the ground; the list and trim; the presence and condition of cargo in the holds; the characteristics of the ground at the flooding site. A detailed diving survey establishes: the class, type, and name of the vessel; its location and direction; the length along the main deck; the width of the main deck in the midship section; the height of the side; the number and location of main transverse and longitudinal bulkheads. Additionally, the type of rudder, the number of propellers, the configuration of the stem and stern, the location of masts, smokestacks, and other deck devices should be determined; the dimensions of cargo holds and coaming hatchways, the placement of cargo, its nature, and quantity. The nature and approximate amount of ammunition (if the sunken vessel was military) should also be determined and established. Internal inspection determines the presence and quantity of soil in the holds and other compartments with breaches; the presence, quantity, nature,

and condition of cargo in cargo holds and on the upper deck; the position and condition of boilers and main machinery.

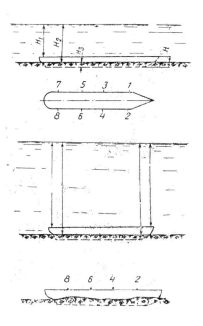

The length of the vessel is determined by the diver using a thin (1-2 millimeters) steel cable or a plant-based cable (measuring line). One end of the cable is secured to the stem of the sunken vessel, and unwinding the coil, the diver takes it along the side to the stern of the main deck. To prevent the line from sagging, the diver ties it to cleats, posts, and other details of the deck as he unwinds it. Simultaneously, he determines the placement of

Fig. 300. Determining the vessel on the seabed

487

hatches and the dimensions of superstructures. For this purpose, he goes to the bow of the vessel, and moving aft again, ties marks on the cable, reporting to the surface what they correspond to. For example, "First mark – bow mast." On the surface, the supervisor of the diving descent records these messages. Upon reaching the stern, the diver ties the last mark at the attachment point of the cable, unties it, and winds it onto the reel, raising it to the surface. Based on the data from the final and intermediate marks, the necessary dimensions of the structural details of the sunken vessel and additional information are determined.

The width of the vessel is determined by the diver using a measuring line at three points, one-third of the length of the vessel from the bow and stern ends, and in the midship section (amidships).

Determining the position of the vessel on the seabed

To determine the position of the sunken vessel on the seabed, buoys must be attached to the bow and stern in the diametral plane. On the surface, the true course of the ship is determined based on the buoys, and the course line is plotted on a plan (tablet). Diving surveys determine the depth of the vessel's submersion, the relief of the seabed around it, the list and trim, and the inclinations of the deck and holds. The depth of the vessel's submersion in the ground is the difference between the height of the side at a given point and the elevation of the side above the ground, determined at several points on each side. The depth is measured to the deck at the side of the vessel, and at the same point, the depth to the ground is determined.

If we denote the measurements at this point as follows:

h – height of the vessel's side;

$h1$ – depth to the side of the vessel;

$h2$ – depth to the ground at the side;

$h3$ – depth of the vessel's submersion in the ground.

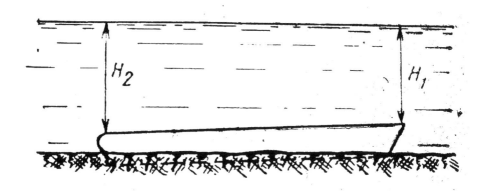

Fig. 301. Different of the sunken vessel

Then h3 is determined by the formula: **h3 = h1 + h – h2**

Points 1, 2, 3, 4, 5, 6, 7, 8 indicate the locations of depth measurements. The depth of the vessel's submersion in the ground is determined at the same points used for depth measurements to the ground when preparing the depth tablet. This information allows for determining the relief of the seabed, the submersion of the vessel in the ground, the list, and the trim of the vessel. In this case, the diver from the deck of the sunken vessel, at certain points marked by the work supervisor, checks the accuracy of lowering the lead to the ground or the deck of the vessel and reports his location and characteristic points of the vessel. The measurement results are plotted on sketches of the vessel to scale, and the obtained points on each side are connected, showing the level of the ground at the sides of the vessel. The submersion of the vessel in the ground is determined during the same period when determining the length of the vessel using a measuring line. The diver, moving along the vessel, ties marks on the line at certain structural elements of the vessel, and at these points, with the participation of the diver, the distance from the deck to the ground is determined using the lead. The list of the sunken ship is established by measuring the distances from the water surface to the deck near the sides.

Knowing the difference in the depth of submersion of the deck at two sides in one cross-sectional plane and the width of the deck, the list angle is determined:

$$h = h2 - h1, \sin\theta = h / b$$

where: b – width of the vessel;

h – difference in depth;

h1, h2 - depths to the deck at the sides of the vessel.

The list of the sunken ship can also be determined using a diving pendulum clinometer. For this, in the middle undamaged part of the deck, the diver clears a place from foreign objects and places the clinometer. When working with a clinometer pendulum, the list angle is determined on the deck in two or three different places.

The difference of the sunken vessel is determined as the difference in depth to the ends of the vessel. The difference is denoted as ΔT:

$$\Delta T = h2 - h1$$

where: h1 – depth to the bow end; h2 - depth to the stern end.

The nature of the ground is determined by external inspection and sampling with a probe at various points, classified according to the corresponding table. If the vessel has sunk in shallow water, the ground survey is conducted in the direction of the presumed towing after its lifting. Simultaneously, from a boat, the depth is measured in a strip 50 meters wide on each side. Based on the measurement data, an act is drawn up.

Determining the hull damage of the vessel

Diving surveys establish the nature of damage to the sunken vessel, the locations, and sizes of breaches, fractures in the vessel's hull. The dimensions of breaches are measured with rulers or measuring lines by placing marks on them. The shape of the breaches is determined by a template taken from its edges, or by tracing the contour of the breach on a sheet of plywood or from boards. The simplest template consists of a wooden block with extendable planks, which are secured with screw clamps. The diver sets the template so that the planks, with their ends, snugly fit against the edge of the breaches. The diving survey may include obtaining other necessary data in each specific case. Based on the survey, a report is prepared, including the results of the diving survey with sketches of the vessel's position on the seabed and the existing damages. During the preparatory work for lifting the vessel, its position on the seabed may change, and the list may increase. Therefore, immediately before lifting, it is necessary to conduct another diving survey and specify the vessel's dimensions, the depth around it, the position of the vessel on the seabed, and the condition and nature of the hull damage.

Lifting of sunken vessels

Depending on the depth of submersion, the size of the vessel, and its condition, the method of lifting the vessel is chosen, and a working lifting project is developed. For lifting vessels submerged in shallow waters, where the upper deck is entirely or partially above the water surface, the most commonly used method is water pumping. This method involves pre-sealing the breaches and sealing standard openings (illuminators, hatches, doors, etc.) in the sides and in the submerged part of the deck and superstructures. Water is pumped out of the vessel's compartments through hatches or specially cut openings in the deck located above the water level, allowing for full or partial restoration of its buoyancy. If the vessel's deck is completely underwater at a depth of 1 – 1.5 meters, water pumping from the compartments, after their sealing, is carried out through specially made metal or wooden shafts.

These shafts are installed on the coamings of hatches or cutouts in the deck under the supervision of the diver. The diver seals the shaft's contact area with putty and wedges. When lifting vessels from shallow depths, lying keel up and standing on a level keel with significant, hard-to-repair damages in the bottom part, the method of water displacement from compartments with air can be applied. Compressed air is supplied to pre-sealed compartments through blow-off hoses introduced by divers into the breaches or standard openings farthest from the water surface.

Small vessels can be lifted by floating cranes of the corresponding lifting capacity. In this method, divers conduct the rigging of the sunken vessel underwater. Small vessels sunk near the shore, with a gentle slope of the seabed and the absence of large stones or other obstacles on the seabed, are pulled ashore by tractors using winches attached to specially made and dug-in earth anchors. In this case, divers secure a bridle on the sunken vessel and attach a towline to it. The most labor-intensive and complex method is the lifting of the vessel with rigid ship lifting pontoons. All major work in this method is performed by divers.

In the work to inspect the vessel, divers are involved in cleaning the trenches near the sides of the vessel to lay pontoons, flushing the tunnels in the ground under the vessel's bottom, running rope guides into the tunnels, ensuring the passage of lifting slings into the pontoons, conducting underwater rigging, and ensuring the leveling of pontoons. The number and type of pontoons needed for lifting the vessel, as well as their placement along the length of the vessel, are determined by calculations during the development of the lifting project. The positions of the pontoons are marked on the drawings, and the distances from the pontoons' hatches to characteristic points or structures of the vessel are determined based on them. (On vessels, "hatches" are through longitudinal or round holes used for cable routing or anchor chains. Depending on the purpose and location of the hatches, they are called: in the bow - "cable," in the middle of the vessel (amidships) - "towing," in the stern - "stern" or "spring"). These distances are measured and marked on the layout line with knots or

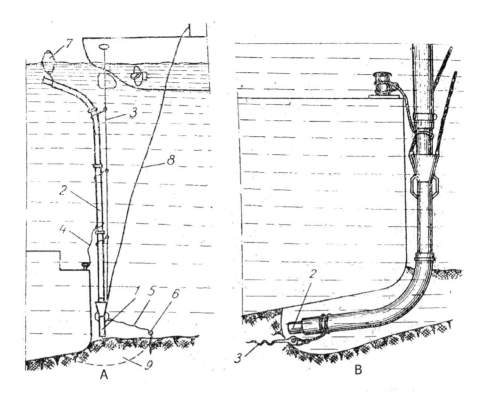

Fig. 302. Scheme of trench flushing: A – soil suction tooling for flushing the initial trench: (1) – soil pump; (2) - discharge hose; (3) – unloading rope; (4) - attachment of the discharge hose to the ship's deck; (5) – rope; (6) – stopper; (7) - buoy holding the end of the discharge hose; (8) – air hose; (9) – contour of the initial trench. B – soil suction tooling for tunnel flushing: (1) – receiving hose; (2) – receiving grid; (3) – corkscrew.

marks. The layout line is fed to the diver on the sunken vessel from the surface. The diver attaches the measuring line to a pre-marked structure of the vessel and pulls it along the deck along the side.

In places coinciding with the marks or knots on the layout line, ropes with ballast at the end (plumb bobs) are attached to the railings, bitts, or other details. The ballast at the point of contact with the ground indicates the beginning of the tunnel. The same work is performed on the other side of the vessel.

The plumb bobs are not removed until the tunnel flushing is completed. The tunnel flushing begins with washing the initial trench. For its washing in soft soils, it is sufficient to use a pneumatic soil pump. Dense soil, such as clay or sand and shell, is washed away by a stream from a hydraulic monitor barrel before the receiving opening of the soil pump. The depth of the initial trench should be 1 – 1.2 meters below the vessel's bilge, and the slope of its walls should prevent soil sliding.

The equipped soil pump is lowered to the work site along a guiding rope previously secured by a diver. During the descent, the diver must be moved to a safe distance or raised to the surface. Before starting the soil pump, the diver secures its discharge hose with a strong rope to the nearest ship structure with slack needed for subsequent deepening of the soil pump to the specified depth.

The diver attaches a piece of canvas rope to the bracket of the soil pump, the free end of which is securely tied to the head of a heavy ballast or a screw-in anchor in the ground. The length of this rope should allow the free movement of the soil pump across the entire area of the flushed trench. Only after this, the soil pump is supplied with working air, and the diver, moving the soil pump within the specified area, systematically washes the soil layer to the planned depth. In case of clogging of the receiving opening, the soil pump begins to float within the slack of securing ropes. In this case, the diver must move to a safe distance and command to stop the air supply to the soil pump. If the surfaced soil pump has lifted the diver with it, he descends to the ground along the rope leading to the ballast or stopper, moves away from the trench, and then commands to stop the air supply to the soil pump.

After that, the diver cleans the receiving opening of the soil pump, and the work continues. Cleaning a clogged soil pump without stopping the air supply can lead to suction, depressurization, and rupture of the diver's diving suit. Depressurization of the diving suit can lead to the compression of the diver and the emergence of circumstances threatening the health and life of the diver. To prevent the danger of burying the diver in the soil during the flushing of tunnels under the hull of a sunken vessel and when cutting deep trenches, the slopes of the side trenches, as well as the edges of the trenches, should be made gentle.

Before continuing the tunnel flushing, the soil pump is re-equipped from the flushed trench. This involves pulling and clamping with brackets one or two bends of the receiving hose with a coarse-mesh receiving grid at the end onto the receiving pipe. This tooling allows keeping the pneumatic part of the soil pump constantly in a vertical position. The tunnel flushing is carried out with the mandatory use of a hydraulic monitor barrel with a non-reactive attachment. The correctness of the flushing direction is determined by the diver based on the riveted or welded seams of the ship's bottom sheathing; transverse seams should be located along the tunnel. To facilitate control over the flushing direction, a stopper is used, which is screwed into the end wall of the tunnel and is screwed in as the ground is washed away from it.

Tunnels of small length (up to 4-5 m) are washed from one side along the entire length, and long tunnels are washed simultaneously from two sides towards each other. A small bridge between two opposite branches of the tunnel is usually not washed but pierced with a diving pneumatic needle. Air exiting from the front end of the needle facilitates its movement in the ground and simultaneously indicates the place where it pierced the bridge. The diver, finding the end of the needle, introduces a thin steel rope into the "ear" and secures it with a reliable knot. Then he pulls the needle back in the opposite direction. The rope comes out after it. After pulling the end of the rope to the surface, a rope of large diameter is added to it and introduced into the tunnel under the supervision of the diver. This action is repeated to insert a guide with a diameter of 21-29 mm, with the help of which a lifting sling is pulled into the tunnel. During the pulling of the guide and the introduction of the sling, the diver should be next to the tunnel and control the movement of the ropes.

In case of jamming (rope entanglement), the diver, after relieving the tension from the rope, releases the entanglement and directs the rope in the right direction. It is forbidden to grasp the rope with your hand, adjust it during pulling.

The lifting sling, introduced into the tunnel, is secured by divers to the ship's deck structures, and its hook is laid on the deck. During the flushing of tunnels under the ship's hull, divers are required to constantly observe safety rules. Advancing forward through the tunnel, the diver must periodically check the clearance of the tunnel behind him. In case of soil erosion or slippage, the diver should turn the hydraulic monitor barrel in the opposite direction and clear his way out. If necessary, a second diver descends to provide assistance.

Rigging of ship lifting pontoons and gin hooks

Rigging of pontoons and gin hooks by divers is carried out during the lifting of sunken vessels. Rigging is preceded by attaching the lifting slings to the standard devices of the sunken ship, and in their absence, pulling conductors and lifting slings under the hull of the sunken ship is carried out after flushing the respective tunnels.

Attaching the sling to the lifting hook

To the rigging site, a guiding steel cable is led and attached near the lifting hook or behind it. The lifting sling is attached to the guiding cable with a sliding bracket, and with the ship lifting bracket hung on it, it is paid out to the depth. The sliding bracket is fastened on the lifting sling at some distance from the hook, so that the diver can freely turn the hook of the sling in the desired direction and bring it to the hook for fastening. The sliding bracket is secured on the lifting sling at some distance from the hook so that the diver can freely turn the hook of the sling in the desired direction and bring it to the hook for fastening. The diving descent for this work is carried out after paying out the sling. Under the supervision of the descended diver, the sling is additionally pulled or released to such a position where the bracket will be at the hook, and the slack of the sling will be sufficient for fastening the bracket. In rough seas, the sling may change its position relative to the hook, so it is necessary to pull out the pin of the bracket in advance and keep the bracket open, then bring the bracket over the hook, and, choosing a convenient moment, close it with the pin. Some designs of hooks allow pulling the lifting sling through them. In this case, after paying out the sling, the diver inserts a working shackle into the hook and attaches it to the hook of the sling. After that, by pulling the shackle and paying out the sling, they pull it through the hook. To the hooks of the pulled sling, the diver attaches guiding ropes, with the help of which the hooks of the sling are aligned to the required position.

The lagging method of rigging pontoons is used when lifting ships sunk at shallow depths or raised from great depths to the last step, as well as during combined rigging. For lagging, the pontoons are laid in pairs with the sides against the side of the sunken ship and connected by lifting slings. The length of the lifting slings should ensure their passage through the hatches of both pontoons and connection with each other. For rigging to the lifting slings, divers alternately attach guiding ropes from each side, along which the pontoons are paid out to the sides of the ship. After paying out, the diver on the pontoon watches the passage of the hooks of the slings through the hatches and determines the length of the slings required to connect them on the pontoon. Then, stops are placed on each sling, they are laid over, and the brackets or connecting devices of the pontoon are connected.

The rigged pontoons, by supplying some air to their middle compartments, are put afloat, and if necessary, they are moored (secured) to the ship's strong rigging. Mooring is used to prevent the sliding of lifting slings and pontoons along the hull of the ship in case of significant differential pressure during the surfacing of the ship, as well as pulling slings from side to side. Mooring is divided into transverse and longitudinal. Transverse mooring is carried out by divers with steel cables: one end of the cables is attached to the pontoons, the other to the deck devices located in the area of pontoon rigging. For longitudinal mooring, to secure the cables on the deck of the ship, devices are selected outside the area of pontoon rigging: for bow pontoons – to the stern; for stern pontoons – to the bow. The mooring cables installed must be well tensioned and securely fastened. Rigging of pontoons in weight is carried out by the stepwise method of lifting ships from great depths. The pontoons are installed at distances from the surface, determining the lifting of the ship to the first and second steps. In some cases, pontoons are installed and lagged in weight, and at significant depths.

Rigging in weight can be carried out using steel musings inserted into the lifting slings, as well as by connecting pontoon straps to the lifting slings using brackets. To do this, guiding ropes are attached to the lifting slings, then the pontoon with attached pontoon straps is paid out along the guides. Under the supervision of the descended diver, the hooks of the slings are brought close together, pulling or releasing the pontoon. With the hooks close together, the diver connects them with a bracket. To do this, he extends the pin, positions the bracket over the hook of one lifting sling, closes it with the pin, and secures the pin with a safety wire. The second sling of the pontoon is connected in the same way to the lifting sling. When rigging in weight, care should be taken to ensure that the brackets are not in the 'open' position. Rigging the gin hook of ship lifting devices and cranes involves throwing the hooks of the lifting slings onto the hooks and securing them with retaining devices. Throwing the hooks onto the hooks is preceded by setting up guiding ropes to the lifting slings and paying out the gins to the work site. To do this, divers lead and secure two guides for the slings. The guides are delivered to the depth along with the descending divers on the diving bell platform. The guides should be attached to the slings below the hooks at a distance of about one meter. To prevent the guide rope from slipping along the sling, it should be wrapped around the sling twice and closed with a working bracket. After releasing the guides, they are tightly tensioned, and toggle brackets are inserted into the gin hooks. The gins are paid out to the depth along them. Under the supervision of the descended diver, the gins are pulled or released to a position where the hooks of the slings are at the level of the gin hook. Choosing a convenient position for the gin hook relative to the hooks, the diver throws and hooks one sling onto the horn of the gin hook, then the other sling. After throwing the slings onto the horn of the gin hook, the guides are released, and the sling hangs on the hook. The thrown hooks on the horn of the gin hook need to be secured with retaining devices. To reduce the volume of diving work, one sling of the lifting sling is hung on the gin hook on the surface before pulling the sling through the blocks or under the ship's keel.

Diving work on fishing vessels

The work of divers on fishing vessels has become widespread. In case of damage to the side keels of fishing vessels that catch and pull nets, divers cut them with an underwater cutting torch or weld them. Ropes or leads (buoy ropes) of drifting nets on the propellers of trawlers are cleaned by divers, as mentioned earlier. Here they inspect and repair herring stops, clean nets and trawls, and perform work on the underwater part of trawlers. Most often, they inspect the lower edge of the nets to ensure a tight fit to the ground. Pulling underwater a particular buoy rope that holds the net in weight, the diver indicates that it needs to be released.

The edge of the net that has hit the rocks is thrown away downstream. A torn net is sewn with nylon thread or a patch is applied to the damaged area, which is provided to the diver in the form of a roll from above. Nets or trawls caught on irregularities in the bottom are freed by the diver. When installing a set net, divers work at depths of 10-15 meters, spread anchors, check the correct placement of the entrance hole of the net, as well as the tightness of the net's lower selection against the ground. Collecting divers are directly involved in the extraction of seafood. Working at shallow depths, they manually collect scallops, mussels, sea cucumbers, sea urchins, and scallops, as well as other seafood in special collection nets (sack nets or geisha nets), after which they bring them to the surface.

Underwater explosive works

Underwater blasting is widely used in various diving operations. The force of underwater explosions destroys rocks, clears fairways, digs trenches, breaks ice jams, dismembers sunken vessels, and disposes of sunken explosive objects. In order to clear the waters to ensure navigation in certain areas of bases and ports, individual areas of water are cleared of sunken vessels by simultaneously detonating a series of explosive charges. To obtain initial data for choosing a method of clearing the bottom of a sunken vessel, determining the design and weight of explosive charges, and the location of their placement, a diving survey of the sunken vessel is carried out.

During the survey, the following are determined: the position of the sunken object on the ground; the nature of the ground around the object (mud, sand, rock, or other type of ground) at a distance of 50 meters; the possibility of divers approaching the hull plating, walking on the deck, and inside the object; the possibility of placing elongated explosive charges around the hull, along the sides, and on the deck; the possibility of placing concentrated charges of large weight inside the hull to scatter dismembered parts throughout the waters. Underwater explosive works are carried out only by diver-blasters. Descents for the execution of underwater explosive works are made by divers who have additional qualifications as diver-blasters. Underwater explosive works are allowed to be carried out only under the direct supervision of a specialist authorized to supervise underwater explosive works. The Unified Rules for Conducting Explosive Works are the main guiding document for conducting underwater explosive works. It is prohibited to carry out underwater explosive works without communication with the diver.

Explosive means underwater

Detonating underwater charges laid by divers is allowed only by electrical means or with a detonating cord. Detonating charges underwater by pyrotechnic means is prohibited. The following main means are used for underwater detonation: explosive charges (such as TNT, ammonals, ammonites, and other explosive substances); detonator caps; detonating cords; pyrotechnic cords; igniter tubes; boosters; blasting machines; electrical wires, putty, sealing compounds.

The charge of explosive substance is determined by its mass, packed in containers, and prepared for detonation. Charges of the following forms are used: concentrated, elongated, shaped, cumulative. Depending on the explosive substance used in the charges, the charges are made in sealed and unsealed containers. The main properties of explosive substances affect the power of the explosion.

Detonator caps are used to initiate the explosion of explosive charges and consist of metallic cases containing initiating high-explosive material. The bottom covering the lower part of the case has a concavity to increase the power of the detonator cap explosion. The upper open part of the case is used to insert the end of the pyrotechnic cord. The suitability of detonator caps is determined by their visual inspection. During the inspection, attention is paid to ensuring that the cases are not dented, there are no cracks, oxidation, or other damage on their surface, hindering the free insertion of the pyrotechnic cord.

Detonator caps require great care in handling and storage; they should be protected from impacts, falls, heating, friction, and other physical impacts. They should be stored in a dry place separately from explosives in boxes of 100 pieces.

Electric detonators are detonator caps with an electric igniter placed in the case for detonating the detonator cap by heating the bridge with an electric current. Sensitivity and moisture-resistant electric detonators are used for detonation at depths of up to 20 meters. The resistance of electric detonators varies from 0.65 to 2 ohms. For detonation, a guaranteed current strength of 1.5-1.8 amperes is required.

Detonating cord is intended for simultaneous detonation of several separately located explosive charges and for non-cap detonation of charges. The cord is detonated by a detonator cap (electric detonator) attached to the end of the cord with threads or insulating tape. The detonation speed (explosion transmission) of the cord is 6800-7200 meters per second. Underwater, a cord with a diameter of 5.5-6 mm is used. The cord covering is colored red or white (in the latter case, it has several red threads). In use, the detonating cord is relatively safe; it can be cut with a knife, and when ignited, it burns calmly. However, when igniting a large amount of cord, burning can turn into an explosion. The ends of the detonating cord intended for underwater use must be well-insulated with waterproof putty or insulating tape. The detonating cord explodes underwater if it stays in the water for no more than 12 hours.

Boosters

Boosters are intended for detonating charges of large mass. In turn, boosters are divided into types: a - cartridge-booster; b - booster from a TNT block; c - booster from powdered explosive substance and electric detonator; g - intermediate charge of explosive substance. Boosters are made from powdered explosive substances or blocks. Boosters made from powdered explosive substances with a diameter of

3-4 centimeters and a length of 20-25 centimeters, weighing 200-300 grams, are called cartridges. Boosters consisting of a single block weighing 200 or 400 grams are called ignition blocks. Boosters are made only on-site. Igniter tubes or electric detonators are placed in boosters before exploding charges. Premature preparation and equipping of boosters are prohibited. For better detonation of the main charge, the booster is installed underwater as close to its center as possible.

Blasting Machines. Explosive machines are used as power sources for underwater detonation, and in some cases, dry batteries, accumulators, power supply networks are also used.

Wires. For underwater detonation to connect the electric detonator to the power source, two types of sapper wires are used – single-core and two-core

Before the start of explosive operations, the boundaries of hazardous zones must be defined, both along the shore and in the water area, and measures must be taken to ensure the safety of personnel, watercraft, and shore structures within these zones. The leader of the operations must inform the senior officer of the designated area about the upcoming explosive work, specifying the time, location of the work, and the mass (weight) of the charges to be detonated. Explosive work at night is allowed only in exceptional cases.

The personnel participating in the work must be well-instructed in safety procedures for explosive operations, familiar with the explosive substances and accessories used for detonation. Only after this, the descent of a diver with a charge is allowed. Underwater explosive work is carried out from a boat, from the shore, or from the ice. Conducting explosive work from a diving boat or other self-propelled watercraft is prohibited.

When performing work from a boat, it must have explosive experts and one or two rowers in life jackets. The explosive expert is positioned at the stern. Other persons are not allowed to be in the boat. The boat can carry no more than 20 charges with a total mass of up to 40 kilograms. Charges are placed in the stern of the boat in a way that prevents them from moving during transportation. Charges are allowed to be loaded into the boat only by the explosive expert.

It is prohibited to manufacture or modify charges, check electric detonators, check the buoyancy of charges by immersing them in water, fix the insulation of charges or boosters, light fires, or smoke in the boat. It is forbidden to transport other cargo in the boat during explosive work. The boat with charges should be at least six meters away from the diving boat conducting the work, and it can approach only at the moment of delivering the charges to the diver. The explosive expert hands the charges to the diver, after which the boat moves away from the diving boat again. Handing more than one charge to the diver at a time is prohibited. If it is necessary to give the diver several small charges (with a total mass of up to 20 kilograms), they are placed in a basket with compartments, which is handed over from the boat.

Divers with a charge are allowed to descend either along the lowering line attached to the place where the charge is laid or along a guiding thread (if descending from the shore). Charges should not be delivered along the signal or other line, and they should not be lowered on wires or detonating cord. Explosive substances, prepared in packaging or without it, without electric detonators or detonating cord, are allowed to be delivered on a hemp line.

The descent should be careful, avoiding impacts of charges or contact with the wires of objects. When laying and securing charges, care should be taken to ensure that the wires do not get entangled in the equipment. When the diver descends with a charge, the wires must be paid out in a way that prevents them from getting tangled with the hose or signal line. When removing propellers, it is allowed to hand over the charge to the diver from the ship where the work is being done.

The charge preparation should take place in a specially designated area where there is no personnel and explosive cargo. The number of prepared and interconnected small charges handed over to the diver should not exceed four pieces with a total mass of no more than 0.6 kilograms. Long charges made of pyroxylin powder, without intermediate detonators, are allowed to be laid on the ground from non-self-propelled watercraft as they are towed along the route or pulled on a rope under the ice when working with ice. Such charges are detonated using detonators.

Large charges are also laid on-site without means of detonation. After laying the charge, its wires must be secured near the charge. After laying and securing the charge and wires near the charge, the diver must ensure that, when moving away from the charge, they do not catch on the wires or detonating cord. After the diver resurfaces, the supervisor must inspect him and ensure that the wires from the charge or the charge itself are not brought to the surface.

Before detonating the charges, personnel on the shore or on the ice, as well as the diving boat and the boat with charges, move to a safe distance, which is predetermined by the work supervisor or the explosive expert. Before the explosion, other diving boats are notified of the impending explosion by hoisting the "N" flag. Charges are not detonated until diving boats respond to it by lowering their signals, indicating that all divers have exited the water.

Territorial wires with trunk lines are connected by the explosive expert on the boat (on the shore) after ensuring that their terminal ends are disconnected from the power source and short-circuited. Only the explosive expert is allowed to detonate the charges. Before detonation, it should be ensured that all necessary safety measures have been taken, the diver has exited the water, and protection of the boundaries of the hazardous zone is provided.

After the ascent to the surface, the diver-demolition specialist is carefully inspected to ensure that they did not inadvertently bring a charge with them on their equipment. The descent of the diver-demolition specialist for the inspection of unexploded charges is allowed no earlier than five minutes after disconnecting the wires from the power sources when using instant and short-delay electric detonators, and after 15 minutes if a delayed-action electric detonator is used. It is prohibited to raise charges by their ends or wires.

Unexploded charges can be eliminated by detonating other charges laid near the failed ones if the conditions of the facility allow for detonating a large amount of explosives. If, for any reason, the failed charge cannot be detonated immediately, the diver-demolition specialist must notify the work supervisor of this and set a buoy near the charge or, with the supervisor's permission, independently bring the charges to the surface. During underwater explosions, the work of divers and swimming of people are not allowed at a distance from the explosion site: 500 meters for a charge mass of up to 50 kilograms; 1000 meters for a charge mass exceeding 50 kilograms.

When performing explosive work on dismantling sunken vessels where the presence of ammunition is expected, measures must be taken to prevent possible detonation of ammunition.

The area within a radius of 100 meters from the sunken vessel must be surveyed to exclude the presence of mines, shells, and other ammunition. After the explosion of the charges, the wires must be disconnected from the power source, short-circuited, lifted out of the water, and wound onto a spool.

If no explosion follows, the descent of the diver to inspect the charges and perform further work is allowed: after 5 minutes of disconnecting the wires in the case of using instant-action electric detonators; after 15 minutes of disconnecting the wires in the case of using delayed-action electric detonators. It is prohibited to raise unexploded charges to the surface. A failed charge is exploded by another charge. If the failed charge cannot be exploded immediately, a buoy or a post indicating the presence of a charge underwater must be placed near the charge. The number of descents of one diver during explosive work in one working day should not exceed: for a depth of up to 6 meters – 8 descents; for a depth from 6 to 12 meters – 6 descents; for a depth from 12 to 20 meters – 3 descents; for a depth exceeding 20 meters - one descent.

In the event of an approaching storm, explosive work must be stopped. If there are several charges left in the boat, it is moved at least 60 meters away from the diving boat, and it is anchored. The personnel from the boat transfer to the diving boat. Explosive work is stopped in waves exceeding two points or in winds exceeding four points. When performing explosive work from the shore or from the ice, the same rules for delivering, transporting, and laying charges must be followed as in work with watercraft.

§ 30. Underwater technical diving operations

Works related to the inspection, construction, and repair of underwater parts of various hydraulic structures are referred to as underwater technical works. Any works carried out with or without the participation of a diver are called complex underwater technical operations. The main underwater technical works include: diving inspection of the seabed and hydraulic structures; underwater works during the leveling of stone beddings, installation of concrete masses, blocks, piles, and other structures; underwater earthworks (excavation of trenches and pits); laying underwater pipelines and cables; installation of underwater parts of water intakes and other hydraulic structures. All types of diving equipment can be used for underwater technical works.

Diving inspection of hydraulic structures

The preparatory part of underwater technical works includes diving inspections of the seabed and hydraulic structures. The inspection of the seabed is carried out using methods described in the section on searching for submerged objects. Diving inspection of underwater structures is performed to determine their technical condition and the quality of individual elements of the structure, as well as to identify the nature of damage to emergency structures. Drawings of the structures are required for the inspection. Based on the data from the diving inspection, a project for repair works is prepared.

Inspection of underwater pipelines

In rivers and bodies of water, the bottom of coastal areas is often reshaped. In some areas, the riverbed is eroded, while in others, sediment is deposited. Due to the flow, exposed and sagging pipelines undergo oscillatory movements, which can lead to their breakage. Therefore, pipelines, cables, water intakes, and other structures laid in rivers and bodies of water require systematic diving inspection and monitoring during their operation.

Diving inspection of submerged pipelines determines:

1. Compliance of the top of the pipeline backfill with the project and execution drawings.
2. Presence and dimensions of exposed areas at the river erosion site along the pipeline route.
3. Amount of sagging of the pipeline.
4. Presence of foreign objects in the pipeline route.
5. Condition of underwater sections of shore reinforcements.

Before starting the inspection of the underwater pipeline, the diving unit receives an inspection program approved by the organization that owns the pipeline. Below is an example of a diving inspection program for two lines of a 600-millimeter diameter main oil pipeline crossing a river. The lines are laid 30 meters apart in separate underwater trenches and backfilled. Shore reinforcement work is done in coastal areas using stone fill on a gravel-sand foundation.

The technical assignment to the diving unit specifies the following:

1. Conduct a diving inspection of a 60-meter-wide section of the river from the right to the left bank.

2. Determine the top of the pipeline backfill marks and their compliance with project or execution drawings.

3. Determine the placement of the top of the pipeline (upper shell). For this purpose, use a hydro monitor to wash across the pipeline every 50 meters until the upper shell of the pipelines is found at a depth of up to 1 meter. The length of each cross-section should be 10 meters.

4. If, during the washing of cross-sections at a depth of 1 meter, the pipeline is not found, stop further washing.

5. Upon discovering a section of exposed pipeline, determine the riverbed marks and the upper shell of the pipeline at the same point after 5 meters.

6. Determine the length and condition of the exposed pipeline section.

7. Assess the condition of the pipeline's coastal areas and shore reinforcements.

8. Mark the top of the backfill and the upper shell of the pipeline on the longitudinal profile of the pipeline crossing.

The diving unit, upon receiving the task of inspecting the underwater pipeline, must familiarize itself with: the project-execution drawings of the pipeline crossing over the river; the alignment (channel) of the pipeline crossing over the river; and be aware of the water level mark at the crossing. A water level gauge post must be installed in the crossing, marked with special columns on both banks, featuring specific daytime and nighttime crossing signs.

Across the river at the crossing, a measuring steel cable with a diameter of 4 to 10 millimeters is laid, with marks tied every five meters. The cable is secured on the banks, as determined by the project, as water level notches. Moving from the right bank to the left along the measurement cable, the diver stops at a specific mark; from the diving boat, they determine the depth of the river from its level to the riverbed. In this case, the riverbed serves as the top of the backfill for the laid pipeline. Knowing the absolute water level mark and the depth at this point, the riverbed mark is determined. For example, if the water level mark is 120 meters and the depth of the river 50 meters from the water notch is 10 meters, then the riverbed mark at this point will be 120 - 10 = 110 meters.

After determining the riverbed marks, which in this case serve as the marks for the top of the backfill of the laid pipeline, and in case of discovering an exposed pipeline, the diver begins washing the cross-sections. This operation is performed with a hydraulic monitor every 50 meters to detect the upper shell of the laid pipelines. The cross-sections are made in the form of a trench with a bottom width of 1 meter, with slopes of 0.4 meters for fine sand and 0.5 meters for coarse sand. The cross-sections are washed at intervals of 5 meters upstream and downstream from the laid measurement cable until the pipeline is found. If the pipeline is not found during the washing of the one-meter-deep cross-section, further washing at that location is stopped. If an exposed section of the pipeline is found, measurements are taken to determine its position and the riverbed at that location every 5 meters and at characteristic points. The diver checks the condition of the pipeline insulation, whether there is any vibration, the stability of ballast weights (for gas pipelines crossing water barriers), and whether there is any sliding of weights along the pipeline due to vibration. The diver also checks for the presence of foreign objects near the sagging part of the pipeline.

When constructing pipeline crossings over large reservoirs and other significant water obstacles, pipelines in the middle and deep parts are usually not buried. Therefore, during diving inspections of these areas, the main attention is given to determining the sections where they sag.

Familiarizing themselves with the condition of shore reinforcements, divers carefully inspect coastal areas, check the integrity of stone prisms, stone bedding, the presence of depressions in coastal areas, and possible slippage of stone bedding or concrete slabs.

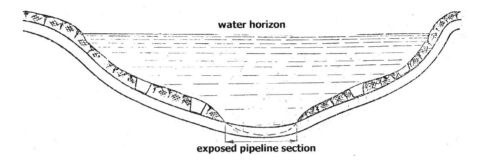

water horizon

exposed pipeline section

Fig. 303. Longitudinal profile of the pipeline

All data obtained during the diving inspection, as well as measurements, are recorded on the drawings and specified in the inspection reports of the laid pipeline.

Inspection of submerged cables across rivers and water bodies

Cable crossings (communication and power cables) are inspected according to a program approved by the organization responsible for the cable mainline laid across water bodies (rivers, lakes, reservoirs, seas).

During the inspection of laid cables, the following are determined:

1. Absence of submerged objects in the cable laying section.

2. Marks of cable laying.

3. Marks of the top of the backfill of the laid cables.

4. Presence of exposed sections of underwater cables.

5. Condition of coastal reinforcements.

6. Marks of the top of the backfill and cable laying.

Inspection of water intake structures

Diving inspection of the submerged parts of a water intake structure is usually carried out after the passage of floodwaters. A water intake structure typically consists of a head, a pipeline (self-flowing or siphonic), and a pumping station. The head and pipeline are considered submerged parts of the structure. Flooding of the head sometimes hinders water supply to the pumping station. Erosion of the riverbed around the head may cause displacement. During the diving inspection of the head, the following are determined: marks of the river and water bodybed; top marks; condition of the head; position of the stone bedding under the head and around it; depth of the water saturation layer around the head; marks of the top of the backfill of the submerged sections of self-flowing (siphonic) pipelines; condition of coastal reinforcements at the water intake structure.

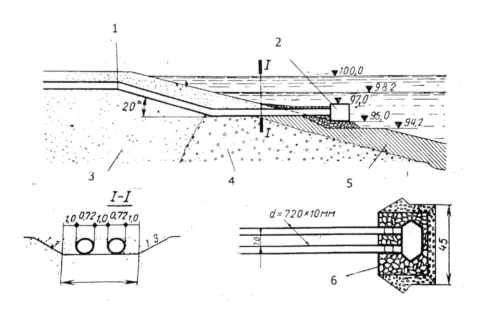

Fig. 304. Water intake structure diagram: (1) - the limit of underwater technical works; (2) - the head; (3) - fine-grained sand; (4) - sand with gravel admixture; (5) - clay; (6) - stone embankment.

In the "Unified rules for occupational safety in diving operations", great attention is paid to safety techniques during underwater technical works. Diving works at water supply structures are carried out according to an approved hourly schedule coordinated with the administration. Before starting work, units are partially stopped or shut down. Additionally, turbine regulation release devices are closed, and mechanisms for starting units and opening gates are turned off. The water filtration point through the water supply structure is determined by pulling a ballasted bag with pitch on ropes, and minor filtration is checked using a pole with a rubber plate and light ballast. Inspection of large through holes in the structure by a diver is only done under the protection of a wooden shield. At water intake and hydraulic structures, divers can only work with permission and a work permit for the right to make underwater descents on the specific structure, issued by the dispatch service.

Diving operations at water supply structures usually include inspecting the bottom holes and gates. All data from the diving inspection is recorded in the project-execution drawings and in the diving inspection report.

Rectification of identified defects

Divers also conduct periodic inspections of the underwater parts of the entire hydraulic structure, paying attention to various damages, erosion of structures, water filtration in the structure and gates, the condition of water-bearing plates, clogging of water overflow holes with debris, broken ice, and more. When necessary, divers perform gate sharpening or cleaning of trash-retaining grilles. Defects in water filtration through the gates are eliminated by caulking the points of contact between the shields and their support surfaces. If foreign objects are found in the slots of the gates, they are removed before closing the gates. When cleaning sandhoppers or trash-retaining grilles, debris and broken ice are collected in a basket, which is then hoisted up. When inspecting hydraulic structures, it is essential to strictly observe safety precautions, as in the presence of through damages, there is a possibility of entanglement of the hose, signal line, and even pressing against the site of damage or pulling into the hole of the diver.

Inspection of structures made of massifs

The purpose of the inspection is to determine the technical condition of piers, wharves, embankments, and other hydraulic structures. The inspection of structures made of massifs includes the following tasks: special attention is paid to the condition of the slope of the stone bedding and the lower row of masonry (damage or shifts); inspection of the stone bedding during the laying of massifs; inspection of proper massif laying; detection of cracks and other damages (attention should be given to areas with exposed reinforcement, the presence of caverns, and breaches). During the inspection, the diver moves vertically along the guide rope or horizontally on the platform. If a shift of massifs or a tilt of quay walls is discovered, the diver uses a ruler and plumb bob to measure them.

Inspection of piling and pile constructions

When inspecting piling structures, the diver must carefully examine the angles, joints of transverse walls, and other fastenings. Upon discovering damages, measurements are taken using a ruler or a measuring rod. When checking pile constructions, the diver, using a clinometer or plumb bob, determines whether the piles deviate from the vertical axis or not. Upon discovering defects (dents, wood splitting), the diver, using a sounding lead, determines the distance from the water surface to the damaged area, making vertical marks on the structure's wall. When inspecting piling and pile constructions, attention should be paid to wood damage by shipworms, cracks, concrete damage, rust on metal structures, as well as areas with exposed reinforcement in reinforced concrete structures. Descents onto hydraulic structures are made after divers familiarize themselves with the structure and its operating principles. Before descending to inspect the underwater part of a hydraulic structure, it is necessary to determine the stability of its individual elements, the falling of which could threaten the safety of the diver. Descent for inspecting the condition of slipways, railways, and docks should be carried out after all underwater mechanisms have completely ceased operation. When working near dams with through damages, devices to protect the diver from suction should be used.

The search for damaged areas is conducted with a slackened rope or a long pole. Descents during the raising of various gate devices are allowed only if it does not lead to a sharp increase in water flow in the descent area, and the water flow rate is not dangerous for the descent. Lifting or lowering gate devices can only be done after the diver has surfaced. If the presence of a diver is required during the descent of the device to observe its correct installation, the diver is allowed to be only above the device without slack in the hose and signal line. Diver's operations in servicing navigable canals include inspecting the bottom of the underwater part of the water area, cleaning drainage and receiving culverts, laying anchorages for navigation marks, and other diving works.

The diver inspects the bottom, holding onto a steel rope previously laid across the canal and lowered to the bottom. As the ground is inspected, the rope is moved along the wall. When inspecting a lock threshold, it is necessary to descend from the external side of the gate. In case of jamming with various objects, such as stones, the diver removes objects to the external side of the gate. For the safety of the diver during the descent, the lock operation is stopped. Divers are not allowed to inspect trenches and pits during the operation of scrapers, hydromonitors, and other soil removal means.

Diving operations in the construction and restoration of underwater structures

Divers involved in underwater work on hydraulic structures must be familiar with their design and undergo preliminary safety training. Diving operations in the construction and restoration of massif structures involve preparing the foundation for the structure and monitoring the laying of massifs. Preparation of the foundation includes: removal of soft soil; construction of a stone bedding; measurements of the prepared stone foundation; underwater concreting.

When performing earthworks, the diver must first determine if there are any electrical cables or pipelines in the area. If present, electrical cables are de-energized and grounded, and the pressure in pipelines is reduced to 1-2 bar. For small areas, divers remove soft soil using soil washing equipment and a soil pump. In areas where soil is removed with dragline buckets or grabs, the diver's task is to wash away irregularities in the soil using a hydraulic monitor. When washing trenches and pits and their walls, the slopes must be gradual to avoid collapses. When using high-pressure pumps to wash the soil with several divers simultaneously, they should be at least 10 meters apart. Divers should not release the hose until the hydraulic monitor has stopped. Stone dumping and filling of excavations are done using steamers, barges with open bottoms, and in winter, with ice, using closed wooden chutes. Divers are responsible for installing and relocating the chutes. The next stage of work is leveling the beds. With the proper laying of ordinary massifs, three types of bed leveling are distinguished: rough, careful, and very careful. During rough leveling, the diver distributes stones into depressions. Careful leveling is done using guide and control rails made of narrow-gauge rails, with their placement checked using a measuring rod. During very careful leveling, the diver fills depressions and gaps between large stones with gravel or, conversely, removes excess stones. During the leveling of the stone dumping, additional stone backfilling should not be done without notifying the diver. If stones are added without troughs or pipes, the diver must surface.

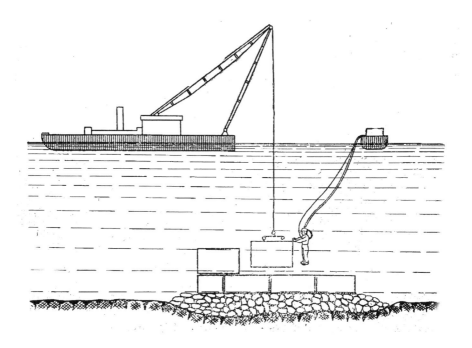

Fig. 305. Diver's position during lowering of a massif

Massifs are placed on the prepared bed using a floating crane under the supervision of a diver. The diver can inspect the installation of massifs only after the descent of the structures has stopped. The diver descends after the lowered massif reaches the ground or is suspended no more than 20-25 centimeters above the ground. In case of its movement, the diver must be on the upper part or on the side that will not come into contact with the adjacent structure. Special attention is paid to the hose and signal line to ensure they are not pinned by the lowered structure. The suspended massif is rotated by the diver in the required direction, and when it is precisely above the designated laying location, a signal is given to the surface to lower the massif. After lowering the massif to the designated location and checking its correct installation, the diver must release the keys for lifting and lowering the massif and hand over the slings. The installation of the next massif is carried out in the same way. Divers should not be lowered or raised on gripping devices and sharp parts of structures. When restoring massif-laid structures, divers prepare the surface (filling in excavations and clearing debris). Using a hydraulic monitor, divers clean soft soil from the stone dumping. When massifs change position or shift, they need to be rearranged. In such cases, the work of divers involves keying the massifs or lifting them with slings. Then the massifs are moved by a crane for proper laying. During the descent of the massifs, the diver guides them manually or with the help of rigging. Inter-massif seams formed during laying are sealed by divers with stones or concrete.

Underwater concreting is carried out when sealing holes in the hull of ships and in the construction, repair, and restoration of hydraulic structures. Aluminous and Portland cements of grades 75, 100, 150, 200, 250, 300, 400, 500 are used for concrete production. Cement is a component of concrete, and sand and gravel of different fractions or other bulk components are used as fillers. For sealing holes, it is best to use concrete in a proportion of one part cement, two parts sand, and one or two parts gravel. The mixture of cement with sand and water is called a cement mortar, and a cement mortar with fillers is called a concrete mix. Concrete strength accelerators include calcium chloride, hydrochloric acid, and liquid glass. Water for preparing the concrete mix should not contain fats, vegetable oils, oil, or acids. Sea water reduces the strength of concrete. Concrete is prepared using concrete mixers or manually. In the manual method, the required amount of gravel or other filler is poured onto a flat surface or a wide container with an open top. Sand is poured over it, followed by cement. All these components are carefully mixed with shovels, after which water is added to the mixture. Mixing is done until the concrete has a homogeneous mass and the consistency of thick paste. In the method with a concrete mixer, it is put into operation, then the required amount of cement and a certain amount of water are poured into it, followed by adding sand and gravel or other filler. Mixing in the concrete mixer is done until the concrete has a homogeneous mass and the consistency of thick paste.

Methods of underwater concreting

Concrete is delivered and laid in various ways: in bags and tubs; by vertically moving; by the "rising solution" method; by concrete pumps and by vibration method. The diver must prepare the concrete laying site well, thoroughly clean the surface from rust, oil, and other contaminants. The area to be poured with concrete is enclosed with a wooden formwork. When sealing small holes, the diver covers it with metal reinforcement made of wire or round iron. For large bottom holes, rails or beams are laid. The concrete pouring from boxes, laying in bags. When sealing a hole, concrete is poured from above in bags and tubs at small intervals to prevent it from setting. Pulling the plug at the bottom of the tub, the diver pours the concrete mass onto the damaged part into the formwork, leveling it slightly with his hands and tamping it down.

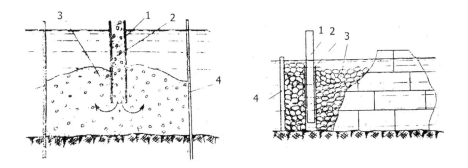

Fig. 306. Underwater concreting: A - using vertically moving pipes: (1) pouring pipe; (2) concrete mass; (3) laid concrete; (4) pit enclosure. B - method of rising solution: (1) pouring pipe; (2) shaft; (3) rubble masonry; (4) formwork.

Concrete is delivered only upon the command of the working diver, who, when lowering the load, must move away. The diver tightly arranges bags with concrete in rows on the reinforcement. After laying two layers of bags, he punctures them with a sharp steel rod, puncturing the third layer along the second, and so on. Underwater concreting by the vertically moving method is used in underwater technical work using pouring pipes with a diameter of not less than 20 centimeters and lifting mechanisms to move the pipe vertically.

Divers inspect and prepare the pit, level its bottom, install the formwork, seal the gaps between the formwork and the pit bottom, as well as between the walls of the formwork. The upper part of the pipe has a funnel. The concrete mix is continuously fed through the pipe installed in the center of the concrete structure. As the level of concrete rises, the pipe is gradually withdrawn, but in such a way that its end is always below the surface of the concrete mix. The diver must monitor the arrival of concrete to the laying site and observe the end of the pipe to ensure it is immersed in the concrete. The pipe is raised on his command. Underwater concreting by the "rising solution" method is used in the construction of massive embankments, piers, quays, foundations of hydraulic structures, and other hydraulic structures. A sand-cement solution is introduced into the stone dumping through pouring pipes. Rising upward, it fills the rubble masonry and creates a strong monolith. Pipes with a diameter of up to 20 centimeters are installed in enclosing lattice shafts or placed in large fillers.

In the process, the pipe is gradually raised, but with the calculation that its mouth is immersed in the laid solution to a depth of at least 0.8 meters. In this method of concreting, divers perform the same work as when concreting by the vertically moving method. Observations on the spread of the solution can be made through special holes made in the formwork.

Underwater concreting with concrete pumps

The apparatus designed for transporting a continuous and uniform flow of concrete through pipes is called a concrete pump. The outlet of the concrete pump pipe, through which the concrete mass is delivered, should be positioned below the surface of the concrete. As the concrete fills the pipe, it is raised. The hydro-vibration method is used in underwater concreting with high-frequency vibrators with a large number of oscillations. This method is employed in the construction of driven piles, supports for bridge piers, foundations for lighthouses, and other hydraulic structures that require special structural strength.

When making driven piles, casing pipes are driven into the ground, from which the soil is initially removed, and then the filler is laid, a vibrator is installed, and cement milk is injected. The loose mass is compacted under the influence of vibration. As the casing pipes vibrate, they are lifted, and then reloaded with filler. In underwater concreting using various methods, the diver must ensure the correct positioning of underwater reinforcement, the integrity of the formwork, and the uniform flow of concrete. After the concrete has set, the formwork or cofferdam is removed, and the density of the concrete is determined. If voids are detected, simple structures for additional concrete injection are fixed and set up with the help of divers. After concrete placement, a final underwater inspection is necessary, during which a detailed survey report is compiled.

Diving operations in the construction and restoration of structures

In the construction of embankment-type structures, divers prepare the foundation for embankment structures and observe the movement and installation of the structure, which has been pre-fabricated in an above-water position. The preparation of the foundation for embankment structures and their installation on a stone bed is carried out similarly to the construction of massive masonry. To lower the embankment into place, its compartments are evenly loaded with stones, with the calculation that the embankment has buoyancy close to zero. Before fully loading the embankment with ballast, the diver thoroughly checks its position on the stone bed, after which he surfaces. In winter, embankments are fabricated on the ice above their installation site, lowering them into a cut hole. When restoring damaged embankment structures, the diver clears the damaged areas of stones and wood. In cases where the area is restored using massive masonry, the diver cuts off the damaged crowns of the embankment and clears the space for laying the masonry.

When constructing pile structures, divers clear the soil and conduct a visual inspection of the piles, paying attention to their deviations from the design position, and measure the distances between the piles. Diving is prohibited during the piling of piles with a cofferdam, during the backfilling of stone embankment, during the lifting or lowering of embankment and pile sections, water intake headers, steel threads of pipelines, and other heavy objects. Inspection of the correct laying by a diver can only be performed after the complete lowering of the elements to the laying site.

Monitoring of the correction by packing and leveling to the required position should be carried out by the diver from the outside or from above a safe location. It is not allowed to drive piles, move floating structures if the diver is within a 15-meter radius of the lowering area. When restoring damaged pile structures, divers dismantle the structures and clear the areas for piling piles. Cavities sometimes form on reinforced concrete piles, exposing and rusting the reinforcement. Repairing damages involves preliminary removal of the destroyed concrete with a jackhammer, removal of rust with a metal brush, followed by flushing the cavity with a high-pressure water jet. Then, a formwork is installed over the damaged area, and the diver patches the cavity with a fatty concrete mixture.

Repair of damages in metal pile structures involves the diver replacing individual parts of the structures or filling gaps and voids in them, after cleaning the metal surface from algae, shells, and rust.

Diving operations during pile extension

Damaged piles are cut off and extended with new ones by joining them using metal sleeves secured with two bolts. The sleeves are made from sections of steel pipes, sized to the diameter of the root pile removed by the diver after cutting. The sleeve is slid onto the extended end, secured with a bolt, and handed to the diver in a vertical position. The diver directs it onto the end of the root pile. If the sleeve does not fit, it is gradually adjusted by hitting it with a manual sledgehammer. Then, through the hole in the lower part of the sleeve, the diver drills a hole in the root pile, passes a bolt through it, tightens the nut with a long wrench, and finally tightens it from above using a lever. The holes in the sleeve should be slightly larger in diameter so that the protruding

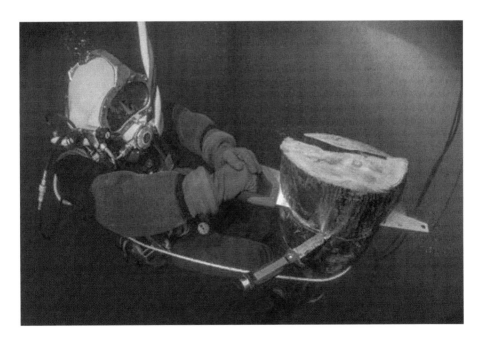

Fig. 307. Cutting of the damaged section of the pile

end of the bolt can pass through them. Depending on the depth, the diver can work from the ground or on a platform.

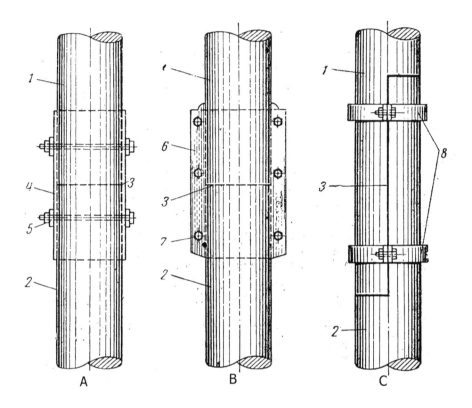

Fig. 308. Repair of damages in pile structures: A – using a sleeve; B – using a clamp; C – using stirrups. (1) part of the extended pile; (2) root part of the pile; (3) joint line of the cut; (4) sleeve; (5,7) bolts; (6) clamp; (8) stirrups.

A widely used method of pile extension is joining with a clamp made of a tube. Presented from above on a lever, the diver secures the clamp to the root pile initially with two bolts. Then, he guides the lowered part of the pile into the center of the clamp and, connecting both parts of the clamp, secures them with the remaining four bolts. When extending piles with the half-wood method, the diver makes a cut on the root pile to the specified dimensions. After that, the prepared extended end of the pile is handed to the diver in a vertical position. Aligning the cuts, he places metal stirrups on bolts.

Diving operations for sealing gaps in a wooden sheet pile wall

When sealing gaps in a wooden sheet pile wall, the diver must first measure the gap, based on which wooden inserts are manufactured on the surface. Balanced inserts are handed to the diver, who then drives them into the gaps using a sledgehammer and secures them with construction brackets. Diving operations during the repair of a metal or pile structure boil down to the replacement of individual parts. Beforehand, divers clean the repair surface from rust, vegetation, and organic formations. Using underwater cutting, they remove individual parts of the pile structure, send them to the surface, and install new parts in their place. Using underwater welding, they secure them in the designated locations.

Underwater welding and metal cutting can be performed by divers with the specialties of 'underwater welder' and 'underwater cutter.' Special electric holders and electrodes are used for these tasks. The welding current is supplied through well-insulated cables, which are turned on and off on the surface only upon the command of the underwater welder. Electro-oxygen cutting is most commonly used, where compressed oxygen is supplied through a tubular electrode. Before starting work, the welding equipment must be checked, the required current strength adjusted, the electrode holder well-insulated, and the return cable connected. The welding unit must be securely grounded, and the viewing glass of the diver's equipment is shaded with filters to protect the eyes of the underwater welder from the harmful effects of the electric arc.

When commencing work, the underwater welder must inspect and clean the welding or cutting area from rust, paint, and dirt. The tasks are performed only in a properly functioning special rubberized

Fig. 309. Underwater welder

drysuit. Underwater welding and cutting must be carried out by divers in suits with attached gloves. In case water enters the drysuit, to prevent electric shock, the underwater welder must command the power to be turned off, then surface. Welding work should be immediately stopped until the faulty equipment is replaced. Similarly, an automatic switch or switch, installed at the descent point, should be present in the welding circuit. Turning the switch on and off should only be done upon the diver's command.

While welding and cutting, the diver must hold the electrode in a way that it does not touch the metal parts of their equipment to avoid burning them. Additionally, to protect the metallic parts of the diver's equipment from electrolysis, an insulating coating, such as lacquer or rubberized glue, should be applied to the diver's helmet and hood. Electrode replacement should be done with the welding circuit de-energized. Touching the electrode to the helmet or hood during work is particularly dangerous. Therefore, the underwater welder must hold the electrode holder with the electrode away from them. Underwater, the current must be turned off during electrode replacement.

When cutting the side plating and inter-bulkhead flanges, measures must be taken in advance for explosion safety—fuel tanks should be filled with water, and the air pockets of flooded compartments should be ventilated with air. Welding and cutting are prohibited in tanks, fuel and gas compartments. It is also forbidden to weld or cut pipes and vessels under pressure. Cut structures that may fall after detachment must be sharpened in advance. When working with a gasoline-oxygen cutting unit underwater, the gasoline cylinder must be secured at a distance of at least 5 meters from the oxygen cylinders. When igniting and burning the gasoline-oxygen cutter, the diver must direct its head downward or away from themselves to prevent potential equipment burn and burns. Placing a burning cutter on the ground headfirst is prohibited, as it may cause clogging of the head and a backfire of the flame.

Fig. 310. Determining the thickness of metal in a structure

Work on the restoration of destroyed or damaged bridges begins with an inspection of the underwater part of the bridge. Divers determine the nature and extent of the damage, measuring its dimensions with a ruler and a foot rule, paying attention to the condition of the stone

527

masonry, pile foundations, etc. The number of damaged piles is calculated, and the method of their removal is determined. Inspecting individual parts of the destroyed bridge, the divers ascertain the depth of burial and their position on the ground.

The next stage of the work is the clearance of the riverbed from the destroyed bridge structures. This is done by underwater metal cutting using electro-oxygen cutting underwater, explosive methods, or sharp excavation and lifting of individual underwater structures or masses. To lift a metal truss, the diver loops lifting straps around it, placing wooden cushions under its sharp angles. When dismantling stone masonry, the diver drills holes in the stones and inserts special keys with lifting straps into them. Large parts of the truss are divided by divers and pulled aside using winches or tractors.

Underwater work in laying pipelines and cable lines

In preparation for laying pipelines and cable lines, preliminary work is done onshore: welding pipes into sections, pressure testing, insulation, and launching the section onto the water. Divers participate in the preliminary examination of the riverbed and trench preparation. Familiarizing themselves with the riverbed, divers determine its relief, soil characteristics, and identify obstacles such as boulders, submerged objects, and depressions. With good visibility, the inspection is carried out with a towed gazebo. In some cases, such as when inspecting the trench bottom, the diver walks around the area along a pre-laid guide rope. Trenches are often developed using special mechanisms: dredges, trenching projectiles, excavators, scraper installations, etc. Sometimes divers perform such work using high-power water jets and soil pumps. In the first case, the diver monitors the operation of a high-power water jet, the hose and nozzle of which are mounted on a frame moved from above. In the second case, they carry out soil washing, holding the hose with the nozzle in the required position. While washing trenches, the diver checks its width every 5-10 meters and reports the data to the surface.

The depth of trench washing is controlled with a foot rule or leveling instrument. In the development of trenches in soft soil, water jet soil pumps of vertical and horizontal types, and pneumatic soil pumps are used. The development of underwater trenches in rocky and hard rocks is expediently carried out by explosive methods. Such work should be carried out by diver-blasters who have undergone special training, strictly observing the safety techniques of explosive works. On a rocky base along the trench bottom, a bedding must be laid. In such cases, sand with fine gravel is supplied from above through a pipe, and the diver levels it with a water jet.

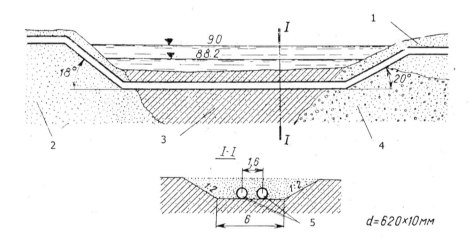

Fig. 311. Scheme of pipeline laying across the river: (1) - fine sand; (2) - medium-grain sand; (3) - loam; (4) - sand with gravel admixture; (5) - pipeline.

After completing the preparatory work, pipelines are laid in one, two, three, or four threads with burial in the trench. Divers participate in lowering the sections into the ground, connecting them underwater, and stuffing the laid pipeline. Individual sections of large-diameter pipelines, aqueducts, and spillways are connected underwater with flanges. Small-diameter pipes are usually laid in a fully welded manner. In recent years, new methods of pipeline laying have been developed. In this case, large-diameter pipeline sections are also welded on the surface, relieving the diver of heavy work. There are several methods of pipeline laying, but we will first talk about connecting large-diameter pipeline sections underwater using flanges. Large-diameter pipes, lowered to the ground in straight sections, are connected by divers with flanges. One side of the section has a blind flange, the other has a swivel flange held by a retaining ring. Flanges are installed on gaskets made of rubber, paronite, fiber, and other special materials. The flanges are brought together using tie bolts. If it is impossible to install tie bolts, then the end of the section is lifted or lowered with a floating vehicle or from the ice. Once the flanges are brought together, the diver places connecting bolts and tightens nuts at two opposite ends of the pipe.

Pipeline laying in trenches. There are several methods of pipeline laying: lowering with supports (stationary and floating); laying by free immersion with water pouring into the pipeline; laying with floating devices with sequential assembly of links (sections) of the pipeline; laying by towing sections (strands) and welding inter-section joints afloat; pulling along a descent path and the bottom of a water barrier. Pulling a pipeline, sometimes ballasted for negative buoyancy, is done by tractors, winches, and towboats. It is especially important that the towing cable is precisely laid along the crossing. The diver monitors the correctness of its laying. In case of cable breakage, the diver searches and sharpens its ends for retrieval to the surface. Before laying the towing cable, divers prelay a thin steel cable, to which the towing cable is attached at the end.

If the pipeline is of considerable length, its individual sections are connected by divers, or their ends are raised for connection from above. When laying a pipeline from ice, trenches can be developed by pneumatic soil pumps, scraper installations, divers using a water jet from a hydraulic monitor. When laying a pipeline, through holes are arranged along the crossing route. Currently, such work is carried out using ice-cutting machines.

Divers inspect trenches excavated by mechanisms, remove foreign objects from them, and also check the laid pipeline. A sound and pressure-tested pipeline is backfilled with soil from a barge, or the diver flushes the trench with a water jet from the hydraulic monitor. To reduce the weight of the pipeline during laying on the bottom, unloading rigid pontoons are often used, secured to the pipeline with plant or steel cable. After laying the pipeline in the design position, the pontoons are sharpened mechanically or with the help of divers. To sharpen a pontoon secured with a plant cable, the diver cuts the cable with a regular wood saw. For sharpening pontoons secured with a steel cable, the diver releases the tackle shackles after removing the load from the pontoon. For the diver's safety during work, the pontoon should be sharpened not during the process of submerging the pipeline, but only when it reaches the bottom of the water body, while filling the pontoon with water. When laying a gas pipeline, to prevent it from floating, a cast iron or reinforced concrete weight is attached to it. Placing and securing ballast weights underwater (half-couplings) is done as follows.

The diver washes out a trench under the pipeline using a hydraulic monitor. Then, the lowered lower half of the weight is installed in the trench under the pipeline using a crane, and the upper half of the weight is installed on the pipeline. After that, the lower half of the weight is lifted by a crane, and after aligning the holes for the bolts, the diver inserts bolts into them, screws them in, and tightens the nuts. When installing hinge cast iron and reinforced concrete weights, the diver monitors the placement of the weight on the pipeline and tightens the nut, which is pre-installed. Since the lower part of the half-coupling is shortened, no trench washing is performed, as they sit well on the pipeline. In this case, washing is only performed up to the level of the bottom of the pipeline.

Inspection of laid pipelines

The purpose of the diver's inspection of a pipeline laid on the trench bottom is to detect and eliminate possible defects, such as insulation damage, voids under the pipeline, deviations from the design elevation, and others. Diver inspection of culverts and large-diameter pipes is allowed only after their laying and slackening of the ropes. The diver should not be ahead of the laid pipe or cable. He inspects cables only after de-energizing and grounding. The diver moves along the pipeline, carefully checks its condition, and installs buoys at locations of detected defects.

Fig. 312. Pipeline repair - coupling installation

Pipeline repair. Various damages to underwater pipelines can be encountered. Depending on their nature (joint ruptures, cracks, through corrosion, punctures, dents, and others), there are many ways to address them. For example: installing supports made of logs or prefabricated boxes; repair by electric welding or using couplings and clamps; replacing damaged sections; repairing damaged insulation.

Voids formed under the pipeline are filled by the diver with soil using a hydraulic monitor or with gravel poured from above through wooden troughs. In places where the pipeline sags, the diver installs pile supports or prefabricated boxes filled with stones. In case of significant erosion of the pipeline (more than 25 meters in length) and a water flow rate exceeding 0.5 meters per second, concrete blocks weighing up to 5 tons are used. They are installed on both sides of the eroded pipeline section. The pipeline is attached to the blocks with angles and channels, after which it is filled with stones.

Small cracks in pressure pipelines are repaired by underwater welding. Individual punctures are closed by placing couplings or patches made from pieces of larger-diameter pipe, followed by welding around them and clamping with clamps. Before welding the patch, the surface of the pipeline must be thoroughly cleaned of insulation. To stop leaks at the flange connection or along the flange of a pressure pipeline, couplings made from two halves of a larger-diameter pipe are used. They are placed on a rubber gasket and secured with bolts.

The gap between the coupling and the pipe is filled with cement mortar supplied from above under pressure. Damaged areas of underwater pipelines operating under pressures up to 50 bars are replaced with inserts connected to the pipeline using compensating couplings. The diver places the top-down coupling onto the insert and tightens it with bolts or welds it. In other cases, special clamps are used instead of couplings, welded around the perimeter.

A non-pressure pipeline is repaired by placing a dense wooden box with concrete poured into it, continuously supplied through a hose or pipe. Gaps between the pipeline and the box walls are sealed with putty. When replacing a damaged section of the pipeline, the diver digs a trench of the specified length or releases the pipeline from ballast; installs and sharpens small pontoons on the pipe and secures the ropes of lifting mechanisms (cranes); cuts an outlet hole for the displaced water to exit the pipe; cuts the pipe into two parts using an electric oxygen cutting torch before lifting them to the surface. After the pipeline has been repaired on the surface, it is lowered to the bottom. Divers inspect the pipeline laid in the trench and flush it.

If the insulation of the pipeline is compromised, the damaged area is repaired as follows: a layer of primer, consisting of 70% petrolatum (petrolatum - a complex combination of hydrocarbons obtained by deparaffinizing petroleum oils) and 30% spindle oil, is applied to the thoroughly cleaned surface using scrapers and wire brushes and wiped with burlap; then, two divers apply a glass fabric bandage with an overlap of 3-5 centimeters, spirally wound with anti-corrosion paste composed of 30% petrolatum, 20% spindle oil, and 50% chrome sludge. The bandage is fed from the top on a hoisting rope. One of the divers, pulling the roll and freeing it from the lowering end, feeds the beginning of the bandage to the second diver, who presses it against the surface of the pipe with both hands. The first diver rolls the roll along the pipe's contour to the lower edge and passes the roll under the pipe before passing it to the second diver for the second part of the pipe's contour. During this process, divers tightly squeeze the bandage with their hands, displacing water from under it.

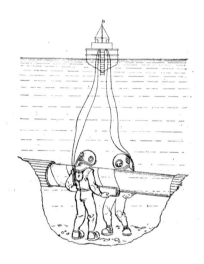

Fig. 313. Application of insulating tape

The second layer is applied using insulating tape with a 50% overlap in width, covering the joints of the old insulation by 20-25 centimeters. This tape is made from staple glass fabric impregnated with a composition of 70% petrolatum, 28% spindle oil, and 2% copper naphthenate (copper naphthenate, representing the copper salt of naphthenic acids with the addition of up to 10 parts by weight of paraffin or petrolatum). Upon completion of the winding, the tape is secured with twine impregnated with tar and covered with a 50% overlap with polyvinyl chloride tape. Polyvinyl chloride tape (PVC) is attached to the pipeline with twine soaked in tar. The insulated section is lined with a lath mat, which is tightened under the pipeline with the ends from the top. The lining mat is tied with tar twine, and after tightly covering the pipeline, it is fastened with wire rope with a diameter of 5-6 millimeters.

After completing the work, divers perform backfilling of the soil under the pipeline and flush the excavated trenches with a hydraulic monitor. The laying of cable trunk lines is carried out using hydraulic cable layers, which simultaneously help erode the soil and lay the cable in the trench. The diver monitors the work of the cable layer and, if necessary, removes obstacles such as roots, stones, and other objects, and also monitors the depth of the trench and the laying of the cable. When laying cables from floating vessels, the payout is done through a special device during the movement of the floating structure. The diver's task is to place the cable in a pre-prepared trench. If the cables are laid in bundles (when several cables are placed in one trench), the diver ensures that the distance between them complies with technical specifications. After laying the cable, the trench is filled with soil. When pulling the cable through protective pipes of the shore well, the diver must be especially careful to ensure that his arm, along with the cable, is not drawn into the pipe. Diving cable repair work includes: searching for and cleaning the cable using a hydraulic monitor; preparing the cable for lifting onto the deck of the floating structure; backfilling into the trench after its repair; checking the position of the cable and covering it with soil. When searching for power cables, a metallic probe should not be used; only a wooden probe should be used. Submarine cables are not repaired.

§ 31. Rescue diving operations

Features of organizing rescue diving operations

Rescue diving operations include underwater activities aimed at rescuing people who have drowned in a water area or remained in partially flooded compartments of a floating or sunken vessel. Autonomous diving equipment is usually used for rescuing those who have drowned in water bodies, while any diving equipment can be used for rescuing those remaining in partially flooded compartments of a vessel.

Fig. 314. Rescuers

The organization of rescue diving operations and safety procedures on ships and in diving services must ensure high readiness for divers' descent and the effectiveness of rescue actions. For these purposes, a standby rescue boat is assigned, which is launched into the water upon the command 'Man overboard' or 'Rescue boat to be launched.' The rescue boat, in addition to rowers, must have two divers equipped with autonomous diving gear.

The readiness of divers on the boat for an immediate dive is ensured by having them wear the diving gear. During rescue operations, divers use signaling buoys individually.

Divers, when rescuing drowning individuals, should approach them from behind, being cautious about potential grabs. A drowning person, losing consciousness, may grab the diver's wrists, neck, torso, and legs, hindering their actions and even posing a threat to their life. To free the diver from the grasp of a

Fig. 315. Diver during the rescue of a drowned person

drowning person, the diver should first attempt to dive. If this technique is unsuccessful, appropriate methods to break free from the grasp should be applied. Rescuing a drowned person in a water area involves the diver inspecting the bottom at the drowning location within visible limits. In cases where the drowned person cannot be immediately found on the bottom, divers conduct a diving search using

Fig.316. Bringing the drowned person

methods such as trawling in concentric circles or other techniques. Upon discovering the drowned person, approach cautiously. If the drowned person is lying on the bottom face up, the diver should approach from the head, grasp the head, and lift. If the drowned person is lying on the bottom face down, the diver should approach from the legs, take hold under the armpits, and lift.

Then, in both cases, push away energetically from the bottom, resurface with the person, and swim with them on their back to the surface. The diver should turn the drowned person onto their back, ensuring their mouth is above water, take hold of them from behind under the armpits, and swim on their back,

Fig. 317. Diver's position during the rescue of a drowning person

using fins. To swim on the side using fins and one free hand, place the drowned person on their back, pass your arm underneath them from below, and grab the forearm of their other arm.

After delivering the drowned person to the boat or shore, immediate first aid is administered, and a doctor is simultaneously summoned. Until the doctor arrives, first aid is provided to the victim, which includes removing clothing that hinders free breathing, clearing the mouth and nose of sand and mud, removing any ingested water, and performing artificial respiration until the victim regains consciousness, stopping only upon the doctor's instruction.

The rescue of personnel remaining in the air pockets of partially flooded compartments of a vessel is organized by the leader of the descent with the assistance of emergency teams, including divers. The success of rescue operations depends not only on the skill and speed of divers but also on providing support from the surface. The rescue of those remaining in partially flooded compartments of a floating or sunken vessel includes establishing communication with the personnel in the air pocket of the partially flooded compartment, sustaining their existence, and rescuing them from the partially flooded compartment. Communication with the personnel remaining in the air pocket of the partially flooded compartment is established by tapping. Subsequently, after laying a hose into the air pocket by divers, the possibility of verbal communication through the hose, similar to a communication tube, becomes available. Communication by tapping is carried out by striking a metallic object against the ship's hull. This type of communication allows determining if there are people in the partially flooded compartments and how many (based on the number of responding taps from the compartment). Sustaining the existence of personnel in the air pocket of the partially flooded compartment is necessary during their preparation for rescue. Depending on the number of casualties and their condition in the partially flooded compartment, two or more divers are sent, bringing with them a hose for supplying fresh air, tested and ready-to-use autonomous breathing apparatus. Drowning individuals are provided with thermoses containing hot drinks (cocoa, tea, coffee), lanterns for illumination, and a towline for guiding movement. If an air supply hose is used, a diver may not be needed. En route to the partially flooded compartment where people are located, divers lay a hose or towline and signal their movement by tapping. Upon reaching the air pocket of the partially flooded compartment, divers establish contact with the casualties, assess their condition, attach the hose for supplying fresh air, provide hot drinks, take measures to position the casualties above the water surface, and, if necessary, seal the openings through which air is escaping from the compartment's air pocket. Then, divers, turning off their breathing apparatus, prepare the personnel for exit from the partially flooded compartment and establish the order and sequence of the exit. Those severely weakened and feeling unwell are designated for exit first. Each diver can facilitate the exit of only one rescued person, provided their condition is satisfactory. If the rescued person's condition is poor, two divers take them out.

After preparing the rescued individuals for exit and a practical check of their skills in using breathing apparatus, divers escort the rescued individuals first, and after their exit, return for the next ones. The escorted individuals remain between two divers, holding onto them and each other with their hands. Divers make stops on the way to assess the condition of the rescued individuals. In case of a deterioration in the condition of the rescued individual, if the rescue is carried out using regenerative equipment, the following assistance is provided: when short of breath, measure the gas in the breathing bag, release excess gas from the bag, assist in oxygen flushing, and in case of heavy breathing, tap on the regenerative box. Unconscious individuals are rescued by two divers. A mask with an oxygen-washed breathing apparatus is put on the unconscious person, and the irritating valve is closed. One diver takes the unconscious person under the knees with the left hand and holds a guide in the right hand, while the other diver takes the unconscious person under the armpits, and both move towards the exit from the compartment. Stops are made along the way to observe the condition of the unconscious person and supply oxygen to the breathing bag of the apparatus.

Methods and rules for performing artificial respiration

At the moment of drowning, when the drowning person involuntarily attempts to inhale, the mouth, nose, and airways may be filled with water, silt, sand, or mud. Therefore, first and foremost, the oral cavity of the drowned person must be cleared. If the teeth of the victim are tightly clenched, their mouth should be opened first using a rotary expander available in the diver's first aid kit.

The branches of the spreader, to which pieces of rubber tubing are attached (to prevent gum damage when pressure is applied), are

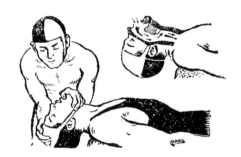

Fig. 318. Head tilt and tongue control

inserted along the cheek behind the last molars, and the mouth is opened by pressing the handles. The handles are placed on a stopper to keep the mouth open. If a spreader is not available, a spoon handle, screwdriver, or other object can be used, wrapped with gauze or a handkerchief. In extreme cases, the mouth can be opened with a finger by placing it behind the

Fig. 319. Medical instrument for mouth opening

molars and pressing on the lower jaw. To keep the mouth open, a piece of cork, wood, or a roll made of bandage or cotton is placed between the jaws. After opening the victim's mouth, the oral cavity is cleared of foreign bodies using two fingers wrapped in gauze or a handkerchief.

After clearing the mouth, proceed to remove water from the airways. For this, the victim is turned face down, and the lower edge of the chest is placed on the thigh of the assisting person, who kneels at the same time. The victim's head hangs down, positioned lower than the pelvis, achieving simultaneous removal of water from the airways and stomach. After removing the water, artificial respiration is immediately initiated. Prior to that, the victim's tongue should be pulled out and secured because, during drowning (or loss of consciousness), the tongue often falls back, presses against the epiglottis, and obstructs air access to the airways.

To control the tongue, a tongue holder from the diver's first aid kit is used. In the absence of a tongue holder, the tongue can be extracted with fingers wrapped in gauze, and then it can be bandaged to the chin with a bandage or any other piece of material.

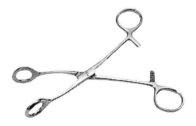

Fig.320. Tongue holder

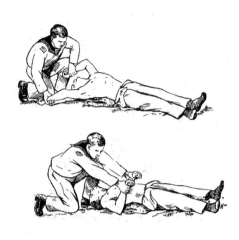

**Fig. 321. Artificial respiration
by the Sylvester method**

Artificial respiration can be performed in several ways, with the Sylvester method being the most common. The victim is placed on their back, with a pillow or roll placed under their shoulder blades to maximize chest expansion. The assistant kneels at the victim's head, takes their hands above the forearms (just above the wrists), on the count of 'one,' pulls them back over the head and holds them in that position on counts 'two' and 'three.' As a result of chest expansion, inhalation occurs. Then, on count 'four,' the hands are pressed against the front-lateral surfaces of the chest, transferring the entire weight of the body onto them, and left in this position on counts 'five and six.' Exhalation occurs when the chest is compressed. After that, the entire cycle is repeated at a rate of about 15 times per minute. The Sylvester method provides good lung ventilation through active inhalation and exhalation, but it cannot be used in the case of fractures and other injuries to the chest and upper limbs. Moreover, in the supine position, even with the head turned to the side, vomit may enter the airways during the victim's involuntary vomiting movements. Artificial respiration by the Schafer method is performed as follows: the victim is laid on their stomach, the head is turned to the side, and the hands are stretched forward (or one hand is placed under the head). A pillow or roll is placed under the chest.

The helper kneels over the victim, at the level of their hips, placing palms on the lower sections of the chest so that the thumbs lie parallel to the victim's back. On the count of 'one,' the hands are applied as shown in the illustration, on the count of 'two,' pressure is applied to the chest, as if pushing it upwards. On count 'three,' the helper transfers the entire weight of the body onto the hands, without bending them at the elbows. Active exhalation occurs. On count 'four,' the helper pushes off with the palms from the chest, and on counts 'five' and 'six' - tilts their body backward. Meanwhile, passive inhalation occurs. The entire cycle is repeated at a rate of about 15 times per minute.

The Schafer method has the advantage that, in the victim's face-down position, the tongue does not fall back, reducing the risk of vomit entering the airways. However, in this method, inhalation remains passive, and less air enters the lungs compared to the Sylvester method.

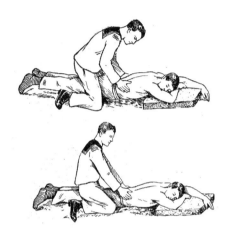

For artificial respiration using the Kallistov method, the victim is placed face down, with bent arms under their head. The helper kneels at the victim's head, placing

Fig. 322. Artificial respiration by the Schafer method

a loop or tied towels under their shoulders and passing them under the arms. The free ends are tied around the helper's neck. The length of the loops is adjusted so that, when the helper straightens their torso, the victim's chest is lifted, ensuring inhalation. When bending the helper's torso, the victim's chest descends, and exhalation occurs. Simultaneously with artificial respiration, the victim can be connected to an oxygen inhaler, providing them with pure oxygen to breathe.

In the Kallistov method, both inhalation and exhalation are passive. However, this method is convenient for use when there is a suspicion of chest injury or barotrauma to the lungs. When methods involving chest compression are not recommended due to the victim's bodily

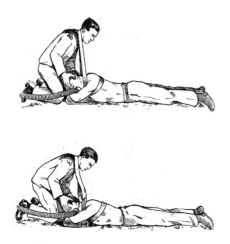

Fig. 323. Artificial respiration by the Kallistov method

injuries, the Laborde method is used in individual cases. This method involves manipulating the victim's tongue, captured by a tongue holder or fingers through gauze, by sequentially pulling it out of the mouth and then lowering it back into the oral cavity. The resulting irritation of the nerve endings at the base of the tongue is transmitted to the brain and from there to the respiratory center, stimulating its activity.

One of the most common methods of artificial respiration is the mouth-to-mouth method. The victim is laid on their back, with a roll placed under the neck so that the head is slightly tilted back. The rescuer stands to the side, supporting the victim's chin and lower jaw with one hand, while using the fingers of the other hand to close the nostrils to ensure that all the air blown in goes into the lungs and does not escape through the nose. Leaning over the victim and pressing their lips to the victim's, the helper exhales, forcing air into the victim's airways. Then, the helper raises their head and inhales. During this time, air exits the victim's lungs. This cycle is repeated in rhythm with normal breathing. As a result, the victim undergoes active inhalation, and exhalation becomes passive.

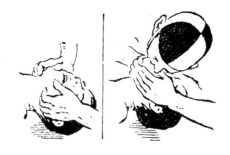

Fig. 324. Mouth-to-mouth artificial respiration

This method is effective because the exhaled air from the helper contains about 5% carbon dioxide, which acts as a respiratory center stimulant and promotes the rapid restoration of natural breathing. Artificial respiration is performed in all cases of drowning when natural breathing is absent. Artificial respiration is discontinued upon the appearance of unmistakable signs of death, which typically manifest approximately two hours after biological death.

Simultaneously with artificial respiration, friction of the torso and limbs is applied, and the body is warmed with warmers placed on the occipital area, neck, and legs.

In the presence of a palpable pulse on the carotid artery and constricted pupils indicating preserved cardiac activity, one artificial respiration is sufficient to restore natural breathing and ensure oxygen saturation of the blood.

If no pulse is palpated, and the pupils are markedly dilated, it indicates that the heart is not functioning, and artificial respiration must be combined with indirect heart massage. Indirect heart massage is performed as follows.

With the palms of both hands placed on top of each other, sharp jolts are applied to the lower part of the victim's sternum. The chest should be depressed towards the spine by at least 3-4 cm. The rate of indirect massage is 50-60 compressions per minute. When compressing the chest, the heart chambers are emptied, and blood is pushed through the vessels.

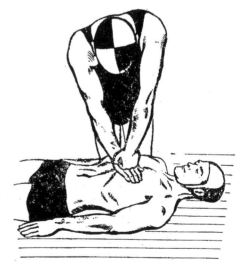

Fig. 325. Indirect heart massage

Fig. 326. Combining artificial respiration with indirect heart massage

After each thrust, the chest expands, and the heart chambers fill with blood. Thus, artificial circulation is ensured. It is better to perform artificial respiration in combination with indirect heart massage with two people. Air should be blown in after every four chest compressions. However, if necessary, one person can perform both procedures. In this case, air is blown in after six chest compressions. Indirect heart massage should be done carefully to avoid damaging the ribs and liver, especially in 'cyanotic' drowning victims. Typically, their liver is engorged with blood and protrudes from under the rib margin.

The application of oxygen through a mask, without stopping artificial respiration, produces a good effect. When the victim regains consciousness and natural breathing is restored, they should be laid on a bed, covered with a blanket, and given a warm drink, keeping them under the observation of a doctor.

Providing assistance for barotrauma to the ear

If a diver feels pain in the ear when descending underwater, they should stop the descent and rise by 1-2 meters to reduce external pressure on the eardrum. After that, they should make several swallowing movements and try to clear their ears. If the feeling of stuffiness or pain in the ear does not disappear, the descent should be stopped, and the diver should resurface. Fig. 351. External and internal pressure on the eardrum In case of a ruptured eardrum in a diver after surfacing, the affected ear should be plugged with a piece of clean cotton or gauze, and the individual should be directed to a doctor. Accessory sinuses of the nose, including the maxillary and frontal sinuses, as well as sinuses in the area of the ethmoid bone, are connected to the external environment by thin channels passing inside the bones. If the mucous membranes covering the inner surface of these channels become inflamed, the lumen of the channels may be partially or completely closed. As a result, phenomena of 'squeeze' may be observed when there is a change in external pressure. If painful sensations occur in the area of the accessory sinuses of the nose during a descent underwater, the diver should act the same way as with 'ear squeeze.

Providing assistance for barotrauma to the lungs

Lung tissue is very sensitive to pressure changes. As a result of a sudden drop in pressure, the lung tissue ruptures. Upon the restoration of normal pressure, air is drawn into the blood through the torn areas of the lungs and pulmonary veins. This air, entering the systemic circulation, causes blockage of blood vessels (embolism). The most characteristic sign of lung barotrauma is pulmonary bleeding, manifested by the discharge of foamy sputum tinged with blood. Generally, this bleeding is not life-threatening, as blood loss does not exceed 100-200 cm^3. The affected person exhibits cyanosis of the skin and lips, rapid and shallow breathing with wheezing, severe coughing, and the pulse becomes rapid and irregular. Swelling in the neck and chest area is sometimes observed, and when pressure is applied to these areas, a characteristic 'crunch' is felt. Such swelling may occur due to the entry of air under the skin, which has escaped through the ruptured lung wall. In some cases, when air bubbles enter the blood vessels of the brain and spinal cord, limb paralysis may occur. The diver brought up from the water is relieved of equipment and a hydro suit that restricts breathing; in this case, the diver is prohibited from making independent movements. Subsequently, the affected person is placed on a stretcher or deck with the head slightly lower than the torso. In this position, the likelihood of air bubbles entering the brain is minimized, as they will be carried by the blood flow to higher parts of the body. The affected person can only be transported on stretchers. If the person is not breathing, artificial respiration is initiated, excluding methods involving chest compression or rapid movements of the upper and lower limbs with pressing them to the chest and abdomen. The best method of artificial respiration in this case is tongue pulling 15-20 times per minute. Inhalation of pure oxygen yields good results in improving the patient's condition. It should be understood that to eliminate the causes of the illness (gas bubbles entering the bloodstream), the patient should be placed under increased pressure for therapeutic recompression.

The treatment for decompression sickness is therapeutic recompression. The removal of formed gas bubbles in the blood and tissues occurs with repeated pressure elevation. Gas bubbles initially decrease in size and then dissolve again in the blood and tissues, thus eliminating the cause of the painful symptoms.

Providing assistance for hypothermia involves removing the person from the water and rapidly warming the body. In the case of mild hypothermia, performing vigorous gymnastic exercises or intensively rubbing the torso and limbs for 10-15 minutes may be sufficient to eliminate all signs of cooling. In the case of more profound hypothermia, the person should be placed in a hot bath or shower at a temperature of 35-40°C, given a hot drink immediately, then laid in bed and covered with warm blankets, applying warmers primarily to the occipital and neck area, as well as to the feet. If necessary, medications are administered to support cardiac activity.

Checkpoint questions for chapter eight:

1. Name four categories of underwater works for divers?
2.
3. What types of works are considered periodic underwater works?
4. Name emergency underwater works?
5. How is the underwater examination of the submerged part of the ship's hull carried out?
6. Name emergency underwater works inside flooded compartments of the ship assigned to divers?
7. Name emergency underwater works outside the ship's hull assigned to divers?
8. How is the removal of propellers done?
9. How is the removal of a ship stranded on a shoal done?
10. Tell about the known methods of artificial respiration?
11. Tell about the methods of searching for sunken objects?
12. How is the lifting of sunken objects done?
13. What works are related to ship-lifting?
14. How is the examination of a sunken ship carried out?
15. What is involved in providing assistance for hypothermia?
16. What underwater works are carried out in fisheries?
17. What is the purpose of using underwater explosive works?
18. How is assistance provided for decompression sickness?
19. What works are related to underwater technical underwater works?
20. What underwater works are carried out in the construction and restoration of underwater structures?
21. Tell about the methods of underwater concreting?
23. How is assistance provided for barotrauma to the lungs?

ABOUT THE AUTHOR

We can say that Alex Fatum (Sevastopol, Ukraine) was destined since he was a child to be a professional diver. It is easy to understand if you were born in a city on the shores of the Black Sea and in a family of fishermen and divers (like your grandfather and father) dedicated to the exploitation of marine farms, in which they cultivated and collected marine mollusks for supply local fish markets. Water was a natural environment for little Alexander.

The day his grandfather counted on him to participate in the refloating of a fishing boat that sank after a sudden storm is marked in his memory. He was only 7 years old, and that fact definitely marked his future. Diving continued throughout his childhood and adolescence. During school holidays, he helped his family as a diver on the fishing boats.

After graduating as a commercial diver in the mid-90s from the Sevastopol Maritime Institute of Nuclear Energy and Industry (now called Sevastopol State University), he began working as a diving instructor at his city's diving school called EPRON, founded in 1931 and specialized in the search and recovery of sunken ships. Since then, he has participated in numerous diving expeditions, studying internal hydraulic dams and performing repairs on coastal hydraulic structures, as well as pipeline installations for oil companies. He has also participated in many ship and cargo rescue operations, in countries such as the United Kingdom, Turkey, South Korea, Poland and the Netherlands. In 2014, Alex moved to Odessa and began working as an engineer in the cultivation and harvesting of mollusks in the fishing industry. In 2017, he became the head of the "Association of Professional Divers and Athletes of Ukraine," where he continues to work to this day.

Since the war broke out in his country, Alex collaborates during the day as a volunteer, helping people in the civilian population who are really in difficult situations and at night, when his family sleeps, he prepares teaching materials such as the 'Basic Manual of the Commercial Diver'. He believes that civilian diving specialists will always be in demand in any country worldwide, especially in Ukraine in the near future. "I think it's crucial to share my experience and knowledge with future generations of divers because after the war, my country will need extensive restoration of its maritime and river infrastructure," Alex told our publishing house.